Morning Celebrations

from My Heart

A collection of Daily Devotionals for Women

By Jeanne Stone Helstrom

ISBN: 1479294020

ISBN 13: 9781479294022

To my loving husband Herb, my beautiful daughters, Kristin, Jamee and Bridgette, and my wonderful godly girlfriends at WomenEncouragingWomen, and my church family, for your love, prayers and encouragement in putting together this collection—to Brock and Bodie Thoene, who encouraged me, gave me words of wisdom, guidance, and much inspiration, thank you all! Also, my utmost appreciation to those who agreed to the tedious task of proofreading, daughter Bridgette Lowry, Auntie Lu Collins, and dear friends Jean Coalter, Kathryn Scaletta and Bev Ingersoll. Thank you, ladies! And ultimately, my praise and thanks go to my heavenly Father for giving me the words—every one. I am so blessed.

Cover Photo by BRIDGETTE LOWRY

"In the morning, O Lord, You hear my voice;
in the morning I lay my requests before You
and wait in expectation." (Psalm 5:3).

INTRODUCTION

Celebrate (Webster): "to commemorate; to proclaim; to honor or praise." **Celebrate** (David): "*They (one generation to another) will celebrate Your abundant goodness, and joyfully sing of your righteousness.*" (Psalm 145:7)

I have enjoyed many, many celebrations over my lifetime ~ birthdays, mine and others', weddings, births, anniversaries, milestones, and a few years ago now, a huge celebration for my retirement from the workforce. We celebrate with parties, gifts, certificates, greeting cards. I love them all. **Celebrations**. All throughout time, God's people celebrated. His word is full of these times ~ the Passover, the Feast of Harvest, the Feast of Weeks, the Feast of Unleavened Bread....many festivals and celebrations.

Over the last several years, during my morning devotional times, I have discovered that this is a time of celebration for me. I find that my mind is fresh in the morning, before the cares of the day start crowding in...and apparently, so did David... "*My voice shalt thou hear in the* ***morning****, O LORD; in the* ***morning*** *will I direct [my prayer] unto thee, and will look up.*"(Psalm 5:3 KJV). What do I celebrate so early in the morning, you ask? As I am writing in my journal, usually after I have gazed outside at the sky and made a cup of tea, I begin to thank God for many things; lots of times I thank Him for the sky, the beautiful stars I see, always hanging right where He put them when they were created by Him, I thank Him for the sleep of the night, that I am able to put my feet on the floor and stand up, I thank Him for a cozy warm home and plenty of food to eat, for my family and friends. And although things are not always rosy, and we don't always have enough money, there are so many uncertainties each day, and we don't know what the future has in store for us....I can thank and praise

Him because *He* knows, and He holds the future in His hands. And I am right where I am because of His plan for my life.

Quite a wonderment to me, also, is that most mornings I wake up with a (Christian) song going through my mind. And more oft than not, the words are somehow exactly what I need to hear for whatever has been concerning me. Does God speak directly to us today? I believe so!! He speaks to me through His word, and through music He has inspired others to write. And so, it is very natural for me to mention song lyrics in a lot of my writings.

Celebrate the Lord with me, His goodness and mercy, and let His love cheer your heart!

And part of my Celebration on this particular morning is due to my being chosen to become a moderator in an online women's encouragement group, after much praying on all sides. I had been asking God for a couple of months after my retirement, to show me where He can use me, and unbeknownst to me, the three moderators of the group had been collectively praying for me as a moderator. See how God works? So it was agreed that I would post a devotional two mornings a week, and I have decided to call it my **Morning Celebration**. Through much prayer, and God's leading, this is a collection of the devotionals I have written, with God's prompting. Each entry is the result of the Father giving me one word, typically, and then He fills me with the rest of the message. Pray for me, ladies, as I embark on this new adventure with you all. And with God. ~ From my heart, Jeanne Stone Helstrom

Unless otherwise indicated, all Scripture quotations are from the New International Version of the Bible. Some scripture is repeated because it's a favorite of the author's

JANUARY 1

A CLEAN SLATE?

I'm not sure there is an official definition for "clean slate" but we use the phrase a lot. It basically means a fresh start, putting the past behind us, an opportunity to start over, a second chance. I didn't hear one New Year's resolution this holiday season, but typically we all end up resolving to do better in the new year...we will lose weight, we will get a better job, we will save money, be kinder, finish that planned project, read our Bible more...it's a good time to make promises to ourselves and to others. But oh, how hard it is to follow through. We can't change overnight. And that's what the changing of the calendar is, just from one day to another. Our problems, concerns and troubles just seem to carry over to the next day, the next year.

God's word tells us *"For I know the plans I have for you, plans to prosper you and not to harm you, plans to give you a hope and a future."* (Jer. 29:11). It's good for us to make plans, but how often do our plans remain only that...plans? God has great plans for us. Oh, I don't know what they are, exactly, but His word tells me I can hope in Him. There is a song we used to sing in church... "Something beautiful, something good, all my confusion, He understood. All I had to offer Him was brokenness and strife, but He made something beautiful out of my life." Many times, our own plans for our lives get in the way of God's plans. Paul said to the Romans (7:15*) "For what I want to do, I do not do, but what I hate to do..."* Sometimes we just can't help ourselves...we slip back into our old habits, day after day, no matter how hard we try to "clean our slates."

So, today we are all putting up our new, clean calendars...the clean slate. We all have regrets from the past 365 days. But we can put those behind us, one day at a time. If we look at all we want to accomplish in the new year, we will be overwhelmed. Oh, it's good to write down goals and work for them, but let's allow God's word and His Spirit to guide us ~ day by day. Here's a prayer I saw yesterday in Dorothy Valcarcel's devotional website, Transformation Garden...

"Lord, I have time,
I have plenty of time,
All the time that You give me,
The years of my life,
The days of my years,
The hours of my days,
They are all mine.
Mine to fill, quietly, calmly,
But to fill completely, up to the brim,
To offer them to You, that of their insipid water
You may make a rich wine such

As You made once in Cana of Galilee."
Michel Quoist

I leave you with that, and best wishes for a Happy and blessed New Year.

JANUARY 2

MORNING CELEBRATION …

"Shout for joy to the Lord, all the earth! Worship the Lord with gladness; come before Him with joyful songs. Know that the Lord is God. It is He who made us, and we are His; we are His people, the sheep of His pasture. Enter His gates with thanksgiving and His courts with praise; give thanks to Him and praise His name. For the Lord is good and His love endures forever, His faithfulness continues through all generations." (Psalm 100).

This is how I feel this morning, in spite of a spring cold (haven't had one in over four years!)…but the sun is shining, and I saw a beautiful starry sky last night displaying God's wonders…I know when I hear the birdsong this morning, the birds are praising God too! The trees and bushes are praising God with their new little buds breaking forth into leaves. And soon, color will cover the earth with flowers blooming. How can we NOT praise Him? God's word says (in Luke 19) *"…if we are to keep quiet, the very stones will cry out and praise Him."* Can you imagine? I wonder what they would sound like…We were made to praise God…even in the midst of our troubles. ESPECIALLY in the midst of our troubles.

I heard a story, many times, about a missionary woman in our church who was in Africa years ago, and she was lying sick and dying on her bed. Her strength was gone and she was getting weaker by the moment. In her anguish she was crying out to God. He spoke to her and brought her attention to a book on the shelf near her bed. She questioned, saying she did not even have the strength to reach out and pick it up, let alone read it. He kept drawing her attention to the book…after awhile she noticed it was a hymnal "Praise & Worship." And then she understood….He wanted her to just PRAISE Him. She began to praise the Lord, laying there sick and near death, and gradually she felt her strength begin to return, and in a day or two, she was up and caring for her family. You see, *God inhabits our praise.* And even when we don't feel like praising Him, even when everything in our lives seems to be falling apart, we must praise Him for Who He is and for His love for us!

JANUARY 3

TELL ME YOUR STORY…

My daughter gave me a beautiful journal-type book one year for Christmas entitled "Mom, Tell Me Your Story." Each page has a prompt, like, why did your parents choose your name, tell a story from your toddler years, what was your first day of school like, favorite family activity, and other questions about my growing-up years…high school, falling in love and getting married…they want to know it all! It will be a great keepsake.

Did you know that God Himself wrote His story for us? It is in book form and contains all we will ever need to know about God, and ourselves for that matter. We are included in His life story. In Joshua 1:8 we read *"Do not let this Book of the Law depart from your mouth; meditate on it day and night so that you will be careful to do everything written in it."* From beginning to end God told us story after story of people just like us who needed Him. They had troubles just like us, they feared the future, like us. They bowed before Him agonizing in prayer seeking His will. And in every story, God was there. God trusted men all through the ages to hear His voice and to write down the words He wanted us to hear. I am so thankful He provided His word that we may know the way. *"Whether you turn to the right or to the left, your ears will hear a voice behind you saying, 'This is the way, walk in it.'"* (Isaiah 30:21). We are no longer obliged to follow all the laws and rituals of the Old Testament (except for the ageless Ten Commandments), but because Jesus came in the form of man and died for our sins, we are now saved by Grace, not by the law. Nor are we required to sacrifice animals to atone for our sin. That sacrifice has been made, once for all, as I Peter 3:18 says: *"For Christ died for sins once for all, the righteous for the unrighteous, to bring you to God."*

All through the Bible are accounts of God guiding His people, rescuing them, teaching and loving them. It's the same for us if we read and listen to what God says in His word. We still hear stories. He still speaks to us. There is another book we must know about… *"Then I saw a great white throne and Him who was seated on it. Earth and sky fled from His presence, and there was no place for them. And I saw the dead, great and small, standing before the throne and books were opened. Another book was opened, which is the* ***Book of Life****."* (Rev. 20:11-12).

Books. Many contain history, but this book contains His story. Our name will be written in that final book, the Book of Life, if we make God first and foremost in our life. If we trust Him for the little things as well as the big things. I want to make sure my name is written in that book…don't you?

JANUARY 4

HEARTBREAK OF PARENTING…

Such a hard and emotional holiday season this has been. I have heard so many people say they sure hope the next year is better than the year we just finished. First, my granddaughter was hit by a truck the day before her 22nd birthday earlier in December, and suffered a broken back, then a week and a half later, 2 days before Christmas, my daughter's dog was killed. Now yesterday, my middle daughter and her two kids moved in with us because she left her husband. It has been a long time coming. I'm so sad for my kids having to go through these troubles. Don't you wish you could just wave a magic wand and make all their heartaches disappear? I sure do at times. And I know they have to go through rough times, just like us ~ being an adult is hard. And *"we know that suffering produces perseverance, and perseverance, character; and character, hope."* (Romans 5:3). But I don't think my kids and grandkids are at that point in their lives yet, when they can actually rejoice in their sufferings, so it's hard for them to understand. They know their mother/grandmother prays for them daily, so do they wonder why her prayers for them are not answered? Aren't they?

I do believe my prayers have not only been heard by our heavenly Father, but answered as well. The answers may not always be what we wished for, like healing, financial prosperity, freedom from trouble. But God does know what we need, before we even ask it. And sometimes His answer is no, or wait. But He is always standing by to help us in all our troubles. The way I know He is answering my prayers is the peace I feel in my heart and mind. It's that *"peace that passes all human understanding."* (Philippians 4:7). It's the peace we feel when we shouldn't be feeling peaceful at all, under the difficult circumstances.

Do you think our Father feels for us the way we do for our children, when we are in trouble? Of course He does. His heart breaks when He sees us going through all the hardships we do, many of them we bring upon ourselves. He has the answers, but we don't always seek them, or take His hand when it is offered to us. He wants to comfort us in our sorrow, to lead us in our confusion, but sometimes we don't want His help. And I am sure His heart breaks, just like ours, for He is a parent, too. His kids run away when they think they can handle their own lives. His kids are hurt and injured. His kids are confused and don't know which way to turn. Just like our kids. That's because we, and they are, His kids. He longs for us to ask Him to lead us, to heal us, to rescue us. Just as we wish our own children will ask us.

I wish for my children and grandchildren, that they will experience God's blessings in this new year. I pray that their eyes will be open to His glorious wonders, and their ears will be listening for His voice. He has promised to never leave us or forsake us. Sometimes we are the ones who leave, but our heavenly Father never does. We can count on it. And He'll heal our broken hearts, and give us peace, and hope. I love that.

JANUARY 5

A NEW DAY...

There is much to be said about a "day." A new day holds much opportunity and promise. We count days. We look forward to a certain day. We are glad when a difficult day is over. We wish someone a good day. We wish OURSELVES a good day. With every sunrise we begin anew. A day is defined as "the period of light between sunrise and sunset." It was created by God. We will never again have yesterday ~ what's past is past. But today is a new chapter in the story of our lives. And it is a gift from the hand of God.

I find that it is SO important for me to spend time with God in the morning, thus starting the day off on the right foot, and setting the tone for the day. We each have 24 hours, every day. We all use those hours differently. Remember that *"This is the day that the Lord has made ~ let us rejoice and be glad in it!"* (Psalm 118:24). And we ask, in the Lord's Prayer, for God to *"give us this day our daily Bread."* (Luke 11:3). We all need food to sustain us, daily. And we need the spiritual food of God's word to sustain us and strengthen us.

There are many things we can do in a day. Some of us cram as many tasks into one day as we can, rushing to and from each assignment, while others take it more slowly, enjoying each project and each person with whom we come into contact. No two people are alike. And no two days are alike. We have no way of knowing what each new day will bring. Sometimes our busy schedules will be interrupted by an unexpected call or visit, an illness, loss of a job, car trouble, loss of a loved one. I try to look at these interruptions as an assignment from God ~ there is a purpose for them. And sometimes they require sacrifice. Jesus Himself was interrupted many times during His ministry ~ when He was headed to a certain place, to see certain people, to perform certain miracles.... *"When she heard about Jesus, she came up behind him in the crowd and touched his cloak, because she thought, "If I just touch his clothes, I will be healed."* (Mark 5:27-28). Jairus came running and begged Jesus to "drop everything" and come and heal his beloved dying daughter. And yet, to Jesus, these were not interruptions. People were His purpose. People were His passion. They were opportunities to display His Father's great love and power.

The phone rings just as we are dashing out the door. Is it possible the caller on the other end is not merely a telemarketer, but someone in need of some encouraging words? Someone needing prayer? Ask God to turn your interruptions into opportunities, and pray that you will use the day wisely. God does not want us to waste any of our days. In John 9:4, Jesus said, *"As long as it is day, we must do the work of Him who sent Me. Night is coming, when no one can work."* Look at each day as a blessing, a celebration! And be thankful.

JANUARY 6

WORDS ~

Did you ever think about the power of words? Remember the school-yard taunt "sticks and stones may break my bones, but names will never hurt me?" This is so untrue. How many of us have called names, or have been called names, that hurt? Or a word spoken in anger or frustration that just won't go away from our memory? There is so much power in words that a single word can change the course of someone's life. And it seems we learn to use hurtful words at a very early age...we don't know how deeply another is affected by the words we speak. When a child is spoken to unkindly, the words can alter his self-esteem and self-image, kill enthusiasm, and actually shape the way he feels about himself. And we cannot take them back once they're spoken. But then, a *kind* word can literally change someone's life, as well. It can plant a seed of encouragement or recognition that would provide a turning point in a person's outlook in life.

Jesus spoke with love and acceptance to those who were shunned by their neighbors ~ we think of Zaccheus, the tax collector, one who was hated by society because of his position and his attitude, but Jesus picked him out in the crowd and gave him His time, made him feel valued, and Zaccheus turned his life around.

Genuine and sincere words cost us nothing, but can be so valuable and mean the world to the one receiving them. Sometimes a person is not used to hearing kind words and may not know how to accept them, feeling uncomfortable or even embarrassed by them. Well chosen words can motivate, offer hope, create vision, and impact thinking. It says in Proverbs 16:24 *"Pleasant words are a honeycomb, sweet to the soul and healing to the bones."* And in 12:18 *"Reckless words pierce like a sword, but the tongue of the wise brings healing."*

Let's be cognizant and careful of the words we use, both spoken and written. Offer a kind word. It can be so powerful.

JANUARY 7

DO NOT BE AFRAID...

"Do not be afraid; have I myself not commanded you? Be courageous and valiant." (2 Samuel 13:28)

Fear is a roaring lion. This lion can paralyze our lives, tear us up, maim us. At one time or another, we are all victims of this beast with its huge paws, extended claws and bared teeth, ready to rip us to shreds. What kinds of things do we fear? Many have faced the fear that their marriage is over. There is the fear of health issues and ensuing surgeries or treatments. The fear that financial problems bring. Fear of being alone. Fear of speaking in public; of asking forgiveness; of what others will think of us; of growing old; of snakes or spiders; of the future ...we all have fear of some sort. Some fear is like a deep anguish that threatens to strangle us. At other times, it is a dull ache that won't go away. It can overpower us, consume us.

David said in Psalm 55:4-5, "*My heart is in anguish within me; the terrors of death assail me. Fear and trembling have beset me; horror has overwhelmed me."* But later in Chapter 55 he also says, *"Cast your cares on the Lord and He will sustain you; He will never let the righteous fall."* (v. 22). Our kind heavenly Father does not give us the spirit of fear ~ that comes from the enemy. Satan loves for us to panic in the face of life's troubles, to run and hide. He laughs! To quote something Joyce Landorf said years ago, "He is acutely aware that he can't take Christ away from us or steal our salvation, but he will do his best to neutralize us into defeated and fatigued specimens of Christianity." He will find that particular panic button and press it over and over again. He wants us to think we live and fight completely alone, and when we begin to feel overwhelmed by life's struggles, it fits in perfectly with his battle plan.

Jesus spoke these words to His disciples, *"Peace I leave with you; My peace I give you. I do not give to you as the world gives. Do not let your hearts be troubled, and do not be afraid."* (John 14:27). The phrase *"Do not be afraid"* is repeated about 365 times in the Bible, incidently. He did say that we would have troubles, but also that He has overcome the world! He knows that we will experience all kinds of anxieties and fears, but He has given us the power of His Spirit to cope with them. Remember, *"I can do all things through Christ which strengtheneth me."* (Philippians 4:13 KJV). We must give our fears to the Lord, and trust Him with them. He alone knows the outcome. And many things we are afraid of never happen anyway. And He will give us the beauty of faith that will never fade.

To quote Gary Wilde, from a daily flip calendar... "Today I can try to remember: Fear loses its power to terrify when I invite it to be my teacher."

JANUARY 8

V-FORMATION...

I love geese. I can hear them honking miles away, and immediately look up in anticipation to see them flying together in V-formation. Oh, sometimes there are only 2 or 3, but many times to my delight I see a whole flock, or "skein" in formation, sometimes their lines are perfect, sometimes pretty wiggly. I know it's gotta be hard to keep in line like that, but God designed them to fly in this aerodynamic V-formation. Even though the V-formation benefits all of the birds, the bird in the lead position has to work the hardest. When this bird tires, it will drop out of the lead position and fall further back into one of the lines of the V. Another bird from further back will rapidly move forward to take the leading position and maintain the formation. The two birds in the furthest trailing positions also tire more rapidly than those in the middle, so these positions are also rotated frequently to spread the most fatiguing locations throughout the flock. The honking we hear is their means of communication, encouraging one another on. Isn't that amazing?

We can take a lesson from the geese. We need each other in our walk of life. Sometimes we stay in formation, following our leader, and sometimes we ARE the leader. Hebrews 10:23 says, *"Let us not give up meeting together, as some are in the habit of doing, but let us encourage one another..."* Sometimes it's hard to stay in line, and sometimes we step out of that formation that keeps us going. Occasionally we want to go and follow a different leader. Frequently the wind is strong and it's cold where we are, and extreme fatigue sets in. If we stay "in V-formation" we will have the support and encouragement of others to help us get through the strong winds of adversity.

Titus 2 teaches us how to be an encouragement to others, and I belong to an online group that has been founded on this chapter. *"Likewise teach the older women to be reverent in the way they live...then they can train the younger women..."* (vs. 3-4). I am so thankful for the women who have come beside me down through the years, all throughout my walk of faith. Sometimes I have been in dire need of help and love and training, and other times I have been able to offer it to someone else. We all need each other. We can take a lesson from nature in so many ways. Let's help each other to stay in V-formation!

JANUARY 9

ASK...

"God insists that we ask, not because He needs to know our situation, but because we need the spiritual discipline of asking." ~ Catherine Marshall.

Asking. We do it everyday. We ask for directions, we ask for advice, we ask questions. Children are always asking, and sometimes their questions annoy us...like "why?!" But this is how they learn. And we'd rather have them ask questions of us, than not to ask at all, or to ask someone else, who is not as qualified to answer. Sometimes we don't have the answer they want, and sometimes we don't have the answer at all.

All our lives we need answers. Answers to the test questions, answers to our financial needs, answers that are hard, or easy, about this or that.

God's word says we should ask. Matthew 7:7 says *"Ask and it will be given to you, seek and you will find…"* and 21:22 says *"If you believe, you will receive whatever you ask for in prayer."* John 14:13: *"And I will do whatever you ask in My name so that the Son may bring glory to the Father. You may ask Me for anything in My name, and I will do it."*

The things we should ask God for are blessings for our marriages, for spiritual renewal and bold faith, for wisdom, for protection, for our families, rest and health, comfort in loss, coping with fear, dealing with temptation, stress, and anxiety. We should pray for a friend who is sick, someone who is graduating or has a new job…well, you get the picture. So many times we ask Him for things that are not important, or that He knows will hurt us.

Jesus tells us that He is the Answer. All our questions must be brought to His empty cross. In Him is all wisdom and knowledge that we cannot get from any other means.

"*Call to Me and I will answer you, and I will tell you great and mighty things which you do not know.*" (Jeremiah 33:3). We can trust any answer He will give us. Too many times we ask God for something, then we go ahead and try to work it out for ourselves, not waiting for His answer. I am learning to wait, as hard as that is sometimes. I would rather wait for His perfect will than to botch it and cause more heartache. I'm excited to see what He has in store for me. Aren't you?

JANUARY 10

FOOT WASHING…

More times than not, my pastor's message corresponds with the same Sunday School lesson I have for my 1st & 2nd graders ~ last week was Servanthood. Don't know how that happens, but when it does, I get a little more material for my class, since Sunday School is after the worship service! The pastor's message was from 1st Samuel 9, about Saul, and how when he was young, he was sent by his father to find the missing donkeys…how his adventure ultimately led him to be anointed by Samuel to be king…although he didn't know it at the time, but he was obedient to his father, and to Samuel, the "seer," and everything he instructed him to do. It's quite a story! Saul was willing and had a servant's heart. My Sunday School lesson was a little different, but still about serving. We came up with lots of ideas about what it means to "wash feet." Our story was from John 13, where Jesus gathers His disciples to wash their feet. The King becoming the Servant. We chose one boy in our class to be a king, and another to be a servant, and we thought of all kinds of jobs each would have. Then I asked what would happen if we reversed the roles, the king cleaning toilets, serving food, feeding the animals, while the servant counted the money, made laws and punished people (the kids' ideas). Then we made a list of all WE could do to be a servant ~ we kept calling it "foot-washing" and I explained that all the things we listed could fall into the category of washing feet. (They were a little grossed out at the thought of washing someone's actual feet!). Some of the things we came up with were, of course, helping mom and dad, being kind, repaying a mean act by doing something nice, listening without interrupting (especially to adults), you get it. These are pretty smart 6-7 year olds!

I attended a foot-washing service in our church many years ago (I have been a member of the same church for over 42 years), and let me tell you, there were many tears and much forgiveness in that service. We were to go to someone who we had an issue with, or someone who was lonely or we did not know very well, or just wanted to encourage. It was beautiful. Do you know that you can "wash feet" every day by doing something kind for someone else? Ephesians 6:7 says, *"Work with enthusiasm, as though you were working for the Lord rather than for people."* It's fun to serve our friends, and even more fun when it's our idea. But has God ever tapped you on the shoulder and asked you to go to someone you'd rather not associate with, especially *"wash their feet?"* Has someone washed your feet lately? (and I don't mean that wonderful pedicure you just had!). Ask God to show you someone who needs a touch of your love and friendship. The world, your city ~ *your church* ~ is full of them! Oh how much we could grow in the Spirit if we would be obedient to His nudgings, and listen to His still small voice.

JANUARY 11

SEARCH ME O GOD...

Psalm 139:23-24 says, *"Search me, O God, and know my heart; try me and know my anxious thoughts; And see if there be any hurtful way in me, and lead me in the way everlasting."*

Here we see the Psalmist, David, asking God to search him, to look into the deepest part of what he is, his own heart. Why would anyone ask this of God? Because we cannot know our own hearts as well as God does. He indwells us, knows every thought, is aware of every feeling…He made us. Earlier in the chapter, David reminds himself that God created his inmost being, that He knew him before he was even born, and sees him, no matter where he goes…David is asking God to test his loyalty to Him, because of wicked men he spoke of earlier.

In contrast to what Solomon had asked God for ~ wisdom, and not money or fame or power ~ David asked that he *"may dwell in the house of the Lord all the days of my life, to behold the beauty of the Lord and meditate in His temple."* (27:4). And even though David had committed great sin, there was a quality in him that pleased God ~ a heartfelt desire for the Lord. And God KNEW his heart, just like He knows our hearts. It took courage for David to pray this prayer ~ "search me, search my heart" just as it takes courage for us to ask the same. It makes us terribly vulnerable before God, but He knows our heart anyway, better than we do. And if we ask Him, He will reveal those places that need to be given up to Him…unforgiveness, hurt & anger, selfishness, anything that would be displeasing to Him. And when we ask Him to lead us in the way everlasting, it means we are willing to be corrected and sanctified by God's loving hands. May this be the desire of our hearts.

JANUARY 12

NEVER STOP MOVING…

I have rheumatoid arthritis, and the motto of one of the advertisements for pain medication is "Never Stop Moving." I find that is true…I tend to stiffen up and become more sore in my joints and muscles if I don't get enough exercise. I do have to keep moving, exercising, walking, bicycling, whatever…All my life I've had what some would call "nervous energy." I always have to be doing something. Even to this day, I can't just sit ~ I have to be at least reading a book or *something*, not just sitting idle.

I think our faith is the same way. Just as we need to exercise our bodies to keep them strong, we must exercise our faith to keep it stimulated as well. Yes, we believe, but Jesus said *"If you have faith as small as a mustard seed, you can say to this mountain, 'Move from here to there' and it will move. Nothing will be impossible for you."* (Matthew 17:20). Do you have enough faith for when the going gets tough? Faith to get you through every day, and every circumstance, no matter how difficult? Exactly what is faith, anyway? Paul told the Hebrews that *"Faith is being sure of what we hope for and certain of what we do not see."* (vs. 11:1). We have faith that God created the universe by His command. Abel, Enoch, Noah, Abraham, Moses, and many others, even Rahab, the prostitute, lived out their faith by offering their sacrifices, following through on God's plan, going where they had not been before...all their stories are outlined in Hebrews 11. Mary had faith in something that sounded completely bizarre. But God had said it, and she believed it to be true. Because *"without faith, it is impossible to please God."* (vs. 6).

We must strive to grow in Jesus' image, living out His teaching and instruction in our own lives and being an example of His divine compassion. We must not become complacent in our Christian walk. If I were to become neglectful of my exercise, I would come to the point where I could not move much at all. I know I must keep moving in order to keep my body limbered up and able to function. The same is true of our faith. God wouldn't make us promises and fail to fulfill them. Promises like, *"I will never leave you or forsake you."* (Heb. 13:5), or *"The Father Himself loves you."* (John 16:27), or *"The Lord will always lead you..."* (Isaiah 58:11). If we believe these, and other promises, we will have the victory over our troubles in life. We will still have trouble, but Jesus said, *"Take heart! I have overcome the world!"* (John 16:33). Faith heals, faith saves, it strengthens and purifies, it encourages. Just as *"The apostles said to the Lord, 'Increase our faith!'"* (Luke 17:5), we too can ask God to increase our faith. Don't let it grow weak and frail. *"Let us fix our eyes on Jesus, the Author and Perfecter of our faith..."* (Heb. 12:2). And share it with others so they, too, may have the hope we do.

JANUARY 13

ONE TOUCH...

My prayer this week has been that God will guide me with His counsel. So, I go where I find that ~ to His word. *"The Lord will guide you always; He will satisfy your needs in a sun-scorched land, and will* ***strengthen your frame****.You will be like a* *well-watered garden, like a spring whose waters never fail."* (Psalm 73:24). I am sure I have read this passage many times ~ even recited it. But I have never locked on to the phrase "strengthen your frame." And I surely do need my frame strengthened! I am in the midst of making a decision whether to add another medication for my RA that my rheumatologist is recommending. There are many possible side effects that are quite frightening. So I took a list of questions to him and he answered them all, and then some. It looks like I may go ahead and begin this drug next week. One of the things the doctor told me was that it's very likely I could go into remission with this medication. Would this be the "strengthening my frame" part?

I believe that God arranged it so that we could take advantage of the medications available to us, if they help us. I hate taking them. But I do like it when they make me feel better. God gave scientists and physicists the knowledge to develop these drugs for our benefit. I know that many times we abuse those drugs and they do more harm than good. I am doing what I can to keep moving, exercising, keeping active ~ but my frame is indeed bent from age, and disease, and will most likely become worse through the coming years. I do know this…when I cross over Jordan, my body will instantly become straight and perfect. I also believe God can do it while I am still here on earth. Whether He chooses to or not is solely His call.

It took only one brief touch of the hem of His garment to bring healing to the believing woman who'd been bleeding for twelve years. And it took one touch to turn Lot's wife into a pillar of salt. God did so much with just one touch…healed the sick and the blind, raised up the lame, wiped out entire armies, put the stars in place, created us! I must be obedient and trust Him in everything. He has already touched my life in so many ways. Paul said in Philippians 4:12-13, *"I have learned to be content whatever the circumstances…I have learned the secret of being content in any and every situation…I can do everything through Him who gives me strength."* So, though I pray for wellness everyday, I still trust Him that my life will be a testimony to HIS strength, whether I am free of my pain, or not.

JANUARY 14

LORD, USE ME…

We all have different gifts and different talents, and sometimes throughout our life, those will change. What we used to think was valuable in the eyes of God are now falling away and other talents take precedence. Some we have we are not even aware of. But God puts people into our lives and into our paths who need exactly what we have. He may not use us in the same capacity He did before, but that doesn't mean we are less valuable in His eyes, and to His kingdom. God uses us for His purposes, and *"His ways are not our ways."* (Isaiah 55:8). Many times we forget how important we are to the process of evangelism. We sometimes believe that if we were not the one to actually lead a person to the Lord, that we had no part in their salvation, but it's not even close to the truth. We are role-models, we send a note, we are behind-the-scene pray-ers, encouragers of teenagers and children, we wash the dishes after the church potluck. Our lives speak volumes.

Have you ever befriended a newlywed couple who has just moved in down the street from you? Or stood on your porch as the little child from next door made his or her way to the school bus, waving, smiling and watching to make sure they got there okay? What about visiting someone who is lonely, or "loaning" $5, not expecting it to be repaid? Giving a hug, or a smile is no less important than writing a check to the missionary offering. There are those around us all day, every day, that need a touch or a kind word. We have no idea how much they are hurting. Sometimes it's us who are hurting. And we are the ones who need that kind word, that hug. There are times when we believe that nobody knows, or cares about what we think or how we feel.

"Lord, when did we see You hungry and feed You, or thirsty and give You something to drink? When did we see You a stranger and invite You in, or needing clothes and clothe You? When did we see You sick or in prison and go to visit You? The King will reply, 'I tell you the truth, whatever you did for one of the least of these brothers of Mine, you did for Me.'" (Matthew 25:37-40). Our Father notices when we say an encouraging word to someone else, He notices that hug, or that tear we shed while praying for another.

I am retired. For more than 25 years I worked at a job and felt fulfilled for the most part, felt that I was contributing to society in some vital way. I especially felt that I was contributing to my family's needs, although some of those needs were being neglected to make way for others. So, working wasn't the perfect solution, either. I did, many times, have opportunity to live my life in the workplace as a testimony to the Lord. So now that I'm not out there working anymore, sometimes I may feel like I am no longer a worthy servant.

But I still have opportunity to talk to my neighbor, to love and nurture my grandchildren, to share my faith with others. I don't have to be standing on the corner proclaiming the promises of God for people to be touched by my life (thank goodness!).

Jesus said, *"You are the light of the world."* (Matthew 5:17). Even if we never say a word, His light will shine forth out of us. He has chosen us, individually, and placed us right where we are at this moment to fulfill His purposes. Sometimes we know what they are, sometimes we don't. We need only keep our hand in His mighty hand, and He will lead us, and use us, and bless us in ways we never imagined. *"As for God, His way is perfect."* (Psalm 18:30).

JANUARY 15

WISDOM FROM GOD...

". . . and if you call out for insight, and cry aloud for understanding, and if you look for it as for silver, and search for it as for hidden treasure, then you will understand the fear of the Lord, and find the knowledge of God. For the Lord gives wisdom, and from His mouth comes knowledge and understanding. He holds victory in store for the upright; He is a shield to those whose walk is blameless, for He guards the course of the just and protects the way of His faithful ones." (Proverbs 2:2-8).

Lord, thank You that You alone make these ~ wisdom and knowledge ~ available to me for the asking. It doesn't mean that I will wake up one morning and instantly be wise and full of knowledge about godly things, but it does mean that the experiences of this life will develop these qualities in me if I ask. And I believe that to be true.

But in order to gain wisdom and insight, I must be always asking, always listening to Your voice through Your word, always obeying. You have the answers and solutions to every challenge we go through and endure in life, no matter how big or how small, how important or how seemingly insignificant. You care about all of it. You WANT to give us wisdom. You WANT us to know the secrets of a happy life in Christ.

So, I have come to the realization that at the end of every experience in my life, I will either be wiser, more sensible and shrewd, or I'll be foolish. So, of course, I constantly pray for wisdom!

James 1:5 says, *"If any of you lacks wisdom, he should ask God, who gives generously to all without finding fault, and it will be given to him."*

JANUARY 16

A BORROWED PRAYER

from Thomas Merton goes something like this... *"My Lord God, I have no idea where I am going. I do not see the road ahead of me. I cannot know for certain where it will end. Nor do I really know myself, and the fact that I think I'm following Your will does not mean I am actually doing so...But I believe that the desire to please You does in fact please you. And I hope I have that desire in all that I am doing... Therefore I will trust You always though I may seem to be lost, and in the shadow of death. I will not fear, for You are ever with me, and You will never leave me to face my perils alone."*

Wow ~ I feel like this often. Lost, no idea where I'm going, wanting so badly to please God, but not sure I am pleasing Him. There are times I know I should be afraid, but I have the peace of God deep inside me. I know He is watching over me. He sees the way I should go, and if I always keep my hand in His, He will lead me.

But life is so uncertain, isn't it? Sometimes the "perils" of life throw us a curve, and things don't turn out the way we expected them to, even if we're sure we are in God's will. I have learned something of late, though. Sometimes it is His will for us to go through suffering, (although He Himself does not *cause* our suffering), because through those dark times, we are forced to look up and put our trust in Him. There is no other way. And through these hard times, we will mature in our faith, grow in our character, and develop perseverance for the rough road ahead.

And the final outcome of our suffering for Christ? *"Blessed is the man who perseveres under trial, because when he has stood the test, he will receive the crown of life that God has promised to those who love Him."* (James 1:12)

Even when it doesn't feel like you're doing anything special for God, or that He doesn't even notice the little things you do, be assured He sees you. He knows your heart, better than you do. And soon this race will be over and we will step forward for that prize, a crown of glory!

JANUARY 17

CHILDREN...

"Only be careful, and watch yourselves closely so that you do not forget the things your eyes have seen, or let them slip from your heart as long as you live. Teach them to your children and to their children after them." (Deut. 4:9).

Wow ~ that in itself is quite an assignment. It says we are to live in such a way that our children, *and* our grandchildren, will learn our faith from us. Seems simple, right? Raising children is a joy, but it can also be exasperating, and scary. We continually ask God for patience, wisdom, rest ~ peace and quiet. And, of course, those things usually come after our hair is gray and our children have moved out. I have wisdom now. I have a lot of patience with my *grand*children. My hair is gray.

I share this prayer with David... *"Since my youth, O God, You have taught me, and to this day I declare Your marvelous deeds. Even when I am old and gray, do not forsake me, O God, till I declare Your power to the next generation, Your might to all who are to come."* (Psalm 71:17-18). Some of us are fortunate to have had loving Christian parents, and knew about God's love from our childhood. Others of us have had to search and find Him for ourselves. But either way, we are admonished to teach God's love to our children and our grandchildren. And we have learned from our mistakes. And God is always there to forgive, holding out His loving arms to us.

Jesus said, *"Let the little children come to Me and do not hinder them, for the kingdom of God belongs to such as these...and He took the children in His arms, put His hands on them and blessed them."* (Mark 10:14, 16). Don't you love this picture?

Today, I bring my little grandson, David, named for the Psalmist, to the arms of our loving God. David will undergo exploratory brain surgery in just a few hours. He's only 8. Oh, he's been down this road several times before. But that doesn't make it any easier. He's a brave little boy, He loves Jesus and knows He'll be with him...so, I pray for David, his parents, all our family (who will all be gathered in the hospital waiting room), for the surgeon and assistants, for his quick recovery. God is so faithful! And I am so thankful!

JANUARY 18

THE TRIP...

Lists...Passport ~ check. Electricity converter ~ check. Camera recharged ~ check. Clothes packed ~ check. Last minute stuff, like toiletries, snacks, book, Bible and journal ~ to come. It takes a lot to get ready for a trip. I hope I don't forget anything. And then, in three days, rising very early, we will load a bus to the airport. 13 days in the Holy Land, the trip of a lifetime. The best part is that two of my three siblings will go along on this much-anticipated tour.

Just last Sunday I was talking to my first- and second-graders about Abram and Lot, and when God sent them into another country. We talked about the reality of that journey. No cars, airplanes, ice chests, or fast-food places to stop along the way. I don't really think they could picture the scene as we discussed it, of the people walking, or riding camels and donkeys, somehow lugging all their earthly possessions, food, clothes, tents (I reminded them their tents weren't like the lightweight nylon ones we have now that go up in a matter of minutes), men, women AND children, not to mention all their sheep and cattle, walking, walking. There were no moving vans, no U-Haul trailers. They had no opportunity of travel to other continents, unless, of course, they took the "slow boat to China." And, well, travel conditions across this wilderness left much to be desired. It was desert, mostly. And mountains. Very rocky. Dusty. They had no maps. They depended on God, who told them, "*...go to the land I will show you.*" (Genesis 12:1). I wonder how long it took them to pack? Certainly longer than me, with my one suitcase and a carry-on. And of course, the trip itself could have taken *months*.

I think of other journeys we read about ~ the long trip through the wilderness for the Israelites when they finally were able to get out of Egypt, (that one took WAY longer than necessary), the trip to Bethlehem for Mary & Joseph, and in her delicate condition. Or, the trip to the Cross. That was a lifetime in the planning. And when the disciples encountered the Savior after His resurrection, he told them, *"Peace be with you! As the Father has sent Me, I am sending you."* (John 20:21). All these travel arrangements were made by Almighty God. There will be one final journey we all take ~ and our safe arrival at our final destination depends on our careful planning, following the roadmaps laid out for us, persevering through the hindrances and detours this life has to offer. If we are faithful, and depend on His guidance, we will arrive safely in the *"land flowing with milk and honey."* (Ex. 3:8). Paradise. The place prepared just for us. This coming trip for me will be just a tiny taste of that glorious place. Walking where Jesus walked will be nothing short of feeling close to Him.

JANUARY 19

HANDS...

I love looking at hands. There are small hands, large hands, strong and weak hands. Old, gnarled and calloused hands, and tiny little fresh hands. I think I like to look at the two last types the best. Those wee little hands of a baby or toddler, the way they explore everything, feel everything, learn what's HOT and what's cold...but it's those old wrinkled and arthritic hands that fascinate me most. I like to wonder where those wonderful hands have been in their lifetime. All the hard work they have done, and the tender loving that has come from them. Hands. One day as I was teaching first grade Sunday school, a little girl who was sitting beside me was gently touching my hand...she was pushing on the puffy vein that was sticking out through my thin and wrinkled skin. I just went on like nothing was happening, smiling in my heart. Here was another person fascinated with hands.

There is a new sweet-voiced recording artist named J.J. Heller who sings "When my world is shaking, heaven stands ~ when my heart is breaking, I never leave your hands... Your hands that shaped the world are holding me..." What a thought! The very hands that put our planet, and all the rest of the planets, together, placed them in orbit, made the grass, trees, and animals, actually hold me when I am troubled. There's a song we used to sing when I was younger, "He's Got the Whole World in His Hands." It's true, you know. Sometimes it doesn't seem like it, but God is aware of everything that is happening in our world, and in our lives. And "He is in control," a phrase I hear more and more these days.

And why wouldn't God care about us, His prized possession, His masterpiece? He laid the foundation of the world, He formed each snowflake, each star, He stretched out His hand over the Red Sea, He wrote the 10 Laws on tablets of stone with His fingertips. He can move mountains, hold back armies, close lion's mouths, bring down fire from heaven to prove His mighty power, even stop the sun (!). But His touch, with those precious nail-scarred hands, is also gentle, loving, kind and soothing. *"For I am the Lord your God, who takes hold of your right hand and says to you, Do not fear, I will help you."* (Isaiah 41:13). And we say... *"My soul clings to You;Your right hand upholds me."* (Ps. 63:8). There are so many things God's hands do that we don't even think about, we can't see, and will never know. So many ways He helps us that we don't realize.

My trusty little book, "At the Name of Jesus" (by Sarah Hornsby) says, "Jesus is God's HAND. Through Jesus, God acts to make Himself and His ways known. Healing, signs, and wonders take place through Jesus. He says...Let God be near to you today. Let His burning, recreative touch rest on you now. [But He uses us, too]... You are part of My body. Will your touch bring someone into God's Presence today? '*And now, Lord, take note of their threats, and grant that Thy bond-servants may speak Thy word with all confidence, while Thou dost extend Thy hand to heal, and signs and wonders take place through the name of Thy holy servant Jesus.*'" (Acts 4:29-30 KJV). Will you be His hands? Will I?

JANUARY 20

FILL ME...

What does it mean to be filled? Webster says it means "to put as much as possible into a container, or space; to take up the whole of; to supply things needed; to satisfy hunger..." When we've just eaten a large meal, we affirm that we are "full." I once applied for a class that was already filled to capacity. When something wonderful happens in our lives, we are filled with joy. Or, we can be filled with dread, or fear, as well. In 2 Chronicles, 7:1, *"...the glory of the Lord* ***filled*** *the temple."* In Psalm 72:19, David proclaimed, *"May the whole earth be filled with His glory."*

There is a relatively new song by Chris Sligh entitled "Empty Me" which tells of the only way we may be truly filled with His own Spirit...the words of the chorus are:

"Empty me of the selfishness inside
Every vain ambition and the poison of my pride
And any foolish thing my heart holds to
Lord empty me *of me so I can be filled with you."*

The first time I heard that song on the radio, it took my breath away. We get just a little taste of the little things of this world and, like the Prodigal son, we want more. Doesn't matter if it's money, recognition, power…chocolate, the more of these things we hold dear in our heart, or anything that becomes so consuming to us, other than God's Holy presence, then the less room there is for God and His sovereign Spirit. John 3:30 states: *"He must become greater; I must become less."* I'm not saying we should never be recognized for the good things we do ~ but, we should be sure to give God the glory. And we do need money in order to live and feed our families, and keep a roof over our heads, but we should not become greedy ~ we should thank Him for His provision, recognizing it comes from Him. And it's not wrong to love chocolate ~ but some of us love it TOO much! As for power, let's be filled with HIS power… and the only way to do that is to empty ourselves. Let that be our prayer. It will change our relationships, our priorities, and we will be blessed beyond measure.

Paul wrote to the Philippians, 4:8: *"Finally brothers [and sisters], whatever is true, whatever is noble, whatever is right, whatever is pure, whatever is lovely, whatever is admirable ~ if anything is excellent or praiseworthy, think about such things."* Empty me, so I may be ***filled*** with the Holy Spirit.

JANUARY 21

WORSHIP IS FOR ALL AGES…

I was reading in Joel 2 where the Lord proclaims *"return to Me with all your heart, with fasting and weeping and mourning…for He is gracious and compassionate, slow to anger and abounding in love…"* (vs.12 & 13). It was after the locusts had come through and devoured their land, and as the people of Zion were pleading for deliverance, the prophet declared a holy fast, "*…call a sacred assembly. Gather the people, consecrate the assembly; bring together the elders, gather the children, those nursing at the breast. Let the bridegroom leave his room, and the bride her chamber."* (vs.

15,16). This assembly didn't just call for the elders and the adults, or for just certain chosen ones...but ALL the people, all ages, the elderly, young nursing mothers, little children, newlyweds... "gather the people."

We include our children in worship services at our church. There are certain Sundays when they do have "children's church" downstairs, and we have a nursery for the very tiny ones, but there are always children, of all ages, in our services. And once a month they have their own special section they get to sit in, right up front. My own children were usually present when they were growing up. We wanted them to learn that worship is sacred. We wanted them to learn the hymns they would sing when they, too, were grown up. We explained communion to them at an early age and they were allowed to partake of the sacraments when they understood. And now, my grandchildren are such a blessing to me, as well. We must have trained our children right, because they have always included their own children in our worship services, and the little ones have been reverently enjoying our communion times for a few years.

The one, or two, things that really touch me are when our little 7-year old granddaughters sing at the top of their lungs (on key, and getting the words right) the choruses and songs we sing as a congregation, and how they readily go forward to pray with someone who has gone to the altar...this is usually our children's director, or one of the teens they adore, but last Sunday, an older man found our little Alizabeth kneeling quietly beside him with her little hand on his shoulder. My heart melted! I can only imagine how he felt! And I love that an act such as this is not stifled by anyone who might believe the children have no place in the service, especially praying at the altar. Oh, believe me, there are some who would think that. But what a blessing they give us in their simple faith. My heart is filled with joy when I think of the generations in our own family (four, so far) who have worshipped and grown together in our church. I feel truly blessed.

So next time you're in church and you hear a baby cry, or a child who must be shushed, or you see a young couple gazing lovingly at one another, or an elderly gentleman nodding off...just remember that God has called ALL people to come into His presence for worship. How else will the little ones learn? We are all part of the body of Christ, young and old. God will bless us all, regardless of our age or standing. After all, Jesus said, *"Let the little children come to me, and do not hinder them, for the kingdom of God belongs to such as these."* (Luke 18:16).

JANUARY 22

JESUS IS ENOUGH...

There is a song I've heard countless times on the radio, and one we sing in church as well, entitled "Enough." Some of the lyrics are: "All of You is more than enough for all of me, for every thirst and every need, You satisfy me with Your love, and all I have in You is more than enough..." Did you ever think about that? In our society, we want so much, don't we? We want it all, in fact. We seem to never be satisfied. We want more friends, more money, more to eat, bigger houses, better cars, all the electronics, and when more are invented, we want those too. And when our lives begin to fall apart, we think all these things will solve our problems and bring us happiness. And when they don't, we want still more.

Jesus is sufficient...He is enough...He is all we ever need. When He truly is Lord of our lives, we can enjoy contentment in any situation. When we desire Him with all our heart, soul, mind and strength, His love fills up all other needs in our life as well. And what He gives us, we can share with others. Only as we empty ourselves can He fill us to overflowing with His loving Holy Spirit.

"*And He has said to me, 'My grace is sufficient for you, for my power is made perfect in weakness.' Most gladly, therefore, I will rather boast about my weaknesses, that the power of Christ may dwell in me.*" (2 Corinthians 12:9). Paul had the right idea here. If anyone was entitled to NOT be content, he was. His life was not going as HE had planned it. Yet, he had given himself fully to God to be used for His ministry, and although he had everything to be DIScontented about ~ beatings, prison, poverty, illness...he still praised God and was thankful in each circumstance. Paul recognized that God's power would be manifested in his own weakness. After all, if Paul were powerful enough to get himself out of his undesirable circumstances, how would that give glory to a Savior? But Christ WAS glorified in Paul's situation. And all the more can He be glorified when we come to the end of ourselves and our resources. An old song in our hymnal puts it this way:

"He giveth more grace as our burdens grow greater,
He sendeth more strength as our labors increase;
To added afflictions He addeth His mercy,

To multiplied trials He multiplies peace.
"When we have exhausted our store of endurance,
When our strength has failed ere the day is half done,
When we reach the end of our hoarded resources
Our Father's full giving is only begun...
"His love has no limits, His grace has no measure,
His power has no boundary known unto men;
For out of His infinite riches in Jesus
He giveth, and giveth, and giveth again."
(Annie Johnson Flint)

Oh, it is SO like Him. Instead of trusting in ourselves, or in our own resources, let's allow Him to show us His great mercy and grace. Our needs can never be greater than His provision. He is enough!

JANUARY 23

ALL HIS PROMISES...

"Yet he [Abraham] did not waver through unbelief regarding the promise of God, but was strengthened in his faith and gave glory to God, being fully persuaded that God had power to do what He had promised." (Romans 4:20-21). Yesterday I was reading in "Streams in the Desert" about God's promises. Another paraphrase of that 21st verse is: "Being absolutely certain that whatever promise He is bound by, He is able also to make good." (Weymouth). I love God's promises. I read them, somewhere in His word, every day. F.B. Meyer said "There is hardly any position more utterly beautiful, strong, or safe, than to put the finger upon some promise of the Divine word, and claim it. There need be no anguish, or struggle, or wrestling; we simply present the check and ask for cash; produce the promise and claim its fulfillment; nor can there be any doubt as to the issue."

God's promises are not empty promises written just to fill up a book. His promises are true and living. And nothing is too difficult for Him. Our Father delights in meeting our needs and strengthening our faith. Each week when I send my husband off on a bus trip, I pray that God will watch over him all the way... God promised... *"For the Lord watches over the way of the righteous."* (Psalm

1:6) and… *"The Lord watches over you ~ the Lord is your shade at your right hand; the sun will not harm you by day, nor the moon by night. The Lord will keep you from all harm ~ He will watch over your life; the Lord will watch over your coming and going both now and forever more."* (Psalm 121:5-8). And so I claim this promise for my husband as he drives away, praying it back to God. And for my children as well. My youngest daughter and her husband just flew off to the Dominican Republic last week ~ I had a deep peace that they would be safe and well. And they returned late Sunday night, safe and well! My heart overflows with thanks!

God said *"I will never leave you nor forsake you."* (Joshua 1:5). I believe He is constant! The Lord promised to give us strength, and wisdom if we ask for it, and joy in our troubles. He said He'd bless us if we give ~ and it's true! He has also promised us eternal life if we walk with Him, and I realize that my body is getting more and more feeble as my years go by, but I know when God's purpose for me has been fulfilled here on this earth, I will walk forever with my Friend in heaven! He *promised!* And this gives me hope. All His promises are true, and I know if we stand firmly on His promises, we will not fail. There is a song that says, "All Your promises are true, I will lift up my eyes to You for You're all that I need and by faith I receive the wonderful things You will do. All Your promises are true, I will lift up my eyes to You, when my heart starts to fail, Lord Your strength will prevail, and all You have said You will do…"The scriptures are full of God's promises to His children. Take God at His word. What kind of a God would He be if we couldn't believe what He says? And my favorite: " *'For I know the plans I have for you' declares the Lord, 'plans to prosper you and not to harm you, plans to give you a hope and a future.'"* (Jeremiah 29:11).

JANUARY 24

COMFORT FOOD…

Oh, we all have some sort of comfort food, don't we? Special foods that make us feel good. We eat it when we are happy, when we are sad, or anxious. I actually have several. Peanut butter is one. Tea, though not exactly a "food" also gives me comfort, for whatever reason. Some people need ice cream, some chocolate. Others will need a whole meal, or many of them...some of us eat too much of our comfort foods. Most of the comfort foods we eat are familiar delicious foods, usually home-cooked, "like Mom used to make." They are nostalgic, most times something sweet. These foods bring back warm memories of our childhood, or a special occasion. But usually they are easy to prepare, or just to grab without preparation. Did I mention French fries? Sometimes the urge will hit me as I am passing by Wendy's or some fast-food place, and I have to turn in and order "just a small fry, please." And really, not even for my comfort...I'm not feeling particularly sad, or anxious, about anything ~ I just want French fries! Thankfully, I don't do this often!

God is the maker of all our foods...well, not ALL of them, really. Numerous foods today contain so many foreign or man-made ingredients, we can hardly call them food, and certainly they are not nutritious! He created an array of delicious foods, full of nutrients, for our health, our enjoyment, for medicinal purposes, and as if we did not think they were enough, we "improved" upon His offering. He had us all taken care of. I believe if we had stuck to the foods He provided for us, we would be healthier and would not have all the diseases and health problems we have today. Some of the foods we eat are very close to being plastic, it's scary. God said, *"I give you every seed-bearing plant on the face of the whole earth and every tree that has fruit with seed in it. They will be yours for food."* (Gen. 1:29).

Paul made reference to food when he was talking to the Corinthians about their spiritual maturity, *"Brothers, I could not address you as spiritual but as worldly ~ mere infants in Christ. I gave you milk, not solid food, for you were not yet ready for it."* (1 Cor. 3:1-2). And Jesus said to His disciples, when, after a hard day, they thought he should eat something, *"I have food to eat that you know nothing about."* (John 4:32). Jesus found satisfaction in doing God's assigned work... *"My food," Jesus said, "is to do the will of Him who sent me and to finish His work."* (4:34). Remember, Jesus fasted forty days in the wilderness, obedient to the Holy Spirit...and when tempted by Satan, He answered, *"Man does not live on bread alone, but on every word that comes from the mouth of God."* (Matt. 4:4). Bingo! This is our *real* comfort food...the Word of God. When I am tired, or sick, or anxious, or sad, or afraid, I find more comfort by turning the pages of the sacred Book than I ever would in French fries, ice cream, or peanut butter. God's word is food for our very souls. It supplies us with all we need. It is nourishment from above. Jesus IS our Comforter. He cheers us with strength and hope in our times of trouble or grief. It is HIS Spirit which comforts us. Like manna from heaven! It's all we need.

JANUARY 25

TO APPEAL...

I got a bill the other day from my insurance company which included a ridiculous charge of $124 for a "surgery" performed in the office. That was way over and above my co-payment for the visit. The doctor had looked at a little "lesion" or pimple, if you please, on my face that had been there for a long time, and froze the cells by spraying a solution from an aerosol can. Hardly "surgery." I could have done that myself. The definition for surgery is: "removal of diseased parts or tissue by cutting." There certainly was no cutting, or otherwise touching by any instrument.

I decided today to appeal this charge. The dictionary says to appeal is "to make an urgent and earnest request for a decision, opinion, help, sympathy, etc.; to call upon some authority or person for a decision, etc.; to pray and supplicate with humility in entreaty implying the request is addressed to God, or to a superior authority"...Ahh...so an appeal would be the same thing as a prayer...my letter was kind of like that. I begged the insurance company, in a nice way of course, to reconsider the ridiculous charge.

We make appeals all the time...to our children, for some task we wish they'd do for us; I receive appeals from telemarketers all the time, for a charity, or some other good cause; politicians are making appeals quite often for votes of the people...we make appeals to God for many things.

So, what kind of a charge do we appeal to God for? He's already paid the price for our sin, and believe me, there is no way I could ever afford the cost for my pardon. And yet, He paid it willingly ~ without my even asking Him to. But we do need to ask, we need to make an appeal to Him, for forgiveness. Just as His word makes appeals to us to live a righteous life, to be perfect, to love our brother (and sister), to encourage one another, to pray without ceasing. So, *"Let us then approach the throne of grace with confidence, so that we may receive mercy and find grace to help us in our time of need."* (Hebrews 4:16). As soon as we utter His name, He is ready to listen to our appeal.

JANUARY 26

DECISIONS...

We make decisions every day, all of us. Some are easy, some are hard. Some decisions are regular every day, like, what to wear, what to fix for dinner, what to watch on TV. We choose whether to ride or walk, drive or fly, call, email or text. Sometimes we ask for help making a determination, such as how a certain dress looks on us, asking for someone else's opinion of a book, or a restaurant, or a doctor. Big decisions, like relocating to another city or state, require a lot of consideration.

Yesterday my oldest granddaughter had to make a very difficult decision about an ongoing situation, and the decision she made was very mature and wise, although it was heartbreaking for her. And she was not alone. Her family stood behind her and supported her decision. It's hard for parents to watch their children agonize over a resolution, and sometimes they take a long time. Parents want to help, they want to just take care of it for them. But the child will not gain wisdom from having someone else solve the problem.

I have had to watch my own children make decisions in their lives, and although I have been there to offer counsel, they made up their own minds to do what they thought best. And yet, it wasn't best. Our own hearts broke many times. But we were always there to stand by them, to help them, to pray with them.

It's like that with our heavenly Father. Many times I have made a wrong choice, knowing it was against what God's best would be for me, but sometimes, because we don't see things as God sees them, we think we know what will work. God doesn't stand there with His hands on His hips, shaking His divine finger at us saying, "I told you so!" Instead, He lovingly takes us in His arms and comforts us, and loves us. And He forgives us. We learn to trust Him. And eventually we are able to make wise choices, welcoming His guidance and counsel. There will even come a time when we don't want to make ANY choices or decisions without first going to God. *"Trust the Lord with all your heart, and lean not on your own understanding; in all your ways acknowledge Him and He will make your paths straight."* (Proverbs 3:5-6). Satan, of course, would want us to make unwise choices. He likes nothing better than for our plans to fall flat. He wants us to become impatient in waiting for God's perfect timing in any circumstance, and to just jump ahead, doubting that God will answer our request. His voice screams out at us, but God's voice is tender, never forceful.

When you have an important decision to make, whose voice are you listening for? *"If any of you lacks wisdom, he should ask God, who gives generously to all without finding fault."* (James 1:5). I want the wisdom that my heavenly Father gives ~ don't you?

JANUARY 27

LET HIM BOAST...

It seems like there is a lot of boasting going on these days. We hear it on the television, not only in advertisements about certain products, but also in speeches made by people in the political realm. Children boast about what they know or what they can do, or the stuff they have, or how strong their dad is! Parents brag about their children. I guess we all boast, sometimes without thinking about it, or realizing it.

God had appointed Jeremiah prophet, put words in his mouth and told him to proclaim whatever He commanded to Israel. The Lord had a whole speech to give him, and Jeremiah spoke it to the people. It wasn't pretty. He reprimanded them. Reminded them of their earlier devotion to the Lord, and then how they had sinned greatly and fallen away. And He pronounced His judgment on them, still giving them *another chance* to make it right, and He promised to bless their nation if they turned back to Him. Sometimes we think (personally) maybe God forgot, since our sin was a long time ago. God doesn't forget, unless we've repented. Does it sound like He may have been speaking to us? He warned them, in detail, of great disaster and destruction coming their way, then... *"'Should you not fear Me?' declares the Lord. 'Should you not tremble in My presence?'"* (5:22). What is wrong with us?! We don't fear Him OR tremble in His presence. We are not ashamed of our conduct ~ and the Lord says, *"Stand at the crossroads and look; ask for the ancient paths, ask where the good way is, and walk in it, and you will find rest for your souls."* (6:16). He has made the way very clear to us in His word. And yet, we disobey Him, blatantly. Again, He said to the people, *"Obey Me and I will be your God and you will be My people. Walk in all the ways I command you, that it may go well with you."* (7:23). They still did not pay attention to Him, the Sovereign Lord, who loved them deeply.

God did not give up, and in the midst of their disobedience and boasting, He said, *"but let him who boasts boast about this: that he understands and knows Me, that I am the Lord who exercises kindness, justice and righteousness on earth, for in these I delight."* (9:24). Now, that's not all the story. God and Jeremiah were actually holding a seminar for these people in the desert, and it goes on and on. And God is still trying to get these truths into His people's hearts and minds, yet today. We are not getting it. We don't understand why God doesn't hear our prayers, why He doesn't heal us, why he doesn't send relief for our hardships. And we continue to boast about what good people we are, and what accomplishments we can take credit for. Like Paul, let us say, *"May I never boast except in the cross of our Lord Jesus Christ..."* (Galatians 6:14). Isn't it about time we started telling others what God has done for us, instead of what we have done for Him?

JANUARY 28

JANUARY....

After the snow and frigid temperatures, came the rain. This is the part of winter that is so dreary to me, and although it is a little warmer, I am sometimes chilled to the bone because of the dampness...and then usually the snow and cold returns, after everyone gets used to the warmer temps, and looking forward to spring!

January is also a favorite time for football enthusiasts, although I cannot imagine sitting outside on cold bleachers in below freezing temperatures in sleet just to say I was able to watch my team win, or lose.

I am thankful for my warm home, comfy bed and plenty of blankets and sweaters. Hot tea and soup warms me from the inside out. Flickering candles help to warm the late light of morning and the early dark of the evening. Not that they put out a lot of heat, but they lend to a cozy atmosphere. But then I think of the homeless people we have among us. We may encounter someone in the store, on the street...in church...and not be aware of their plight. They do not have the comforts of home as we have – not a roof over their heads or a hot meal. Oh, there are several homeless shelters, and soup kitchens around, but they leave much to be desired, especially where family is concerned. Some offer a room, a bed, and a meal, but not much comfort for the loneliness.

Jesus said, *"For I was hungry and you gave me something to eat. I was thirsty and you gave me something to drink. I was a stranger and you invited me in, I needed clothes and you clothed me. I was sick and you looked after me, in prison and you came to visit me..."And when they asked,"Lord when did we do all these things?"Jesus answered,"Whatever you did for one of the least of these brothers of mine, you did for Me."* (Matthew 25:35-40).

January is almost gone, but there are still a few months when we will experience bitter cold and darkness. Think about those less fortunate who will have frost-bitten fingers, cramping stomachs from lack of food, fatigue and loneliness, and no where to sleep...and find ways to help, whether it is carrying a few extra pairs of gloves in your car, or an extra coat, some granola bars, socks. Give of yourself, in Jesus' name. You will be blessed.

JANUARY 29

MIRACLES...

We really see miracles everyday, even when we don't recognize them. On Sunday my daughter Bridgette ran/walked in the Susan G. Komen "Race for the Cure." She was so proud to be a part of that event. She is a cancer survivor, although not breast cancer. On Saturday she donated 10" of her hair to Locks of Love. To each recipient of a wig made with donated hair, that is a miracle, a gift of love. For weeks, Bridgette has been collecting donations for this cause, and she exceeded her goal. She was very proud of that. She said the survivors, all miracles, wore a special Survivor T-shirt, and at an appointed time, after the race, each one released a pink balloon into the air. She said it was breathtaking. Hundreds of miracles all together in one place! What a thrill!

Sometimes it's easy for us to get caught up in a "cause" and volunteer our time and resources, without realizing the sheer miracle that has taken place in the lives of many others who are involved. Jesus did many miracles during the few years of His ministry. He turned water into wine, He cast out demons,

He healed many diseases and illnesses ~ He even brought the dead back to life. *"Jesus of Nazareth was a man accredited by God to you by miracles, wonders and signs, which God did among you through Him..."* (Acts 2:22). He still does miracles today. We have seen many of them in our own ladies' groups...Andrew is a miracle, little Noah is cancer-free, Nancy found a new job because she trusted God, Heather was ultimately healed when she was taken to heaven, and through her faith many people were touched deeply. Betty's recent car-accident could have inflicted more serious injury, but it didn't. Even the miracle of friendship and encouragement for one another gives us hope. We have seen hearts changed, marriages reconciled, relationships mended, finances provided. These are all miracles from God's hand. We don't know how He does them, but we know we couldn't have. Sometimes situations and circumstances are out of our control and we see no hope for change. *"But nothing is impossible for God."* (Luke 1:37). He alone offers us hope.

The dictionary's definition of miracle is: "an event or action that apparently contradicts known scientific laws and is hence thought to be due to supernatural causes, especially to an act of God; a marvel." Many people will tell of a near-death accident in which "someone" carried them to safety, or they were unhurt in the midst of terrible wreckage. Miracles don't just involve people ~ all of God's creation is a miracle. Look at the rose, how perfectly formed it is and how it opens up, it's fragrance. Or the birth of a baby which is planted by a seed, grows in its mother's womb, and comes forth at the appointed time, a fully formed human being. And the instinct of a wild animal in finding food and caring for its young. How the stars and planets stay in their places in the sky.

Let's open our eyes to the things we take for granted, which can only be done by God's own hand. And thank Him for His big, and little, miracles in our own lives.

JANUARY 30

THE TRIP OF A LIFETIME...

I recently was privileged to spend thirteen days in the Holy Land, and what a thrill to see the places Jesus walked and lived. There were 21 of us, including one 8-year-old child and two teenagers, who all had an incredible time. Our tour guide made the trip, really. A fine Christian man who knew of all the places and quoted the scriptures with his heart ~ not only *by* heart, but he lived them. What a learning experience for all of us!

There was a place on the mountain (one of the many) that our guide pointed out as the "crossroads," and I immediately was thrilled because one of my favorite scripture verses is Jeremiah 6:16, *"Stand at the crossroads and look; ask for the ancient paths, ask where the good way is and walk in it, and you will find rest for your soul."* And oh, did we climb mountains, and ancient stone steps, and we descended deep into the earth to explore tunnels and caves. Each one had particular significance. We even visited a deep and huge cave called a "columbarium," where the ancients raised pigeons and doves to be sold for sacrifices. Who knew? And the Western Wall where we also witnessed the celebrations of a few Bar-Mitzvahs. The ancient customs still go on.

Some of the favorites were Caesarea, Mt. Carmel, Nazareth, the Jordan Valley, the Dead Sea, Masada, Qumran, Ein Gedi, Tzippori, Jericho, and Bethlehem. We hiked up hills in the Judean Wilderness, visited the Temple Mount, Dome of the Rock which is now closed to everyone but Muslims, and the Garden of Gethsemane. We wandered through the narrow Hezekiah's tunnels, gazed on, and in, the Garden Tomb and at Golgotha. And experienced a beautiful and private communion service right there in the Garden.

There is something to be said about the Mediterranean diet...it's wonderful. Our hotels served huge buffets each morning and evening full of wonderful salads, breads, meat dishes and fresh fruits, including dates and figs, of course! We ate well, yet I still managed to lose a couple of pounds because of all the walking we did!

I know it was God who made this trip possible for me... *"Delight yourself also in the Lord and He shall give you the desires of your heart. Commit your way to the Lord, trust also in Him and He shall bring it to pass."* That's in Psalm 37:4-5, and it has long been a favorite of mine.

There was much fellowship, and deep friendships were nurtured. I missed out on the huge snowstorm we had at home, but it was worth it. I wouldn't have wanted to be anywhere else!

JANUARY 31

GREATER IS HE...

I received news yesterday that some author friends of mine have had their beautiful Christian website hacked by Muslim extremists. This is not the first time. When someone is doing something great for God, the enemy tries his best to thwart their efforts. They have a wonderful blog, full of so much knowledge, which gives ALL the glory to God for everything they write in their books, and all that happens in their lives. It is so disturbing that one, or a few, jealous people think they have the right to terrorize good people like these, who only proclaim the truth. I pray for God's protection on them and their work, and that from this moment on He would put His hedge around their website and their lives, and family, an invisible impenetrable shield so that they can go on proclaiming the truth as they have done in years past. I pray also that God would encourage them in their work so they *"do not become weary in doing good, for at the proper time we will reap a harvest if we do not give up."* (Gal. 6:9).

I love what a friend shared yesterday from "Streams in the Desert" about God's victories, and how it sometimes looks like the enemy is winning, but then God comes in and upsets all the work of the enemy, and "turns the way of the wicked upside down." And here's the phrase I love... "Thus He gives a great deal *larger* victory than we would have known if He had not allowed the enemy, seemingly, to triumph in the first place." So what sometimes looks like the enemy getting the upper hand, is really just a precursor to his ultimate defeat. And God's timing is perfect in it all.

So, I pray for my friends, that the Lord will give them the strength to persevere. I know they are not the type of people to give up so easily. *"But one thing I do: Forgetting what is behind and straining toward what is ahead, I press on toward the goal to win the prize for which God has called me heavenward in Christ Jesus."* (Philippians 3:13-14). Please help me in lifting up these beautiful people in prayer, that God will show them the blessing in their suffering. *"Greater is He that is in me than he that is in the world."* (1 John 4:4)

FEBRUARY 1

TIME...

This morning I was marveling that another month has begun, and at how fast time seems to go by, for some, at least. Well, it's time the way WE see it, anyway. But to God, *"a thousand years [in Your sight] are like a day that has just gone by."* (Psalm 90:4). We are so driven by time. The clock, the calendar, the oven timer...we stress about never having "enough" time. But we're all given 24 hours. In fact, that's not even a sure thing. We have no guarantee that we'll have this afternoon, let alone tomorrow. And when we step into God's presence, time will stand still ~ we won't even measure it, for any reason. Eternity. Hard for our finite minds to grasp. Schedules? There won't be any. Deadlines? They won't exist. No time limits forevermore. *"Can you fathom the mysteries of God? Can you probe the limits of the Almighty?"* (Job 11:7).

So, how do you spend your time, anyway? one might ask. Well, if you have a career, you spend time driving, in meetings, on the phone, with customers, on the computer, generating and printing reports, making lattes, flipping hamburgers, scanning products through a cash register. Even if you stay at home you're still on the phone, the computer, shopping, cooking, driving, washing and drying, cleaning, appointments...and once in awhile there is time for a book or a TV show. If we get up early enough we may spend a few minutes in God's word, or running or working out. Our days are full to the brim. We all have the same amount of hours, yet, some seem to be able to get much more done than others.

Psalm 90:12 says, *"Teach us to number our days aright, that we may gain a heart of wisdom."* I'm not so sure I know exactly what that means. God is the only one who knows the number of our days. But what I think it might mean is that we should take extra care to make our lives and our days count for Him, asking for the wisdom He alone gives us. Is our time spent caring only for our own needs? Or do we set our own plans aside to care for one in need of encouragement, love, help, affirmation, discipline?

I like to think of God as joyfully anticipating our arrival in heaven, just as we have felt when we had a special, unbelievable surprise waiting for someone we love. We can hardly wait until they get home, or until we meet them, so we can see the amazement and wonder in their face, and share their delight. *"No eye has seen, no ear has heard, no mind has conceived what God has in store [prepared] for those who love Him."* (I Cor. 2:9). This world will pass away. For some of us it will be sooner than for others, but God's timing will be perfect. God's sense of time is secret to us. He had no beginning, and He will have no end. And when we are in His presence, and time will be no more, we will have eternity to figure it out!

FEBRUARY 2

PREDICTIONS...

Have you ever made a prediction? It's pretty easy to do. Certainly we hear them all the time. I think the most common is a weather prediction...we especially pay particular attention to them this time of year, in the winter. We plan our travel by what the forecast is. But many times ~ they are dead wrong. In fact, lately, where I live, they are seldom right. This doesn't mean that the meteorologists are incompetent, or don't know what they are talking about... it only means that the weather patterns can change course and take a turn, and miss us completely.

This week, as every year, we tuned in to a little fat creature known as a groundhog, Punxsutawney Phil, who apparently can tell us if spring will be early or on time, just based on whether he sees his shadow or not when he emerges from his hole. This, of course, is absurd, but what started out as superstition and legend, has now become a tradition...all over the world. We are duped if we think one little rodent in one certain town can predict the changing of the seasons on every continent. The seasons are naturally going to change ~ our world was designed that way.

The weather is not the only prediction we make ~ we can predict someone's behavior, especially if it has been typical; we can predict trouble when certain situations obviously lead up to it...there are religious cults who forecast the "end of the world" by even going so far as to name dates. In Acts 1:7 Jesus said, *"It is not for you to know the times or dates the Father has set by His own authority."* In fact, *"No one knows about that day or hour, not even the angels in heaven, nor the Son, but only the Father."* (Matthew 24:36). So, if not even Jesus knows the time of His return, how is it that men on earth can claim to know it? None of us can even know if we'll have tomorrow, although we make plans for it.

There are many mysteries. We can do a lot of guesswork and speculation. Horoscopes tell you how to plan your day by predicting all kinds of things... how your job will go, how your love life will develop, if you'll have bad or good luck, and many of them are utterly ridiculous, but there are great numbers of people won't even begin their day without first consulting their zodiac sign. But the only One who can truly see into the future is our heavenly Father. Believe it or not, He knew our future before He even created us. He wants us to trust Him, and not the ideas of men. *"Trust in the Lord with all your heart, and lean not on your own understanding."* (Proverbs 3:5). Are you anticipating the events that are foretold by the psychics, or relying on the promises of God, put forth in His word to us, to lead and guide us, and to provide for all our needs?

FEBRUARY 3

STORMS

What a beautiful storm we had last night. I love thunderstorms. We'd been waiting for it for two days...you know how dependable weather forecasts are! Did you know that lightning "fixes" nitrogen in the air breaking up molecules that fall to earth onto the grass to green it up? Isn't that amazing? *Natural* fertilizer. It was cloudy all day, then during dinner we began to hear the thunder roll, then a few flashes of lightning. I opened a window so I could hear it...I don't know why ~ but I always feel so cozy in a storm (when I'm inside!). God created the storm ~ *"He made the darkness His covering, His canopy around Him ~ the dark rain clouds of the sky. Out of the brightness of His presence clouds advanced, with hailstones and bolts of lightning..."* (Psalm 18:12). After the storm, I stepped outside into the stillness, hearing the raindrops still dripping from the trees. The sky was black in the direction the storm was heading, but that just made the double rainbow all the more brilliant! I stood there and gazed at it for a few minutes, just praising God. The sun was just setting, and the western sky was bright behind me, but the most amazing color, between orange and yellow was appearing in the east, a huge cloud, almost mushroom-like, bright against the dark gray sky. I am so in awe of God's handiwork. Never in my lifetime could I think of colors to put into the sky, or the flowers, or the layers of the earth.

Our lives are like the storm sometimes. We have some beautiful days, but then something begins to loom overhead ~ finances, relationships, crises ~ like the clouds forming and building gradually, and then the storm breaks and thunder crashes, and unless we are under the shelter of His wings, where it's cozy and safe, we are faced with fear, and uncertainty, and danger. Sometimes we run, looking for a safe place, a shelter. Our heavenly Father, Creator of all the universe, the earth, the sun, moon and stars, and yes, the storms, is waiting with His loving arms wide open. We are safe. He has promised to never leave us ~ He's with us always, even through the storms of life. And when the storm is past, and the sun breaks through ~ we see that He has been right there beside us through it all.

FEBRUARY 4

THE WONDROUS OLIVE TREE...

The Olive Tree has been called "the tree that never dies." Although it doesn't reach maturity until some time between 35 and 150 years, many olive trees in the Mediterranean have been estimated to be 1,700 years old. (Some say even older). When they are mature, they produce regularly and indefinitely.

When I was in Jerusalem, in the Garden of Gethsemane, a huge, gnarly tree was pointed out by our guide to be the oldest tree in the garden, and possibly in the world. Some have said 2,700 years old. How can that be? you ask. The olive tree, if left undisturbed, never dies. As explained to me, "When you look at those trees, with their thickened bark, hollowed centers and massive, twisted limbs, what you are seeing are shoots which have pushed through the earth from the root system of an original tree, and grew into complete trees in themselves. These new outer trees then sometimes fused around an aging, decaying center, to form a new ring of life. If an olive tree is cut down at the base, those new shoots will still spring up around the stump." David wrote in Psalm 128:3 *"Your children will be like olive shoots around your table."* Saul was referred to as the offshoot of the sycamore tree, while David was an offshoot of the olive tree.

This is amazing to me. No wonder there is so much reference to the olive tree in the Bible. And it is used in so many ways...the olives are a precious food, of course, and olive oil is valuable, which has been used for many things down through the ages ~ burned in lamps as a source of light, an ointment to heal wounds. It was prized by cabinet makers for adding luster and beauty to wood products. Olive oil was actually used to ease the movement of the great stones used to build the pyramids. And the most powerful symbolic significance is that of anointing. The word Messiah comes from the Hebrew word for anointing, or, the Anointed One. Hosea 14:7 says, *"His branches shall spread, and His beauty shall be as the olive tree."*

Just a simple little thing like a bottle of olive oil we use in cooking, and olives we love to put on pizza, but such an ancient and valuable commodity, with so much significance....

FEBRUARY 5

GETHSEMANE...

"They went to a place called Gethsemane, and Jesus said to His disciples, "Sit here while I pray." He took Peter, James and John along with Him, and began to be deeply distressed and troubled. "My soul is overwhelmed with sorrow to the point of death," He said to them. "Stay here and keep watch." Going a little farther, He fell to the ground and prayed that if possible the hour might pass from Him. "Abba Father," He said, "everything is possible for You. Take this cup from me. Yet not what I will, but what You will." (Mark 14:32-35).

Gethsemane was an oil press, being in the midst of many olive trees. It's also referred to as the "site of the agony." It was here that Jesus faced His most difficult decisions, choosing whether or not to go on to accept the penalty of death on the cross for our sins. It was the hardest decision of His ministry. He would have to bear our guilt and the sins of the whole world ~ billions of people, not just from His time, but time to come.

Gethsemane is not just a sacred place, but a time, a position we all find ourselves in at one time or another. It's a place of deep agony. A time when the cares of the world are *pressing* in on us. When was the last time you were in Gethsemane? I was there physically when I visited, and I have never been the same. But I have been there several times since then, in my heart, when those difficult decisions have to be made, when in anguish we seek the answers to many of life's struggles. We've all been there, and some of us are there now. Gethsemane. The place of sacrifice ~ *"not my will, but Thine be done."*

In a way incomprehensible to us, Jesus' suffering satisfied the demands of justice and made mercy available. Then, at the cross, victory came, when He said *"It is finished"* and died, but then the resurrection, just as He promised!

And so, because of Gethsemane, His and ours, we can rise victorious over all our trials and the perils of life. And we may know He is God Almighty's Son and it was all done to redeem us.

FEBRUARY 6

TO BE STEADFAST...

Jesus is steadfast. He turned His heart and life in the direction of the Cross, and stayed on that path throughout His life, until it was finished. God requires us to be steadfast, and to remain determined to stick to our right choices no matter how difficult the way becomes. He promised to be with us and help us. The enemy will push at us until we stumble and fall, but we must remain on that narrow path; it's the only way to Life.

David said, *"My heart is* ***steadfast****, O God; I will sing and make music with all my soul. Awake, harp and lyre! I will awaken the dawn. I will praise You, O Lord, among the nations; I will sing of You among the peoples. For great is Your love, higher than the heavens; Your faithfulness reaches to the skies. Be exalted, O God, above the heavens, and let Your glory be over all the earth."* (Psalm 108: 1-5). I hadn't considered that my waking up with a song in my mind and in my heart was "awakening the dawn." What a beautiful concept. Does this come from having a heart that is steadfast?

Many times we are overwhelmed by forces outside of our control. Paul invites us: *"So then, brethren,* ***stand firm*** *and hold to the traditions which you were taught by us, either by word of mouth or by letter."* (2 Thess. 2:15). He also tells us to *"keep your spiritual fervor, serving the Lord."* (Romans 12:11). No one ever said it would be easy to serve God. So many times it feels like we are spinning our wheels and getting nowhere. And often we feel like giving up. But God wants us to remain steadfast. Steadfast in prayer, in our praise to Him, in our obedience, and in trusting Him. No matter what.

"Create in me a pure heart, O God, and renew a ***steadfast*** *spirit within me."* (Psalm 51:10). God has promised to never leave us, no matter how far away we stray, no matter how many mistakes we make. Let's keep our hand in His

and stand firm through every trial. *"He will keep in perfect peace him whose mind is steadfast."* (Isaiah 26:3).

FEBRUARY 7

PROCLAIM IT!

"I proclaim righteousness in the great assembly; I do not seal my lips, as You know, O Lord. I do not hide Your righteousness in my heart; I speak of Your faithfulness and salvation. I do not conceal Your love and Your truth from the great assembly." (Psalm 40:9,10).

Who is the "great assembly?" In David's day, they were members of the Great Synagogue, those representatives of the Law who occupied a place in the chain of tradition between the Prophets and the earliest scholars known by name, including sages and prophets like Ezra, Nehemiah, Mordecai, Daniel, Simeon the Righteous, Haggai, Zechariah, and Malachi, and in Jewish tradition they numbered 120. So, who would be our great assembly in this day and age? Just the leaders and teachers of our churches and synagogues? The people we go to church with? Or, how about those we work with, live near, travel alongside, or see in the grocery store? What about our children and spouses?

I believe that all of these deserve to know about the righteousness of Jesus, and will see our own righteousness as we live out our lives in front of them, mingling every day with them in our different walks of life. Sometimes it's downright frightening to speak up and tell someone about God's love for us, and for them. But, *"God hath not given us a spirit of timidity; but of courage, of love and of a sound mind."*(2 Timothy 1:7) I know there are some times that are not convenient to share the gospel, but our demeanor and kindness is one way of sharing God's love. He said *"Be still and know that I am God; I will be exalted among the nations, I will be exalted in the earth."* (Psalm 46:10). If we don't share His love, someone else certainly will. Or, they will share something altogether false. And *"… if we don't praise Him, the very rocks will cry out."* (Luke 19:40).

Let's let our lives proclaim His righteousness to all we meet, to that "great assembly" around us each day. It was not meant to be hidden away. And it shouldn't be scary to speak up. God will give us the words and the strength. He IS our righteousness. Proclaim it!

FEBRUARY 8

CHOSEN...

Jesus is the Chosen. He is the One the Father sent to fulfill all the law and prophecies of the Old Agreement. *"And a voice came out of the cloud, saying, 'This is My Son, My Chosen One, listen to Him!'"* (Luke 9:35).

We all know what it's like to be "chosen." Or not chosen. All of life involves choices...to be chosen for the team, chosen for the job, chosen as the winner in a contest...we choose our friends, and they choose us. We choose the food we like, homes and furniture, a gift to give, the college we want to attend, our career, our life's mate. An adopted child, once given up or abandoned, is chosen by a loving family. Being chosen requires a big responsibility. Being passed by often hurts, and feels like the painful rejection that it is. Every day we choose, or are chosen. Some choices are very hard to make. And sometimes we make the wrong ones.

"But Jesus says...'I have paid the price, and I have chosen you to inherit with Me all the treasures of the universe.' This is the greatest gift we could ever receive, being in touch with the Source of Love, and allowing Him to flow through us to choose others..." (quoting Sarah Hornsby, "At the Name of Jesus").

Just remember this: *"But you are a chosen people, a royal priesthood, a holy nation, a people* ***belonging to God****, that you may declare the praises of Him who called you out of the darkness into His wonderful light."* (1 Peter 2:9).

No matter what life hands you, how many times you are passed by for the perfect job, the perfect mate, a best friend, just remind yourself that God has chosen you. What greater honor is there than that?

FEBRUARY 9

CONTENTMENT...

"...for I have learned to be content whatever the circumstances. I know what it is to be in need, and I know what it is to have plenty. I have learned the secret of being content in any and every situation, whether well fed or hungry, whether living in plenty or in want." (Philippians 4:11-12).

Just yesterday I was able to teach my 13-year old grandson a small lesson in being content. Not sure if he's fully grasped the concept yet, but I think he's mulling it over...He wanted a cell phone ~ don't they all? But his grades were bad in school. So, his mom made a deal with him that if he brought his grades up, she would buy him a phone this summer. His aunt from the other side, a former teacher, offered to tutor him every day. Lo and behold, the grades came up. AND he was chosen "student of the month" just before school was out. So, at the beginning of summer, he got his cell phone. And of course, he texted the minutes WAY overboard, so that now he owes his grandpa (who signed him up on his family plan) lots of money for the overtime. Grandson has discovered some of his friends have "cooler" phones that do more stuff and he came to Grandpa to see if he could upgrade (already!). Grandpa is a real softie, but didn't feel good about this. Auntie was going to buy the phone for him, but it got complicated in that they needed all Grandpa's pertinent information...finally, we agreed together that the answer was going to be "no."

So, I got to be the heavy. Grandson called yesterday afternoon to find out what the verdict was, and I stood my ground and told him we thought it was not a good time to get another phone, since he'd only had the phone for a month, and because of all the money he still owed Grandpa, (which, granted, he is working to earn), and besides, this would be a good lesson for him to learn patience and to be satisfied with what he has. He was a little disappointed, but said he was OK with the decision. I told him this could be a goal he could work toward on improving his attitude, continued good grades, etc, etc. He really is a sweet kid, and it's hard to tell our grandchildren no, but we had to be practical. 13-year olds don't know much about being practical. So, I told him to look up the above scripture and maybe he would understand...I actually texted it to him!

Jesus' words about this were, *"If you then...know how to give good gifts to your children, how much more will your Father in heaven give good gifts to those who ask Him!"* (Matthew 7:12). Sometimes a good gift to give a child is NOT to give what they ask for...it's saying "no."

FEBRUARY 10

TREASURE...

"Do not store up for yourselves treasures on earth, where moth and rust destroy, and where thieves break in and steal. But store up for yourselves treasures in heaven, where moth and rust do not destroy, and where thieves do not break in and steal. ***For where your treasure is, there your heart will be also."*** ~ Jesus. (Matthew 6:19-21).

I have a lovely charm bracelet. Remember those? Mine has quite a story. It was given to me at the end of my 2-year term as chairman of the local Christian Women's Club, '79-'81. A beautiful gold chain with two charms, an Idaho potato, engraved on the back with CWC '79 -'81, and one that said "90% Angel." I had fun adding charms to it over the years. Some I bought, others were given as gifts. I treasured it. It was about me. A little bowling ball & pin because I had been on leagues for many years, a camera, since I loved taking pictures, a motorcycle, because my husband and I rode one together, a sewing machine, since I was a seamstress, three tiny birthstone rings together to represent my three children, a Star of David charm from Jerusalem, a cross, #1 Grandma...there are many.

One day I couldn't find the bracelet. It wasn't where I "usually" kept it. I looked everywhere, literally, for years. We thought maybe my small granddaughter had picked it up and thrown it into the trash, not that I ever really left it lying around. One morning I was going through a bag of clothes to take to Goodwill, and there were a few items I thought my youngest daughter would be interested in. She took a skirt and a few other things. A few days later, she called to say "I found your charm bracelet! It was in the bottom of my washing machine!" Apparently a skirt I had given her had stored that (now valuable) bracelet in a pocket all those years. I rejoiced, added a couple more charms to it, and put it in my jewelry box. I hardly ever wear it. But it's a treasure, for sure.

How many "things" in our lives do we treasure? Many of us have various collections ~ teacups, books, Christmas decorations, large bank accounts (I've never seen one of those!), but these are all vulnerable to loss. And we cannot take them with us when we die. And many things, like my prized charm bracelet, are put away and forgotten. Nicodemus was a very rich young man, and he asked Jesus how to get into heaven. Jesus told him to sell everything he had and follow Him. Nicodemus' treasures were more important, I guess, because he went away very sad. He couldn't part with his "stuff." (that story is found in John 3).

Things I treasure have changed over the years as I grow in my faith. I have come to treasure my time with God, my Bible, His spoken living word, relationships with those I love, His beautiful creation. Oh, I still have my collections, but I have been known to give some of these things away at times. Paul said, *"But we have this treasure in jars of clay (us) to show that this all-surpassing power is from God and not from us."* (2 Corinthians 4:7). Where is your treasure?

FEBRUARY 11

HORSES AND HEALING...

There are two books I read five to six years ago which intensified the admiration I have had for the magnificent creature, Horse. The books are "Hope Rising" and "Bridge Called Hope" both by Kim Meeder, owner of a wonderful horse rescue ranch in Central Oregon. I am not a horsewoman, but I was so impressed at the miraculous stories of unbelievable rescues, and the way emotionally needy children are also "rescued" when they are invited to meet these horses, each needing physical and/or emotional (mostly emotional) healing. I have kept in contact with the ranch called Crystal Peaks, at times sending a donation, but mostly offering prayer and encouragement for their "operation." It's truly a ministry. Many of the horses they are called to rescue are very close to death, being either abandoned or incredibly abused and injured, starved or neglected, or all of the above. The "therapy" offered to suffering children costs them or their family nothing. The ranch survives on donations alone. It's amazing how healing and hope comes on both sides, the child, and the horse, through something as simple as grooming or feeding, spending time together. Loving.

Last week, my husband surprised me with a trip to the ranch. He didn't tell me where we were going, and when we drove up, I just cried. I had shared some of the stories with him from time to time, but I honestly didn't realize he had been so perceptive over the years of my profound desire to visit the ranch and meet these horses I'd read so much about through the books and regular newsletters I receive. No other gift could have meant as much! I got to meet and love on some of the horses I'd seen only in pictures and words.

These relationships that are formed between the children and the horses are much like the relationship we have with our heavenly Father, who rescues us in the same way, by gently loving us to Himself. Some of us are suffering physically, have been abandoned and are lonely, many of us feel abused and our emotions are injured. Like these children and horses, we are drawn together to God who is reaching out in unconditional love, accepting us just as we are. And the wonderful thing about Him is that He understands where we are. He understands and knows our hurt, our loneliness. *"He was despised and rejected by men, a man of sorrows, and familiar with suffering. Like one from whom men hide their faces He was despised, and we esteemed Him not. Surely He took up our infirmities and carried our sorrows...He was pierced for our transgressions, He was crushed for our iniquities; the punishment that brought us peace was upon Him and by His wounds we are healed."* (Isaiah 53:3-5). He alone is our Hope! And, like those emotionally needy children who come to the ranch, it costs us nothing. The price has already been paid.

FEBRUARY 12

BLESSED SLEEP...

I seldom sleep through the night without getting up at least once or twice. I don't stay up real late, but I am up very early each morning...my body just tells me it's time to get up. Sometimes I feel rested, other mornings, I don't. And I know that many, many people do not sleep well, or at least rest in their sleep, for many reasons...people around the world, in my city, in my family. I pray that I will never take a good night's sleep for granted. David said *"I will lie down and sleep in peace, for You alone, O Lord, make me dwell in safety."* (Psalm 4:8). David wrote this in spite of his deep distress. Stress is one of the leading reasons we are robbed of sleep. Stress ~ over illness, finances, relationships, looming danger...many times we don't sleep because we are hungry, or we've had too much to eat or drink just before bed. Some of us take medications to help us sleep.

God designed our bodies to need sleep after a long day of work or activity. Not only do our bodies need restoring sleep, so do our minds. But most of the time our minds stay active during the night, even while sleeping. Frequently we forget that God gives us rest. We battle with all the problems of life, and we fail to remember that God is watching over us, even in our turmoil. We become frustrated and look for relief everywhere else, but don't remember to turn to God, who is waiting to soothe us with His words, holding us in His arms until the morning light. God wants us to rest, because then we will be at our best to follow the natural rhythm of the life He has created...work, play, eat, sleep...work, play, eat, sleep...Every once in awhile, while I was working, I would become so tired I couldn't sit at my desk. I would go downstairs to our lunch room, usually deserted mid-afternoon, lie my head down on the table, close my eyes, and relax just to the point of dozing, and I would feel rested enough to finish the day. A power nap? Just what we might need sometimes.

Some day we will be in a place where we will not need sleep, because there will be no night. Our bodies will be transformed, never to need recharging again. *"Yes," says the Spirit, "they will rest from their labor, for their deeds will follow them."* (Rev. 14:13). I believe the last part of that verse means that we have been faithful to God in keeping His commands. His concern is that His people are working, making every effort to overcome Satan in every way. That's hard work! Hebrews 4:10 says, *"For anyone who enters into God's rest also rests from his own work, just as God did from His."* Many refer to death as "falling asleep." Well, I believe it is at that moment that we become fully awake and vital, and really begin to live! It will be a time of rest from our labors, yes, but truly a time of eternally living!

FEBRUARY 13

A THORN IN MY FLESH?

"There was given me a thorn in my flesh, a messenger of Satan, to torment me, Three times I pleaded with the Lord to take it away from me. But He said to me, 'My grace is sufficient for you, my power is made perfect in weakness.' Therefore, I will boast all the more gladly about my weaknesses, so that Christ's power may rest on me. That is why, for Christ's sake, I delight in weaknesses, in insults, in hardships, in persecution, in difficulties. For when I am weak, then I am strong." (2 Corinthians 12:7-10).

I have many rose bushes, and of course, the most beautiful flower also sports those deadly thorns! I have come out of my garden with puncture wounds, deep scratches, ripped clothing, blood dripping. Sometimes they scratch you as your arm passes by, and sometimes they grab on, not letting go. Thorns are brutal. But I keep going back for more! The beauty of the roses is worth it somehow. I've heard it said that the rose is "God's autograph."

Hmmm...have you ever wondered exactly what Paul's thorn in the flesh was? He had plenty, for sure. And before he knew Christ, Paul *was* the thorn in others' flesh! Sometimes we think of our thorn as being physical and health problems, or someone who bothers us by their mere presence. Some see it as a particular sin or weakness that often torments, and we just can't shake it. Maybe it's a lack of perseverance, a lack of trust, anything we tend to struggle with on a regular basis. I've heard a few people say "that woman/child/man is a thorn in my flesh!" So it can be the irritating personality or habits of another person. Maybe we're quick to judge, or we carry grudges.

Paul also refers to this thorn as a "messenger of Satan." It may seem that if we grow *too self-assured of our own righteousness*, God will permit one of Satan's messengers to afflict us. And we need to be careful as to how we respond to this affliction. We are each accountable for our own sins and shortcomings. And instead of boasting in our own strength to overcome the evil, we should boast in the Lord's power and strength, revealed in our weakness. That's why Paul could say he *delighted* in weaknesses and hardships, because then God's own ever-present power could be seen. He didn't complain or whine, but he SANG and praised the Lord in the midst of his turmoil!

Did you ever think of your "thorn" as being a "fellowship of pain," sharing in the Lord's suffering? It should teach us to be grateful and to see the miracles opening up before us, mostly that miracle of God's love and healing. He's standing by to show us His power and give us *His strength* in the midst of our pain, and to bring us through it.

FEBRUARY 14

LOVE WITHOUT WORDS...

In 1st John 3:17, I read this: *"If anyone has material possessions and sees his brother in need but has no pity on him, how can the love of God be in him? Dear children, let us not love with words or tongue but with actions and in truth."*

I love "random acts of kindness," don't you? I love seeing them taking place, I love being the recipient of them, and I love doing them. It's a chance to make someone's day better. Not that we have to go about obviously looking for something nice to do for someone, but the "random" part is just being on the lookout for an opportunity to help. You hear about people who pay at the toll booth for the person behind them, you read about a little child making a purchase for a sick mother, but doesn't have enough money, so the person in line behind him pays the difference. There are so many ways in which we can make someone's day. Our next door neighbor "secretly" fertilizes my lawn when he's doing his own, or he prunes my trees when I'm not looking. And we have been the recipient of bags of groceries when the funds were low, or gone, not knowing who left them on our porch.

My husband and I were on a motorcycle trip a few years ago in Montana and stopped at a lodge for breakfast when a family with three small children came in, looking pretty bedraggled. They had been hiking and had all their gear on and it began to snow, so they wanted to come in out of the weather. They ordered, and while they were eating, my husband went up to pay our bill, but asked also for theirs. He hadn't planned on doing that, but as we sat there, he was more and more compelled to do this act of kindness. They never found out who paid, of course, and that's the fun of it. Their day had started out kind of hard, with the weather, and trying to maneuver their small children in and out of their warm clothes and backpacks, and I'm sure they talked about that restaurant bill most of the day. And we received the blessing, just knowing that we helped in this small way.

William Shakespeare wrote: "The quality of mercy is not strained; it droppeth as the gentle rain from heaven; upon the place beneath; it is twice blessed; it blesseth him that giveth and him that takes."

And from Martin Luther King, Jr.: " *Agape* is understanding, creative, redemptive goodwill toward all men. *Agape* is an overflowing love, which seeks nothing in return. Theologians would say that it is the love of God operating in the human heart. When you rise to love on this level, you love all men not because you like them, not because their ways appeal to you, but you love them because God loves them."

Even the smallest gift of your time, delivering a latte to someone you know is having a busy day and will not get a break, taking a meal to a family where there is a new baby, fixing a kid's bike, picking up litter, looking for ways to make someone else look good. There are so many little, seemingly unnoticed, acts of kindness that won't take up much of our time...be on the lookout.

FEBRUARY 15

ALL ALONE...

Valentine's Day just came and went, and my Valentine was out of town. But it's OK because we celebrated with a nice dinner beforehand. And we were in touch throughout the day. But I think of those who are truly alone, elderly people whose loved ones are in a nursing home and don't recognize them. Or those who are the patients, or residents, in assisted living communities who seem to be forgotten. A day like this must bring with it loneliness and sadness. And there are the widows and widowers, or divorcees who have no one, for any holiday.

I have a dear friend who is one of the growing number dwelling in assisted living...she knows she may never go home again. Her husband is gone, and both of her children live far away. I have adopted her. Not that I don't have my own children near, but because I DO. I know what it's like to see them often, sometimes daily, and how special that is. I know I will be taken care of if I am ever in her shoes. I know that I miss my own mother immensely. I took my friend a Valentine and some sugar-free truffles. She was thrilled. She told me she loves me. She does that every time I visit her. That's what makes it worth it. Today is her birthday and I have been invited by the staff for lunch and a little party. I love making her feel special. My Bible says that we should *"look after orphans and widows in their distress..."* (James 1:27). And He Himself is a *"Father to the fatherless, a defender of widows...He sets the lonely in families..."* (Psalm 68:5-6).

Oh, I know, sometimes being alone for a short time, even a few days, isn't bad...I like my solitude once in awhile...but for those who are all alone day in and day out, night after night, there is such an unpleasant sense of emptiness. *"Look to my right and see; no one is concerned for me. I have no refuge; no one cares for my life."*(Psalms 142:4) David cried out to God while he was in the cave in the wilderness, and was questioning whether he would even live. But then he realized that GOD was his *"refuge, his portion in the land of the living."* (vs. 5). God desires for us to have companionship and fellowship. And He knows what it's like to be abandoned and forsaken ~ He experienced that loneliness Himself in the wilderness, on the Cross...

But Moses spoke for God when he said, *"Be strong and courageous…for the Lord your God goes with you;* ***He will never leave you nor forsake you****."* (Deut. 31:6). What a promise, what an antidote for our desolation. Just to know that when everyone else forgets us, leaves us alone, our heavenly Father never, ever will. When you feel so lonely that your heart is breaking, be confident and trust in His promise. *"The righteous cry out and the Lord hears them; He delivers them from all their troubles. The Lord is close to the brokenhearted and saves those who are crushed in spirit."* (Psalm 34:17-18). Even when you don't feel the Lord is near, He is. You're not alone.

FEBRUARY 16

WHAT'S IN A NAME…?

Ever think about names? Real, given names, nicknames, pet names…of our seasons, Winter, Spring, Summer and Autumn, "Fall" is a nickname. In North Idaho Summer is also known as "road construction" season! Sometimes we have nicknames, given for various reasons. There are terms of endearment, such as honey, sweetheart, darling or sweet-cheeks, as we refer to our loved ones. I am known as Jeanne, Honey, JR, Mom, Sis, Grandma and Grammy. In scripture, God changed the names of many people, according to some accomplishment or direction their lives had taken, or a plan He had for them. Names were chosen for the meaning of them. Today, we name our children after ancestors, or search lists for the combinations that sound just right. Some parents simply make up names.

Jesus has many names as well…Father, Son, Holy Spirit, and a host of others…Savior, Redeemer, Creator, the Alpha and Omega, Almighty, Ancient of Days, I Am, Bright and Morning Star, Abba, Lord, Emmanuel, Brother, Messiah, Master, Lamb of God, Lily of the Valley, King of the Jews…well, I could fill this page, of course. There are many songs written about the names of Jesus. His names, and the mention of them, bring comfort to us, for He is also known as Comforter. His word says, *"Salvation is found in no one else, for there is* ***no other name*** *under heaven given to men by which we must be saved."* (Acts 4:12). How could we know that we could stake our lives on the name of a man?

Philippians 2: 9, 10 says, *"Therefore God exalted Him to the highest place, and gave Him the name that is above every name, that at the* ***name of Jesus*** *every knee* *should bow, in heaven and on earth, and under the earth, and every tongue confess that Jesus Christ is Lord, to the glory of God the Father."*This means everyone ~ sinner or saved. Even the devil himself will bow his knee to Jesus on that last day! Such power in a Name. Jesus is not unapproachable ~ call Him what you like ... the Hope of Glory, Fountain of Living Water, Jehovah, Truth, the True Vine, the Way, Abba (which actually could mean "Daddy."). Whatever your need is, He will be that for you, Friend, even Husband. Call out His name today. He will hear you, no matter what name you call.

FEBRUARY 17

HARMONY...

"God made the earth by His power; He founded the world by His wisdom and stretched out the heavens by His understanding.When He thunders, the waters in the heavens roar; He makes clouds rise from the ends of the earth. He sends lightning with the rain and brings out the wind from His storehouses." (Jeremiah 10:11,12). So, everything God made is, or should be, in harmony with everything else. I mean, look at how the seasons change, and how each season has its own distinction and properties...everything is in harmony. God made it all to work together. There are certain plants created for food for certain animals, there is even one particular moth created just to pollinate one particular flower ~ plant life dies in the winter and comes back to new life in the spring...

Webster defines "harmony" as: to fit together; combination of parts into an orderly whole; agreement in feeling, actions, ideas, interests; the pleasing combination of two or more tones in a chord, etc. I love harmony in music. God created our voices to be different from one another, yet when blended in music, they make a beautiful sound ~ harmony. Paul wrote to the Romans in 12:16: *"Live in harmony with one another. [KJV says,"Be of the same mind..."]. Do not be proud but be willing to associate with people of low position. Do not be conceited."* And Peter repeated later, *"Finally, all of you, live in harmony with one another; be sympathetic, love as brothers, be compassionate and humble. Do not repay evil with evil or insult with insult, but with blessing, because to this you were called so that you may inherit a blessing."* (3:8-9).

Lord, help us. We have come so far away from Your plan for us! Cause us, in this time of economic turmoil, when pride and power have taken over the governments of the world, to turn our eyes upon Jesus once again. Draw us back to Your heart. You are our only hope for harmony in the world once again.

FEBRUARY 18

THREE GUYS IN A FIRE...

"Whoever does not fall down and worship will immediately be thrown into a blazing furnace." (Daniel 3:6). Of course, we know this from the story of the three young men who worked for the king, Shadrach, Meshach, and Abednego, who were truly thrown into a furnace because they would not bow down and worship a huge golden statue King Nebuchadnezzar had set up in Babylon. When these three fellows, who were Christians by the way, refused to bow down, some astrologers noticed and tattled on them to the king. The king gave them another chance. He repeated the rules to them. But they replied they were not worried about the fire ~ their God would rescue them. The audacity! The faith. (We had so much fun with this story in my 1st & 2nd grade Sunday school class last week).

Now, I think this was a huge furnace. I haven't researched it, but I have seen the stones in Israel that were made to construct the walls of Jerusalem, and I know they were made by men. Of course, we know bricks have to be baked to harden, and these are not ordinary bricks, but probably about as big as a van, give or take a cubit or two. So, in order to bake these, their ovens had to be large. Large enough for three men ~ four? ~ to be walking around inside. This is what the king saw when he looked. But who was that fourth man? When he finally let them out of the furnace, he was astonished that their clothes and skin were not burned, not even the hair on their heads was singed. They didn't even smell like smoke. Oh, yeah, after this, Nebuchadnezzar believed and praised God.

So, what does this story have to do with us today? Have you ever felt like you have been thrown into a fiery furnace? Oh, I don't mean like the one these boys were thrown into. But how about the fiery trials we go through from time to time? Many of us will be lucky to get through this economic "crisis" unscathed. How about mistreatment ~ by a boss, a parent, a "friend?" Or a misunderstanding, a punishment we didn't deserve...an illness, a loss...Isaiah 48:10 says: *"See, I have refined you, though not as silver. I have tested you in the* ***furnace*** *of affliction."* Are we strong enough to say no when a "king" tells us to believe or worship or act in a way that is not glorifying to the King? When a boss orders us to do something that isn't honest? Who will be watching us to see if we'll be burned up? Our God will reward us if we stand firm in our trials. Remember, He is in there with us, standing beside us, protecting us. Refining us, as pure gold. *"When you walk through the fire you will not be burned, neither will the flames kindle upon you. For I am the Lord Your God."* (Isaiah 43:2b-3). What a promise!

FEBRUARY 19

SONGS OF DELIVERANCE...

"You are my hiding place; You will protect me from trouble and surround me with songs of deliverance." (Psalm 32:7)

This astounds me, the thought of the Lord singing over me with "songs of deliverance." What a comfort! I think back to the many times when my children were small when I sang to them to comfort them, to help them fall asleep. It makes perfect sense that my heavenly Father would soothe my soul with song. Maybe this is why I love the Psalms so much. After all, God is the Creator of music. But none of the music on earth, no matter how sweet and inspiring it is, will ever match what we will hear in heaven. The angels all have perfect voices, and so will we when we join them. We will *"sing to the Lord a NEW song, His praise in the assembly of the saints."* (Psalm 149:1). The song of redemption, the angels will not be able to sing. They haven't experienced that transformation, that saving grace. Wow, what a picture! Can you imagine it?

All throughout scripture we find music...Mary sang from her heart before giving birth to the Savior; Zechariah, after John's birth; Deborah, in the book of Judges; David, of course, was a musician who played the harp and wrote the beautiful psalms and was called "Israel's singer of songs;" Job asked, *"Where is God my Maker, who gives songs in the night?"* (35:10); and in Isaiah, the whole world sings... *"Shout for joy, O heavens; rejoice, O earth; burst into song, O mountains! For the Lord comforts His people and will have compassion on His afflicted ones."* (Isaiah 49:13). And of course, there were Paul and Silas who sang praises after being beaten and thrown into prison...(Acts 16:25).

I thank God that I always have a song in my heart, and going through my mind in the morning when I awake. It's God's voice ~ God's music ringing in my soul! No matter if I am happy, or if I have concerns that weigh me down, God still puts a song in my heart. It just happens. And we are admonished all through scripture to "sing unto the Lord." Sing for joy, sing of His great love, sing of God's strength. *"Sing and make music in your heart to the Lord, always giving thanks to God the Father for everything in the name of our lord, Jesus Christ."* (Ephesians 5:19,20). And if you don't have a song, pray and ask God to give you one. He is faithful.

FEBRUARY 20

REDEEMED!

"For you know that is was not with perishable things such as silver or gold that you were redeemed from the empty way of life handed down to you from your forefathers, but with the precious blood of Christ, a lamb without blemish or defect." (1 Peter 1:18).

My friend, Webster defines "redeemed" as: recovered, having the fee paid, set free from captivity, ransomed, rescued, delivered from sin and its penalties; honor, worth & reputation restored.

We don't use this word, "redeemed" very much anymore, unless we're talking about cashing in coupons. There are many songs written about the redeemed...Let the Redeemed, Redeemed and I Love to Proclaim it, Song of the Redeemed, I am Redeemed, We the Redeemed...but you know what I was thinking? We are the only ones who can sing that song. Although we read about the beautiful choirs of angels, the hosts of heaven who lift their songs of praise to God, singing "worthy is the Lamb," and "holy, holy, holy," they don't know the song of redemption. They have not experienced the washing by the blood of the perfect Lamb, they don't know the thrill of being forgiven or redeemed. They don't know what it's like to hear the voice of the Shepherd, guiding, leading. They have never been held captive by sin, not ever had the need to be delivered from bondage.

And yet...they praise Him and worship Him all day and night long. Shouldn't we, His redeemed, be singing the song of the redeemed even louder and longer than the angels do? We are the ones who have something to praise Him about. *"My lips will shout for joy when I sing praise to You ~ I, whom You have redeemed!"* (Psalm 71:23).

FEBRUARY 21

HE WAS THERE...

In the song, "You Were There," by Avalon, the words hold such assurance that God is always with us. The first verse is:

"I wonder how it must have felt when David stood to face Goliath on a hill. I imagine that he shook with all his might...until You took his hand, and held on tight..."

Ever feel like you're facing Goliath? Oh, it doesn't have to be a giant soldier with a huge sword and shield...your Goliath can be any obstacle or challenge you face, day in and day out. Something seemingly insurmountable ~ a job, a confrontation, illness, the bills...

And then again:

"So there he stood upon that hill, Abraham with knife in hand was poised to kill. But God in all His Sovereignty had bigger plans, and just in time, He brought a lamb..."

Has God told you what you must do, but you are afraid to obey Him? It's scary when we get orders from our heavenly Father, for a task that we know is impossible to accomplish ~ in OUR power. God never asks us to do the impossible but that He won't be giving us HIS power to do it. In fact, if we are obedient in what He asks, He is actually the one who will be doing it. We are only the vessel through which He will act.

We must learn that *"His ways are not our ways."* (Isaiah 55:8). My goodness, He made the universe, and He alone keeps it from crumbling into dust. He sent His only Son who hung on a cross so that we would not have to be left in the dark ~ the song goes on... *"Every moment, every planned coincidence just all makes sense, with Your last breath."* God was the power in David's swing, and He was the calm in Abraham. He is the God who understands and will give us the strength to face the Goliaths in our life, and the peace to do what He asks us to do.

Remember Jesus' words, *"My grace is sufficient for you, for My power is made perfect in weakness."* (2 Corinthians 12:9). Just know that when you stand and face the enemy, when you are at the bottom of a hill that seems impossible to climb, when you are weak and have no strength left and you want to give up, He is there, right beside you. And He understands. Put your hand into His big powerful hand and He'll go through with you. He cannot fail.

FEBRUARY 22

GOD'S GENTLE TOUCH...

"For You created my inmost being; You knit me together in my mother's womb. I praise You because I am fearfully and wonderfully made; Your works are wonderful, I know that full well." (Psalm 139:13-14).

OK, I have written about this subject before, God's fingerprints, but I heard the song on the radio this morning by Steven Curtis Chapman, "The Fingerprints of God," and it stirred my spirit and reminded me of just how much God's hands are on me, all the time, every day. The song describes us as a "Masterpiece that all creation quietly applauds...fashioned by God's hand and perfectly planned to be just who we are..." There will never be another creation exactly like us, like you, or like me. And sometimes we suffer a broken heart, or we are discouraged because things aren't going well in our lives, but we don't see ourselves as God sees us. Often we let man's perception of who we are interfere with the confidence God can give us as His child.

Can you actually feel the warm and soothing touch of an unseen God? Author and musician Jennifer Rothschild, who lost her vision at the age of fifteen, explains how God's touch works from the inside out, warming the heart, mind, and soul. It lifts weights that eyes could never see. It washes away the anguish of guilt, the bite of fear, and the ache of loneliness. With the gentle pressure of His hand on our shoulders, we can find our way through the darkest of nights. She wrote about it in her book, "The Fingerprints of God."

"*When I said 'My foot is slipping,' Your love, O Lord, supported me. When anxiety was great within me, Your consolation brought joy to my soul.*" (Psalm 94:18-19). Be assured that God's eyes are always on us, and we are covered by His great love. When it feels like things are falling apart all around us, and we can't feel His presence or His touch, just remember that His touch is so gentle that sometimes we are not even aware of His arms wrapped around us. But He is there. He promised in Matthew 28:20 He always would be.

FEBRUARY 23

THE CLOCK IS TICKING...

I love the old-fashioned wind-up alarm clocks. My Grandma had them all over her house, Big Bens and Baby Bens, and when I would stay with her, I remember her going from room to room each night, winding them all up. That was all I heard while falling asleep. For some reason it was a comfort to me. I can't remember a time when I didn't have one of my own on my bedside table. I no longer need the clock's alarm ~ my body wakes up on its own at the same early hour each day, but I love the ticking. We have a cuckoo clock, and a mantle clock that ticks and bongs...and I have clocks of some kind in each room. I noticed that I have four in my living room alone. Most of them have batteries, but some are wind-up. They still all tick.

It's important for us to keep track of the time. We have appointments, or not. I love to be on time, if not a little early, wherever I go. Some members of my family don't actually leave until it's time to be there! (This is a thorn in my side!). In Ecclesiastes 3:1 and following, we read the beautiful passage which has been quoted and sung down through the ages, *"To everything there is a season and a time to every purpose under heaven; a time to be born and a time to die; a time to plant and a time to reap; a time to kill and a time to heal; a time to tear down and a time to build; a time to weep and a time to laugh; a time to mourn and a time to dance; a time to scatter stones and a time to gather them; a time to embrace and a time to refrain; a time to search and a time to give up; a time to keep and a time to throw away; a time to tear and a time to mend; a time to be silent and a time to speak; a time to love and a time to hate; a time for war and a time for peace."* I wasn't going to include the whole passage, but somehow, I couldn't cut it short...

We each have 24 hours every day. It's important that we do not waste a minute. Time seems to be going by so fast. Our children are young, and we "turn around and they are grown with babes of their own" as the song says. It's true. It seems like time is running out for our world as we know it. All through scripture there are warnings that the time is short, but I think we are on the threshold of end-times right now. Jesus told a parable of Ten Virgins. They knew the bridegroom was coming, but not sure of the exact hour. Five of them were ready, had oil in their lamps and extra to take along. The other five ran out of oil along the way and had to turn back to buy more. And this is when the bridegroom came and took the five who were ready and watching with Him to the wedding feast. The others were turned away ~ it was too late. (Matthew 25: 1-13). The moral of the story… *"Therefore, keep watch because you do not know the day or the hour."* (Vs. 13).

Seems to me it's a good idea to be prayed up and ready, because Jesus will come *"like a thief in the night."* (1 Thess. 5:2). The clock is ticking, and soon our time will run out. Let's use our 24 hours wisely, and be ready and watchful. We may only have today.

FEBRUARY 24

DELETE...DELETE...DELETE...

Last night I was checking out my email address book. Did you know that everyone who emails YOU, even junk email, ends up saved in your address book, as well as those you email? I deleted almost 100 names of "people" I didn't even know! Just taking up space in my address book. There for no apparent reason. I would never use them again…But while I was selecting the names I wished to delete, a thought came to me…I wonder if God does this with His book of names? Well, it says in Exodus 32:33, *"The Lord replied to Moses, 'Whoever has sinned against Me I will blot out of My book.'"* Sounds like it could happen.

In Daniel 12:1, speaking of a time of great distress, which I think we are in right now, *"But at that time Your people ~ everyone whose name is found written in the book ~ will be delivered."* Well, this sounds more promising. I'm relatively sure God doesn't sit up there with His heavenly eraser and keep score, or sit at His great computer in the sky with His finger poised on the delete button, just waiting for us to mess up, and when we are saved, He writes our name in the Book of Life, but when we sin, He erases it, but then… when we repent He writes it in again. He has given us the Holy Bible, our instruction manual for life, telling us how we should live in order to inherit eternal life. It's pretty simple, really. It's life that makes it hard. With His help we can do it.

Did you ever take part in a contest, or try out for a team, and then have to wait for that final day when the director, or teacher, or coach or whomever, would stand up and read the names from a list? And you felt that anticipation deep down in your stomach, like butterflies, just listening for your name, not sure, but hoping you made it and that your name will finally be called? This is what will happen on that last day, when all the people of earth will stand before Him while He reads our names, or not, from the Book of Life. We CAN know for sure. There is NOT limited seating in that heavenly banquet hall. "Whosoever will" may come. Jesus Himself said in the last book of the great collection of books, Revelation 3:5, *"But he who overcomes will, like them [some of the saints], be dressed in white.* ***I will never blot out his name*** *from the Book of Life, but will acknowledge his name before My Father and His angels."* Do you have a reservation? Is your name written in the Book?

FEBRUARY 25

HOT, COLD...HOT, COLD...

This is the time of year when we turn up the heat in our homes and cars, then pretty soon we're too hot...and although the weather isn't ever hot in the winter, at least where I live, it does get balmy on days like we've had this week, even though spring is still months away, requiring only a light jacket... but then we will plunge to sub-freezing temperatures in a matter of hours, producing snow...we wear more sweaters, heavier coats. If you're like me, you pour a cup of coffee, or tea (in my case), go sit down to read, or work at your desk, and pretty soon, you remember to take a drink and it's cooled off...so you stick it back into the microwave and heat it up again...and again. Hot, cold...

Many of us who are around my age, which I won't disclose here (!), experience hot and cold within seconds. Our own body's thermostat goes haywire and we suddenly peel off that extra sweater, or run outside to feel the relief of the cool air. Then, almost immediately, we are cold again, because our internal thermostat realizes we were hot, so it turns down the heat...my goodness... this is miserable.

Jesus had something to say about being hot, or cold... *"I know your deeds, that you are neither cold nor hot. I wish you were either one or the other! So, because you are lukewarm ~ neither hot nor cold ~ I am about to spit you out of my mouth."* (Revelation 3:15-16). The water supply in Laodicea had to be piped in from the mountains, and by the time it got there, it was lukewarm, and somewhat smelly at times...this could have been what Jesus was referring to, but He could have been reprimanding lukewarm Christians as well...we cannot do much for the kingdom or the cause of the gospel if we aren't really committed to Jesus and if our life doesn't show spiritual enthusiasm. He doesn't have much use for "casual" Christianity, but wants us to be fervent in our study and our witness. Tepid water isn't very palatable, and a tepid heart indicates spiritual indifference.

I don't like my coffee or tea lukewarm, nor my iced tea or soft drink languid. It should be refreshing, at the temperature it was meant to be. I desire to have my spirit refreshed, as well. If I don't study God's word each day, talk with Him in prayer, follow where He leads me, and share His love with others, my faith becomes stagnant. I want to be "on fire" for my Lord. Anything less than all I have will keep me from becoming a dynamic Christian, and cause a barrenness in my soul. I would be useless to Him. Pray that God will use you. Don't be a "middle-of-the-road" Christian, but joyfully follow Him where He leads, beside the refreshing streams of living water.

FEBRUARY 26

STEPPING STONES...

As I was writing in my journal this morning, I was thinking about who would find and read my journals (I've finished 62, all written in those pretty wordless books). I looked back and realized, with a little surprise, those have all been over a fifteen-year period. Oh, I kept prayer requests in calendars and date books long before that, but not really the "diary" type. I must have learned this from my mother, although she didn't really train me in journal-writing. I remember seeing her write things in her little green canvas-covered lined notebooks since I was very young. They all matched. I wish I could find all of them. She wrote many of those over the years. Although they didn't usually capture the deep prayers of her heart, they recorded events and wishes and prayers for the day.

So, as I prayed this morning on the last page of book #62, I asked God that when I am gone, and my kids find my journals, that there would be nothing contained in them that would ever cause them, or their children, to stumble, or have a tainted view of their mother's and grandmother's faith, that instead of being a stumbling block, my heartfelt words would be stepping stones for their own walk of faith. I have never gone back and read what I've written in any of them, but I know I did my share of complaining to God. I did, however, and still do, make sure I give Him praise and thanks for everything that has happened in my life, whether hard times or good times. And I'm sure those prayers have changed over the years as I've grown and matured in my own faith.

David said, *"Since my youth, O God, You have taught me, and to this day I declare Your marvelous deeds. Even when I am old and gray, do not forsake me, O God, till I declare Your power to the next generation, Your might to all who are to come."* (Psalm 71:17-18). My main reason for beginning to journal in the first place was to gain a closer relationship to my heavenly Father, and writing it all down has kept me focused in my prayer life. Every day I write scripture on the pages, and every day I pray on the Word. I *"let my requests be made known to God"* (Philippians 4:6) and I am careful to give Him the praise for the outcome, whatever His will is…I sometimes write lyrics to songs which inspire me (is that a surprise?), or a poem, I include photos of those I'm praying for, I even have little Brooklynne's (my new great-granddaughter) footprint on the page for the day she was born, because I took my journal to the hospital, and the nurse was most gracious to stamp her little inked foot there. I have traced my grandchildren's hands in the pages then prayed for them inside the wobbly image.

My journals will be a record of my faith – stumbling block or stepping stones? I hope and pray it's the latter.

FEBRUARY 27

A SPECIAL BIRTHDAY…

It's my youngest daughter's birthday February 28th. And February 29th is my oldest daughter's birthday, one she only gets to celebrate every four years. Yes, she was born in a Leap-Year. A special time. When it wasn't a Leap Year, we would celebrate it on the day before. So for her fifth birthday, we presented her with a baby sister! But we always had separate birthday parties ~ they were five years apart, after all. We tried celebrating on the same day a time or two, but we realized it actually took a little away from each of their special dates. Oh, every birthday is special. I would actually let my girls and their little friends eat their cake off my good china dishes, and drink their punch from my good crystal goblets at some of their parties. Not one ever got broken!

There are lots of special birthdays, when you think about it. Many expectant parents who are due to deliver on or around the New Year, hope to deliver on New Year's Day. Or, a special sequence of dates, such as 10/10/10 are desirable birth dates to give our offspring. Not that the day we were born bears any significance to who we are and how unique or distinctive our life is. In fact, each day we are given is a celebration. I love to watch my two-year-old great granddaughter as she learns a new word or idea almost every single day. She is excited at every new discovery. She celebrates each day.

I think that's what God meant for us to do. Celebrate each new day. Every day is a fresh start, no matter how much we messed up the day before. And all through time, God's people have celebrated. And messed up. And celebrated again. There seemed to be a Feast scheduled for many things...some of the popular feasts are Passover, Unleavened Bread, First Fruits, Pentecost, Trumpets, or Rosh Hashanah...you get the idea. And of course, when there was a wedding, the feasting went on for days. My family celebrates birthdays that way, too, kind of. Each of my daughters has a circle of girlfriends who celebrate each other's birthdays together, then we have a family birthday party as well. There might be another celebration in which the birthday girl is taken out to dinner or lunch by another friend, and the celebration just goes on and on.

I think God meant it to be that way. We are all special to Him ~ He made us! It's wonderful when our family and friends desire to honor our birthday with observance of how special we are to them. I do realize that not everyone celebrates birthdays in the same way, if at all. Some wish for a celebration, but it doesn't happen. I will tell you this ~ God celebrates you, every single day. *"All the days ordained for me were written in Your book before one of them came to be."* (Psalm 139:16). His eyes are on us every day of our lives. He gives us the immeasurable gift of a new day when we wake up. He paints a beautiful sunrise and sunset for us, and causes His flowers and trees to bloom in the spring. His rain is a gift to water all those living and growing things. The smiles and the giggles of my great-granddaughter are such a gift, so fresh from the hand of Creator-God. And if I had nothing else in life, the gift of eternal life is essential ~ *"For it is by grace that you have been saved, through faith ~ and this not from yourselves,* ***it is the gift of God****..."* (Ephesians 2:8). If you have received that gift, you have a spiritual birthday, one that should be celebrated every day. Never take it for granted. Happy Birthday!!

FEBRUARY 28

WINTER WORRIES...

Lots of people where I live in Idaho actually thought winter was over, and spring was right around the corner, but it has come back with a vengeance. We've had harsh temperatures and blizzard conditions the last two days, with snow piling up to over a foot...this storm, anyway. I love winter. This snow and cold doesn't bother me. A lot of our residents complain about the winters, and I'm not sure I understand why they are living here, knowing we get snow, and spring does not come in February, no matter what a fat, furry little creature says!

Normally, I just take the snowy weather in stride, but yesterday my oldest granddaughter and her husband, and their baby, my first great-granddaughter, left Idaho for South Dakota to visit friends. This was their first ever road trip. And when they left, we were having a blizzard. They started to change their minds about going, but all the arrangements had been made and their friends had taken a few days off from their jobs to visit with them. I was proud of them that they had grown up and were off on their own, but I admit, I was worried about their safety. It so happened that the weather improved the farther east they went, until the last, then they had snow again, in fact, white-out conditions! But, they arrived safely this evening.

Also, yesterday, my oldest daughter started a new job, 35 miles to the south of us, near the Indian reservation, and had to drive in the blizzard on mountain roads. She let me know when she arrived there, and she had made it with a few minutes to spare. Okay, two down. This morning my husband left on another trip to southern Idaho, driving a charter bus full of high school students. This would take him over a treacherous mountain pass, notorious for bad conditions in the winter. Right up to the last minute, we wondered why the school didn't cancel the trip. Another blizzard during the night and this morning cancelled schools in the area, but the trip was still on. Needless to say, I have done a lot of praying, more than usual, for my family's safety in their travels. Yesterday I was a little preoccupied with thoughts of their safety. OK, I was a nervous wreck! But I trusted God to get them all where they needed to go.

God heard all of my prayers. Everyone arrived at their destinations with no troubles. God promises to watch over us and take care of us, day and night.

"For He will command His angels concerning you to guard you in all your ways; they will lift you up in their hands so that you will not strike your foot against a stone." (Psalm 91;11-12). I have written that verse in emails, and text messages to my loved ones this week, and re-read it several times myself. I am so thankful we can count on our heavenly Father to watch over us. David was very aware of God's protection over him, and he said in Psalm 121:8, *"The Lord will watch over your coming and going both now and forevermore."* I get such comfort and deep peace from these words.

More storms will come, storms of many kinds, not just snow and rain and wind. But life brings storms as well, in the night, all day long, and sometimes for days and weeks on end. Some of these storms are of our own making, others are caused by outside influences ~ family relationships, work, illness, financial trouble, and disaster. *"Jesus said, 'Don't let your hearts be troubled. Trust in God, and trust in Me.' "* (John 14:1). *"Give all your worries to God because He cares for you."* (1 Peter 5:7). I used to think that I shouldn't bother God with my little worries, but someone said that I might as well, since He would be up all night anyway! There is nothing that our heavenly Father does not care about, and nothing He cannot do. If He can get my beloved family members through the snowstorms, and over the ice and snow covered roads safely, I know He is watching constantly and will protect us all in our comings and goings. I praise Him over and over!

FEBRUARY 29

TELL THEM....

I have a fairly new friend who needs Jesus in the worst way, and after reading some comments she made yesterday, I sense the urgency to tell her. She has alluded to the fact that she's not a believer, doesn't need prayer, but if we want to pray, go ahead...she's always been able to "fix" whatever problems that come up. But she is facing a huge crisis in her life and is pretty desperate right now. And so I have asked God for a word, and this is it...

"For whosoever shall call upon the name of the Lord shall be saved. How then shall they call on Him whom they have not believed? And how shall they believe in Him of whom they have not heard? And how shall they hear without a preacher? And how shall they preach, except they be sent? As it is written, 'How beautiful are the feet of them that preach the gospel of peace, and bring glad tidings of good things!'" (Romans 10:14-15).

OK, so how distinct is that? I have a job to do…well, God will do it, but I must obey Him and TELL her! And what was my hint that she needs Him so badly? She was going back to the hospital for yet another surgery and was feeling very discouraged, could not see any light at the end of the tunnel. She couldn't focus and was only concentrating on the negative in her life, her bleak future. She had tried, in her own power, to be a good person, but knew that she faced a future without happiness. She had no hope in tomorrow. She had built her life on a shaky foundation and was feeling like it was all beginning to crumble away…

My goodness ~ how clear is the urgency there? This is one of those ripe fields, ready for the harvest. I must tell her! I don't know how she will accept my letter, just coming home from the hospital (she lives in another country), but if she never writes to me again, at least I will have told her about Him. Today I will write the letter. I will pray before I write, and I'll pray as I put it into the mailbox. God will do the rest.

Is there someone in your life who needs to hear about Jesus? Someone who is desperate, but may never admit it like my friend has? Will you be the one to tell them? It's not our job to save them, only to tell them. God will do the work in their heart. Oh, I can't wait to see the outcome of this…and if I don't see it in this life, I will later! We must tell them!

MARCH 1

IT'S SO QUIET…

I have had such a busy weekend! I had plans for a nice quiet weekend. Two of my grandchildren stayed overnight on Friday night, Saturday was full with visitation, shopping, and a memorial service, Sunday with church, then a birthday celebration dinner for one daughter, with a party following for cake & ice cream. We cut that short to make it to our first Easter cantata choir practice and distribution of the music, then topping it all off with our children's talent contest at church, which was delightful. Brought the same two grandchildren home Sunday night to sleep over again so mom and dad could spend the day together, shopping for her birthday and just enjoying each other's company.

In the midst of all this, the weather has been terrible, rain and snow (mostly snow) and much wind. My oldest grandchildren are traveling again, coming home from their trip east last week, not feeling very well, and my husband is driving bus again through snowy mountain passes expecting to be home pretty late. But my house is finally quiet. The television is off, the little voices are gone, and I just hear the wind and the clocks ticking, along with the occasional sound of a car driving through the slush in the road behind my house. It's pretty peaceful. But I'm still a little stressed about everyone who is traveling in these winter conditions. God has reminded me several times this week, and I've passed it along to my kids, that His angels are hovering over them all along their way, *"For He will command His angels concerning you to guard you in all your ways..."* (Psalm 91:11). I have referred to that very verse many times, and it's good to remember it. After my older daughter made a "white-knuckle" trip home from her job tonight, over a mountain highway, I asked her if she heard the angel wings over her car. She said, "Psalm 91, right?"

God tells us in His word not to be afraid. In fact, I've heard that the Bible has about 365 verses containing that phrase, "do not be afraid" and so I think God is serious about it! That would actually be one 'do not fear" verse for every day of the year. And each day He wants us to know He is with us. *"So do not fear, for I am with you; do not be dismayed for I am your God. I will strengthen you and help you; I will uphold you with my righteous right hand."* (Isaiah 41:10). We actually do need a measure of courage to get through each day. For one thing, we have no idea what each day holds for us. We may have plans for the day, or the weekend, but those can change in a moment. God alone knows what lies ahead for us, each day, each hour.

So, as I sit in my quiet house, waiting for my husband to arrive home from his grueling bus trip, I will rest in the peace that He has given me. Although the weather is ferocious, the roads are dangerous, and my loved ones are out there somewhere traveling, God says to me, *"Be still and know that I am God."* (Psalm 46:10). He is still in control. He is paying attention to my concerns. I will enjoy the quiet...

MARCH 2

MY PRAYER FOR KRISTY...TO TOUCH THE HEM OF HIS GARMENT.

"As Jesus was on His way, the crowds almost crushed Him. And a woman was there who had been subject to bleeding for twelve years, but no one could heal her. She came up behind Him and touched the hem of His garment and immediately her bleeding stopped.

'Who touched Me?' Jesus asked. When they all denied it, Peter said, 'Master, the people are crowding and pushing against You.' But Jesus said, 'Someone touched Me. I know that power has gone out from Me.'" (Luke 8:42-46).

This woman had visited many doctors, had tried many treatments, none of which could help her. This day she knew Jesus would be coming near, so as weak and ill as she was, she tried to get close enough to Him, and without causing a stir in the crowd, only wanted to come close enough to reach out, her fingers extended, and barely touch the hem of His cloak. She was determined not to give up when there was still a chance she could be healed. And suddenly, He knew! He felt the power go out from Him and knew someone had touched Him. Oh, there were people all around Him, pressing in on Him, but this was a different, deliberate, desperate touch. Once discovered, the woman admitted touching Him, and told Him why. *"Then He said to her, 'Daughter, your faith has healed you. Go in peace."* (v.48).

My dear precious friend, Kristy, (many other names can and have been inserted here) has been sick for a long time. A very long time. Like the woman in this account, she has been to many doctors who have not been able to help her. She has a family she cannot take care of, and she is worried and scared, trying desperately to trust God.

Lord, You know Kristy ~ You made her. I pray that she would have the faith to reach out and touch just the hem of Your garment, and that Your healing power would go out to her. She is discouraged and frightened. Even in the midst of so many pressing against You now, calling out Your name, I know You see her, just as You saw and knew the woman of old who reached out. And I know it is not Your clothing that would heal her, but her persistence, her faith... Your divine power. She is Your child, Lord, and she needs You now. You are fully aware of her vulnerability and the stretching of her faith. And when it is all said and done, please let Kristy be strong and blessed for having gone through this fiery trial. Bring her out victorious, and may Your holy name be glorified through it. You are the Great Physician. Amen.

MARCH 3

PERFECTION...

"The law of the Lord is perfect, reviving the soul. The statutes of the Lord are trustworthy, making wise the simple. The precepts of the Lord are right, giving joy to the heart. The

commands of the Lord are radiant, giving light to the eyes. The fear of the Lord is pure, enduring forever. The ordinances of the Lord are sure, and altogether righteous. They are more precious than gold, than much pure gold; they are sweeter than honey from the comb. By them Your servant is warned; in keeping them there is great reward." (Psalm 19:7-11).

Do you see that? Everything about our Lord is perfect, trustworthy, right, radiant, pure, sure and righteous. More precious than pure gold. His laws, ordinances, precepts, statutes, commands, are all we need to live as He meant for us to live. So why is it that man has made all his own rules? We have proven, (just take a look at our world and the condition it's in today), this doesn't work. God had made a perfect world with everything we needed for a perfect life. That didn't last long when man decided to do things his own way. Can you imagine God's sadness as He has looked down, over the centuries at the mockery we have made of Him and His pure and perfect love for us? And can you envision what our world would be like today if we had stuck with God's laws and precepts? There would be no violence, no sickness, no selfishness, no frowns, no jealousy, no hate…sounds like heaven, doesn't it?

I would pray, along with David, *"May the words of my mouth and the meditation of my heart be pleasing in Your sight, O Lord, my Rock and my Redeemer."* (vs. 14).

MARCH 4

TWO PRIDES….

God said, "*I hate pride and arrogance…*" (Prov. 8:13). Also, *"Pride goes before destruction, a haughty spirit before a fall."* (16:18). We have seen so much "pride and arrogance" in our government, and in the world of celebrities, and I believe this is the kind of pride God is talking about when He says, *"Do not be proud, but willing to associate with people of low position. Do not be conceited."* (Romans 12:16). We learn this kind of pride at a very young age. We express our desire to "do it ourselves" and we take on the attitude of "see what I did?" There is a certain amount of pride that we can take in our accomplishments, but we must give the glory to God for giving us the talent and ability in the first place.

There is another kind of pride, the kind that made my heart swell. My oldest daughter and my oldest granddaughter, both graduated together from college ~ they received their Certified Medical Assistant degrees. My granddaughter is the very busy mother of a 6-month old little girl, and yet she had a beautiful gold cord hanging around the shoulders of her gown ~ she graduated with honors. They have both received much encouragement from our family. It's true life hasn't been easy for either of them, but they chose to rise above the difficulties and they certainly shined at their graduation, like the stars they are! It was quite a moment. They were just glowing. It was a huge accomplishment for them. It's good for us, as parents, grandparents, and friends, to say "I am SO proud of you!" to *"encourage one another daily"* (Hebrews 3:13).

I know that these two beautiful women will not hold it over anyone else's head that they have done this thing...they will just go on to get jobs and do the best they can to help others. They will be proud of what they can do, proud of what they have learned ~ but not prideful in themselves. That's a hard word to understand, isn't it? Is pride good, or is pride bad? If it brings us to be puffed up or conceited, then it is the kind of pride God warns us not to have. If it encourages us to go on helping others, and glorifying God in the process... then be proud, but we must be careful that pride doesn't consume us. In the end we will hear the pride of our Father, when He says, *"Well done, good and faithful servant!"* (Matthew 25:21).

MARCH 5

GOD OF MY PAIN...

"He will wipe every tear from their eyes. There will be no more death or mourning or crying or **pain**, *for the old order of things has passed away."* (Revelation 21:4).

This is a promise I have clung to for many years, and especially in the last few. We all have pain of one sort or another, either physical or emotional, and sometimes both. And often one will affect the other. God knows about pain. Sometimes He takes it away, sometimes He doesn't, but He has promised to always be right by our side. *"I will never leave you nor forsake you."* (Hebrews13:5). Sometimes in our greatest pain, our darkest moments of suffering, it may feel like He has turned His back and walked away from us. But He does not do that. He calls for us to praise Him, even in our suffering. Paul did. Job did. And even though at times it felt to them like God had indeed forsaken them in their misery, He had His eye on them constantly.

I had great pain this past week, so bad on Sunday morning I contemplated not going to church. But I am a Sunday School teacher, and I love being in His house. My attitude has always been, "I will hurt if I do it, and I will hurt if I don't do it" ...so I may as well go ahead do it. I didn't want to miss something great. People tell me they can tell I'm in pain because they can see it in my eyes, even though I am smiling....I love these people of God, these friends who know me and love me. And pray for me. I KNOW many were praying for me, friends and family. About a month ago I was mistakenly given the wrong size syringes for my critical weekly RA medication, and so I had been *under*-medicating myself without realizing it. As my pain continued to intensify, instead of being alleviated, I tried to reason why this was happening. I finally made the discovery last week, but couldn't talk to the doctor's office until Monday. I needed a "booster" to hold me over until I took my next shot, still four days away. On Monday morning I woke up in much less pain! I hadn't even begun the extra meds yet, and I immediately knew people were praying for me. I should have continued to feel worse, but I was better!

During the time my pain was building, for several weeks, I talked to God about it many times, and still I was able to thank Him and praise Him for what He was doing in my LIFE, if not in my body. I know that suffering builds character, and I want to be able to be a witness to God's wonderful grace through anything my body would be suffering. It seems such a waste of time to mope around feeling sorry for myself. It is far better to praise Him ~ not for the pain, but in it. And well, maybe for it too, since I know there are valuable lessons to be learned. Not that I would ASK for it, but I am thankful God knows about me and sees me. He made me, after all....and I can say with Job *"Though He slay me, yet will I trust Him!"* (vs 13:15). And in Job 23:10: *"when He has tested me, I will come forth as gold."*

MARCH 6

EXERCISE...

Ugh! Are we ready? Spring is coming...I'm off to Jazzercise class this morning...but I've been going all year, 3 days a week. It's hard for me because I have rheumatoid arthritis, but I must keep moving. And I try to get in some exercise every day. So, most days I ride my bicycle as well, if not outside, then the one in my basement. It takes discipline, doesn't it? Exercise, which is good for our body, isn't always fun, and it takes time out of our busy day.

Just as physical exercise is good for our bodies, we need to exercise our minds and our hearts with the Word. I believe the more we get our minds and hearts "in shape" for coming trials, the better we will come through them. And we *will* have them. Jesus said, *"In this world you will have trouble. But take heart! I have overcome the world."* (John 16:33). Many scriptures make reference to "the race" of life. Paul alluded to this in his letters, this one to the Galatians: *"You were running a good race. Who cut in on you and kept you from obeying the truth?"* (Gal. 5:13). Oh-oh…someone cut in? Yes, this happens in a race. Just when we're feeling pretty confident that we are well on our way and there is smooth sailing ahead, someone cuts in on us and brings us down. We stumble, we fall. We are tempted to just lie there in the gravel, and give up. It's too hard. We are tired. But there is a reward, a prize, if we stick to the program! Oh, we may not get a medal, or a trophy, but the satisfaction of having a healthy body and a healthy mind will be worth the effort.

As Paul said in his 2nd letter to Timothy, *"I have fought the good fight, I have finished the race, I have kept the faith. Now there is in store for me the crown of righteousness, which the Lord, the Righteous Judge, will award to me on that day…"* (vs.7,8). And again to the Hebrews, *"Therefore, since we are surrounded by such a cloud of witnesses, let us throw off everything that hinders and the sin that so easily entangles, and let us run with perseverance the race marked out for us. Let us fix our eyes on Jesus, the author and perfecter of our faith, who for the joy set before Him endured the cross, scorning its shame, and sat down at the right hand of the throne of God."* (vs. 12:1,2). So, no race or exercise program in our lives will ever be as difficult or as grueling as the one our Savior went through, for me, for you. And He has promised to be with us, to give us strength for the journey…and a crown when we come through the finish line.

What are you doing to get into shape? An exercise program requires regular, scheduled workouts, not just a few calisthenics here and there. So it is with our spiritual "workouts." Schedule a time each day to get into the Word, and be faithful in this, and you'll be surprised how healthy you'll feel.

MARCH 7

CHANGES...

My goodness...if someone had told me a month ago we would go through all the changes we have in the last 30 days, I would have turned around and run the other way! Sometimes, change is good...if it changes our perspective. Some changes make us stronger. Jesus said, *"I tell you the truth, unless you change and become like little children, you will never enter the kingdom of heaven."* (Matthew 18:3). Well, I was a kid once, for quite a few years, and my parents, and others, kept telling me to grow up. So, now I see in the Word, that we are to become like little children. When we grow up, we think we know it all. So, when something major happens, like stroke, it causes us to step back and take a look at the things that are really important. Maybe families need to pull together a little bit closer. Maybe a husband and wife are too wrapped up in doing their own things.

I have learned in the last four weeks that the world will wait for me. My exercise class will still go on, and will still be going when I am able to return. The stores will not close down if I don't run out and shop in them. There are things I can do in my home that will keep me close to my spouse, not needing to hover, but just to be here when he needs me. I have also learned that the Lord will not let us starve if my husband's paycheck is not coming in. Jesus said about His provision, "*...do not worry about your life, what you will eat or drink, or about your body, what you will wear. Is not life more important than food, and the body more important than clothes? Look at the birds of the air, they do not sow or reap, or store away in barns, and yet your heavenly Father feeds them. Are you not much more valuable than they?*" (Matthew 6:25-26). God has reassured me with this scripture over and over again, whenever worry starts to creep in.

The change in our status has shown me that many, many people, friends and family, really do care about us and are praying for us. Some have offered help. Many have visited, and some of these we haven't seen in a long time. Lives are being touched that we may never have even met, had this illness not taken place. *"For my thoughts are not your thoughts, neither are your ways My ways, declares the Lord."* (Isaiah 55:8). Who are we to say what is best for us? I never would have picked this predicament for our lives right now ~ or any time. But I have to trust that God in His Sovereignty knows what is best for us.

And as if this change in health isn't enough, we ended up having to put our beloved dog down last week, and just yesterday have adopted a "new" dog, and so we have even more adjustments to make. But God gives us the strength we need, *"My grace is sufficient for you, for My power is made perfect in weakness."* (2 Cor. 12:9). And I know He is making me ready for the ultimate change, if I just stay faithful... *"we will all be changed ~ in a flash, in the twinkling of an eye, at the last trumpet."* (I Cor. 15:51-52). So, I can either go through life kicking and screaming, or let myself be led by the Father's hand all the way, learning through the hardships, so that I will be ready for that last change. The trumpet *will* sound.

MARCH 8

IN SICKNESS AND IN HEALTH...

For better or for worse...we have had those times in our marriage when everything seems to go well and we are happy, and then the bottom falls out and it seems we have almost lost interest and don't have the strength to go on. But through prayer and diligence and God's grace we grow a little more deeply committed to each other, and to our relationship.

For richer, for poorer...although we have never been what I would define as "rich," there were years when both of us were bringing home paychecks and we were comfortable. But it seems we've had more of the poorer days, especially in recent years, times when we just didn't know where the next sack of groceries was coming from, or how we would pay the mounting bills. It causes us to trust more deeply in God's provision.

This is the year we both go on Medicare, and I've been looking forward to the time we might actually have a little money to put away, monies that aren't going for the high medical insurance premiums. But sickness has struck, in a big way. Oh, we've had illnesses before, both of us, but nothing as serious as stroke, that "S" word that we all dread. It comes without warning. My husband's hit during a surgical procedure. I'm grateful he was there with his doctors present, and they immediately began diagnosing and treating. Still, the damage was done.

And, so, we go on from here. It's all about Love. God imagined and sanctioned marriage; *"The Lord God said, 'It is not good for man to be alone. I will make a helper suitable for him.*'" (Gen. 2:18). And He gave us guidelines about how to love each other, respond to each other's needs, and care for one another. *"Wives, submit to your husbands, as is fitting in the Lord. Husbands, love your wives and do not be harsh with them."* (Colossians 3:18,19). And He gave us the "Love" chapter, 1 Corinthians 13 ~ the whole thing tells us just what love is. Jesus included in His rundown of the parables, the part about us taking care of one another..."*when I was sick you looked after me...*" (Matthew 25:36), and later He happened to mention that whenever we took care of anyone in any way, we have actually done it to our Savior. (verse 40).

Well, with God's divine help, I will see my husband through this time of illness, loving, encouraging, helping...since I did sign on to take care of him "in sickness and in health." And someday soon, we will enjoy the blessings of good health once again, and give all the glory to God.

MARCH 9

MUCH INSPIRATION...

We talk about the storms of life, the uncertainty of our days. We can never know the future ~ and honestly, I don't think I would want to! I read in Ecclesiates 3 that there is a time for everything...*to be born, to die, to plant, to uproot, to kill, to heal, to tear down, to build up, to weep and to laugh*...and the list goes on, and on, including everything in life. The writer says, *"I have seen the burden God has laid on men. He has made everything beautiful in its time."*(vs. 10-11). I'm not exactly sure what that means, except that I have seen evidence of it in my lifetime. A thing we have deemed as disaster has brought about a beautiful end, giving glory to our Maker.

It's been a few days since my husband's stroke, and this is certainly not something we planned for. It has really thrown our family for a loop. But immediately people began praying for us, and they still are, and I was encouraged by God's word right away. And immediately, people around us, doctors, nurses, began to be touched by our deep faith. The first verse of scripture that was shared with us in the very beginning of this calamity is Acts 2:25-26 ~ *"I saw the Lord always before me. Because He is at my right hand, I will not be shaken. Therefore, my heart is glad and my tongue rejoices; my body will also live in hope because You will not abandon me to the grave."* From this point on, my mind was full of

God's promises, such as, *"Surely I am with you always, even to the end of the age."* (Matt. 28:20). I began praising the Lord from the very beginning...what else was I to do ~ despair? I asked God to give me a positive outlook, and He said, *"If any of you lacks wisdom, he should ask God, who gives generously to all without finding fault, and it will be given to him. But when he asks, he must believe and not doubt."* (James 1:5,6).

When the days begin to wear on me, my heavenly Father assures me that *"when I am weary, He is my strength,"* (Is. 40:31), and *"When I'm afraid, He's my courage."* (Deut. 31:6). Then David reminds me, *"Why so downcast, O my soul? Why so disturbed within me? Put your hope in God, for I will yet praise Him, my Savior and my God."* (Psalm 42:5). He goes on to say, *"God is our refuge and our strength, an ever-present help in trouble. Therefore we will not fear though the earth give way and the mountains fall into the heart of the sea..."* (Psalm 46:1-2).

God told me, through His word, not to fear because He's with me, (Isaiah 41:10), and that I can have peace in troubled times, because He's the overcomer, (John 16:33), He said that I should *"cast my cares on Him and He would sustain me ~ He will never let the righteous fall."* (Psalm 55:22). He promised me that He will work it all out and make something good out of the bad. (Romans 8:28). And so, how can I doubt promises like that? From the Almighty God of the Universe? Who else am I going to believe?

Well, I don't know where to stop...I may have to do a part II!

"Because of the Lord's great love, we are not consumed, for His compassions never fail. They are new every morning ~ great is Your faithfulness! I say to myself, 'The Lord is my portion: therefore I will wait for Him.'" (Lamentations 3:22-24).

MARCH 10

INSPIRATION...PART II...

So, yes, it has been a pretty scary week, to say the least. But, then it's always frightening when we think about what may be coming, and what we don't know. We keep getting encouragement from doctors and therapists, with no particular timeline. We have no idea when my husband may return back to work. And the bills are mounting. So, God has been speaking to me more and more, holding me in His arms ... He's so big, such a comforting Father. He tells me, *"So do not fear for I am with you, do not be dismayed for I am your God. I will strengthen you and help you. I will uphold you with My righteous right hand."* (Isaiah 41:10). And later, in John 16:33, Jesus says, *"I have told you these things so that in Me you may have peace. In this world you will have trouble. But take heart! I have overcome the world!"* I have to keep remembering that God sees what is out there ahead, and He is already working on the solution. *"His way is perfect!"* (Psalm 18:30).

"For God did not give us a spirit of fear, but of power, and of love, and of a sound mind." (2 Tim. 1:7). I have already seen this sound mind in my husband, and I praise God every day that he can still understand and reason, even though he cannot speak ~ yet. And so, we really can *"know that in all things God works for the good of those who love Him, who have been called according to His purpose."* (Romans 8:28). His purpose? What kind of a purpose would there be in an illness like this? Or any? Well, as I mentioned earlier, in Part I, I have observed and known God to be working in relationships we are forming with those taking care of him (my husband). We have already become fast friends with a doctor and a nurse, on a personal level as well as professional. We have been able to talk to them about God. This alone could be the reason for my husband's stroke. That seems a little far-fetched...but does it, really? God uses ordinary people, and unlikely situations to reach those who may otherwise be unreachable. Was some mother or grandmother praying for these individuals, that God would send someone (like us) to them with the good news? We'll never know.

And God continues to speak to me through His word. He says, *"Cast your cares on the Lord and He will sustain you; He will never let the righteous fall."* (Psalm 55:22). These are not just poetic or hollow ideas. These are the timeless words spoken by a Holy God. This life intends to bring us down, but *"Because of the Lord's great love, we are not consumed, for His compassions never fail. They are new every morning ~ great is Your faithfulness! I say to myself, 'The Lord is my portion: therefore I will wait for Him.'"* (Lamentations 3:22-24).

Okay, you get the idea. We get our strength from the Lord, the Creator of heaven and earth. Nothing that happens to us is an accident, but God uses every situation, every heartache, to bring about glory to His name. And believe me, His name is being glorified in our lives. I can stand and testify to His love every day!

MARCH 11

LIGHT...

"I am the light of the world. Whoever follows Me will never walk in darkness, but will have the light of life." (John 8:12).

Have you ever been afraid of the dark? Many of us have been afraid as children, but we have grown up, and if we are still afraid of the dark, we don't like to admit it. It seems childish. I'm not actually *afraid* of the dark, I just don't like to try and find my way in the dark, whether I'm driving, or walking through my house in the night. We have a couple of night lights, one on the hood over the stove, and one in a terrarium (which used to be a fish tank) in our bedroom that gives a nice soft glow. When our grandchildren spend the night, we leave one on in the guest room as well as the guest bath. A little light just makes it easier to find our way through the darkness.

There are times when the darkness is good...the stars shine more brilliantly when it's darker, movies are easier to watch in the dark, and sleep is more restful when it's dark. But there are so many uncertainties in the darkness...what was that shadow? Did something move? We trip over things. Run into things. We can't read in the dark. The batteries are dead in the flashlight! But some people like the darkness...Jesus said *"Light has come into the world, but men loved darkness instead of light, because their deeds were evil."* (3:19). See, it's easier for people to sneak around and get away with wrongdoing at night because they think they won't be seen.

Jesus said that we are *"the light of the world. A city on a hill cannot be hidden, neither do people light a lamp and put it under a bowl. Instead they put it on its stand, and it gives light to everyone in the house. In the same way,* ***let your light shine before men****, that they may see your good deeds and praise your Father in heaven."* (John 5:14-16). It is so much easier to find our way in the light. There are so many things in life that cause darkness, or uncertainty. But Jesus is the Light. And if we follow Him, He will lead us safely. And in heaven, *"The city does not need the sun or moon to shine on it, for the glory of God gives it light, and the Lamb is its lamp."* (Rev. 21:23).

Thank you, Father, for the light of your Word, the light of Your presence. And for sending Jesus, the Light of the world. Amen.

MARCH 12

A HARD DAY….

It's been a hard day, Lord. My dear husband was frustrated to tears. I feel helpless, although I know I am supposed to be helping him. I am the help mate you gave him. But, I am not able to carry this. And I am so weary ~ not strong enough.

But Your word says *"My grace is sufficient for you, for My power is made perfect in weakness."* (2 Cor. 12:9). And so, Lord, I have to commit my weakness 100% to You. I need to depend on You to do what I cannot do. You are my Strength.

Let me be astonished at what You can do in my circumstance through my tired and weary self. You alone will enable me to become strong in what I must do. Give me power to resist the discouragement the devil uses to defeat me. I desire You with all my heart. Fulfill Your purposes in me and through me.

Touch my husband in these coming days and weeks as he becomes stronger. Deliver him from the prison of this stroke and heal his speech. Give him the determination to get better, no matter how difficult it is for him, for me. Help us to daily remember that You love us, and You have not left us alone. Wrap Your arms around us and show us the light at the end of this long, dark tunnel.

And then help us to remember to give glory and praise to Your name as You guide us through to the light. Amen.

MARCH 13

THE HOUSE CALL…

When I was a little girl, I remember our family doctor coming to our house to take a look when one of us was sick. It was common practice years ago. "Doctoring" has changed much over the last few decades. It used to be that the family doctor would do it all ~ every kind of exam, X-rays right in the office, stitch up cuts, set broken bones, perform any surgery needed, they would even prescribe medication right over the phone. Now there are different doctors for every ailment ~ specialists. I have nothing against specialists. This is a good thing, because the doctor can concentrate on and be the expert in any given medical field. But there are so many, and when my family doctor in early days used to see me for everything, he could also know me and know everything about my health history. In this day and age, it's hard to get to know the doctor. It's like you're always seeing a stranger. And house calls are non-existent.

Except for one doctor I know. This is my husband's cardiologist/surgeon. This wonderful doctor visited my husband almost daily while he was hospitalized for his recent stroke, and when he was transferred to our local hospital for rehab, the doctor still called me several times to check on him. He even drove over to our city on a Saturday to visit my husband while he was in the rehab facility. Well, that's very noble and caring, you might say. But this same busy and popular specialist also came to our home last week and visited with us for nearly two hours, talking not only about my husband's health, but about many things, our families, dogs, travel, faith...an incredible event not to be taken for granted. And this was repeated last night, when he drove the 70-mile round trip for another home visit. Nothing professional, no medical equipment was brought along, no examination was preformed...just friendships and conversations shared. We have cherished these times.

Jesus was like that. Although he wasn't identified as a "doctor" but as a teacher, or rabbi, He was the Great Physician, who *"went through Galilee teaching in their synagogues, preaching the good news of the kingdom, and* ***healing every disease and sickness among the people."*** (Matthew 4:23). He had a group of "associates" that traveled with Him, His disciples, and He spent much time training and teaching them as well, giving personal attention to each one. He truly cared about the well-being of each one, and of those people who needed Him in the communities He visited. And He didn't just set up a conference, or series of meetings, He personally visited in the homes of those who were in need...He raised up a little girl who had died, and a little boy as well, and a good friend. He healed a woman right on the street who had been ill for twelve years and had been to many doctors with no answers for her illness. He made the blind see, and the lame walk. He performed many miracles. He gave hope when the people were in despair. He calmed fears. He loved.

Our doctor friend has mentioned that he never really gets to know his patients because they are typically in his office for such a brief time, for consultations before and after surgical procedures. But because of my husband's stroke, and the subsequent extra care that has ensued, he said he has gotten to know more about my husband, his character, his deep faith, our family... he shared this with us during one hour-long visit in the hospital. They don't make doctors like this anymore. House calls are unheard of. It is no accident that we were led, or referred to this special doctor. I believe our meeting was ordered of God.

I don't know why strokes happen, or why it has touched our family. But I do know that God is using this experience to reach others. He has given us hope through His word, caused us to trust in Him more deeply, and we can give testimony to His power and strength just by the way He upholds us through this difficult time. Doctors and nurses, and therapists are seeing that too. It will make a difference, in our lives, and those around us.

MARCH 14

IT'S RAINING...IT'S POURING...

Remember that little jingle we used to sing? The old man is snoring...one of those nonsensical little tunes that were fun and everyone knew. Well, it is raining here, in fact...really pouring! Literally. We often use the same phrase when we are overwhelmed by a string of "bad luck," such as one problem or disaster after another, as has been true in our family of late. First it was my husband's stroke – several weeks ago now. Then more recently, our beloved elderly dog got so bad we had to put her down. We voiced the little ditty – "when it rains, it pours." Well, today we learned that my husband's car is in dire need of repair, to the tune of over a thousand dollars we don't have. Since he hasn't been working, that's income we can't count on.

I have learned never to ask "what's next!?" Because the minute you ask a question like that, you find out the answer soon enough! So, instead of throwing up our hands and giving up, we just continue to plug along, one day at a time, because what else are we going to do? I know that God is fully aware of our struggles. He told us we would have them. He wants us to trust Him with every hardship that we encounter. 1st Corinthians 10:13 says, *"And God is faithful: He will not let you be tempted beyond what you can bear. But when you are tempted,* ***He will also provide a way out so that you can stand up under it."*** This is good to remember. He wants us to know that whatever comes our way, with Him by our side, we can overcome it.

It's in times like these that I think of Job, and Paul. I've been thinking of them, and reading about their woes, a lot. I really can't imagine that my life can ever get as bad as Job's did. And yet, God did not leave him, through all of that! Job knew it, too. He proclaimed many times that he would be faithful to God. He had to. What choice did he have? He made several statements that showed his deep faith. 5:9: *"He performs wonders that cannot be fathomed, miracles that cannot be counted."* And vs. 18: *"For He wounds, but He also binds up; He injures, but His hands also heal."* 13:15: *"Though He slay me, yet will I hope in Him."* What else do we have if we don't have hope?

Paul is another one who inspires me in these uncertain times. He was beaten, jailed, hunted, and stood trial for his preaching. He was shipwrecked. But it didn't stop him from proclaiming Jesus. *"Believe in the Lord Jesus and you will be saved ~ you and your household."* (Acts 16:31.). He said, *"I consider my life worth nothing to me, if only I may finish the race and complete the task the Lord Jesus has given me."* (20:24). When he and some other prisoners were about to be shipwrecked, he advised them, *"Last night an angel of the God whose I am, and whom I serve, stood beside me and said, 'Do not be afraid…'"* (27:23). Paul resolved to persevere, to run the race, to hope in God's love. How can we do less?

Although, as Donna Partow once titled one of her books, "This Isn't the Life I Signed Up For," I am convinced that nothing happens to us that God doesn't know about or allow. I believe that if we persevere as Paul admonishes, we will reap rich blessings and God will teach us "unsearchable things" as we obey Him and trust Him, and draw ever closer to His side. Paul also observed, *"I consider that our present sufferings are not worth comparing with the glory that will be revealed in us."* (Romans 8:18). We will be more than conquerors. *"And we know that in all things God works for the good of those who love Him, who have been called according to His purpose."* (vs. 28). We may never know what God's purpose is in our suffering, but know that He has a plan for us in it all. I have already seen miracles.

MARCH 15

BEING WATCHED…

I know that God sees us as we go through the trials and struggles of this life. At the very beginning of David's Psalms, we read, *"For the Lord watches over the way of the righteous…"* (Ps. 1:6). And 33:14, *"From His dwelling place He watches all who live on earth ~ He who forms the hearts of all, who considers everything they do."* He places His angels all around us as well. I know of many of them... Dr. K, Jennifer-Anne, Pastor Ron, Merle, Robyn, our kids, Katherine & JT, Bill & Stephanie, our church family...these are our doctors, nurses, therapists, family and neighbors who have supported us in the last few weeks and have been there for us contributing their prayers and encouragement. They have each been placed in our lives *"for such a time as this."* (Esther 4:14). That's a different story, the account of Esther, but still shows God's hand in "arranging" certain people, certain meetings. None is by accident.

I thank my heavenly Father for making them available, and for stirring the hearts of specific people, placed in our lives by His own design. Not only have they been a blessing to us, but I believe in some way we can be, and have been, a blessing to others as they have watched our own faith to grow in the midst of our troubles.

I remember when my children were small and I would watch them play outside, making sure they didn't go too fast, or climb too high, or wander too far away. I wanted to make sure my eyes were on them at all times, and that they were safe. I even stood over their crib or bed and watched them sleep. What a feeling in my heart. God, our heavenly Father, is fully aware of when we are too high, or we wander too far away. He is concerned about us when we are hurt or sick. Sometimes He is not successful in getting us to slow down, or turn around, before we run into trouble. Many times we think we know what is best, and God is always waiting there with His arms outstretched.

Yes, we are being watched. But I believe Satan is watching us too. He's hoping we will turn away from our Maker in our times of trouble. He discourages us and puts doubt into our heads. He lies. And others are watching as we turn and give glory to God. Just this morning my husband shared with me that he had seen another man this week who had had a stroke and did not have the freedom to walk easily, or use his arm, which hung helplessly at his side. He said that causes him to count his blessings. It is a blessing he didn't have more damage than he did. It is a blessing he was with his doctor when trouble struck. Is it a blessing he had the stroke? Maybe. It depends on who is watching, and what they see in our lives. May they see the faith that is growing deeper as we depend on God's strength. May they see the character that is developing through perseverance in troubled times. May they see God's healing hand day by day.

"Be exalted, O God, above the heavens, let Your glory be over all the earth." (Psalm 57:5).

MARCH 16

A STUDY IN GRACE...

Our ladies Bible study group is going through a book by David Jeremiah titled "Captured by Grace" ~ subtitled, "No One is Beyond the Reach of a Loving God." It's all about the author of the hymn, Amazing Grace, John Newton, his wayward life, and all the hardships he endured before he realized the fullness of God's grace. It also contains many examples of Paul's life, his sufferings, and the grace shown to him. I believe I could even say, as many of us could, that I am a study in God's amazing grace. I know what it is to be a recipient of God's unmerited favor.

The weeks are marching on now since our lives have been turned upside-down by stroke. It was by God's grace that it wasn't worse, that my husband can still walk, eat and basically take care of himself, though not right at first, but those things came back rather quickly. The frustrating part is his inability to speak, although that is slowly returning. It has been difficult to communicate with and for him, and to take care of all the phone calls, and requests that he makes. It's easy to become discouraged. These times challenge our faith. But God has given grace enough for each day, and we have to remember, we have "inside information," because in Romans 8:28 Paul said, *"And* ***we know*** *that all things work together for good to those who love God, to those who are called according to His purpose."* John Phillips said that "God's purposes cannot be thwarted." That's good to know.

When we are believers in Christ, we are standing upon the very Rock that will never crumble, even though it seems the world around us is crumbling. Paul is not merely making an observation that maybe God is in control ~ he reminds us that we **can know** this for certain. Not a thing on this earth can touch us without passing through the will of God. Even when we are so distraught we cannot pray, *"We do not know what we should pray for as we ought, but the Spirit Himself makes intercession for us with groanings which cannot be uttered."* (Romans 8:26). We, and our sufferings, are part of the big picture. Many details are still a mystery to us, but God said, *"For I am God and there is no other; I am God and there is none like Me, declaring the end from the beginning, and from ancient times things that are not yet done, saying, 'My counsel shall stand, and I will do all My pleasure'...indeed, I have spoken it; I will also bring it to pass. I have purposed it; I will also do it."* (Isaiah 46:9-11). This is our assurance that there are no limits in

God's ability to handle all things that come our way. There is no way we could see what has been planned for us from the very beginning of time, but I know whatever the outcome, it will bring glory to God.

We have some bad days here and there, but these are things that God uses. They are part of the puzzle, with God holding that final piece that will make it a beautiful picture. Nothing about us, nothing that happens to us, is unusable within His plan. So, *"let us not become weary in doing good, for at the proper time we will reap a harvest if we do not give up."* (Galatians 6:9). He shows us His great grace every day. To ask for it has become part of my daily prayer!

MARCH 17

WIND CHIMES...

The wind is blowing hard tonight...I think it's blowing Spring in...but I love the sound of the wind chimes hanging on my house in about three or four areas. It's such a peaceful sound in the midst of the tumult of the wind.

Reminds me of how far I've come since I began journaling. I wrote in my first journal about 15 years ago, how fearful I was of the wind. We lived in an area which had hundreds of tall pine trees, I was always afraid one of them would fall on our house, and in fact, I strategized which one, and right where it would fall, because of the direction the wind typically came from...right on top of the wing where our master bedroom was! As it turned out, we did actually have a tree fall on the house in a summer windstorm, which contained a rare funnel cloud for this area, but it wasn't the tree I had picked out, and it fell on a different part of the house. During this same storm, we actually stood in our front yard and watched trees snap in half all around the perimeter of our development, one right after another, some falling on houses, some on cars...fortunately, no one was injured. It was quite a violent, freak tornadic-type storm, in the heat of summer. Frightening.

I began to really pray in earnest that the Lord would take away my dread of the wind, and help me to trust Him more to take care of me and my family. I started to look up scripture verses about fear and write them into my journal, and then pray on them. Next, I looked up verses on faith and trust, and asked God to strengthen my faith. I certainly didn't want to cause my children to become fearful of the wind because I was. We had already mastered thunderstorms and actually enjoyed watching them.

And so began my writing of journals. As I began to pour out my heart to God about many things, often looking up scriptures to help me deal with things like fear, pain, trust, I also started looking up verses about salvation, and praying these for my loved ones who weren't saved. Peace, in the midst of every storm. And so on...my concordance is a valuable tool!

And that brings me to now, and while the wind is blowing outside, although I still don't like it, I am resting and believing that God will take care of us. And there are the wind chimes. We have collected them over the years, not a lot, only four or five, but I love the peaceful sound they make in the wind. Some of them are high tinkling sounds, and others are a deeper, richer tone. In many of Bodie Thoene's novels, she talks about how when a special Spirit from God came to one of the characters, they would hear the tinkling of wind chimes. I think of that now every time I hear them, and it reminds me that God's Spirit is with me, protecting me from harm.

God is in the wind, for He created it. It has a purpose. It can be a gentle breeze or a strong and powerful and destructive thing. I prefer the former, but always, it reminds me of our powerful and majestic God. And I feel His Spirit.

MARCH 18

STRENGTH FOR WHAT LIES AHEAD...

Does any of us know what tomorrow will bring? I mean, we do know some things...we here in North Idaho already know that the schools in our town are closed again tomorrow because of too much heavy snow on the flat roofs of most school buildings. And where I live, many roofs have collapsed, and businesses closed due to the volume of snow. We know we have appointments, errands, etc. Some of us even know what we will fix for dinner tomorrow. But there are situations and events that are beyond our control, unexpected circumstances which may arise that we're not ready for. There will be surprises, trauma, unpleasant, and pleasant news.

Do we worry now because something *might* happen tomorrow that we're not expecting? God wants us to live victoriously, not in fear of what tomorrow may bring. In fact, He *enables* us to live victoriously. Instead of fretting about what may come our way tomorrow, we should dwell on the fact that God lives within us. Think about the power that gives us in this life. *"For the eyes of the Lord range throughout the earth to strengthen those whose hearts are fully committed to Him."* (2 Chronicles 16:9). God uses today's difficulties to strengthen us for tomorrow. He equips us to be honest, to take a stand, to be true. Whatever we do, it is His grace that saves us. His hand that gives us strength.

We have a myriad of uncertain tomorrows ahead of us. A new president, with many changes in our government. Some of us will have job changes, and some will have life changes. May we always seek Him to keep our minds clear and our hearts pure, His word bringing triumph to our lives.

MARCH 19

GRATITUDE...

I ran across this in a little *Day Brightener* book this morning... "Gratitude. More aware of what you have than what you don't. Recognizing the treasure in the simple ~ a child's hug, fertile soil, a golden sunset. Relishing in the comfort of the common." There are so many simple and common things in life that usually are overlooked, because we are searching for something more, something bigger and better.

Ever watch "Little House on the Prairie?" Most of us have. Our children looked forward to that show every day after school, and my 34-year old daughter still watches it often, along with her children. There was something wholesome in the lives of the Ingalls family. The children went to a one-room school house, played with sticks and rocks, and each other, developing relationships. Their meals were simple, yet nutritious, they learned skills and worked hard, and appreciated everything they had. Their home, their land, each other.

But look how far we have come away from that era...we have SO much, yet we only want more. We want so much that mothers don't stay home with their children anymore. We want so much, we are in deep debt. Are we not satisfied with warm homes, plenty of clothes and food to eat? Have you noticed the things our children and young adults are interested in now? ~ electronics, games, computers...so much so, that they have retreated inside themselves, and no longer communicate with parents or one another. Are they learning to be grateful? We shop just for the sake of shopping, *in case* we see something out there we don't have yet. Can we not be thankful for the simple things, God's creation, music, each other? Hebrews 12:28 says: *"Therefore, since we are receiving a kingdom that cannot be shaken, let us be thankful, and so worship God acceptably, with reverence and awe..."* Wow. If we are faithful in our thanksgiving to God, and worship Him as we should, we will have as our own, a whole kingdom! Then who will need all that other "stuff?"

MARCH 20

LONG-AWAITED SPRING...

It's coming. There are signs everywhere. Tulips and daffodils, hyacinth and crocus are pushing their leaves up through the softening ground. Birds are searching for places to build their nests. The brown in my grass is disappearing. Although we didn't have a particularly hard winter this year, the coldness and dreariness has lasted just as long. I'm always ready for sunshine and warm days after the "long winter's nap!" The first page of the Bible says, in Genesis 1:14-15, *"And God said, 'Let there be lights in the expanse of the sky to separate the day from the night, and let them serve as signs to mark seasons and days and years, and let them be lights in the expanse of the sky to give light on the earth.'"* Our Creator specifically designed the seasons to follow one another, and so we know it will come ~ Spring. There is already evidence of it...it is lighter in the morning and in the evening ~ the days are longer. It happens like clockwork. People have already been working in their yards. Ball teams are practicing. And soon the world will be painted with every color as the trees and flowers begin to bloom. There will be new life everywhere!

Our lives are much like that. There are seasons that we go through...some seem longer than others, like when we're waiting for Spring to arrive, and we see encouraging signs, but then it turns cold again. Some difficult circumstances in our lives seem to be almost over, but then there is a setback, and it seems to take so long. But just as we have the promise of Spring, we also have the promise of God that He will remain faithful through all our hardships. *"Let us not become weary in doing good, for at the proper time we will reap a harvest if we do not give up."* (Gal. 6:9). It would be just like the garden we plant in the spring...we have to nurture it, water it, keep the weeds back, feed it, and when the plants are mature, we may enjoy the bounty we have so carefully tended. When we are faced with tough times, we cannot give up, or we will sacrifice a great blessing that is in store for us. *"Being confident of this, that He who began a good work in you will be faithful to complete it until the day of Christ Jesus."* (Phil. 1:6). Many of us will become tired or discouraged and give up on our gardens before they begin to flourish, but know this ~ our heavenly Father will never give up on us! And though we become discouraged in our circumstances, there will be an end to our trouble after God has nurtured us, pruned us and shaped us. And when we are mature, that is when our fruit will show. Just as we have automatic sprinkling systems for our lawns and gardens, and water them regularly, we must stay close to the Source of Living Water so that our souls will be ready for the harvest. For it's Jesus who gives us new life!

MARCH 21

WINGS

"He giveth power to the faint; and to them who have no might He increaseth strength; Even the youths shall faint and be weary, and the young men shall utterly fall. But they that wait upon the Lord shall renew their strength. They shall mount up with wings as eagles, they shall run and not be weary, they shall walk and not faint." (Isaiah 40:29-31 KJV).

I love this verse – it gives me so much hope. And I love eagles. They are one of the most magnificent of God's creatures. I have researched a little about the bald eagle and am amazed to learn that when they approach "old age" between 30-40 years old, they really do begin to "renew" themselves. They know they must go through a painful period of transformation and renewal, or do nothing and await death. For about 5 months, the eagle trains itself to fly beyond the high mountains, build and live in its nest, and cease all flying. Since its beak grows very long and curved, it "sands" it down and breaks it off on the rocks, and after a new beak grows it then removes its gnarled claws, and then its long, thick feathers. It *waits* quietly while this process is completed. Then it will soar again in the sky with renewed youth and strength, living on for another 30 years. This is so fascinating to me – it's all by the Creator's design.

The symbol of the eagle is used about 38 times in the scriptures. Eagles mate for life. They are committed to their families and care for their young and guard them from harm. *"Like an eagle that stirs up its nest and hovers over its young, that spreads its wings to catch them, and carries them on its pinions."* (Deut. 32:11). What a wonderful example of parenting. The young eagles don't want to step out of their "comfortable" nest – and we are sometimes like this – we become complacent and don't want the growing experience. Many times the scriptures refer to God "carrying His children on eagle's wings." In Psalm 103:5 we see that our spiritual youthfulness is renewed ~ it's a time to get rid of what's weighing us down, holding us back, aging us spiritually ~ to give up sinful habits, give in to the Holy Spirit. The eagle does not "flap its wings" as other birds do, (they are so heavy it would be an expenditure of too much energy), but wait for just the right time, then soar on the wind. Sometimes we jump out too soon and flap our wings, wasting strength, instead of waiting for God's timing, His answers, His direction. And the eagle is one of the cleanest birds ~ but if they are held in captivity, they become very dirty. God created us, like the eagle, to remain pure and holy. This will only be possible when we hope in God, and wait for Him to renew our strength, preparing us to be molded into a new creature ~ to be zero again, be still again, be quiet again. And sometimes this renewal process will be painful, like the eagle's.

And "eagles seem to have a premonition of death. At such a time they will fly to a high place and fasten their talons to a rock. With dignity and majesty they die looking into the setting sun. What a glorious picture of God's eagle Saints! When it's time to depart this world, they find their feet *firmly planted* on the solid Rock Christ Jesus, and their eyes fixed with wondering gaze on the Son of Righteousness. Then with eagle wings and unfettered joy, they soar to glory!" (this adapted from Rev. W.C. Greiner).

The storms of this life can actually form strong, godly character so we can face the winds of adversity. God bless each one of us as we "mount up with wings as eagles" and renew our strength in Him!

MARCH 22

WAITING...

Maybe one of the hardest things we have to do in life is to wait. We wait all our lives, everywhere we go...in traffic lines, in grocery lines, in hospital waiting rooms, at home in our closets ~ on our knees. When we're little we wait for Daddy to come home, we wait for Christmas. Seems like such a time-waster, doesn't it? We wait for news, we wait for special days, we wait to feel better, we wait for babies to be born, for seasons, for people. It's tough to wait.

The Psalmist said "*Wait for the Lord, be strong and take heart, and wait for the Lord.*" (Ps. 27:14) and again in 130:5 ~ *"I wait for the Lord, my soul waits, and in His word I put my hope…"* I wonder how much time went by between those two verses ~ weeks? Years? It would take me a lifetime to write all that David wrote. How much asking went on during that time? Did David think the Lord would *ever* answer his prayers and his cries? Did he ever lose faith?

My husband is a builder by trade, and has been struggling with two homes that he's been trying to sell ~ one for two years, the other for a full year. The waiting has been hard, since this is his livelihood. But I must say, the Lord has provided for us while we wait. And what are we learning? To *trust* Him! Sometimes it takes awhile. And Isaiah says: *"Yet the Lord longs to be gracious to you; He rises to show you His compassion. For the Lord is a God of justice. Blessed are all who wait for Him!"* (30:18). How many of us have prayed, "Lord, give me patience, and give it to me NOW?" Paul said, in Colossians, *"And we pray this (that the people would be filled with knowledge) in order that you may live a life worthy of the Lord and may please Him in every way, bearing fruit in every good work, growing in the knowledge of God, being strengthened with all power according to His glorious might so* ***that you may have great endurance and patience****, and joyfully giving thanks to the Father Who has qualified you to share in the inheritance of the saints in the kingdom of light."* (1:1-12). So there you have it ~ why we wait. The waiting in our lives produces endurance, and this is where patience comes from. And throughout all history, people everywhere have been waiting. And we still *"wait for the blessed hope ~ the glorious appearing of our great God and Savior, Jesus Christ!"* (Titus 2:13).

Let's not give up hope. Waiting is part of life. It's hard, but it'll be worth it all when we see Him!

MARCH 23

KINDNESS…

"And God raised us up with Christ and seated us with Him in the heavenly places in Christ Jesus, in order that in the coming ages He might show the incomparable riches of His grace, expressed in ***His kindness*** *to us in Christ Jesus."* (Eph. 2:6-7).

People are unkind. We treat each other despicably sometimes. We learn this behavior as small children. It's the selfish nature we are born with. I hate it. God hates it. But He is full of grace, and He shows us a kindness and gentleness that no one else ever can. Some people go through their lives, unfortunately, never knowing the kindness that can heal, and cleanse. They are beaten down and made to feel worthless by their circumstances, or they can be made to feel undeserving and wretched by one single word, spoken harshly.

There is a story I heard a long time ago which impacted how I look at other people...a dad and his two children were traveling on a bus, and the children were acting unruly, getting up and walking around, being noisy, and the other passengers were getting upset with them when finally, someone said to the father, "Can't you see that your children are disrupting the whole bus? Can't you get them under control?" The father then told this person that they have just come from the hospital where their mother had died, and the children were acting out their grief and frustration. He was too despondent himself to correct them at the time.

This reminder has caused me to look at people in a different way, wondering what circumstance has caused them to act the way they have...giving them the benefit of the doubt. We never know who has just heard a bit of bad news, or what they are going through in their own lives. One thing I know ~ Jesus will never treat us as anything less that God's precious creation. His loving-kindness is better than life itself.

Remember to treat others as Jesus said, in the greatest commandment, *"Love one another, as I have loved you..."* (John 15:12). Offer kindness whenever you can. You may be the only person who does on this particular day.

MARCH 24

PROMISE OF PRAYER...

In church on Sunday we had a visiting missionary family who spoke to our congregation about their work in a foreign field. I think most churches invite missionaries to come and speak from time to time. At the close of the service we were invited to visit the "missionary table," piled high with books, pictures, and brochures about many various child sponsorship and giving opportunities. They sometimes will pass out a card or a bookmark with the family's picture on it as a reminder to pray for them. I have several of these, tucked away safely in my study Bible. As we take the card in our hand, we promise our prayers for their safety and health as they return back to their field.

We run into a friend in the supermarket we haven't seen in a long while, and as we visit, we learn of some hardships they've gone through since we last saw them. We say we will pray for them, and then we go our way. Or a call comes from the church secretary asking for prayers for a certain parishioner, or a situation, and we say, "I will pray." But then what happens? We forget, or the card gets misplaced, or we become caught up in our own troubles and wish someone would pray for US. What humbles me most, though, is that when I see that person again, or when the church secretary calls with an update, can I say, "I prayed for you?"

I have often prayed that God will bring someone to mind that I should pray for, and sometimes He will do that, even in the middle of the night. It's not just a coincidence that a name will pop into your head, causing you to wonder what's going on in their lives and puzzled why you're suddenly thinking of them, but it is a call for prayer. And we don't need to know what's wrong ~ we need only to pray. God is fully aware of their concerns. I sometimes think, though, that our participation in praying for others isn't necessarily for the others' benefit, but for our own. We learn to trust more deeply in God, we grow in our own faith and discipline, and perseverance when we pray for others. It's good for us. And it's a command. James 5:16 says, *"Therefore confess your sins to each other and pray for each other so that you may be healed. The prayer of a righteous man [woman] is powerful and effective."* And Paul told the Ephesians, *"I pray also that the eyes of your heart may be enlightened in order that you may know the hope to which He has called you, the riches of His glorious inheritance in the saints, and His incomparably great power for us who believe."* (1:18-19).

There are many promises we make...to our children, to the bank, to ourselves...but the most important one to keep is the promise to pray. When someone tells me they are praying for me, I rest in the potential that I don't have to come up with the answers, and I don't even have to think up the words to pray in my agony, but someone is lifting me up to the throne of the Almighty, and I take such comfort in that. I don't have to really even explain my situation, God already knows anyway. What a faithful friend, one who will promise to pray, and then follow through.

MARCH 25

A SONG IN THE NIGHT...

There has been a program on Moody radio for years and years called "Songs Through the Night" with the very gentle, smooth-voiced commentator, Mike Kellogg, (among others), giving encouragement and playing songs of hope and peace, all the way through the night. I haven't listened for a long time, but at times, when I'd be driving at night, or staying up late, I would listen, especially when going to sleep, and the calm voice, along with the beautiful hymns, relaxed me so I could sleep. I think the program is meant to do that ~ to give calm, and peace, and encouragement when we are troubled.

There's just something about singing. God created music. Job said, *"Men cry out under a load of oppression; they plead for relief from the arm of the powerful. But no one says, 'Where is God my Maker, who gives songs in the night?'"*(vs. 35:9-10). "Night" doesn't always necessarily mean that period of time between sunset and sunrise when we sleep. Sometimes the night is not a restful time for us to restore our strength for the next day's work. To many, it can be filled with terror, alarm, and dread. It can be the darkness that comes from loneliness, illness, feelings of utter abandonment. There are often nights of sorrow, nights of persecution, nights of doubt, bewilderment, anxiety, oppression, of ignorance. "The dark night of the soul" can be such a time of spiritual crisis when we are seeking God with all our might, feeling as though we have lost hope and God is not there, and no one cares. But sometimes in the quiet of the night, if we listen to the silence, we can hear God's harp ring out from the breezes, crickets, from the stars and planets, from the waves of the ocean, almost chanting...the sweet music of His love.

Paul and Silas had been beaten brutally, and thrown in prison. Yet, in the mire and the pain and the darkness, God gave them a song... *"At midnight Paul and Silas prayed and sang praises unto God; and the prisoners heard them."* (Acts 16:25). What a sound that must have been in the night ~ echoing through the cold darkness of that dungeon, surely causing a stir among the other prisoners and guards. Even in their exhaustion and through their pain, they had no fear, because they trusted their God. And they sang praises to Him! In the midst of their suffering.

It's easy to sing in the daylight...when things are going well for us, when the sun is shining, when our cup is full. But it's not natural to sing when there is trouble, when it is dark. But God gives us a song in the night. God IS our song in the night. "*The Lord is my strength and my song.*" (Exodus 15:2). "*He put a new song in my mouth.*" (Psalm 40:3). Just remember that God, who gave us a song in the daylight, does not leave us in the night. He's watching over us constantly. He is there in the thickest darkness, "*surrounding us with songs of deliverance.*" (Psalm 32:7). "*Weeping may endure for a night, but joy comes in the morning.*" (Psalm 30:5). It's imperative for us to listen for that faint song in the dark of our night. The melodious chimes of His Spirit singing over us.

MARCH 26

A NEW FRIEND...

Will Rogers once said "A stranger is just a friend you haven't met yet." Now, I will say, some strangers I wouldn't want to get close to at all...we warn our children to "stay away from strangers." And, I do have some friends, even family members, who are quite strange at times! But I met a new friend, a very nice lady, a couple of weeks ago in our Mall who sells tea in a kiosk. I have been a tea consultant for about four and a half years, until the company just went out of business at the end of last year...and so I was drawn to her because of this common interest. I stopped, and we began talking about tea (what else!?). I told her about the company I had been affiliated with, we shared tea knowledge, and I took her brochure and went on my way. Last weekend I stopped by again and talked a little more with her. We both share a profound love for tea. Then last night, I went by and visited again, and actually bought some tea from her, and I found out that she is a Christian sister. That cinched it for me...she is my friend! We each shared a little about our faith, and I told her I would pray that her business does well. I am sure I will be visiting with her again, many times in the future.

The book of Proverbs has lots to say about friends...in 17:17, "*A friend loves at all times.*" All times? Even when you disagree, or offend one another? And in 18:24, "*...but there is a friend who sticks closer than a brother [sister].*" I can believe this...some of us have brothers or sisters whom we haven't spoken to in a long time. And in 27:10, "*Do not forsake your friend...*" One day while Jesus was talking to His disciples, He told them this, "*Greater love has no man than this, that he lay down his life for his friends.*" (John 15:13). Could you do that? Now, I cherish my friends, all of them, new and old. And I am rich in friendships. But I'm not sure

I could lay down my life for one. I could give them money, offer to babysit for them, drive them to the doctor or the store, visit them when they're sick, share Jesus with them…but *die* for them? But, we never know for sure, do we? I have heard of people who have thrown themselves in front of a bullet, or a car, which would have hit their friend, or child, and that's noble…maybe I could…

There was one Person who had no trouble dying for me, though. Jesus actually died and took on sin and death for the whole human race. His death was not a sudden quick death, it was a slow and agonizing death, but He went through with it because He loved me…and you. Because He is our friend, and a truer friend will not be found anywhere. *"Abraham believed God and it was credited to him as righteousness, and he was called* ***God's friend****."* (James 2:23). What an honor. Do you revere your friendships? God does.

MARCH27

IS OUR SUFFERING NECESSARY?

Many times, we believe, through reading scripture, that suffering is actually necessary for Christian growth. Is it essential to draw us closer to God?That's a hard question. Let's look at it this way…suffering is unavoidable in this life ~ for anyone. No matter how careful we are, no matter how guarded we try to keep our lives, we will still suffer, and some more than others. God Himself went willingly into the midst of evil, suffering and ultimately death in order to rescue us. Paul suffered greatly at the hands of those who thought he was doing an evil thing, preaching the word of God. Granted, Paul had a reputation for inflicting plenty of pain and misery to many of Jesus' followers until God got his attention. His life was a complete turnaround. Can you imagine the suffering this once proud and haughty man went through, suddenly being struck blind, hearing the great voice of God, and being humiliated and humbled all at the same time? But his conversion was real and complete. And from that moment on, he was willing to suffer for the cause of Jesus. And he did suffer at the hands of the Romans, and many others. He was shipwrecked, beaten, thrown into prison in shackles, many times over. And when his wounds were healed, they were inflicted again and again. I believe Paul suffered the physical pain from these wounds the rest of his life. They had to have taken a toll on his body.

Yet, to Paul, it was a privilege to suffer for Christ. He said, *"For to me, to live is Christ, and to die is gain...I am torn between the two: I desire to depart and be with Christ, which is better by far; but it is more necessary for you that I remain in the body."* (Philippians 1:21,23,24). He knew his suffering would benefit the believers ~ and they still had much to learn before he left them. Our suffering is a result of our fallen state as a human race, from being separated from God. Living for Christ is not going to guarantee us an escape from misery, but it offers us a way to get *through* the suffering we will surely endure. God knew we would need that. In fact Paul said to the Corinthians in his second letter to them, *"God...has given us the Spirit as a deposit, guaranteeing what is to come."* (5:5). And of course, he's talking about our heavenly home. So, by "taking up our cross" we are not necessarily seeking increased suffering, but it is a voluntary act of love uniting with Christ in His suffering. And, I believe, we can help others who suffer in the same ways that we ourselves have suffered. There is a divine reason for everything we endure here on earth, and when we cross over that river into the eternal life that will be our reward, our prize for finishing this race called life, we won't remember any of the pain or suffering we went through in this life. We will only hear those words of the Savior, *"Well done, good and faithful servant."* (Matthew 25:21).

MARCH 28

APPEARANCES...

"The Lord does not look at the things man looks at. Man looks at the outward appearance, but the Lord looks at the heart." (1 Samuel 16:7). How many times do you let appearances sway you one way or another? We've all heard the old phrase, "don't judge a book by its cover..." but how many of us are guilty of that very thing? I just bought a pair of cozy-looking "therapeutic" slippers through an ad in the Sunday newspaper...it promised to be perfect for all kinds of foot problems, such as arthritis, as I have. They looked so soft and cushy, and touted a sole that would cradle my feet in pressure-free support, conforming to the shape of my foot. They were to cushion every step. When I received them, they were nothing like the picture had shown. They were flimsy, the soles

were so thin I could feel the floor beneath my feet, and they were shoddily constructed. I packaged them up and sent them back, asking for a refund.

Or, have you ever ordered an item from the menu in a restaurant and it was nothing like the picture? Or, started reading a book that looked and sounded wonderful, only to be disappointed in the content, story line or language?

Lately, I have wondered about Spring. Well, I know it is typical to experience every kind of weather during this beloved season, that it teases us with nice sunny days, only to send snow, rain, hail, and wind the next day, or all in the same day. My daughter actually went to the store the other morning wearing shorts and flip-flops, and when she came out, it was cold, windy and rainy! I sometimes think we had warmer weather on some days in the middle of winter. It's downright cold, even when the sun is shining. But, I know from past experience that it will get better, and warmer!

Many things will vie for our attention by their appearances. A new home may have all the outward signs of modern conveniences, cute trim, pretty carpet and tile, but upon further inspection, shows poor workmanship in the structure. Making new friends may prove to be quite a disappointment when at first the friend may go along with your ideas and plans, only to turn against you at a later time.

When I was fairly newly married, we invited friends over for dinner, and I had made a beautiful pumpkin pie, from scratch. After the dinner dishes were cleared away, I cut the pie, and served it with coffee. The little toddler boy of the couple we were entertaining, took a bite of the pie and spit it out, saying "yuck!" Just as his mother was ready to reprimand him for his rude behavior, I also tasted the pie…I had totally forgotten to put in the SUGAR! Yuck was right. It was a really nice pie, with a flaky crust, and my taste buds were ready for it, but it really did taste bad!

Appearances aren't what they seem, a lot of the time. We have often paid a high price for something that turned out to be a cheap imitation. Veneer instead of fine wood, rusty metal instead of platinum, glass in place of crystal, vinyl when it said leather, copy replacing original, I could go on and on…

Are we really deep down inside who we appear to be on the outside? Paul told the Thessalonians, in 5:22, *"Abstain from all appearance of evil."* (KJV). That means we are not just to keep from doing evil, but we are to stay clear away from any guise or representation of anything evil, any wrong-doing. We don't want to *appear* that we are doing anything evil, when we are not. Here's what Paul said to the Corinthians, in (1) 10:31, 32, 11:1… *"So whether you eat or drink or whatever you do, do it all for the glory of God. Do not cause anyone to stumble...Follow my example, as I follow the example of Christ."* Appearances.

MARCH 29

THIS LITTLE LIGHT....

Have you noticed how many songs on Christian radio are about "light" these days? There is a new recording, "This Little Light of Mine" and I remember, as many of you do, singing that as a child in Sunday school. The artist has tweaked it a little, adding some different verses to it, but it's still the same song. I like it. There are others... Light of the World, Light Up the Sky, Go Light Your World, The Lord is my Light, many more.

I love light. At this time of the year, we have more daylight...it lifts the spirits, gives more energy. Light allows the spring and summer flowers to grow and bloom. It's a time when the darkness and dreariness of winter disappears. God is the Maker of light. *"And God said, 'Let there be lights in the expanse of the sky to separate the day from the night...' God made two great lights ~ the greater light to govern the day and the lesser light to govern the night..."*(Genesis 1:14-16). He also made the stars as smaller twinkling lights that would be used to direct men in their travels for centuries. It is important in all we do to have light. Candles have been made and used since the earliest of times to give light in the darkness. Then oils were utilized (and still are, in camping lamps!), and then, one of the greatest inventions was electricity, so all we have to do is flip a switch and the light comes on.

There are flashlights, lights in watches, ovens, refrigerators, doorbells, telephones...when we finally "get" something, or have a great idea, we refer to the "light coming on." Street lights show us where to turn, headlights help us find our way on dark roads, porch lights show us the address, some lights add warmth, but we always need light. The Bible says, *"Jesus is the Light of the world."* (John 9:5). The Psalmist wrote, *"You, O Lord, keep my lamp burning; my God turns my darkness into light."* (Ps. 18:28).

Note: as I am sitting here *at this very moment*, writing this devotional about light, the song is playing on the radio, "Light of the World," following, "Light up the Sky." I rest my case! And I don't find that curious or coincidental at all

~ I just look at it as an affirmation that I'm on the right page just now!...God speaks to me that way sometimes.

Many times in scripture, Jesus is referred to as Light. And at times, we ourselves are called a light, *"I have made you a light for the Gentiles..."* (Acts 13:47). And in Matthew 5:14, Jesus Himself calls US *"the light of the world."*He admonishes us to *"let our light shine before men that they may see our good deeds and praise our Father in heaven."*(vs 16).

We absolutely cannot find our way safely in the dark. We need light. Whether it's in a dark house, on a dark road or path, or a tunnel, or just trying to get through life in a dark world, we need the Light He gives. We cannot exist without it. I'm so glad Jesus gave Himself to be the Light we need. And we have access to it every hour of every day. And in heaven? *"The city does not need the sun or the moon to shine on it, for the glory of God gives it light, and the Lamb is its lamp."* (Revelation 21:23).

MARCH 30

TAKE A HIKE...

Well, it must be a sign of spring ~ people are taking hikes, some in groups and some alone. There are many reasons for hiking, but mostly it's for exercise and fresh air. If you're part of a scouting group, such as girl or boy scouts, hiking is the number one way to earn badges, because of the items they look for, or learn to do, on their hikes. Well, it used to be when I was a girl. My son-in-law often takes his kids for hikes on Saturdays. They look for "stuff" like flowers, birds, bugs, or "signs" of wildlife, if you know what I mean. The kids love it. Sometimes hiking is too strenuous as it usually leads us up hills and mountains.

or a Walk... Walking is one of the best forms of exercise we can do. Doctors recommend it. The gyms and health centers are full of treadmills. And in the last several years, walks are organized for many different causes... cancer awareness, pet rescues, and others. There seems to be a fun run or race for every cause as well. But that leads to triathlons, Ironman, and that's another subject! Paul talks of running the race of life, *"...let us run with perseverance the race marked out for us."* (Hebrews 12:1). Sometimes it does seem like we are racing through life. And many times, we are in such a hurry to get where we are going, we miss a lot of wonderful things. That's why I like walking. It's a lot more relaxing, but still very beneficial for your body. And you can see much more along the way.

Many things are said in the Bible about our "walk." Joshua 22:5 says, *"But be very careful…to love the Lord your God, to **walk** in all His ways, to obey His commands, to hold fast to Him and to serve Him with all your heart and all your soul."* That verse pretty much covers how we should walk. And David puts it like this: *"Lord, who may dwell in Your sanctuary? Who may live on Your holy hill? He whose **walk** is blameless and who does what is righteous, who speaks the truth from his heart…"* (Psalm 15:1,2). So, is it actually possible to have a blameless walk? Apparently it is, because David repeats it later on, in Psalm 84:11, *"…the Lord bestows favor and honor, no good thing does He withhold from those whose **walk** is blameless."* Okay, does this mean blameless in the eyes of men…or of God? Too many times we think we have to try to be perfect and we get discouraged because we aren't. People criticize us and disappoint us, and we disappoint ourselves. We try, and we fail. We want to give up. It's an uphill "hike." But God made us. He knows how frail we are. He is so patient with us. He holds out His hand and helps us get up again. Micah tells us to *"**walk** humbly with your God."* (vs. 6:8). He wants us to ask Him for directions, to follow the path He has laid out for us. And because of God's great grace, it is possible for us to walk that close to Him. Close enough for Him to consider it blameless. He sees our heart. And He will bless.

MARCH 31

DOES GOD HEAR US?

Every day we cry out to God to save us from danger, or illness, from discomfort or fear. And sometimes, it seems He does not hear us. We feel as though we are alone in our suffering. Do we dare think that He would not understand our pain? Or care about it? David said, *"In the day of my trouble, I will call to You, for You will answer me."* (Psalm 86:7). Did David know something we don't know? He read the same scriptures we read. So, we repeatedly cry out to Him for mercy, and it appears He does not answer. We want Him to rescue us from our suffering, from our fears, from hurtful relationships, from illnesses. And we just can't understand His silence.

But then this plea comes to my mind... "*My God, My God, why have You forsaken Me? Why do You hide Your face from Me?*" (Matthew 27:46). And "*Why are You so far from rescuing Me, so far from the words of My groaning? Oh, My God, I cry out by day but You do not answer ~ by night, and am not silent.*" (Psalm 22:1-2). There is much desperation in those words. They are the very words of Jesus, our Lord. He cried out to His Father in His darkest hour. God heard His prayers, but did nothing, or it would appear so. Jesus endured many troubles deep in His soul. He was not only forsaken by His heavenly Father, *"He was despised and forsaken among men, a Man of sorrows and familiar with suffering."* (Isaiah 53:3). He humbled Himself to the point of death on a cross, and God crushed Him and put Him in the deepest darkest depths of the pit. He was burdened with every sin of every man ~ and He suffered sin's terrors for our sake. He didn't deserve this. In the midst of His suffering, His faith called on His Father. All His suffering was necessary to show God's great mercy, even at the gates of hell. More than anyone, Jesus understands our pain and suffering.

We celebrate His victory over death, and all who saw Him saw the glory of God. The Father was satisfied at the deep and profound anguish in His holy soul, and through this sacrifice, we are delivered from the domain of darkness. We will reign with Him in heaven! God does indeed hear our cries for mercy. Let us remember that His timing is perfect ~ His ways are not our ways, but *"His way is perfect."* (Ps. 18:30). We may suffer for a little while, but our suffering is not in vain, it is never wasted. His glory will be seen in us if we stand firm and remain faithful. God promised, *"Never will I leave you; never will I forsake you."* (Hebrews 13:5). He does hear our prayers, but His answer will not come until it is the perfect time. Thank You, Lord, that our lives are in Your hands, and we can trust You to know and understand our pain. Help us as we wait, to remain faithful, to see Your glory in our seemingly dire situation. Amen.

APRIL 1

WHAT TO WEAR?

Did you ever stand before your closet and have trouble making up your mind about what to wear? Oh, if you're a woman, I'm sure you have. I still do, although not as much as when I was working. I would sometimes try on 2-3 outfits before I was satisfied that I had the right one on for the day, or the occasion. It didn't fit right, or it had a spot. This starts early. My three daughters did this, from the time they were about three years old and had learned to dress themselves. About every five minutes they would have on a different outfit, but then all the other ones would be strewn all around their bedroom. This didn't change when they were teens. Their closets were full, and yet, they would lament "I don't have anything to wear!"

Apparently this practice has been carried over from early Bible days… Jesus said, *"Therefore I tell you, do not worry about your life, what you will eat or drink; or about your body, what you will wear. Is not life more important than food, and the body more important than clothes? Look at the birds of the air…and why do you worry about clothes? See how the lilies of the field grow. They do not labor or spin. Yet, I tell you that not even Solomon in all his splendor was dressed like one of these."* (Matthew 6:25-29). I think, really, we do need to concern ourselves with what we're wearing, as far as conservative apparel, and we want to honor God in our appearance, but what Jesus is telling us here is that we should *"seek first His kingdom and His righteousness, and all of these things will be added to you as well."* (vs. 33). We shouldn't expend so much energy on finding the right outfit that it takes away from serving and trusting our heavenly Father.

And just think, when we leave this life, we will have the perfect clothes, not anything ill-fitting or with stains we couldn't get out in the wash, but pure and spotless, gleaming white robes, made for us by the ultimate Designer of the universe! We won't have to worry about how it fits, or if the color is right…it will be perfect, because on that day we will also be perfect! Oh, that's a whole 'nother message!

APRIL 2

FEAR FOR THE FUTURE?

"For God did not give us a spirit of fear, but a spirit of power, of love and of self-control." (2 Timothy 1:7). Do you hear that? God gives us a spirit of power! And of love…and yet, we are afraid. The enemy is the author of fear. He thrives on making us so afraid we are ineffective in our Christian walk. Of course, there are certain things we should have a healthy fear of, but not so much that we are consumed by it.

My friend on the east coast wrote me an email this morning expressing her fear, a fear that is so great she isn't eating right and has trouble sleeping. She has such a fear of the future and of how the elections will turn out, she can hardly function. It consumes her thoughts all day long. I wrote her back and encouraged her that God is in control, and He did not put that debilitating fear in her heart. And I gave her this scripture. Now, I wish it were that easy just to tell someone not to be afraid, but God's word is full of "Do not fears." He tells us, *"Be strong, and do not fear"* and "*So do not fear, for I am with you*." Or this, *"But perfect love drives out fear."* David said *"I will fear no evil."* And God said *"Fear not for I have redeemed you; I have called you by My name; you are Mine. When you pass through the waters, I will be with you; and when you pass through the rivers, they will not sweep over you. When you walk through the fire, you will not be burned; the flames will not kindle upon you. For I am the Lord your God, the Holy One of Israel, your Savior."* (Isaiah 43:1-3).

I know it's not easy to not be afraid, but we do need to remember that God sees what's going on in our world. And He is still in control. But we, as His children, need to stay on our knees and pray for our blessed country. The situation looks grim right now, but it still can be turned around. Nothing is impossible for God.

APRIL 3

FRIENDSHIP....

"A friend loves at all times." (Proverbs 17:17)

"There is a friend who sticks closer than a brother (sister)." Proverbs 18:24)

Friendship. We all want to be someone's friend. Some of us have but a few good friends, others have more than they can count. Friends provide company, a gentle word, a simple gift. Friendship in itself is a gift to be treasured. When we find a true friend, a kindred spirit, a soul mate, we find a support system to get us through every detail of our lives. God sends us these friends. There is something very special about the relationship between girlfriends. A girlfriend is like a sister who fills up the empty spaces, inspires us, encourages us, forgives us. Peter said this: *"Be full of sympathy toward each other, loving one another with tender hearts and humble minds."* (1 Peter 3:8). He could have been speaking to us. Actually, I think he was. Life is so short and we never really have enough time to gladden the hearts of those we walk with each day.

I'm never embarrassed to hug a friend, or hold her hand when she's troubled, or to listen to her cares…or pray with her and for her. Sometimes words are not even needed. We understand each other with our hearts. Much like Jesus does. Yet, He is the ultimate friend. And He said *"You are my friends if you do what I command."* (John: 15:14). Not like my little 6-year-old granddaughters, who when playing together, one of them will be mad and say "You're not my friend anymore!" But the greatest command Jesus gives us is to *"love one another as He loves us."* (John 13:34). If we do that, we are His friend. And God gives us the gift of people who love us, who surround us with loving-kindness. I find that in my Women's groups. How unique is a group of women who mostly do not know each other, but who are brought together in their hearts through the everyday troubles and joys of another? What a support system we can have right here! I thank God for each one of you.

May the warming love of friends surround you as you walk through today, and each day to come. And may you truly be blessed.

APRIL 4

MUST HAVE BEEN THE MOON…

I have a thing about the sky ~ I love looking at it. It's so vast and the scenery changes almost constantly because of the clouds, the colors of sunrises and sunsets, though sometimes it's merely gray. I find myself catching my breath many times because of a sight I will only see once, for only a few seconds. I don't usually reveal what I have written in my journal, but yesterday I was inspired to write the following and I thought I'd share this little part of my heart…

"What a beautiful full moon You gave us last night, and this morning, Lord! It lights up the whole world in this time of deep winter darkness. Your creation, the "lesser light." No matter how often, or how many times I have seen that ancient moon, I am still in awe of its beauty. And there was Orion, too, just hanging in the sky where it always is, right where You placed it so many ages ago! Yet suspended SO close.

"When I consider Your heavens, the work of Your fingers, the moon and the stars, which You have set in place, what is man, that You are mindful of him?" (Psalm 8:3-4). And yet, Lord, You love us more than any creature on earth or in heaven. You take time, and great effort and patience, to teach us to be righteous, how to live our lives to give glory to our Maker. *You honor us*, Lord! And in turn, I pray that my life honors You, though I know in my own effort it will never be enough. Life is such a struggle, but why would we ever turn back when You are our Helper? You work alongside us enabling us to do Your will, giving us strength for the day. You alone, Your word, gives us hope. You *are* our Hope! "

And so, I pray this for each one of us, as we go through the darkness of the waning winter. There will only be a few full moons, and some we won't even see for the clouds that will cover. But still, we know it is there. Let's continue looking up. Look for evidence of our heavenly Father in the little things, as well as the bigger-than-life things. Every living thing reveals His sovereignty ~ look at the feathers of a bird, the symmetry of a pinecone, the snowflakes, the gentleness of a butterfly, the waves of the ocean...answers to prayers that could come from nowhere else. He's all around us, never leaving us. Sometimes we need to just *"Be still and know that I am God."* (Psalm 46:10).

APRIL 5

THE LORD, MY ROCK...

"The Lord is my Rock, my Fortress, and my Deliverer. My God is my Rock, in whom I take refuge. He is my shield and the horn of my salvation, my stronghold. I call to the Lord, who is worthy of praise, and I am saved from my enemies." (Psalm 18: 2,3).

I don't know that I have many enemies, but so many times I feel defeated ~ oh, not in my spirit, but in the circumstances of life. And this year has been especially hard because of the economy. My husband is a home builder by trade, and he has two beautiful new homes that have been for sale for over two and one-half years. He, of course, still has to come up with the interest payment on the construction loans, which somehow God has provided. But it has used up my husband's entire retirement savings, and all of his 401k. We may, in the end, have to give these homes up to the bank. All that money he poured into them will be gone. But, as Job once said, *"Though He may slay me, yet will I hope in Him!"* (13:15). And we have put our trust in Him. What else can we do?

We have watched, with peace in our hearts, how God has provided for us this past year, in the little things, which really turned out to be big things. He provided a record snowfall last winter…for my husband, this was a miracle, since he has a snowplowing business and several accounts who depend on him to clear the snow. God worked out some other situations and has provided some work. I know, these are problems everyone has, but God has come through time and time again and rescued us. Oh, we still aren't out of the woods. We are praying for the economy, our president, the troubles our children are having, trusting our heavenly Father at the same time, keeping our eyes on Him so we don't miss a thing!

"He reached down from on high and took hold of me; He drew me out of the deep waters. He rescued me from my powerful enemy, from my foes, who were too strong for me." (Job 18: 16, 17). He is so good! He has His eye on me all the time. He loves us so much! And this knowledge causes me to count my blessings. We still have our warm and cozy home to live in, plenty of food to eat, family and friends who pray for us…we are SO blessed! And I have learned to praise Him in the hard times, not just for what He has done, and certainly not FOR the bad times, but because He is Almighty God, and the only One worthy of our praise.

APRIL 6

STRANGER IN OUR HOME…

We just attended a Rotary breakfast this morning, and met the girl from Taiwan that we will be hosting in our home for three months, beginning next month. This will not be a new experience for us, as we have hosted four other exchange students in the past 19 years, three of them for the length of a full year. It's been an adventure. Only one of them had had any church background at all. She went home with a deeper relationship with Jesus. The girl before her had no church background, but attended services with us, as well as our youth group, and within the week after she arrived home, she called us and said she had asked Jesus into her heart! My pastor told us we have a mission field right in our own home. Matthew 25:35 says: *"For I was hungry and you gave me something to eat. I was thirsty and you gave me something to drink. I was a stranger and you invited me in…"*

I always look at the exchange program as a way to touch another's life in some little (or big) way. And not only are we making an impact on the student who lives with us, but ultimately on her family as well. But it works the other way too. We learn so much from the students, their heritage, their customs, the skills they bring, the joy of teaching them something new…and most of all, the relationship-building. They become part of our entire extended family. Of course, it takes a lot of effort ~ preparing the guest room, loading the pantry, meetings with the agency, school stuff, transportation … but the lasting memories are well worth the energy. These students become part of our family *for life*. We are still in touch with all four of the previous girls, and have met all their parents, who came to America to meet us.

As Paul said to the Hebrews in 13:2, *"Keep on loving each other as brothers. Do not forget to entertain strangers, for by so doing some people have entertained angels without knowing it."* Sometimes I don't think I am up to another student in my home, but as it is now official, one more time, I find myself getting excited about it. Though we are empty-nesters, our grown children and grandchildren frequently stop in, and our home is never really empty. And best of all, it is filled with love. A love we are able to send home with each student.

APRIL 7

WORTHY…

"Worthy is the Lamb,
Worthy is the Lamb,
Worthy is the Lamb,
Worthy is the Lamb,
To receive power and riches,
And wisdom and strength,
Honor and glory, and praise!
Worth is the Lamb!"

Once again, a song has been going through my mind since I woke up this morning. I love that. Almost daily I wake up with a praise song on my mind. Better than whatever an alternative might be! And what's even better, this song is taken directly from scripture – Revelation 5:12.

Jesus IS worthy. He is deserving of the highest praise from people everywhere. Not only all peoples, but all of His creation praises Him! Have you noticed already the signs of new life? Spring is coaxing the buds on the flowering trees and bushes, little crocuses are blooming already and the tulips and daffodils are pushing up through the ground. Soon the birds will be teaching their young to fly, and bringing them to our feeders. Brown lawns are turning green. It's all by God's great design. This is how the earth praises Him. There is no other person or thing that merits our praise.

You may say you don't have anything to praise Him for, there is so much sadness and hardship in our world, and uncertainties in our future. But I know God is in control. He has already conquered all our troubles. And this alone is reason enough to praise Him ~ just because of WHO He is! And...He is worthy.

As we reflect on this week, and the celebration of the resurrection, let's meditate on God's word. And if you think you can't memorize scripture, sing the scripture songs you HAVE memorized. Same thing. Keep His word alive in your heart. Sing praises to Him. He alone is worthy! *"To Him who sits on the throne and to the Lamb be praise and honor and glory and power, forever and ever!"* (Rev. 5:13).

APRIL 8

THE LAMB OF GOD...

In early times, a spotless, perfect lamb was considered the prime sacrifice for sin. Blood had to be shed to atone for any and every sin. The lamb would be chosen from a personal herd, or one could buy a lamb from a shepherd, only unblemished and perfect. Sometimes the lamb offered in sacrifice had become a family pet, which made the sacrifice even more heart wrenching. If one couldn't afford a lamb, then a lesser animal could be killed, even a dove, but still white and pure and spotless. But then Jesus came on the scene. John 16:33 says, *"...for this reason I was born, and for this I came into the world, to testify to the truth...."*

Jesus was the Lamb of God, His only Son, perfect, unblemished ... nothing else would do. An unbelievable sacrifice, yet those of us who do believe have the hope of eternal life, our sins forgiven by one huge act of love … Jesus, the only perfect innocent One, allowed Himself to be taken out, beaten and cruelly killed so that we could be clean before God. He freely poured out His life's blood for each of us. Willingly, He took upon Himself all our sin, our sicknesses, our loss, our grief. Those things crushed Him in His very soul and spirit even as the lashes, beatings, the mocking crown of thorns, then the agonizing death on the cross, mutilated His body. *"But He was wounded for **our** transgressions, He was bruised for our iniquities; the chastisement of our peace was upon Him; and with His stripes we are healed."* (Isaiah 53:5). It was foretold. And He did it so that whatever bruises and crushes us, our spirits, may be healed. He did it for Love. A love that the world has never seen, before or since. It is no marvel, then, that we can call Him the Savior! And after He was crucified, and the earth shook and turned dark, and the veil in the temple was torn in two, "… *they were terrified and exclaimed, 'Surely He was the Son of God!'"*(Matthew 27:54).

But the story doesn't end here…on Easter Sunday morning we celebrate the fulfillment of His promise to us, that on the third day He would be raised from the dead. Christ the Lord is risen, indeed! Hallelujah! Celebrate!

APRIL 9

BURSTING FORTH!

The early morning sun first gives a soft, then more intense glow just before blazing over the mountain…a hundred birds startled, or perhaps receiving a signal from one other, explode all together from a single tree…the fury of a mountain creek flows strong from the winter's snow melting and building force, forming a powerful waterfall…the buds and flowers are ready to suddenly pop open…baby birds fledge from their nests…a Savior…

Wait. How was it that our Savior emerged from His grave? We know from reading in John 11, the account of Jesus raising Lazarus from the dead, that Lazarus sort of "stumbled" from his tomb, (at least, as I see it) still wrapped in the strips that served as his grave clothes, all around his body and his face. I believe then that his loved ones ministered to him, clothing him and giving him food to eat. But, I can't see our Savior coming out of His tomb in this way. First of all, Matthew 28 says there was a violent earthquake, as an angel came down to earth and rolled away the stone from the entrance of the tomb. I don't really think Jesus needed that stone to be rolled away for Him. He had the power to exit on His own, even coming *right through* the stone that had sealed the entrance. And if the angel glowed with such a bright light, can you imagine what Jesus must have looked like at that moment? I believe Jesus would have burst forth in a glorious light like no one has ever seen! And apparently no one but the angel saw Him coming out from the tomb. Oh, there were the guards, but they fainted when they saw the angel.

More beautiful than the time-lapse photo of a rose opening up, more mysterious than a butterfly emerging from the protection of the chrysalis, more spectacular than a sunrise or sunset, or the most violent of thunder and lightning storms...we can only imagine what that morning was like. No one saw. He was calm and seemed normal when everyone found Him later, except some did not recognize Him...maybe this was because they didn't expect to see Him alive, although He had spoken of this earlier. He *promised* it. Or maybe because there was something about His countenance...a glow? I haven't really thought too much about this, His emergence from the tomb, until just lately after hearing it in a song for the hundredth time. I just know that when the women who loved Him went to the grave to anoint his body, the tomb was empty. He was not there! But because of Who He is, I see His resurrection from the grave as a glorious and powerful event. It couldn't have been any other way, for He was victorious over death! The grave just could not contain His glory any longer!

Twelve years ago, and again this winter, I was fortunate enough to stand inside that very tomb. I walked around, touching the cold walls with my hands, seeing the track where the stone would have rested, and rolled. On my way out, there was a sign on the back of the door which said, *"He is not here, for He has risen!"* (Matthew 28:6). I saw firsthand that this was true. The tomb is empty.

I believe that when we step into heaven, it's not going to be a quiet little entrance, but as we enter in through those gates, heaven will explode for us into glorious light, because His Light will be ever-present, and the voices of a thousand angels, along with all the saints, my parents and loved ones who have gone on before, will be ever praising and worshiping Him Who was triumphant over the grave, and made it possible for us to be, too. That's the way I see it.

APRIL 10

RAISED FROM THE DEAD?

I believe God cares about what we care about. 1st Peter 5:7 says, *"Cast your cares on Him because He cares for you."* Our Lord raised a few people from the dead. We read about Jairus' daughter, who had died, and because of his faith, Jesus went with him to the house, *"and went in where the child was. He took her by the hand and said to her, 'Little girl, I say to you, get up!' Immediately the girl stood up and walked around."* (Luke 5:38-42). Apparently, her death was very recent, because Jairus originally came to Jesus for her healing, *"but as they were on their way, word came to him that she had died."* But then there's Lazarus. Here was one of Jesus' best friends, and he had been dead and buried *four* days. Jesus said a prayer, then *"in a loud voice he called, 'Lazarus, come forth!'"* And he did.

Jesus Himself was raised from the dead, after three days, after a brutal death because of our sin. He has power over death because He is the author of Life. Many times we pray for someone who is dying, and they die anyway. Sometimes, because of some trauma, someone's heart will stop, and can be restarted again. But here's a twist. Does God raise animals from the dead? He made them, that's for sure. He made dogs with the ability to be trustworthy and to be our faithful companions. He made a donkey talk. (Numbers 22:30). Here's my story.

All this week my daughter's older dog, Sheba, has been dying, literally. She's been lethargic, not eating, barely able to move. Having no money for the vet, she tried to care for her the best she could, loving her, trying to coax her out of the doghouse, giving her water...each morning she would go down the stairs from her deck to check on her. Sheba would only lay there and look at her with sad, almost lifeless eyes. And each morning my daughter expected to find her dead. This sweet dog has been the subject of much stress and many prayers, mine, my daughters, and her children's, all week. Last night, she went to the door to let the other younger dog in, and there stood Sheba, wagging her tail! She let her in and cared for her. She went right to her doggie-bed. She ate a little, and this morning she is the same. This is an astonishing and wonderful miracle for my young grandchildren to see. Even if she had died in the night, it was more of a comfort to have her in the house instead of a cold doghouse where she was hard to get to.

OK, she wasn't dead. But very nearly. Not sure if God has healed her ~ she's old and will die eventually.* But this has been a great concern this week to some people who love God ~ and who love that dog. What a way for God to show His love back to us. *"We love Him because He first loved us."* (1st John 4:19).

*Note: After 5-1/2 years, at this writing, Sheba is still alive.

APRIL 11

SIMPLY CELEBRATE!

My very first devotional for the women's group I write for was called "Morning Celebration," because for me each new day is a celebration. I love "watching" the sun come up in the morning, (although in the winter it takes longer!), hearing the first bird songs of the day ~ I love the quietness of the early morning, the peace. It's a simple thing to love. The morning. Well, for some it is. Have you ever watched a small child celebrate the new day? My daughters used to wake up smiling, every one of them, almost every day, even when they were babies. I'm not sure they knew the day was a gift from God, from whose hand they were so fresh…but they were just happy to learn something new and see what the day had in store for them. Young children truly enjoy pretty much any activity. They want to try everything. They are uninhibited, and they trust the people in their lives.

Then they begin to grow up ~ the games become more complicated, more technical. They discover computers, and X-boxes, and MP3 Players. Cell phones. They become competitive, and harder to please. They forget the simplicity of the days when they played with blocks, crayons, cars and dolls, and could create their own games.

Are we like this, as adults? When we first came to Christ we were so excited to learn something new in His word, we were like babies craving that heavenly milk. Even as we matured, and became able to "eat" the meat of the Word, we were fervent about growing in knowledge. But as life crowds in on us, we begin to see more of the troubles looming in front of us, and less of God…although He is still right there, we have backed ourselves into a corner, surrounded by our distress. Jesus said, in Revelation 2:4-5, *"You have forsaken your first love. Remember the height from which you have fallen. Repent and do the things you did at first."* He wants us to come back to Him as little children, when our faith was fresh and new…and simple. *"I tell you the truth, anyone who will not receive the kingdom of God like a little child, will never enter it."* (Luke 18:17). It's pretty clear He wants us to humble ourselves as little children, sincere and open, and knowing that without His help, we can do nothing. Just like a child who needs his Daddy's help, we need our Abba Father's help as well!

We must come to Him with a simple faith, like a child, not letting the complications and entanglements of life pull us in different directions. His hand is always outstretched to us, His arms always open, ready to embrace us, like a Daddy. Let's celebrate the simple, non-embellished life of trusting His truth, when all other is shouting to us from the sidelines. God lovingly made us. He is our Father. It's the natural thing to do ~ trust Him. And celebrate the simple life.

APRIL 12

SPRING RAIN…

Hosea 6:3 says: *"…let us press on to know the Lord. His going forth is as certain as the dawn; and He will come to us like the rain, like the spring rain watering the earth."*

Yesterday we had some rain, after a pretty nice, sunny, but coolish, week. The clear skies have definitely lifted people's spirits and gotten them outside in the fresh air. And even though we have had so much snow here all winter long, and we're welcoming the sunshine and nice weather, the rain is refreshing to the ground and reminds us of the abundant goodness of God, who created and sends the rain. And soon the trees will be leafed out, the flowers will be blooming, and everything will be lush and green once again. But this couldn't happen without the spring rain. And we will no doubt be getting a lot of it in the weeks to come. And we cannot live without it.

Just like the showers of His Holy Spirit raining down on us…we need these as well for our very sustenance. In Jesus' great oracle at the edge of the Sea of Galilee, He said, *"Blessed are those who hunger and thirst for righteousness, for they will be filled."* (Matthew 5:6). Just as water quenches our thirst on a hot day, and the rain freshens and nourishes the earth, so the Holy Spirit quenches our thirst for Jesus, and for holy living. And for whatever seems to be missing in our lives. *"Come, all you who are thirsty, come to the waters…"* (Isaiah 55:1). Let the cool and clean water of the Holy Spirit wash over you and bring refreshing to your soul....

APRIL 13

BIRDS OF THE AIR...

I read somewhere that there are over 9,000 species of birds in the world, and about 315 of them are parrots, who live in the tropics. Now, I watch birds, and I feed them, but I have never seen more than a few species on one given day in my backyard. When I travel, I do see a few more, however. But I am blown away at how many different kinds of birds our Creator has made. And each one has a special name. And here's another amazing bit of information... each bird has a special and unique way of building their nests. Of course, some birds don't even build nests, but "borrow" or steal another bird's nest. They all have their own song, or call. They come in all different sizes, from the tiny hummingbird to the majestic eagle. There are the drab brown/gray birds, and those with every color of the rainbow in their feathers. They eat different foods, some eat anything and everything, others eat only bugs, or only seeds. I once even saw a crow lift off out of a dumpster with a whole hamburger in his beak! Seriously.

Our God provides materials the birds will need for building their nests, and He feeds them, each one. *"Even the sparrow has found a home, and the swallow a nest for herself, where she may have her young ~"* (Psalm 84:3). Sometimes it feels to us like God isn't paying attention to our troubles. We pray, we cry out to Him, and still we have distress and difficulties...but He sees us. He is very aware of our needs. *"Are not two sparrows sold for a penny? Yet not one of them will fall to the ground apart from the will of your Father. Even the very hairs of your head are all numbered."* (Matthew 10:29, 30). I'm sure every beautiful feather is numbered on each bird He made, as well. He cares SO much for His creation, each species ~ animal, bird, fish, and Man. Oh, I wouldn't even want to start counting all the different animals, or fish...each unique from the other.

They all praise Him, in their own ways, simply by doing what they were created to do. And yet, WE are the ones who are created *in His image*, but find it so difficult to praise Him. I've often wondered about that. *"If we don't praise*

Him, the stones will cry out." (Luke 19:40). Can you imagine that? Of all God's creation, we are the ones who can communicate with Him, we are the ones whom He LOVES ~ enough to give His life's blood on a cross so that we may be saved. Are we to only praise Him when things are going well for us? No. David learned to praise God in any situation. He said in Psalm 43:5, *"Why are you downcast O my soul? Why so disturbed within me? Put your hope in God,* ***for I will yet praise Him****, my Savior and my God."* We are to praise God because He is worthy of our praise, not because of the things He does for us. If a tiny bird loses its home, its family, because of vandalism or storm, it simply keeps singing its song and begins all over again, trusting its Maker to take care of it. We are in the palm of God's hand. "His eye is on the sparrow, and I know He watches me." (From the Mahalia Jackson song ~ 'His Eye is on the Sparrow' and my mother's favorite song ever). He cares so much more for us than any other creature He has made.

APRIL 14

MAN'S BEST FRIEND...

For generations, or at least as long as I can remember, dogs have been considered "man's best friend." Granted, there are some dogs who are not necessarily friendly by nature, but for the most part, the dogs we own and love are loyal and devoted to their owners. There have been so many unforgettable movies and TV shows about the friendship of dogs – there was Lassie, Rin-Tin-Tin, Benji, Old Yeller, (wow, I'm dating myself here!). What about Beethoven, Homeward Bound, The Shaggy Dog, Bolt, Petie in the Little Rascals, and the all-time classic, Lady and the Tramp. Their own brand of loyalty moves us and touches our hearts. We make them part of the family, and they are. They're companions to the elderly, used to comfort the terminally ill and have uncannily predicted when their human is about to encounter a dangerous or life-threatening condition, such as a heart attack. We read stories about the family dog who alerted everyone when there was a fire. A dog pulls a drowning friend from a river or lake, or turns on a wild animal threatening someone they love. They see for us, hear for us, and save our lives. And they just love to be with us. I have a friend like this. Her name is Stormy, a Springer Spaniel. I found this quote that just about says it all...

"The one absolutely unselfish friend that humans can have in this selfish world, the one that never deserts them, the one that never proves ungrateful or treacherous is their dog."

~George Graham Vest, Senator of Missouri, 1855

I have another Friend who loves to be near me. He would battle any enemy to keep me safe. He comforts me when I am sad or alone. He cares about me when I am sick or afraid, He goes with me through the fire or the rushing river. This Friend can see the things ahead which I can't see, and He hears my voice when I call to Him. He is a constant companion, passionately devoted to me ~ in fact, He laid down His life for me. He cares all about my desires, my life-long dreams, the things that concern me most, and He wants the very best for me. He is extravagant in His gifts of mercy, grace and unending love. You guessed it, my Friend is Jesus. He wants to be the best Friend we've ever had.

"This is My commandment, that you love one another, just as I have loved you. Greater love has no one than this, that one lay down his life for his friends. You are My friends, if you do what I command you." (John 15: 12-14). Jesus ~ Friend of sinners, Friend of us all. A Friend who will never leave our side. He wants to be your Friend, too.

APRIL 15

WHO IS YOUR KING?

I say this more often than not, but I am so inspired by music ~ generally, when I wake up in the night, and especially in the morning, there are the words to a song going through my mind. I love this. I thank God for it, because I know He speaks to me through music. Christian music comes straight from His word. Our choir has been singing from our Easter musical, "Sovereign Lord" and believe me, it is beautiful. This music has been ringing in my spirit for weeks. This morning I woke up with these words, "He will rule the world, every eye will see Him, coming on the clouds, all of heaven with Him...He will rule the world, Jesus is the King of all the earth, He will rule the world!" And of course, the music and the harmony is breathtaking. Well, I believe God is giving me a message here. He's asking, "Who is YOUR king?"

In our day, in this society, it is so easy to get caught up in so many things and if we're not careful, they become our "king." Things like jobs, family, people we admire and want to be like, TV and movies, with the kids it's cell phones and video games, and they have so many sports and movie heroes that are not favorable or virtuous role models. I always have my dictionary handy, and so I thought I would look up the word "king." It is defined as "a [male] ruler over a nation; sovereign; monarch; something supreme in its class; chief, in size & importance…" There are other kings listed, Kings Arthur, Lear, Charles, James…the Bible talks about a lot of kings, some good, chosen and ordained by God Himself, and others abominable.

I teach first & second grade Sunday School, and one day we had a lesson about kings. (I think it was a specific king, but I don't remember who). We discussed what a king's job was and it was the consensus of the class that kings control the people, of course, boss and punish the servants, count the money, eat a lot, make the rules. On the other hand, the kids decided that the servants worked to make the money for the king, they cleaned the toilets, fanned the king, cooked the food - lots of food, fed the animals, and a lot of other unpleasant things. When I asked them if they thought a *king* would ever do these things, they didn't think so. But then I told them there IS a King who is like a servant ~ who is full of love, who drops everything to listen to people, who is kind, who will do anything for His people…they got it. First and second graders are smart. "Jesus is this King!!"Yes, and the Bible has much to say about this King. *"Great and marvelous are Your deeds, Lord God Almighty. Just and true are Your ways,* ***King of the ages****. Who will not fear You Lord and bring glory to Your name?"* (Rev. 15:3,4). And in Rev. 17:14 He is called *"Lord of lords and* ***King of kings****."* He is King of glory, King eternal… *"Now to the* ***King eternal****, immortal, invisible, the only God, be honor and glory forever and ever. Amen."* (1 Timothy 1:17). Who is your King?

APRIL 16

IT'S GREEN!

My favorite time of spring is when everything begins to turn green and flourish, instead of being brown and bare, and dead. Of course, the rain is what does it, and we certainly have had a lot of that. Even as I write, it is raining ~ again. Last night, just about twilight, I happened to be standing at the sliding glass door, just looking out, and noticed how brilliant green everything looked, even at that hour. And it was raining then…no sun in sight. This morning, before it was even *time* for the sun to rise, which it didn't, there was that glorious green again. What a beautiful color God chose to signal a favorite season. Green. The trees, grass and shrubs are such an electric color of green, and then with the splashes of yellow, pink, purple and red, it's beginning to look really amazing across the landscape. Everything is washed and clean and almost glistening.

Of course, the word "green" has a new meaning in our society today. There are books written to guide us in our work, our homes, our shopping, our disposal of garbage, gas for our cars ~ in "natural" methods of saving our environment. Some of it makes a lot of sense and we should have been doing it a long time ago ~ in fact, some people, naturalists, have been practicing being kinder to our earth for many years.

God Himself said, *"I will send you rain in its season, and the ground will yield its crops and the trees of the field their fruit."* (Lev. 26:4). And each spring, that which appeared to be dead, is given new life, and blooms grow afresh. Jesus made a new covenant with us, and gave us a new commandment, *"as I have loved you, you must love one another."* (John 13:34). And because of His obedience to death on the Cross, we also can enjoy new life. *"We were therefore buried with Him through baptism into death in order that, just as Christ was raised from the dead, through the glory of the Father, we too may have a new life."* (Romans 6:4). *"We are a new creation..."* (2 Cor. 5:17). And at Christ's coming, we shall see a new heaven, and a new earth (2 Peter 3:13)...a new Jerusalem. Everything will be new. (Rev. 3:12).

If we think this beautiful fresh spring is breathtaking, just wait until we see what God has in store for us in the near future, if we remain faithful to Him! This green and floral spectacle we see now will be dim when we walk along those streets in the new City. And, by the way, it is fitting that the emerald is one of my favorite stones, in fact, my birthstone. I understand heaven will be full of them! Green.

APRIL 17

WHAT IS YOUR WORTH...?

There are many people in this world who are worth a lot of MONEY. I don't know any personally, but you see them on the covers of magazines such as Fortune, Forbes, Money, Conde Nast, etc...executives drop their names impressively in meetings and in conversation, there are LISTS that show where these people rank in their worth. In today's economy, I'm certain the rich are still getting richer, but I'm sure not! What determines a person's worth, anyway? Is it the homes we live in, or how many homes we own? The cars we drive? The trips we take?

But Jesus said, *"Do not store up for yourselves treasures on earth, where moth and rust destroy, and where thieves break in and steal. But store up for yourselves treasures in heaven, where moth and rust do not destroy, and where thieves do not break in and steal. For where your treasure is, there your heart will be also."* Matthew 6:19-21).

We have a storage unit. We have used it for ten years, since we moved into our current home, because we didn't want to make room for the extra "junque." But *someday* we will do something with it. It must be valuable. My husband and I went to the unit a few months ago, looking for some things for a garage sale, and it's true, everything was covered with dust and cobwebs, and I didn't even want to touch it. We took out a few things, and then decided we will load the rest up and take it to the dump…someday. It still sits there and we pay the rent. So what's our worth? We are told that earthly riches are not where our worth is. We are worth SO MUCH to God that He sent His only Son, Jesus, to die a cruel death on a rugged cross to save us for Himself. We are so valuable to Him, His eyes are always on us, His ear always tuned to hear our prayer. We are worth more than we can ever imagine.

"For You created my inmost being; You knit me together in my mother's womb. I praise You because I am fearfully and wonderfully made; Your works are wonderful, I know that full well. My frame was not hidden from You when I was made in the secret place. When I was woven together in the depths of the earth, Your eyes saw my unformed body. All the days ordained for me were written in Your book before one of them came to be." (Psalm 139:13-16).

APRIL 18

LORD, I'M TIRED….

Sometimes don't you just drop into bed at night, exhausted beyond imagination? There is so much demanded of us, we grow so weary. Our lives are full and busy, and it seems, so often, there is no time for rest. And when we do get to sit down and put our feet up for a minute, there are interruptions…the phone, the door, someone needing something else of us.

And as if we aren't busy enough with job and home and family, it seems that even if there is a little time we could call our own in a day, we tend to fill it up with yet another thing! And then we get discouraged because we are so tired of fighting life's battles. We struggle just to get the bills paid, keep peace in the family, put food on the table. It's a lot of work. Emotionally, as well.

Jesus says, *"Come to Me, all who are weary and heavy laden, and I will give you rest. Take My yoke upon you and learn from Me, for I am gentle and humble in heart; and you shall find rest for your souls. For My yoke is easy and My burden is light."* (Matthew 11:28-30). Whew...don't you just feel a little sigh of relief? Our Lord wants to give us REST, relief from our weariness, refreshment. He has permanently released us from the burden of our sin, so we can rest in a relationship with Him. We CAN hear His voice, feel His love, and receive His strength. He has promised to never leave us. He restores our soul, and refreshes our spirit. God said, *"My Presence will go with you, and I will give you rest."* (Ex. 33:14). David spoke of this rest in Psalm 62:1... *"My soul finds rest in God alone."*

Of course, we have responsibilities, and obviously we cannot sit around and rest all the time. Nor should we. But in the midst of our work, and play, we must take a few minutes to find refreshment...we need to take a meal every so often...and it really isn't rest if we drive through a fast-food place and eat in the car while driving, is it? As God gives us opportunity for rest throughout our day, we should stop and take advantage of it, if even only for a few minutes. Years ago, my father-in-law used to come home in the middle of the day and lie down for 15 minutes. They didn't call them "power-naps" then, although some professionals speak of these now. Really, this rest-time is essential, for our physical and emotional health.

The 23rd Psalm begins ~ *"The Lord is my Shepherd, I shall not want. He makes me lie down in green pastures, He leads me beside still waters, He restores my soul..."*

Lord, thank you for the rest You provide for us. Help us to know we will be more effective in our life's work when we take time for rest. You care for us, and your provision strengthens us. We need You. Help us to recognize those little bits of time, those still waters, that come along as opportunities for rest, and cause us to give thanks to You for them. Amen.

APRIL 19

LORD OF THE CRISES…

"I lie down and sleep; I wake again, because the Lord sustains me. I will not fear the tens of thousands drawn up against me on every side. Arise, O lord! Deliver me, O my God! Strike all my enemies on the jaw; break the teeth of the wicked. From the Lord comes deliverance. May Your blessing be on Your people." (Psalm 3:5-8).

Oh, this week has been grueling…it feels to us, my husband and me, that we have tens of thousands of enemies coming against us from every side. For several years my husband's business has suffered, yet he hangs in there. His health has suffered because of the stress. For every step forward, it seems we take three or four backward. Our hopes build, then are dashed. Most of the stress is financial. God has truly sustained us through this time. This week, however, my husband landed in the hospital for a couple of days and will be continuing tests on his heart and brain. He's fine now, but he passed out and there are some heart issues. And here's the bomb…they told him he cannot drive for a month. His livelihood is driving charter buses right now. So, this is causing the added stress of no income.

This doesn't seem like much of an encouraging devotional today, but I want us all to remember, that whatever trials we face, whatever we are going through right now, or we will be facing in the future, *nothing* is too big, too impossible for our great and sovereign God. He was with David through many troubles, and in our more than 40 years of marriage, He has seen us through countless crises and circumstances which were beyond our control. He is merciful and compassionate and will not give us more than we can handle. His strength is perfect in our weakness. Helen Keller once said, "Character cannot be developed in ease and quiet. Only through experience of trial and suffering can the soul be strengthened."

And so, *"I know that my Redeemer lives, and that in the end He will stand upon the earth!"* (Job 19:25). All the problems of this life will be over and He will deliver His own. Praise the Lord! The prayers of the saints are covering us. Let His name be glorified in our situation.

APRIL 20

QUICK FIX?

Between last night and this morning I have had computer problems. No online connection. I hate when that happens. Then I have to call my internet provider, and go through the whole rigmarole to get it fixed. The "quick fix" would be to simply re-start my computer, which they always suggest when you call, and I already tried. So, next I have to go through the automated menu, then finally get a technician, in person, give my account number and state my problem. I'm sure this has happened to you as well. But, the first person couldn't help me, so she transferred me to another person and I had to repeat everything I just told her! I have two modems, one for internet, one for wi-fi, and apparently they weren't "talking" to each other. Sheesh!

It seems the more modern our technology, the longer it takes to fix it... that doesn't seem right. Our cars are more complicated these days, and when something goes wrong, it takes more money and more time to fix the problem, especially if it's computerized. The modern conveniences made to save time seem to actually take up *more* of our time!

In our lives, problems loom every day. We would love for God to "fix" them, and we are sometimes impatient for Him to do so. We have relationship problems, health problems, financial problems. David said, *"I waited patiently for the Lord; He turned to me and heard my cry. He lifted me out of the slimy pit, out of the mud and the mire; He set my feet on a rock and gave me a firm place to stand. He put a new song in my mouth, and hymn of praise to our God."* (Psalm 40:1-3). I don't think this happened instantly. It was a process. David wrote a whole book about the process, as we probably could. And it is the process which helps us to grow and become stronger in our faith. It's just like the butterfly or the baby chick struggling to break out of it's cocoon or shell...when someone helps them, they emerge quicker, but weaker. If allowed to go through the toil and the labor of breaking free, they are strengthened. So we are stronger for the struggles we go through.

When the problems of life weigh us down, and we are in a hurry for solutions, we must remember that God's timing is perfect, and He knows how much we need to struggle before we can emerge standing on rock solid ground. And just as we need our technical support for help in fixing our computer problems, we need God's "technical support" in fixing our lives. Hold on to the hope He alone gives, and experience His mercy and compassion. Know that He will "fix" the problem ~ we only need to *"be still and know that He is God."* (Psalm 46:10).

APRIL 21

JESUS, OUR RECONCILIATION...

"Therefore, if anyone is in Christ, he is a new creation; the old has gone, the new has come! All this is from God, who reconciled us to Himself through Christ and gave us the ministry of reconciliation..." (2 Cor. 5:17-18).

Quoting from the little book I love, *At the Name of Jesus*, "The estrangement between God and man, brought about by man's sin, is ended by Jesus' sacrificial death on the cross. Gentiles, as well as Jews, find their true life and spiritual home where Jesus is Lord. Jesus says... When I broke down the walls separating you from other kinds of people, I enabled you to see Me in all who love Me. Take off the blinders put up by your country, your race, even by your denomination, and appreciate Me in people everywhere..." (Sarah Hornsby).

So, God has already reconciled the world, that means everyone, to Himself in Christ. *"We are therefore Christ's ambassadors, as though God were making His appeal through us."* (vs. 20). We have a job to do ~ to love others with Jesus' love. Otherwise His death, this priceless gift He gave, is for nothing. He *became sin* so we could be freed from it. (vs 21).

Colossians 1:19-20 says, *"For it was the Father's good pleasure for all the fullness to dwell in Him, and through Him to reconcile all things to Himself, having made peace through the blood of His cross; through Him, I say, whether things on earth or things in heaven."*

We cannot do it on our own power. We must love others with God's power, with His help. Ask Him to love others today, especially the unlovely, through us.

APRIL 22

PERSEVERANCE...

Our exchange student from Taiwan, Lisa, (real name Yu Hwa), loves our piano. She's never had piano lessons, but has "played around" with the little catchy tunes that drive mothers crazy, because they're played over and over again! Bless her heart, she doesn't give up until she gets it right. My own girls begged for piano lessons, and nine months into them, after NOT practicing even near enough, gave up. Well, same with me. I would LOVE to play the piano, my beautiful little spinet that belonged to my husband's grandmother, and I did take lessons a couple of times. The first time was in a "recreational" piano class at our local college which turned out to be a disaster for all kinds of reasons. I got my money back from that one. But, I had a book! And try as I might to figure it out on my own, it was just too difficult while trying to raise three little children. I kept telling myself that when I was old, I would take it up again. Well, a few years ago, I took private lessons, but by the time I drove there on my lunch hour once a week, and realized just how much it was costing, I gave that up too. But, I had a book! I managed to learn 3-4 songs out of it, and I've promised myself that now that I'm retired, I have the time to practice more, but I want to sound like Jim Brickman…NOW!

Last night, Lisa said to me, "you have to tell me when you're sick of this!" Well, I won't, not on your life. She is determined to get it and will sit there literally for hours. She does not read music, but plays by ear. She even makes up stuff that sounds really good. I believe she could write music. She's amazing. James said, in 1:4, *"**Perseverance** must finish its work so that you may be mature and complete, not lacking anything."* That pretty much sums it up. So, even though Lisa gave up and went to bed, having learned half the song, she will finish learning it. I know she will. Even if it takes weeks. Her desire and the beauty of the music is what drives her. It's in her soul. What an example!

Last weekend our city hosted the Ironman triathlon. There was a story in the paper the next day about a woman who had made it almost the whole way…bicycling, swimming, then running all day, over 16 hours, a total of 140.6 miles, and within about three minutes of the finish line and the midnight deadline, her knees buckled and gave out, she collapsed, wailing because she was so close. She yelled, "I'm not ending it like that!" and people ran to her, helped her get up, and she pushed ahead on shaky, rubbery legs, making it through the finish line before toppling again. She didn't win, but her perseverance paid off and she was a finisher! And a hero to many who cheered her on.

And as Paul said to the Hebrews, in 12:1, *"Therefore, since we are surrounded by such a cloud of witnesses, let us throw off everything that hinders and the sin that so easily entangles, and let us run with **perseverance** the race marked out for us. Let us fix our eyes on Jesus, the author and perfecter of our faith, who for the joy set before Him endured the cross, scorning its shame, and sat down at the right hand of the throne of God. Consider Him who endured with such opposition from sinful men, so that you will not grow weary and lose heart."* Oh, that's long, but there was no good place to stop! I needed that whole thought. What would have happened if Jesus decided halfway through His assignment that the race was too hard, too difficult, and He didn't have what it took to finish? What if He concluded that the suffering, the ridicule He heard over and over, wasn't worth it? Where would that leave us? It would mean that I would have to suffer and die for my own sins. And you would. I am so glad Jesus persevered, aren't you? I think Lisa is an inspiration to me. I want to sit down at my piano, probably when she goes home, because I don't have a chance right now, and stay with it until I learn something. Until I have a breakthrough! How about you? What race are you running? Stick with it, run to the end, and receive your reward.

APRIL 23

DON'T WORRY…BE HAPPY!

Webster defines **Worry:** "to cause to feel troubled or uneasy; make anxious; to feel distressed in the mind." **Anxiety**: "a state of being uneasy; apprehensive; having misgivings." **Concern:** "to cause to feel uneasy or anxious; a matter of interest or importance; interest in or regards for a person or thing." **Fear:** feeling of anxiety caused by the presence of danger, evil, or pain; terror, fright; respectful dread…" you get the picture. They are all related, and one leads to another. Joyce Landorf, in her book "The Fragrance of Beauty" (1976) defined worry as a "scampering mouse." This little mouse of worry scampers all over our souls, over our face, our hands and our body motions. It can cause us to be jumpy, talk non-stop with defensive and critical comments. Sometimes self-pity works its way in there, too. Worry borrows unknown trouble from tomorrow… "*Who of you by worrying can add a single hour to his life?…Therefore, do not worry about tomorrow, for tomorrow will worry about itself. Each day has enough trouble of its own"* ~ Jesus. (Matthew 6:27, 34).

Worry affects our ability, mentally and physically, to act wisely in a situation, to think logically. Here's what worry can be to our bodies: a poison in the blood, a drain on inner vitality, a stiffening in the joints, a hardening of the arteries, causing of an ulcer…and much more. (Quoting from Joyce Landorf again). Worry also becomes a habit, and can hold like a death-grip on our whole life. It blinds us. It's useless. Although it is natural for us to worry, it is not in God's plan for us to spend every waking hour worrying over each detail of our lives. "The woman who worries misses all the sunshine of life because she's forever expecting the rain." (JL). And this is when it becomes sin to worry, when we allow it to take over our thoughts. It reveals a lack of faith in God's ability to work out the details.

So, what it boils down to, is if we would concentrate our thinking on *"whatever is true, whatever is noble, whatever is right, whatever is pure, whatever is lovely, whatever is admirable ~ if anything is excellent or praiseworthy ~ think about such things."* (Phil. 4:8). And practice the calming beauty of prayer. Oh, and Happiness? Good pleasure, joy, contentment. Jesus can give all this in exchange for our worry.

APRIL 24

PRUNING...

Last night I pruned some of my beautiful willow trees. My husband has been giving me grief about them because the branches hang over the sidewalk and he has to duck to walk under them. I hated to start chopping them! These are trees I rooted myself and planted them as tiny twigs, 8-12 inches high, 10 years ago. I have pruned and shaped them lovingly over the years, but, it had to be done. They are the Austrian willows that changed into "weeping" willows this winter under the weight of our record snowfall. I just cried. I thought they would be ruined. But amazingly, even after months of being weighted down by the snow, the branches sprang back up when the snow was melted enough to release them. It was not only painful emotionally for me to prune them because I LIKED the shape and the look of them, but my arthritis has been flaring up in my hands, swelling fingers and joints...and so it was very painful physically for me, too. But I didn't dare turn my husband loose on them!

As I was working those big pruning shears, I was thinking about how God has to prune and shape us, His own creation, His children. He starts us out as tiny "twigs" and lovingly and carefully prunes and trims us as we grow up, then standing back, looking at us with delight, He notices other imperfections. We are human, after all...so, He begins the pruning process again. The pruning knife here is the Word of God, according to Hebrews 4:12. *"For the Word of God is living and active. Sharper than any double-edged sword, it penetrates even to dividing soul and spirit, joints and marrow; it judges the thoughts and attitudes of the heart. Nothing in all creation is hidden from God's sight. Everything is uncovered and laid bare before the eyes of Him to whom we must give account."* So, it is only when affliction leads us to this discipline of the Word that it becomes a blessing; the lack of this heart-cleansing through the Word is the reason why affliction is so often unsanctified. As we yield ourselves humbly and heartily to the teaching of the Word by the Spirit, the Father will do His blessed work of pruning and cleansing anything that hinders His Spirit's work in our lives.

As I stand back and look at my trimmed trees, they really don't look so bad. And this pruning will allow them to grow and flourish in the years to come. And I will probably prune them again as they need it. So, I welcome God's pruning in my life so that His purposes will be fulfilled in my life! I wouldn't want it any other way.

APRIL 25

FRESH FAITH…

This time of year, people are beginning to mow their lawns, and I love that smell of the fresh-cut grass. And what about the wonderful scent of fresh-baked bread, or brownies? I have mentioned this before, but I love the clean crispness of fresh notebook or journal pages before I begin writing. Freshly washed sheets on the bed, crisp lettuce in the salad, a fresh paint job on the house. Here's one of my favorites ~ huge fresh-baked cranberry-oatmeal cookies from the store bakery. They package them by two in the deli. Good with *fresh* coffee…there are so many things that are just better when fresh.

Often I think about my faith ~ is it fresh, as well? We used to have testimony services in Sunday evening church. Many would stand, ready with their testimony, but at least half of those were, shall we say, not fresh? Oh, the person was grateful for the way God had saved them ~ 15-20, or even 50 years ago, and that God had gotten them through many rough places, but what they shared was not recent, or up-to-date. The radio station I like to listen to has a couple of hours once a week, called Faith-Filled-Friday where people are invited to call in and tell of a recent answer to prayer, or a way God has strengthened their faith in just the past week. There's just something more credible about a new story that one can identify with, and it will sometimes prompt someone else to share.

I believe God wants us to talk about the things He does for us. Some of our miracles are just little things, but we can bolster the faith of another by sharing it all. Philippians 4:4 says, *"Rejoice in the Lord always…"* That pretty much means every day. And in 1 Peter 3:15, *"Always be prepared to give an answer to everyone who asks you to give the reason for the hope that you have…"* If our faith, and our experience, is not fresh and up to date, how can we share it with others in a way they'll believe. *"Yet this I call to mind, and therefore I have hope: Because of the Lord's great love we are not consumed, for His compassions never fail. They are new every morning; great is Your faithfulness."* (Lamentations 3:21-23). If God's mercies are new **every morning**, how can we share a stale faith?

APRIL 26

SHOWERS OF BLESSING…

"I will send showers, showers of blessings, which will come just when they are needed." (Ezekiel 34:36). There was a little chorus we used to sing in church… "Showers of blessing, showers of blessing we need, mercy drops 'round us are falling, but for the showers we plead."

We've been having a lot of showers here in North Idaho, and really, they are a blessing, because it can get very dry in the summer and then we have the dreaded forest fires. The moisture helps to keep the forests from getting too dry. Of course, that time will come this summer when it does get hot and dry. But every bit of rain helps. I cannot help but thank God for them. Our lives sometimes become dry and parched and we long for these showers of God's blessings. Too many "things" weigh us down, and we tend to become very concerned and busy about the responsibilities and matters of life. Soon, our prayer life, our Bible-reading and devotions become shorter and sparse, and somewhat "dry" and bland. We begin to feel farther away from God.

David had times like that, I think, much like we do. Here's what he said in Psalm 103:1-5: *"Bless the Lord, O my soul, and all that is within me bless His holy name. Bless the Lord, O my soul, and forget not His benefits; Who forgiveth all thine iniquities; Who healeth all thy diseases; Who redeemeth thy life from destruction; Who crowneth thee with lovingkindness and tender mercies; Who satisfieth thy mouth with good things, so that thy youth is renewed like the eagle's."* (KJV). This follows a Psalm of lament, a cry for help, in the prayer preceding it, as throughout the book of Psalms we see David crying out to God in anguish and despair, then followed by praise for the God who rescued him...God certainly showered blessings upon David, all through his life, as well as hardships.

Sometimes we are the recipients of blessing from our heavenly Father, but we don't realize what we are receiving are actually blessings. Sometimes the hard times are blessings. We have all heard stories of someone who was traveling and their flight had been postponed or they were late and missed it for some reason, only to learn the plane crashed, killing everyone aboard. Or, you get into a long line at the grocery store and it's not moving very fast, and you are getting more and more antsy to get through it, but someone behind you looks troubled, and you begin to share with them and make their day a little bit better. What about an illness, that through treatment of it, the doctor discovers something else that could have been far worse if found at a later time? These are blessings. My friend visited Washington D.C. with her family, and they arrived the same day as the shooting at the holocaust museum. They had a visit scheduled in a day or two. It was a blessing they weren't there on that day.

Are there "showers of blessing" that come down on you everyday that you don't recognize? **"There shall be showers of blessing: This is the promise of love; There shall be seasons refreshing, Sent from the Savior above."** He is showering us with His blessings, we just need to go out and stand with our face and our hands upward and comprehend and receive, and thank and praise Him!

APRIL 27

LISTEN TO THE BIRDS...

Lord, listen to the birds this morning. I have not fed them yet and they sound a little bewildered. Maybe a little bit angry, or at least indignant. Is that how we sound to You when we think You're not paying attention to us? When we think You're not answering or even hearing our prayers, that You don't even know where we are, or that we're hungry? Of course, if I never put food out for "my" birds, they would still not go hungry, because You feed them. They are Your creation and You care about them. They're delightful to You....

And so it is with me. Do I sometimes feel like You're out of tune with my needs, with my fears and concerns? *"O, Lord, You have searched me and You know me. You know when I sit and when I rise; You perceive my thoughts from afar. You discern my going out and my lying down; You are familiar with all my ways. Before a word is on my tongue, You know it completely, O Lord. You hem me in behind and before; You have laid Your hand upon me. Such knowledge is too wonderful for me, too lofty for me to attain. Where can I go from Your Spirit? Where can I flee from Your presence?"* (Psalm 139: 1-7).

Lord, I am so glad You never, ever take Your eyes off me. No matter where in this world I am, You see me and You are covering me with Your umbrella of protection. Just as You care for the birds of the air, and every living creature, even the flowers that only last for a few days, You care even more for me, and for my needs. And everything I have is Yours. I am so grateful. *"Let everything that has breath praise the Lord!"* (Psalm 150:6).

APRIL 28

WATER OF LIFE...

"In the beginning God created the heavens and the earth. Now the earth was formless and empty, darkness was over the surface of the deep, and the Spirit of God was hovering over the waters." (Genesis 1:1-2). This tells me that water was one of the very first things God created. When He created the earth, water was part of it. There were seas and oceans. It hadn't yet rained on the earth. I don't know ANYTHING about chemistry, but I do know that water has many physical and chemical properties, that were there at the beginning. For eons, scientists and chemists have studied and experimented with water. One thing I know, we can't live without it. We can live for a period of time, even long periods of time, without food, but not water. It is essential to life, and to our body's functions.

We see water everyday. For those fortunate to live near lakes, as I do, we can use it for recreation. It makes for beautiful landscaping and scenery. Our plants, grass and trees need water to survive. We experience water in many forms – ice, snow, hail, rain, clouds...it's refreshing, and yet, it can be devastating, as we have seen in hurricanes and ravaging record snowfalls.

Jesus is the Water of Life. He is the source of the supply of living water that gushes forth from the fountain, the essence of life, His blood. *"Jesus answered and said to her, [the woman at the well] 'Everyone who drinks of this water shall thirst again; but whoever drinks of the water that I shall give him shall never thirst; but the water that I shall give him shall become in him a well of water springing up to eternal life.'"* (John 4:13,14). We see many references to water throughout scriptures. A huge flood. God turned the Nile into blood. He held the Red Sea back. Water gushed forth from a rock. Jesus changed the water into wine. Baptism. Fishing. It's very important.

Are you thirsty? Jesus alone quenches that thirst. *"But blessed is the man who trusts in the Lord, whose confidence is in Him.* ***He will be like a tree planted by the water that sends out its roots by the stream****. It does not fear when heat comes; its leaves are always green. It has no worries in a year of drought and never fails to bear fruit."* (Jeremiah 17:7-8). That's where I want to be. Tapped right into that Living Water.

APRIL 29

KILLDEER...

I have been watching a couple of killdeer parents in the street in front of our house for a few days. They are so pretty, and almost as fun as quail to watch as they run all around. These have been "signaling" danger by a shrill call...I always know when they are around. Sure enough, early this morning the babies (four of them) left the nest, and we were fortunate enough to see them running across the street (and there's always a little straggler!), and through the neighbor's yard. I have read that they won't return to their nest once they've fledged, so I guess they are off to bigger adventures. I don't understand why they have their nests on the ground, and sometimes out in plain sight, but God created them that way. It's dangerous, but He watches over them.

But, aren't we kind of like that, too? We don't always stay away from danger and where it's safe. We live on the edge. Sometimes circumstances around us cause us to be in danger, but other times we dare to stray away from God's hand and get ourselves into risky and sometimes perilous situations. God always has His eyes on us, no matter how far away we are from Him. David said in Psalm 69:16-18, *"Lord, answer me because Your love is so good. Because of Your great kindness, turn to me. Do not hide from me, Your servant. I am in trouble. Hurry to help me! Come near and save me; rescue me from my enemies."*

And so, in our trouble, we look up. We trust and believe in Him who made us. God's love never fails. When we are weak, He is strong. And He is faithful to watch over us, even when the way seems so dangerous. Like the little killdeer, and all the other creatures He made, He never takes His eyes off us. He is our Protector. He will keep us close to Him.

APRIL 30

TURNING THE CALENDAR...

"Teach us to number our days aright, that we may gain a heart of wisdom." (Psalm 90:12). I love turning the page on my desk calendar ~ it's so clean and uncluttered...so far. I look back to the previous month and wow ~ every block has several things written on it ~ meetings, appointment, classes, birthdays... what a busy month it was. Then I turn to the new month ~ empty. Well, there are a few things written in, but it won't take long to fill it up too. There is a bridal shower and a wedding, a day to get my labs done, then a doctor's appointment, my grandson's tonsillectomy...

In the midst of all my busy-ness, I try to make every day count for something eternal. I ask the Father to help me to make a difference in someone's day, even by something as simple as a smile, a phone call or sending a card, or a secret prayer. The Bible says in Psalm 103:15,16, *"As for man, his days are like grass, he flourishes like a flower of the field; the wind blows over it and it is gone, and its place remembers it no more."* I was going to stop there, but let's go on...verses 17 & 18 say, *"But from everlasting to everlasting the Lord's love is with those who fear Him, and His righteousness with their children's children ~ with those who keep His covenant and remember to obey His precepts."* What we do with our lives right now will last through generations to come. I'm praying my actions will be ordered by God, I will follow His precepts even when the way seems difficult.

Sometimes we just go on day after day without even thinking of what kind of an impact we are making on our family, friends, or acquaintances. Many of us wake up dreading the day. I admit, there are certain things I dread, but I always try to celebrate the morning and the new day, and ask God to show me what great and mighty things He has in store for me. I know that *"With the*

Lord, a day is like a thousand years, and a thousand years are like a day." (2 Peter 3:8). What we do today in His name will go on through eternity, though we may not see the end result in our lifetime. But there will be a day when the calendar has run out, we won't need to write those appointments in ever again... *"for you know very well that the Day of the Lord will come like a thief in the night."* (1 Thess. 5:2). It will suddenly be over, all our striving and work will be finished. No more appointments, only one grand meeting, with our Lord in heaven. I want to make sure I don't miss that one!

MAY 1

WE ARE VALUABLE...

"What is man that You are mindful of him, the son of man that You care for him?" (Psalm 8:4).

Years ago I heard a story about a little boy with a good attitude, who said "God made me and God doesn't make junk!" And over the years we have probably all heard that sentence many more times. And it's true. I was just reading in a daily devotional that I received this morning emailed from the Presidential Prayer Team people, and here's an excerpt from it...

"Astrophysics? Particle physics? These studies range from the macro to the micro. And the incredible twist they discover, according to Joel Primack and Nancy Abrams, a husband-wife team, is that humankind is at the center of it all. In their book **The View from the Center of the Universe**, they say, 'Physically, humans are the geometric mean of the largest part of the visible universe...man is made up of the rarest substance in the universe, atoms beyond helium, which accounts for less than 0.1% of the universe.'

"Don't you feel more significant in God's design now? He knows what scientists are only beginning to discover – that you are wonderful! Your Heavenly Father created you in *His* image, only a little lower than the angels. He made you for a good reason and you are valuable! Therefore, glory in the fact that not only is God intimately mindful of you, He desperately loves you."

And each one of us is so unique, there is no other just like us, like you or like me, in the universe. That's incredible to me. He didn't just "pop" us into existence, though. He painstakingly crafted and designed each one of us in our mother's womb, another unbelievable miracle. *"For You created my inmost being;*

You knit me together in my mother's womb. I praise You because I am fearfully and wonderfully made; (Psalm 139:13). I love that! We were made on purpose! We are not a mistake, but specially crafted as an artisan lovingly and expertly crafts his creations of beauty.

Our life is a gift from God. What we do with it is our gift back to Him.

MAY 2

TO PARDON....

"Then Peter came to Jesus and asked, 'Lord, how many times shall I forgive my brother when he sins against me? Seven times?' Jesus answered, 'I tell you, not seven times, but seventy times seven.'" (Matthew 18:21). Peter must've thought that answer from his Lord was pretty unbelievable. In fact, it IS pretty unbelievable. Can anyone really forgive someone that many times? 490 times? Is that per day, or per lifetime? Still, is it possible? For the same offense, even?

Jesus also said, a little while before, *"But if you do not forgive men their sins,Your Father will not forgive your sins."* (Matthew 6:15). Oh-oh...that changes things a little, doesn't it? So, does that mean ALL sins, or just certain ones? But, you ask, what if they do it again? And again? Seventy times seven. Forgiving, and asking forgiveness is not easy. And it's costly. But it must be kept up to date. Sometimes we say we're sorry, but are we really? It's like the little child whose parents make them say they're sorry for being mean to another child, and they finally whisper, 'sorry!"They don't mean it from their heart. Mom made them say it.

When you've been hurt terribly, it is very hard to forgive the other person. I've had some very hurtful, sometimes devastating things happen to me at the hands of another person, but when I realized how *freeing*, for me, it is to forgive them, it was so much easier. I realized I was in bondage to that person's sin...sometimes when a person hurts us, they don't realize it, but we wallow in the pain of it, and it controls how we act. Sometimes bitterness and anger and hatred will result from unforgiveness. We must realize that there are some things we cannot change. Sometimes the wrong will be repeated again. It's possible that God will not change certain people in our lives. He may not take away the problems, even if we forgive over and over again. We will always have differences with one another. But He will give us the *grace* to accept them.

Forgiving is love in action. And God's love never fails. After all, He pardons us, over and over again, doesn't He?

Jesus' forgiveness is the ultimate illustration of love, for He said, even as they were killing Him, *"Father forgive them for they know not what they do."* (Luke 23:34).

MAY 3

SO BLESSED...

I am naturally one to count my blessings. I have always been a positive thinker, one to look on the bright side, to look for the good in people...most of the time. I know how blessed I am to have my whole family near me. Two daughters live within two blocks of me, and the other a mile away. That means all my grandchildren are also close, and they love to stop by. Yesterday, my newly-turned-13 year old grandson, Matthew, stopped by on his new bike just to visit because his friends couldn't "play." That's exactly what he said. I'm so glad he isn't too cool to still be a little boy at heart. He helped himself to iced tea in the fridge, and sat down in Grandpa's recliner, and just started visiting with me. We talked about his braces he'll be getting in a few weeks, college ~ for goodness sake, he's only in 7th grade ~ and the possibility of him going into the military after high school. He played with the cat, and just wasn't in a hurry to leave. I reveled in that, in those few minutes when he was all mine and I had his undivided attention. It was a precious time.

We also have the opportunity to babysit the younger ones often. Sometimes they take walks with their parents and stop in for a few moments. I see them almost every day. And I feel blessed in so many other ways ~ in my friendships, my health, a comfortable home that, in spite of the economy and unreal financial difficulties, we have not lost, and we don't take this for granted, not for a minute...these things are all evidence of God's rich blessings in our lives.

God's blessings are many, and He promises to bless those who *"keep His statutes,"* who *"fear the Lord,"* who *"walk in the light of His presence,"* who are *"faithful,"* all these found in the Psalms, and of course, the one I love in Proverbs 31, *"Her children [and her grandchildren, my paraphrase] rise up and call her blessed."* And we have the Beatitudes from the sermon on the Mount, listing all God's blessings to the poor in spirit, the meek, the peacemakers, the persecuted, the pure in heart ~ all of those things I wish to be, and try to be, but realized a long time ago I cannot be without God's help and His power in my life. Not that everything has been rosy in my life ~ there have been many dark and hard times over the years. But God has used each difficulty to teach me something valuable about His love and His care for me, and cause me to put my trust in Him, and I would never change that. And there are many "little" blessings each day that, if I'm not careful, I would take for granted…the blessing of quiet solitude in the morning, watching the sun rise, the beauty I enjoy in His creation, a wonderful cup of hot tea, laughter, a dependable car, eyesight and good hearing…I could fill pages. Last night we saw a beautiful red deer, (usually they're more gray), a young buck with his rack covered in velvet, enjoying the grass in a neighbor's front yard. He didn't care that we turned our bikes around and came back to watch him, and to "talk" to him.

But the greatest blessing of all will be on that day when I face my Savior and hear Him say, *"Well done, good and faithful servant."* (Matt. 25:21). And when He bestows on me that crown, my great reward, it will be worth it all.

MAY 4

HUMILITY…

I attended our city's National Day of Prayer service, at the City Hall, which, in itself, is a miracle in this day and age. I wondered if this would be the last time Christians would be able to have a day of prayer like this, unafraid to stand in a public place and proclaim the love and power of God? And I thought how powerful our prayers would be when, in cities all across America, on a certain day, at noon in their individual time zones, people would be praying for 3-4 hours in the middle of the day, all in one accord. I was excited, and of course, the scripture in 2 Chronicles 7:14 came immediately to my mind, as it does often… *"If My people, who are called by My name, will humble themselves and pray, and seek My face, and turn from their wicked ways, then will I hear from heaven and will forgive their sin and will heal their land."* And verse 15 goes on to say, *"Now My eyes will be open and My ears attentive to the prayers offered in this place."*

God calls us to be humble, not proud and puffed up, or powerful in our own might, but bowing before Him, the Sovereign God of the universe, the only One who can fix this mess we've gotten ourselves in. It must begin in our hearts. At the City prayer service, one of the pastors spoke and prayed for *humility* among the American people. This impressed me most. And he did what none of the other pastors did, he knelt at the microphone as he offered his prayer. He invited others to kneel before God, in humility, as well. I think almost every knee was bowed, and as I knelt there myself on the concrete sidewalk, feeling the discomfort of that position, I thought of what a "sacrifice of praise" it was for people with arthritis and bad knees and backs to kneel anyway. God said we should humble ourselves, and pray.

The National Day of Prayer has passed, but I would pray we would not let our prayers of yesterday fade away as the days and weeks go by, but that we would continue to offer up in our daily prayers our President, our entire governmental system, national, State wide and local city leaders, the residents in our counties, the schools, our military men and women and their families, asking for repentance and revival, and for God's outpouring of grace and mercy upon us all!

O God, please bless America!

MAY 5

A HEART LIKE GOD'S...

"Create in me a pure heart, O God, and renew a steadfast spirit within me." (Psalm 51:10). Is it possible for anyone but God to have a pure heart? This would have to be a heart free from defects, faultless, blameless, free from sin or guilt... perfect. It seems unconceivable. And yet, Jesus said, *"Be perfect, therefore, even as I am perfect."* (Matt. 5:48). Yet, how can we, fallen man, ever expect to be perfect in His sight? It is humanly impossible. My body is far from perfect, my mind less than impeccable, and my heart is full of selfishness and pride.

"But the Lord said to Samuel, 'Do not look at his [David's brother's] appearance or at the height of his stature, because I have rejected him; for God sees not as man sees, for man looks at the outward appearance, but the Lord looks at the heart.'" (1 Samuel 16:7). There it is. It makes no difference how WE see ourselves, or each other for that matter. What is important is that God looks at our heart. He knows it's impossible for us to be perfect, to have a pure heart like His, in our own strength. But David was "one with God," he molded his heart and his spirit into

the likeness of what he saw. He beheld the beautiful heart of God by what God showed him. David prayed, *"Show me Your ways, O Lord, teach me Your paths; guide me in Your truth and teach me, for You are God my Savior."* (Psalm 25:4-5). David sought after God with ALL his heart. David was not perfect by any means, but he was striving after God's heart, even as a young boy.

We have an advantage that David didn't have, however ~ the example of Jesus' life here on earth, and the Cross. That speaks intensely of God's heart. I'm not saying we must give our lives for all mankind as Jesus did, or that we must sacrifice everything we have to be like Him. But we do need to see things the way He does in order to have a heart like His. Oh, sometimes we do, don't we? We try to be kind and compassionate, unselfish, caring...but then sometimes doubt creeps in, and maybe a little impatience, and pretty soon we're being critical or indignant...It's so important that we are communing with Him hourly throughout our day, minute by minute, in order to hear what He says to us, to be who He wants us to be, to have a heart like His. It takes sheer obedience in everything. Charles Spurgeon said, "You must keep all earthly treasures out of your heart, and let Christ be your treasure, and let Him have your heart."

"I will give them an undivided heart and put a new spirit in them; I will remove from them their heart of stone and give them a heart of flesh." (Ezekiel 11:19)

It involves having the knowledge of God's presence in our lives, and the unrestrained joy of that knowledge. God wants to give us the perfect heart, a heart like His. And with God, nothing is impossible.

MAY 6

THE RACE...

All of our life is a race, did you ever think about that? When my kids were little, they would race to see who could finish their meal first, or get to the swings first at the park. When they started school, there were foot races, and relay races, testing, trying to beat the clock. We race through our days, day in and day out. There are marathons, for which athletes train vigorously, pushing themselves to beat their last time. We race frogs, pigs, go-carts, horses, lawnmowers, and dogs. And there is the "rat race." I think occasionally we are all caught up in that one, as we race through our day.

Luke said in Acts 20:24, *"I consider my life worth nothing to me, if only I may finish the race and complete the task the Lord Jesus has given me ~ the task of testifying to the gospel of God's grace."* Someone said we need to slow down and "take time to smell the roses." I have noted that some people don't even realize there ARE roses, or clouds, or trees, or sunsets…they are definitely in too big a hurry. But sometimes, like being a runner in a marathon, we feel like we just cannot take another step. We can't make it to the finish line, no matter how much we have trained. Life is too hard, and there are obstacles we didn't expect thrown into our path. We start out with that joy and energy and confidence, but as we race on, the problems of life tend to weigh us down ~ worry, personal wounds, anger…and we don't hear those standing on the sidelines cheering us on…and we don't notice Jesus waiting at the finish line with His arms wide open.

Paul wrote to the Hebrews, *"Therefore, since we are surrounded by such a great cloud of witnesses, let us throw off everything that hinders and the sin that so easily entangles, and let us run with perseverance the race marked out for us.* ***Let us fix our eyes on Jesus,*** *the author and perfecter of our faith, who, for the joy set before Him, endured the cross, scorning its shame, and sat down at the right hand of the throne of God. Consider Him who endured such opposition from sinful men, so that you will not grow weary and lose heart."* (v. 12:1-3).

That "great cloud of witnesses?" Aside from being that huge group of the righteous ones who've gone before us, they are the faithful friends and loved ones who pray for us and encourage us daily, and some we don't even realize are praying for us. And we, of course, are part of that great cloud as well, when we lift our brother or sister in prayer. And at the end of our race may we say, as Paul did in his second letter to Timothy, *"I have fought the good fight, I have finished the race, I have kept the faith. Now there is in store for me the crown of righteousness, which the Lord, the righteous Judge, will award to me on that day…"* (v.4:7-8). All our life is training for that day when we will receive the prize. Don't lose heart!

MAY 7

FIREFLIES…AND OTHER LIGHTS…

I have been reading Patsy Clairmont's book, "Catching Fireflies." She talks about moments in her childhood when the children caught fireflies and put them into a canning jar, and watched their light. She even used to take her jar to bed with her, for a "nightlight" but then when she was asleep, her parents would come in and take the firefly jar outside and free them for another night. What great memories. I, too, remember fireflies, or lightning bugs...are they the same? I don't think we have ever had them here in North Idaho, but when I was a child and we traveled as a family, we would experience the awe and joy at seeing these little creatures lighting up their corner of the world, or, at least the roadside bushes. I don't think my own children or grandchildren have ever seen them. I once bought my daughter, as a gift, a quart canning jar which had electronic "fireflies" inside, run by battery. It was cute, and, hey, it's the next best thing.

Can you imagine why God even made the tiny little firefly? He really seemed to be into "light." It was actually the first thing He spoke into being, "*'Let there be light,' and there was light.*"(Genesis 1:3). The next lights that showed up, four days later, were the moon, sun and stars, all lights of differing degrees and intensity. And lightning! I like to think that maybe He created lightning even before any of these other lights, just to have a little fun now and then, flashing here and there. I love lightning. And He got really creative when He brought into being the awesome aurora borealis...and of course, the rainbow. As much as we try, we can never duplicate any of the light God has created. Our world would be a very dreary, and quite frightening, place without light. So, we have porch lights, headlights, pool lights, flashlights, candles, and kitchen sink lights. We put night lights in our bathrooms or in the hall just in case we get up in the night. And Christmas. Oh, Christmas! Don't we love the lights at Christmas? Everything is lit up to the hilt...our houses, our trees, the streets downtown and store windows...and of course, Christmas is when we celebrate the real Light that came into the world. *"Jesus said, 'I am the Light of the world. Whoever follows Me will never walk in darkness, but will have the light of life.'"* (John 8:12). I believe that God didn't create darkness, but that darkness is the absence of light. *"He separated the light from the darkness."* (Gen. 1:4). Not only is Jesus the Light of the world, He calls us to be light as well... *"In the same way, let your light shine before men, that they may see your good deeds and praise your Father in heaven."* (Matthew 5:16). We cannot be this light without the energizing power from the Holy Spirit in our lives.

And, just as the Bible begins with light, it also ends with reference to light, in Revelation 21:23, *"The city does not need the sun or the moon to shine on it, for the glory of God gives it light, and the Lamb is its lamp."* I want to go there. And when I do, I'll bet there will be a few fireflies, too!

MAY 8

SHACKLES...

Webster defines shackles as "1. a metal fastening to gird or bind the wrists or ankles of a prisoner; 2. anything that restrains freedom of expression or action..." In the song "He Touched Me" the author sings about being "shackled by a heavy burden, 'neath the load of guilt and shame..." Paul called himself *"an ambassador in chains"* as he continued to share the gospel while being held in prison ~ in shackles. (Eph. 6:20).

These past two weeks I have felt a little like that. Oh, I wasn't being held against my will ~ or was I? My husband had a fainting episode two weeks ago and while awaiting the results of many tests on his brain and his heart, to rule out the possibility of a seizure, mainly, the doctors had forbidden him to drive. And so he was dependent on me to drive him to appointments, to the bank, other errands. At first I felt a little like a caged animal ~ some of my own freedom had been taken away. I had to be "at the ready" whenever he needed to go someplace. But then I began thinking of how he must feel, having to depend on someone else to get him where he needed to be. He felt fine, he wasn't an invalid, just not allowed to drive, maybe for a month! I talked to the Lord a lot about this. And I decided I was my husband's helpmate, and no matter how inconvenient, during this time I was to be at his beck and call. I had to realize that he was also in bondage.

Sometimes we are prisoners of circumstances, and other times we place ourselves in the position of bondage by our disobedience. Christ came to earth and willingly died on the cross so that we could be free from bondage, from the chains of fear, resentment, selfishness, anger, inferiority, unforgiveness... sometimes we cannot change the circumstances, but God can change our hearts. It's highly possible that He will not change others who make our lives uncomfortable, and He may not take away our problems, but He will give us the grace to accept them and live with them. It's a promise: *"My grace is sufficient for you, for My power is made perfect in weakness."* (2 Cor. 12:9).

Well, the good news is, yesterday after the doctor's appointment, my husband was declared safe to drive. No seizure activity had been detected in the brain scan or EEG. After having his wings clipped for a *mere* 2 weeks, he was free to drive again. What a difference that made in his demeanor. Jesus once said *"I tell you the truth, everyone who sins is a slave to sin…So if the Son sets you free, you will be free indeed!."* (John 8:34, 36). We don't have to carry our burdens and remain enslaved to sin. Jesus has taken away our chains, unlocked our shackles so that we can enjoy the freedom of serving Him.

MAY 9

THE BIG FISH…

"But the Lord provided a great fish to swallow Jonah, and Jonah was inside the fish three days and three nights." (Jonah 1:17). This is one of the first Bible stories we learn when we are children, and it's pretty impressive. And unbelievable. But I believe it ~ because it's included in God's word, for a purpose. The story isn't totally about a man being swallowed by a big fish, but it's about *disobedience* to God. God told Jonah to go to a sinful city, Nineveh, and preach against their wickedness, but instead, as we know, Jonah ran away in the other direction. And that's when he got into all kinds of trouble. He caused trouble for other people too, people who were not even involved in his predicament. And suddenly Jonah's problem became their problem, almost to the detriment of the whole group…

The theme of this part of the story is disobedience. How many times have we heard God's voice telling us the way to go, and we don't think we can do what He asks, so we run from God in the opposite direction? There's more…

As soon as that fish swallowed up Jonah, he changed his tune. He began to seek God, and prayed to Him from the belly of the fish ~ in essence, he was running TO God. Jonah realized he was out of the will of the Father. So, God caused the fish to spew Jonah out onto the beach, and Jonah headed then to Nineveh and saw that God was right…it was a very large, important, and wicked place. Just like sometimes when we think if we do God's bidding, it will be easy ~ sometimes it's not. Sometimes it's discouraging, hard, and we wonder if it's worth it. But the important part is our *obedience* to God. If we are obedient, HE will do the work.

Well, the end of the story is that Jonah walks away, after preaching to the people, and has a temper tantrum. He complained to God that they were so bad they didn't deserve for Him to save them! Aren't we grateful that God thinks each one of us is deserving of His grace, and mercy and love? Do we think others are not deserving of His love? Let's let God be the judge of that, and just be obedient to His calling in *our* lives.

MAY 10

ALL GOD'S CREATURES...

"And God said 'Let the land produce living creatures according to their kinds; livestock, creatures that move along the ground, and wild animals, each according to its kind.' And it was so..." (Genesis 1: 24). I love animals. Dogs, cats, horses, birds, deer... turtles? We had a real different kind of morning yesterday...my youngest daughter picks me up regularly for our exercise class, and this particular morning, we rounded the corner by the high school near my house and she did a double-take and quickly pulled over to the side of the street. There crawling along the sidewalk was a good-sized turtle. No kids around, no houses in fact, except a few across the busy street. Had the turtle actually escaped and crossed that busy street? I jumped out and rescued the creature, while she found a box in the back of her van to put him in. Then we were on our way, astonished and wondering where in the world this critter came from. We went a few blocks up the same street, and found another creature that was not so fortunate. A dog had just been hit by a car, and a lady had run into the street, losing her shoe in the rush, and was bending over the dog, who appeared to be deceased. There was a man standing there with her, I assumed the man who hit the dog, since there was a car pulled over on the side. We were saddened...such an array of emotions in just a matter of a few minutes.

We will be watching the lost and found ads in the paper for the next few days, but it looks like the kids *may* be permitted to make this turtle, "Viking," named for the mascot of the high school where he was found, a summer project, at least. We'll see how they do with that responsibility. As for the dog, his owner and family will be spending some sad and lonely days.

This experience caused me to think that God Himself must also go through quite an assortment of feelings and emotions every day when He looks down and sees all the trouble His people, His creatures, get into. Some of us run out into dangerous places, some of us are rescued from impending peril. Some of us heed His direction and leading, others of us turn our backs and go our own way. I know God feels happiness at looking down on many of us, and disappointment and dismay when He sees the behavior of others. Sometimes we break His heart, and other times He's so proud of us! He wants so much to just reach down, take us by the hand, or place his hands on our shoulders, and just turn us around so we will go in the right and wise direction. But He has given us a free will, and He will not force us. We make our own choices, and sometimes suffer the consequences. He will only love us, and welcome us into His arms when we come running back.

God cares about all His creatures. We are all valuable to Him. He wants to protect us all from harm. He feeds the wild animals. He watches over the sparrow. And we are much more precious to Him than all else in His creation. *"For You created my inmost being..."* (again, Psalm 139:13). Of all the creatures God has made on earth, we are His masterpiece! What a thought!

MAY 11

TO SAY GOODBYE...

Today we will say goodbye to my brother-in-law, who died last week after a five-year battle with two different kinds of cancer. And we wonder why God allows so much suffering to some of His good people, when He simply and quickly takes others home, in their sleep, or in a sudden tragedy. I do know that now my brother-in-law is not suffering from the effects of the chemotherapy which ravaged his body (isn't it supposed to heal?) and does not need the relief that morphine gives, if someone administers it often enough...He was well-loved, and many friends and family came to visit in his last days.

Now he is in heaven, he's received his reward that was promised to him for his righteousness. He reached out to so many during his life, and now he is reaching out to Jesus. He's the lucky one ~ sitting at His feet, basking in the radiance of that heavenly place. It's a celebration. I know his reunion with his loved ones who have gone on before was joyous. And now he is whole and well.

Psalm 116:15 says, *"Precious in the sight of the Lord is the death of one of His saints."* God knows how much misery and anguish this one has gone through, and His God-heart is tender and merciful, as He welcomes him into His arms.

Now death is no longer a concern for our brother-in-law, as he will live eternally with our Lord, totally free of pain. And I'm sure our loved one would say this to those of us who miss him: *"I have fought the good fight, I have finished the race, I have kept the faith. Now there is in store for me the crown of righteousness, which the Lord, the righteous Judge, will award to me on that day ~ not only to me, but to all who have longed for His appearing."* (2 Timothy 4:7,8).

Jesus' appearing will come to all of us at one time or another…it came last week to my brother-in-law. Whether we join him one by one, or together in the Rapture, we will see Him. *"He has been sent to bind up the brokenhearted… to comfort all who mourn…to bestow on them a crown of beauty instead of ashes, the oil of gladness instead of mourning, and a garment of praise instead of a spirit of despair."* (Isaiah 61: 1-3). Nothing on earth compares to the joy we will know when we take that first step into heaven, where our soul longs to be. God prepared a mansion for our brother, and Jesus has given us hope that we will see him again some day. And for those of us left here to mourn, God gives peace and comfort.

MAY 12

OUR MOTHERS…

An idea that has taken hold on Facebook this week is to replace your "profile picture" with one of your mother. Suddenly pictures of older mothers are showing up. And very nice things are being said about moms. It's really amazing to see. Of course, I couldn't resist putting in a picture of my dear sweet mom from her high school graduation in 1945. It's a beautiful picture. My mom was a beautiful woman, inside and out. This will be the ninth Mother's Day that I have not had her around. I miss her. A lot. Every day there is something I would love to tell her, or ask her. Lots of the latter. There are plenty of ancestor-type questions I still need to ask. I wish that she could cuddle her first great-great-grandchild on her lap and watch that chubby little face giggle in delight. Every day I look in the mirror, I am reminded of her, for as I grow older, I'm looking more and more like her. I wonder how much my heart is like hers? There are many things I love that she loved. There are feelings she had about certain things that I feel the same about. She was a prayer warrior. I'm trying to be one. I know she had a great influence on the woman I would eventually become. She loved her children passionately. So do I. She was impeccably faithful to her marriage. That has been of solemn and earnest import to me as well. I had a good teacher.

God has given mothers a huge assignment ~ *"Train up a child in the way he [she] should go, and when he is old he will not turn from it."* (Proverbs 22:6). I believe that means we should be living in such a way as to show our children the right way to go. Our job is crucial to their development. We are to not only give care and nurturing, but we comfort them when they are ill or hurt, or frightened. The Lord said, *"As a mother comforts her child, so I will comfort you."* (Isaiah 66:13). I believe God has many of the "motherly" instincts, since he put them into us from the very beginning of time. Jesus even likened Himself to a mother hen in Matthew 23:37, *"...how often I have longed to gather your children together, as a hen gathers her chicks under her wings..."*

I have three daughters. And they are all mothers. I have implored my heavenly Father to help me be a good mother to them, all their years, so that in turn they would know how to be good mothers to their children. Many times they have lamented that it's hard, they thought they were failing, for one reason or another. I have assured them they are good mothers. Because they are. I know some of you who are reading this do not have good memories of your mothers, growing up, or even now. My heart hurts for you. It was God's plan that mothers would teach us all we should know about life. But sometimes, they teach us the wrong things, or nothing at all. If your mother was not there for you in a loving and caring way, please know that your heavenly Father wants to fill in that voided area of your heart. Although you will, as I have, make mistakes along the way, He wants to help you with your own children, teach you to nurture and love them as a mother should. There is no other love like a mother's...except God's. And He said, *"I will love you with an everlasting love..."* (Jeremiah 31:3). We can count on that.

MAY 13

MY MOTHER'S SHOES

Years ago, maybe 20 or so, my mother found her graduation shoes in a closet, a beautiful pair of navy blue soft leather high-heeled pumps with rounded toes, and the little rows of perforations, like men's wing-tip shoes, in perfect condition...She asked me if I'd like them, because we wore the same size, and I said, yes, although they were not really in style then, but maybe someday I would wear them. Well, I put them away, someplace special, and didn't really think about them again until last winter, when I saw the exact pair of shoes in SEARS! The precise style from 1945 had come back! I got excited, and when I came home I began looking for them. Of course, we had moved since I stored them away, and if you're like me, there are boxes of things that you put away in the basement, and don't think about again, for a long time ~ or until you need something that's in them. I couldn't find them. They weren't where I thought they should be. But, I kept looking, and I even prayed that God would help me to remember which box they were in. In a couple of days, I found them. Since I now have arthritis in my feet, I didn't think I could wear them, but I put them on and they felt so comfortable, and I did wear them to church one Sunday, and I had to show them to everyone and tell them the astonishing story about my beautiful 67-year old shoes. My mother's shoes.

Then I got to thinking about what it meant to wear my mother's shoes. Wow. Could I even fill them? (Since Mother's Day has just past, I thought this would be a good time to share my thoughts). My mother has been gone eight and a half years, and I miss her terribly. She was my friend, my confidant, and she loved me fiercely, and I her. Every once in awhile I see a certain trait, or expression, or hear a tone of her voice in myself. What an honor! I love the things she loved. I "inherited" many of her favorite books, and they have become my favorite books. Treasures. She never, ever interfered in my married life, even when my problems broke her heart, but she was always there for me when I came to her ~ about anything. She remembered so many details ~ birthdays of my friend's babies, for goodness sakes! She journaled, loved to write letters, prayed everyday for her children and grandchildren. She was hopelessly devoted and faithful to my dad (who just passed away four years later, and who missed her so painfully). She taught me how to be a wife, a mother, a friend, and about God's great love and mercy. And she showed me, by her own example, how to pray and trust our heavenly Father. She left a legacy of faith for her children that I hope to leave for mine, and theirs. I thank God for her, and pray for a little bit of the wisdom and grace in my own life that she possessed. And I know her spirit is with me as I still walk on this earth.

Not all of us have such wonderful memories of our mothers. I pray that God will bring to mind those special times spent with our moms, and if we don't have mothers, He will provide someone to love and pray for us and our families. And if not, Isaiah 66:13 says: *"As a mother comforts her child, so will I comfort you."* This is God speaking…He can, and wants to, fill any void in our lives. He has in mine!

MAY 14

THE VIRTUOUS WOMAN…

"A wife of noble character, who can find? She is worth far more than rubies. Her husband has full confidence in her and lacks nothing of value. She brings him good, not harm, all the days of her life….she is clothed with strength and dignity; and she can laugh at the days to come. She speaks with wisdom, and faithful instruction is on her tongue…her children arise and call her blessed; her husband also, and he praises her…a woman who fears the Lord is to be praised." Bits and pieces of Proverbs 31 (vs. 10-12, 25-30). I am fascinated by this woman. Can anyone ever really become that perfect? I love this passage, but I fall SO short of this description. Although…I came close once.

I was out garage-sale shopping with one of my married daughters, and she was discussing some of the troubles one of her sisters had had when they were all younger, talking about a discussion they'd had earlier. She was asking her why she was rebellious, and talking about that, then she told me she couldn't understand it because "we had perfect parents!" Well, when they were teenagers, none of them thought that. And, of course, we WEREN'T perfect parents. But they were all grown up now, and looking back, they realized we weren't so bad. Well, this is something I thought I would have to wait all my life to hear, if ever! I was stunned. I didn't comment, but like Mary – I "treasured it in my heart." And I did not let it go to my head, but thanked God that somewhere along the way, I did *something* right. And the first thing that came to my mind was *"her children will arise and call her blessed!"*

I don't think it is an accident that this passage was included in the Bible, at the end of a book of good advice for living…the "epilogue" as it's titled in my Bible. God is the Master Designer and made us women very special. He means for us to be women of strength and dignity, no matter what comes our way, speaking with wisdom, and having kindness as our rule. He wants us to have a sense of spiritual things, victory over temptations, concern for others, a sense of humor and wonder at God's creation. We need to be honest, balance our priorities, and grow in the knowledge of His word. If it were not possible to become this Virtuous Woman, He would not have included this instruction.

We are each responsible for our own learning of God's ways. We may not have the ability or resources to "buy a field" or own a business, but we can be hospitable and care for others, especially our families. Joyce Landorf put it this way, in her book The Fragrance of Beauty: "The woman who has asked Christ into her heart has the same fantastic potential as a rose bush. She may not understand (or look forward to) the losses of the pruning season, but she knows pruning means growth, not death. She looks to God for her strength. She feeds daily and regularly on His words, and her roots grow deep into the soil of His love." We all have this potential. God designed us this way on purpose.

MAY 15

WHEN I WAS A CHILD...

"When I was a child, I talked like a child, I thought like a child, I reasoned like a child. When I became a man, I put childish ways behind me." (I Corinthians 13:11). When we grow in our faith, we lay aside the little Sunday School songs, like The Lord's Army, Jesus Loves Me, Jesus Wants Me for a Sunbeam, Head and Shoulders, Knees and Toes, If You're Happy and You Know It, and many more, and sing the more "mature" Christian songs...Amazing Grace, Showers of Blessing, Higher Ground, Wonderful Grace of Jesus...you get the idea.

And when we grow up, and we have our own children who are in Sunday School, once again we sing those little songs, teaching our youngsters of God's love. But the songs that move our own hearts are the ones found in the hymnal. We grow up, and become "mature Christians." Paul says we should leave the milk behind and go for the meat of God's word. (Hebrews 5:12). He says that sometimes we are slow to learn, and need someone to teach us the elementary truths of God's word. Do we not pay attention? Is there too much going on all around us for us to "get it?" Paul has much to say about this in Hebrews 5 & 6. If we don't keep learning God's word, hiding it in our hearts, living it each day, we'll grow stagnant in our faith. And Jesus Himself said that even though we study the scriptures diligently, if we do not **come to Him**, we will not have eternal life. (John 5:39, 40). But He also said,*"I tell you the truth, anyone who does not receive the kingdom of God like a little child will never enter in."* (Mark 10:15).

So, what is it? Do we stay as children, or do we grow up? Well, of course we must grow and mature in the knowledge of God, but we must come with the simple faith of a child, who comes to Jesus uninhibited by things of the world. Children believe so much easier than adults do. Life is simpler for therm. I think we try to make it more complicated than it really is. Yes, we must find wisdom and understanding, yet believe with the simplicity like that of a child. Jesus said in Matthew 18:4: *"Therefore, whoever humbles himself like this child is the greatest in the kingdom of heaven."* Humility is a particular attribute of children that is naturally lost when we become grown-ups.

We don't need to stay like children insofar as we don't eat the "meat of the word," and don't progress into deeper spiritual knowledge and wisdom, but we do need to come humbly to Him, sincerely trusting His love and instruction, and desiring to please Him with our lives.

MAY 16

MORE ON MOTHERS...

Mother's Day has just past. I had such a sensational day with my children and grandchildren, I can't let it go just yet! Since my three daughters live close to me and I see them all the time, it isn't really unusual that we get together often. But they all made Mother's Day so exceptional I was almost overwhelmed with happiness and blessing. There were five mothers in my home on Sunday, my daughters, my oldest granddaughter, and myself. My youngest daughter had spent countless hours perusing old photos and secretly putting together a wonderful DVD slide show of each of our families, one for each of us. Set to a very moving song, "My Daughter's Eyes," it was a loving gift of enormous worth. It's just a little plastic disk, but there is so much contained in it. Memories, all good. I am blessed. I thought of the verse in Proverbs 31:28... *"Her children rise up and called her blessed..."*They all blessed me abundantly that day. Not only did they bless me, God has blessed me with each one of them, and their families.

There are mothers everywhere ~ at church, the grocery store, the doctor's office, driving down the street...I am aware many of them are not as blessed as I am. Some of them don't know where their children are. Some of them spent Mother's Day alone, weary, scared, empty, insecure, ill, hungry... lonely. For several of us, our mothers are gone...in heaven. My own mother has been gone over eight years now, and I still miss her as much as I did when she first went away. I often wonder if I did enough for her...if I honored her sufficiently. I spoke to her frequently on the phone, always wanting to report something new the children, or grandchildren did or said, or accomplished. I could always ask her anything, any bit of information I needed about anyone in the family, or friends. I knew she always prayed for me, and for my brothers, and our families. I could count on that. She taught me so much. I want to be like her. I am like her, I see it in so many ways. I had a wonderful role-model. Her instruction and nurturing are still with me.

As for Sunday...I cannot forget the warm feeling I had the whole day long, and like Luke 2:19 says of Mary, when the shepherds came to worship the Christ child, *"She treasured up all these things and pondered them in her heart."* My children are a gift from God, precious and treasured, more valuable than gold or silver. And they make me feel that way, too.

MAY 17

HE MADE ME...

"O Lord...You know me. You know when I sit and when I rise; You perceive my thoughts from afar. You discern my going out and my lying down; You are familiar with all my ways." (Psalm 139:1-3). What an awesome thought! With all the babies born each day, all across the world, His eyes are on EACH one, all our lives! I'm so glad I serve a God like this.

We all have something wrong. Something that our bodies are suffering through. Or if not us, we know someone close to us who has an illness of some kind, and we hurt with them. But our bodies are designed by God, our Heavenly Father, who is Sovereign above all other gods. It's not that He made a mistake when He created us, no, not at all. *"So God created man in His own image, in the image of God He created him; male and female He created them."* (Genesis 1:27). We live in an imperfect world. Oh, it WAS perfect when God created it, but sin ruined it. And the foods we eat today are far from the foods God created for our nourishment "in the beginning." So, our bodies suffer with maladies and illnesses that have worsened through the years. What I'm saying is that God understands our infirmities; He took them all on Himself on the Cross. He suffered immeasurably so that when our imperfect lives come to an end, we will indeed be perfect in His presence. Our Father wants to draw us closer to Him, and many times through our suffering, that is what happens ~ where else are we to go? Let's realize that our suffering is temporary, and trust that God sees us in our discomfort and anguish, whether it's for ourselves or others. After all, He made us and He understands our bodies, and our very souls. Praise Him that He is always standing by!

MAY 18

BIRTHDAYS

"Teach us to number our days aright, that we may gain a heart of wisdom." (Psalm 90:12). There it is again, the part about numbering our days. We really don't know how many days/years we will live ~ only God knows that ~ tomorrow is never a sure thing. I am having another birthday, and my family will celebrate with me. I have already received several birthday greeting cards, and a few gifts, from friends. Birthday celebrations make us feel very special. And we are, for God made each one of us an individual, different from any other. *"I praise You because I am fearfully and wonderfully made!"* (Psalm 139:14). I consider each birthday a blessing from God. I have learned to thank Him for each new year, and each new day He gives me to live. The Bible tells us our normal lifespan is 70 years. Some of us will live longer than that, others a much, much shorter period of time. And we never know. We can make plans, but we can't count on them coming to fruition. All we can do is live our lives the best we can for His purposes. James 4:14 says, *"For what is your life? Life is but a vapor that appears for a little time, and then vanishes away."* It's like the steam evaporating from a boiling pot, or your breath vanishing in the cold air, a

wisp of smoke rising from a campfire, or the mist that hangs over a lake in the early morning. Ask God for wisdom every day. *"The wisdom that comes from heaven is first of all pure, then peace-loving, considerate, submissive, full of mercy and good fruit, impartial and sincere."* (James 4:17). I want this kind of wisdom, and each year that I watch my children raise their children, I see them gain a little more wisdom through the trials and relationships, just as I have, and I feel a little wiser for having taught them throughout my own life.

MAY 19

THOUGHTS OF AN OLD WOMAN...

"I will lie down and sleep in peace, for You alone, O Lord, make me dwell in safety." (Psalm 4:8). I was so thankful for my good night's sleep upon waking the other morning, this verse came to my mind. For one thing, the Lord has restored my strength and my health after being sick for about a week, when my nights were restless and listless...it's so good to FEEL good, and sleep well. Then I read back a little bit, well, to the very beginning of the Psalms, to Psalm 1. *"Blessed is the woman [my paraphrase] who does not walk in the counsel of the wicked or stand in the way of sinners, or sit in the seat of mockers. But her delight is in the Lord, and on His law she meditates day and night. She is like a tree planted by streams of water, which yields its fruit in season and whose leaf does not wither. Whatever she does prospers."* (Psalm 1:1-3). I so want to be this woman, and to have such a desire for His word and His law, that it comes to my mind in every situation. I want to have my feet rooted along the lush, green banks, close to the source of that Living Water, the Holy Spirit who can take away anything that does not belong in my life ~ anything selfish or impure. I want to be nourished by His truths, to love easily, and share the joy that He has given me.

I don't know how many more days or years I will have on this earth, none of us does...but I want to make the best of each one He gives me. Each day is a gift, and I am thankful for it. It's true ~ He chose me before He even made the world, to be holy and blameless in His sight. I can't even imagine that He stood there, knowing of each and every child who would be born throughout all time and loving each one already. He had a plan to restore each child to

Himself. I'll never understand His fathomless ways, but I do know He loves me beyond what I can ever imagine.

"Now to Him that is able to do immeasurably more than all we ask or imagine, according to ***His power that is at work within us****, to Him be the glory in the church and in Christ Jesus throughout all generations forever and ever!"* (Ephesians 3:20-21). And that's another thing that is astonishing to me…that the God of the universe has given me, a mere, ordinary woman among 6 billion people, His power just by proclaiming and speaking Jesus' name! I still have so much to learn ~ and I am OLD! I pray for His wisdom to soak up as much as I can in the days I have left, and to share it freely with others.

MAY 20

NO ONE LIKE ME…

"When I was woven together in the depths of the earth, Your eyes saw my unformed body. [And You LOVED me!] *All the days ordained for me were written in Your book before one of them came to be."* (Psalm 139:15-16). Can you tell by now that this is one of my favorite passages in the Bible?

This is my journal entry for yesterday morning… "And Lord, I know, that as I was being formed by Your tender and loving hand, You were designing me, with all my genes and cells, to be just exactly who I am now. You created me *unlike* any other person. My hair, skin, eye color, size, character, and personality are unique to only me. Oh, there are family resemblances, but no one is exactly like me. You are the Awesome Creator! And, what is more amazing to me is that You know where I am every moment, every day. You know and understand my joys, my heartaches, my fears, my struggles. I don't have to utter a single word, and You know the cries of my heart. You see into the very depths of my soul, even when I don't know what's there."

"O Lord, you have searched me and You know me….Before a word is on my tongue, You know it completely, O Lord. You hem me in ~ behind and before; You have laid Your hand upon me. Such knowledge is too wonderful for me, too lofty for me to attain." (Psalm 139:1-6).

"I am so blessed, Lord. I can never, ever give You enough thanks for Who You are to me, and, who I am to You! Savior, Redeemer, Father, Healer,

Defender, King, Lord, my Pillar, Burden Bearer, Restorer…Your names never end."

"Your mercies are new every morning!" (Lamentations 3:23).

MAY 21

THE PURPOSE IN MY LIFE…

"Listen to Me…you whom I have carried since you were conceived, and have carried you since your birth. Even to your old age and gray hairs I am He, I am He who will sustain you. I have made you and I will carry you; I will sustain you and will rescue you." (Isaiah 46:3-4). Have you ever wondered why you were born? Why you exist? I can truly say I have never wondered that. Oh, I'm not saying I knew my purpose in life at an early age, but I just never questioned or doubted God. Really. I guess my upbringing was such that I just took all I was taught as gospel. My parents loved me, and loved God, and I would say confidently they taught me well by their example.

I know that every town I lived in and every person I met was on purpose, even when I was little. My parents' friends made an impact on me. I can still remember some of them from my childhood. Sometimes we lived near relatives, and sometimes we lived far away from them. But we always found people to love. I lamented about going to so many different schools, always being the new girl, not having very many friends, and then leaving those I had made. But I can say that every one of them made some kind of a difference in my life. And I wouldn't trade that experience for anything now.

"Whether you turn to the right or to the left, your ears will hear a voice behind you, saying: 'This is the way; walk in it.'" (Isaiah 30:21). I know that God ordered each day, each step I took, each place we lived. I know that everything I was involved in, Sunday school classes, youth groups, Bible studies, was part of His plan for my life, leading right up to this present moment. I can look back through the years and see how He has guided my steps, how every situation or circumstance I found myself in, no matter how difficult it was at the time, led me to who I am now, in Him. All the things that happened to me, good or unpleasant, or downright

frightening, were part of His plan. He has chosen me to walk down many paths, and I have grown, and been blessed. He has corrected me when I have done it wrong. My heavenly Father has heard all my prayers and seen my difficulties. And best of all, He has forgiven me. He has filled my heart with joy and hope.

Don't get me wrong. My life has not always been rosy or without pain. But I have always had the knowledge that the Lord has been with me.

He said, *"Fear not for I have redeemed you; I have called you by My name; you are Mine. When you pass through the waters, I will be with you; and when you pass through the rivers, they will not sweep over you. When you walk through the fire, the flames will not set you ablaze. For I am the Lord, your God."* (Isaiah 43:1-3). And somehow I knew that. I have been through those rivers, and those fires. I never felt alone. I knew He loved me. He always will.

MAY 22

OLD PEOPLE...

They are everywhere, but mostly on the roads, and at the grocery store, I think. You gotta watch out for them...they drive real slow (some of them shouldn't be driving), and they walk real slow. I went to the grocery store yesterday, and the parking lot was real interesting...SLOW drivers, being very careful, actually, watching so that they won't hit another car. They truly have all the time in the world, they're not in a hurry. Well, there I was, trying to back OUT of my parking space, and three cars were taking their time in my row, either pulling out, or in. One of them came in the wrong way so she was swinging wide to pull into the space next to me correctly. Oh, my goodness. Then another car behind me was not moving (but this was a young person, just smiling) because someone else was in front of them. Then it hit me...well, not literally!...that *I am one of them!* Yes. I'm another year older this week, and I'm sure my hair could not get any whiter. I just had to chuckle. And I had to wonder what I look like to other drivers. *Younger* drivers.

We really do need older people, though. I love to sit and visit with them ~ they have so much knowledge and wisdom, and history. *"Is not wisdom found among the aged? Does not long life bring understanding?"* (Job 12:12). Of course it is, and it does. We grow wiser and more knowledgeable with each year, and each experience, bad or good. The longer we live, the more mistakes we have opportunity to correct. We have occasion for more learning, more loving, more teaching, more forgiving. I find myself reading and learning and writing, and growing, more than I have at any other time of my life. And I realize that it is a waste of time to worry. God is so good to take care of us, and I trust Him more and more. Now and then, younger people don't really want to learn from an older person…they don't want their advice. They just don't realize how valuable their counsel is. So, they learn life's lessons the hard way. But, so did we. David said, in Psalm 71:17-18, *"Since my youth, O God, You have taught me, and to this day I declare Your marvelous deeds. Even when I am old and gray, do not forsake me, O God, till I declare Your power to the next generation, Your might to all who are to come."* And sometimes, we need to just live our lives in front of them, and they will come to us when they realize they are ready to learn from us.

Max Lucado has said, "Your last chapters can be your best. Your final song can be your greatest. It could be that all of your life has prepared you for a grand exit. God's oldest have always been among His choicest." (from *He Still Moves Stones).* I don't want to pass up the opportunity to make a difference in a young person's life, or, another old person's, for that matter. I want to use every day I have to the fullest. And I *want* to get older! Actually, that would mean…more birthdays!

MAY 23

A WOMAN FASHIONED BY GOD…

There are many books written, and Bible studies given on the "Proverbs 31 Woman." There is so much wisdom and good advice given in the book of Proverbs, but I keep going back to chapter 31. I have prayed over the years, many, many times, for God to make me into this woman.

The exhortation begins like this: *"A wife of noble character, who can find? She is worth far more than rubies. Her husband has full confidence in her and lacks nothing of value. She brings him good, not harm, all the days of her life."* The chapter goes on to say how hard she works for her family and her community, but this part is what I love, and it is my prayer every day: *"She is clothed with strength and dignity; she can laugh at the days to come. She speaks with wisdom, and faithful instruction is on her tongue. She watches over the affairs of her household and does not eat the bread of idleness. Her children arise and call her blessed; her husband also, and he praises her. Many women do noble things, but you surpass them all. Charm is deceptive, and beauty is fleeting, but a woman who fears the Lord is to be praised."* (v. 25-30).

I know there are many days we do not FEEL like being this woman of noble character. We want someone else to be noble for us. There are times we feel like we have NO dignity – no one respects us, no one listens. Our strength has run very low. And we have moments when we long for wisdom from someone else, because we simply don't KNOW what to do. We aren't strong enough to be everything for everybody.

But then I remember ~ God made me like this! God made women in such a way that we can withstand the rigors and hardships of life. He made us to be the moms and the wives because we are strong, yet tender and gentle. But He also made us to need Him. And without Him, all of these responsibilities become too much for us, and sometimes the task is impossible.

I am so glad He made me a woman, and that He has told me He will always be there to help me through whatever my family and I must face each day. And the last verse (v. 31) of Proverbs 31 says *"Give her the reward she has earned..."* That will make it all worth it!

MAY 24

HERE BY ACCIDENT?

My husband's mother had been told after the birth of her second child, she should never have any more children ~ it could be dangerous to her health. So the doctors performed a tubal ligation to alleviate this risk. Ten years later my husband was born. So, my husband was always (jokingly, I'm sure) referred to as an "accident" or their "oops" child. Naturally, hearing these kinds of comments as he was growing up, he began to feel deep inside that he hadn't been wanted...certainly not planned. His birth was a mistake. This of course caused him to go through life with a "chip" on his shoulder, and an inferior impression of himself. Oh, his parents loved him, they prayed for him, and they wanted all the best for him. They brought him up in the church and *"trained him up in the way he should go."* But he still had that gnawing feeling that he wasn't really wanted. To this day, whenever something doesn't go just right, or he perceives someone may not like him, it accelerates his feelings of inadequacy. How sad to have lived one's whole life feeling unwanted, even by loving family members.

In Rick Warren's book, The Purpose Driven Life, his second chapter is entitled "You are Not an Accident." He says, "God…planned the days of your life in advance, choosing the exact time of your birth and death…He never does anything accidentally, and He never makes mistakes. We are the focus of His love and the most valuable of all His creation." On the first page, in the dedication, Mr. Warren quotes this:*"It's in Christ that we find out who we are and what we are living for. Long before we first heard of Christ…He had His eye on us, had designs on us for glorious living, part of the overall purpose He is working out in everything and everyone."*(Ephesians 1:11 Msg). I was so glad to read this excerpt to my husband.

I have spent much of my married life lovingly reminding my husband, by both words and deeds of acceptance, that his birth was not a mistake, but it was indeed a *miracle.* I'm still not sure that he sees it as that. His feelings are deep and have been life-long. But he trusts our Lord, and I pray that God will bestow a certain measure of grace on him, and he will begin to realize his worth in God's eyes, and the talents he has as God-given. God has blessed him with wonderful skills in carpentry, and a beautiful singing voice, which he loves to use in praises to our Lord. I pray he will soon realize what is God's purpose for his life. We all have a specific purpose in life, a reason we were born, though some may not yet be aware of that objective. Ask God to show you His purpose for your life. Study His word every day. We are the "tools in His hands, to be used for His good purposes." And repeating one of my favorite verses, from Jeremiah 29:11, *"For I know the plans I have for you, declares the Lord, plans to prosper you and not to harm you, plans to give you a hope and a future."* God makes no mistakes!

MAY 25

HUMMINGBIRDS – LITTLE GIFTS FROM GOD…

I've learned there are over three hundred different species of hummingbirds. With their unbelievable fast wing-beats, 1260 per minute in fact, and a long tongue that can lick their food up to 13 licks per second, they are a fascinating little creature. And because of their fast heartbeat and breathing rate, they need an enormous amount of food each day. Many species seem very gentle and peace-loving, but others are very territorial, and will chase away not only other hummers, but larger birds as well, from their nesting areas or food. I've read that they come to rely on feeders and food supplies year after year, and if these are no longer available, they could die. That's why they come back to our feeders each summer ~ they seem to remember where each one is. They have incredible endurance and stamina, but they also know when they need to rest, and will go into a deep sleep for up to 12 hours and replenish their strength.

These tiny creatures are one of God's many miracles and a good example of evidence that God is Creator. Job 12:7 says, *"But ask the animals and they will teach you, or the birds of the air, and they will tell you…"* and verse 9: *"Which of all these does not know that the hand of the Lord has done this?"* The evidence is everywhere, from the loudest thunder, brightest lightning, farthest star, and the tiniest hummingbird. I can just imagine God's huge Creator-hand forming that tiny little bird, with its long bill & tongue, delicate wings that can move faster than any others, its migratory instincts. And they can hover by flapping their wings in a figure-8 pattern. Who but our God could have thought of such a thing? It is a remarkable little miracle.

And if God spent the time on these incredibly delicate little birds, how much more has He spent on us, His masterpiece? Sure, the hummingbirds have very intricate little systems, and everything works in cooperation with all the parts. But humans have a soul, we think and love and hurt and reason, unlike any other creature. If there is ever a time when you are feeling insignificant, think of all He has made, and how complex the universe is, how intricate we are. *"And let everything that has breath praise the Lord!"* (Psalm 150:6).

MAY 26

REPRIMAND…

As I've said before, I teach a Sunday School class of first and second graders ~ such a sweet age…sometimes! In the almost 15 years I have taught the class, I've had at least one unruly child, typically a boy, each year. We have had many foster children who have attended our church with one or two foster families, and they have been, at best, difficult at times. But I love these children, and so I keep on teaching them. For the most part they love and take part in the stories and songs. We take the full two years learning the books of the Bible in a fun song, and the Lord's Prayer, and even the older ones I've taught previously will stop in to say, or sing, these with us occasionally.

During the past year, I had six to seven girls and one boy in my class. This sweet-tempered boy has pretty much held his own with the girls, and we have made him feel special. There was an incident one Sunday, however, where one of the most amiable girls humiliated him in front of the rest and when I arrived in the classroom, he was sitting in the corner crying. The little girl sweetly apologized, we talked about it, recalling all the lessons we have had concerning how we treat each other, and I finally had to take him to his father's class because he couldn't be consoled, didn't want to stay. And the hard part was calling the girl's mother, because she really isn't a bad or troublesome girl.

The memory verse we'd been learning for that past few weeks is Proverbs 20:11, *"Even a child is known by his actions, by whether his conduct is pure and right."* I had defined the word "conduct" and we had discussed at length exactly what this verse means. The curriculum during the quarter also included several stories about young people who have done the right thing and how God honored their actions.

Found this in the Bible: 2 Timothy 4:2 says: *"Preach the Word, be prepared in season and out of season; correct,* ***rebuke*** *and encourage ~ with great patience and careful instruction."* I have always tried to teach in this manner. Our heavenly Father gave us the best example of this discipline...when Adam and Eve sinned, he drove them out of the Garden and basically excommunicated them. Sodom was forewarned of destruction if they didn't clean up their act. They didn't, and God destroyed the entire city. Jonah disobeyed God and made big trouble for himself as he became dinner for a huge fish. Jesus even rebuked Satan when a boy was demon-possessed. Jesus rebuked the wind, as well, and the storm, Peter, the fig tree, and even His own mother. But Jesus also said, at the end of His holy Book of books, *"Those whom I love, I* ***rebuke*** *and discipline. So be earnest, and repent."* (Rev. 3:19). As parents, we know we have needed to discipline our children from time to time. It's a big job keeping them on the straight and narrow. And it's heart-breaking when they choose to go their own way. Imagine how hard it is for God to take care of His children. All of us. And how heart-breaking it must be for Him that we keep on in our sin.

The Good Book is full of guidelines and commands to ensure that we lead a godly life, and if we don't follow those rules and laws, we get into trouble

~ in traffic, in the classroom, financially, in relationships, and with the law. A Proverb repeats, *"Listen to My instruction and be wise; do not ignore it."* (8:33). That's what I try to teach my 6- and 7-year olds. And that's what God tries to teach us through His Living Word. Sometimes we need to be corrected. We'll talk about that another time…

MAY 27

ROOTS…

Just this spring I have noticed some little red shoots coming up through my lawn, and I am suspicious that these may be from my two lovely quaking aspen trees. I planted these trees at least eight years ago along the back fence, along with some Austrian willows, which all grew very fast and are beautiful trees. Our neighbor sadly had to take out the aspens in his yard last year because they were sending up shoots all over his lawn. I thought we were just lucky, although we have had many problems from the surface roots of the willows. So, now I am dismayed at what may become of my trees, ALL of them in our back yard. We have already had to remove two of them because their roots invaded the neighbor's yard next door ~ under the fence! Apparently these kind of trees will have shallow roots if their moisture supply isn't deep enough.

I've told this story before ~ for several years, while I was growing up, my family moved quite often, and I was forced to change schools many times, leaving what few friends I had behind, and facing the task of making new friends in new neighborhoods and schools. I often felt that I didn't have any roots. Any real place I could call home, any real lasting friendships. Then in my junior year of high school, we returned "home" to Idaho after my dad's retirement from the Navy, and I found that I did indeed have roots, right here at home. I became reacquainted with many friends I had when I was younger. And with the loving Christian upbringing of my parents, I realized I had these roots all along. I was determined my own children would have the roots I didn't think I had, and they have grown up in the same town, same school district, all their lives. So have their children. And we have rooted them also, in Christian upbringing as both our parents did with us.

In the parable of the sower, we read about seeds that were scattered on different kinds of soil…rocky places, weeds, pathways…just as in some of the ways we receive God's word: *"The one who received the seed that fell on rocky places is the man who hears the word and at once receives it with joy. But since he has no* ***root****, he lasts only a short time. When trouble or persecution comes because of the word, he quickly falls away."*(Matt. 13:20-21). We must make sure that our faith is strong, and our roots go deep into God's word. *"But his delight is in the law of the Lord, and on His law he meditates day and night. He is like a tree planted by streams of water, which yields its fruit in season and whose leaf does not wither…"* (Psalm 1:2-3). Daily reading and meditating on God's word is like drinking freely of the water that is offered to us. Living Water. *"And I pray that you, being rooted and established in love, may have the power together with all the saints, to grasp how wide and long and high and deep is the love of Christ, and to know this love that surpasses knowledge ~ that you may be filled to the measure of all the fullness of God."* (Ephesians 3:17-19). The only way to do this is to make sure that you have put down deep roots beside the streams of Living Water!

MAY 28

NO GOD, NO PEACE ~ KNOW GOD, KNOW PEACE…

Jeremiah 7:23 says, "…*but I gave them this command: Obey Me and I will be your God and you will be My people. Walk in the ways I command you, that it may go well with you.*"These are the words that God sent Jeremiah to speak to the people of Israel when they had turned their backs on Him. In fact, the book of Jeremiah is full of God's warning and pleading to the Israelites to turn back to Him. And yet, *"they did not listen or pay attention; instead they followed the stubborn inclinations of their evil hearts."* (vs. 24). Does this sound like us today? "We the People" have strayed so far away from God's grace, how can we expect to have peace of our own making, when it is sought in anger and violence, terror and greed?

When you think of peace, what comes to mind? Is it a gurgling brook beside a beautiful meadow in which you are lying, gazing up at the clouds? Or is it late at night when all the kids are finally in bed asleep and all is quiet in the house? Do you think peace is the absence of war? The cat curled up and purring beside the fireplace? Is peace what you have when all your bills are paid and there is money left over? Peace is defined as "freedom from disagreement or disorder; harmony; absence of mental conflict; serenity; calm; quiet…" But what about in the middle of a storm, or in the midst of conflict? Can we have peace then, really?

Jesus said, *"Peace I leave with you; My peace I give you. I do NOT give to you as the world gives. Do not let your hearts be troubled and do not be afraid."* (John 14:27). When our Savior uttered these words to His disciples, they were troubled and feared the future. They were not feeling peace. But Paul assured the church that *"…the peace of God, which transcends ALL understanding, will guard your hearts and your minds in Christ Jesus."*(Phil. 4:7). This would be a peace that is unnatural, at best. Peace in the midst of the storm. Like when He rebuked the waves that were tossing the tiny fishing boat all around on the sea ~ *"Peace!"* Peace when you are facing a huge and overwhelming medical diagnosis. Peace when the in-laws are coming over for dinner. Peace on your first day at a new job. God can give it in every situation. Not only is it the absence of conflict between people, it is the deep assurance we can have in our hearts that our Sovereign God who made the universe is in control in our lives. He alone is the God of Peace.

MAY 29

LETTERS TO THE EDITOR…

Do you ever read the Letters to the Editor? I do. And sometimes I write them. We write letters to express our opinion, or complaints, our empathy, our thanks, for some item that is public or we feel it needs to be. These letters are usually about something we are deeply concerned about ~ politics is a biggie, or animal rights, or we are simply adding our vote to someone else's concern. It may be to inform the public of some injustice that has been done, or thank an unknown hero…someone who came to the rescue in a difficult situation. The editor cannot usually DO anything about that which concerns us, except to let the public know about our feelings. And sometimes the letter we write doesn't get published in time to make any kind of an impact, and we are disappointed, watching for it, not seeing it. When we do finally see our letter, sometimes we are a little embarrassed, and we wish we hadn't written what we did in haste. But it's too late. It has been said. Occasionally another reader will answer our concern in their own letter, or at least support us in our cause.

Our prayers are kind of like Letters to the Editor. We voice our complaints, our concerns, our suggestions, to the heavenly Father, who hears us. He doesn't make them public, and He actually CAN do something about them, even if only to give us peace in our time of need. Jeremiah 33:2-3 says, *"This is what the Lord says, He who made the earth, the Lord who formed it and established it ~ the Lord is His name: 'Call to Me and I will answer you, and tell you great and unsearchable things you do not know.'"* See, this is the difference between the editor, and the Father. The editor hears (reads) our petitions, but he has no power to change our situation. Our heavenly Father, the God of the universe, hears our every cry, or whisper or whimper, and He not only hears us, He cares and will answer. He may not answer right away, but His timing will be perfect, and there is a lesson in the waiting. He has the sovereign power to answer every prayer, no matter how little and insignificant it seems, or how huge it may be to us... Our prayers mean something to Him, and our words are not wasted. And He actually knows our need before we even ask. He cares. We need never be embarrassed about what we say to Him. He knows our heart. Let's remember to always thank Him as well, for answered prayer, and for the seemingly "unanswered" prayers. But, let us never fail to ask. Only God can see our future and in His infinite wisdom and perfect time, He will answer.

MAY 30

GRANDCHILDREN...

Oh, what a blessing these little ones are! And what an awesome responsibility. As we watch our own children struggle to raise their offspring, making the same mistakes along the way that we did, we want very much to tell them the things NOT to do. It's like another chance for us at parenting ~ a fresh new generation. Sometimes our parent-children will ask us for advice. I try not to give it unless they ask. They will lament to us when things don't go right. And sometimes they don't want our input. They do collaborate with other new parents their own age, who are going through the same troubles.

I couldn't imagine raising children without God's help. I spent a lot of time in prayer for my children, even when they were tiny, even before they were born. And especially when they began to grow up. We had all our children dedicated in church soon after their birth, and somehow I must have thought that would insure that they would grow up to be perfect children, walking with the Lord. It actually just got harder and harder. And those three sweet little girls are now raising their own children, after dedicating them all in church, soon after their birth…some situations are different than they were for me, but there are still struggles. The book of Proverbs offers some hope to parents. Prov. 19:18 says, "*Discipline your son, for in that there is hope…*" And the ever-famous and well-used Proverbs 22:6: "*Train a child in the way he should go, and when he is old he will not turn from it.*" I've often asked, "How old??"

When my grandchildren (some of them) grew up, I recognized my children, their mothers, in them. And I believe I recognize myself in my girls. They are just younger versions of ME! But, in spite of the feelings at times that I had failed as a parent, I must have done some things right, because my sweet girls, all now in their 30's, have risen up many times and called me blessed! And I truly am! Mother's Day and my birthday have recently passed, and they did what they could to make me feel very special and honored. Actually, I find that they don't wait for a special occasion to show their love to me. And, my grandchildren are learning to follow suit. Psalm 71:17-18, says, and I repeat, "*Since my youth, O God, You have taught me, and to this day I declare Your marvelous deeds. Even when I am old and gray, do not forsake me O God, till I declare Your power to the next generation, Your might to all who are to come.*" I showed my children that prayer is very important with every stage of our lives, and they, in turn, are teaching their own children the same thing. I am truly blessed. My kids aren't perfect. My goodness, I know I wasn't perfect, either…oh, that is another part of the story ~ I saw my own parents also praying and teaching me and my siblings the very same things about God and His mercy. You see what David was saying about generations? And I have yet another generation beginning with my 3-year old great-granddaughter! Our work, and joy, never ends.

There was a song when I was little, "Be Careful Little Eyes What You See…" and that song has recently been incorporated into a Christian song entitled "Slow Fade" which talks about being careful where we let our feet and our eyes and our ears go, about gray areas, and sin, and staying close to the Father…

So, just because our kids are grown and raising their own kids, that doesn't mean our work is done. We need to pray more than ever for those precious young souls, no matter how young they are. Pray for these new, and not-so-new parents which are our children. Jesus said, "*Let the children come to me… for the kingdom of God belongs to such as these.*" (Luke 18:16). Our children and grandchildren are freshest from the hand of God. They are a gift. Be thankful for them, spend lots of time with them, teach them, and never stop praying for them.

MAY 31

I AM LOVED...

So, a few weeks ago I celebrated another birthday...I won't say which one, but the numbers are getting pretty high! It was quite a week...I think I celebrated almost every day. Monday I had much needed massage therapy. Tuesday was to be lunch with a girlfriend, whose birthday is the week prior, and though we've always celebrated it together with lunch, she was ill and we had to postpone that one. Wednesday (the actual day of my birthday) I was fortunate to get together with four friends I attended high school with *eons* ago. That was really special. That evening my family surprised me at a church dinner with a cake, and all the grandkids were there too. And after the dinner, Bible study class had goodies and a card for my day. Thursday, cake and a card at another Bible study, and Friday lunch with two more girlfriends. Then Monday, my beloved brother took me for coffee and a bagel early in the morning. I believe we are finally done with the celebration.

All of this attention makes me feel very special. In fact, it is affirmation that I am very much loved. Many greetings to me that week spoke of love and best wishes, conveying the gift of friendship, desiring for me a year full of good health, and much joy and promise. Some sentiments were humorous, some short and sweet, while others were deep and profound. All were loving.

But the greatest message of love for me is sent from my Savior. His word is like a big birthday card full of loving messages to me. I'm sure He was thinking of me when He created the world (John 17:24). I know He saw me as I was growing inside my mother's womb (Psalm 139). He sees me wherever I am and sends His angels to surround me and protect me (Psalm 91:11). He knows what's in my heart (Psalm 19:14). He sees me when I am hurting (Job 5:18). He is with me when I am alone (Hebrews 13:5). He shows me the right way to go (Psalm 25:4). There is no greater love than that of my Savior (John 15:13). He is the God of Love (Psalm 117:2). Even if I had no friends, and if no one remembered my special days, or greeted me lovingly, He would still be right beside me.

But I am one of those people who is blessed beyond measure. I have the love of my family and friends, and best of all, the unfailing love of my heavenly Father. If I had nothing else, that is enough.

JUNE 1

WANT GOD'S POWER...?

"I pray also that the eyes of your heart may be enlightened in order that you may know the hope to which He has called you, the riches of His glorious inheritance in the saints, and His incomparably great power for us who believe. That power is like the working of His mighty strength, which He exerted in Christ when He raised Him from the dead." (Ephesians 1:18-20). Can you believe that? We, as believers, can have the same power God used when He raised Jesus from the grave! That is utterly amazing! How can that be? Well, Paul wanted his hearers to be flooded with light in their inner beings, as revealed by God Himself. Paul wanted them to know this unsurpassed power. But also that it is not our power, but His. We cannot accomplish what He calls us to do in ourselves, but actually HE will accomplish it.

This is the resurrection power we can experience, but He is the one who demonstrates it in and through us, the miracle of His resurrection power ~ *"for us who believe."* (v. 19). To realize this power is, of course, to be willing to obey what He says, what He has called us to do...the loving, and forgiving, caring for the unlovely, trusting Him like a little child. That doesn't seem so hard....does it? Sometimes it is impossible! When someone hurts us deeply, when circumstances are out of our control and make our lives miserable, when we're lost and confused and don't know which way to go, when all we want to do is lash out at someone who has wronged us, when we're in so deep we don't think we can ever get ourselves out...this is exactly when God's power can be made visible in our lives. When we are at our weakest. His promise to us is this, *"My grace is sufficient for you, my power is made perfect in weakness."* (2 Corinthians 12:9). When we say "I can't!" God says, "I can!" The secret is in the believing!

JUNE 2

THE LORD'S TEMPLE...

When I was young I heard a pastor say that our bodies are the Lord's temple and we should take care of them, what we do with them, what we put into them. I have always remembered that. Recently I was reading a devotional by Mike Wolff in which he referred to the "city of God's holiness" which is not built by human hands, but is indeed in our very hearts. He went on to say that "God's holy habitat is the joy of all who live by faith." Imagine! That "mighty fortress" and "bulwark never failing" is within our own spirit. He has made our hearts and souls His domain. I don't have to go looking for Him, or "wait for the day" when I will bodily be in that city, but I can know beyond a doubt that He is in me right now. *"Do you not know that you are a temple of God and that the Spirit of God dwells in you?"* (1 Corinthians 6:19). I love the freedom of not having to make an appointment to enter into the "holy of holies," but I can walk right into His presence any time, any day. In fact, His presence is right with me all the time. He promised in Hebrews 5:5, *"Never will I leave you; never will I forsake you."* Did you see that? "NEVER." He will never leave us to flounder on our own, to find our own way, or to figure out our own solution. Oh, but many of us choose to do just that, don't we?

It doesn't make sense NOT to trust God. What He says in His word, He will do. I cannot imagine getting to this point in time without Him, without His intervention in my life, keeping me from harm and disaster. I have never had any reason not to trust God. Many times my life has not gone the way I had hoped it would, many things happened along the way that I didn't plan on or want, but I never blamed God, and I never stopped trusting Him. What else would I do? He did not promise that we would have a smooth path with no troubles if we trusted in Him. Jesus said, *"In this world you will have trouble. But take heart! I have overcome the world!"* (John 16:33). And since He lives right here in us, in our temples, we can be overcomers too, in every way. We have instantaneous access to His power since he resides deep within us. What a thought! "*Christ in you, the hope of glory!"* (Paul, Col. 1:27). It is way beyond my feeble understanding. The Holy of Holies, right inside of me. Turn your back on the world and walk around in your temple. When you seek Him, you will find Him. He's there.

JUNE 3

A FAITHFUL FRIEND...

I just finished watching the movie "Bolt" with my 6-year-old granddaughters. It's a cute animated movie about a little girl and her dog…a heart-gripper. Many movies have been made about dogs, the "faithful friend" and "man's best friend," etc., ie. Old Yeller, Lassie, Benji, Beethoven, Lady and the Tramp, Homeward Bound, Eight Below, just to name a few of the top ones. No doubt we have seen at least a few of them over the years. They are nearly always heartwarming stories about the relationship and bond between a dog, or dogs, and their owner/master, mostly involving children. Many true-life stories about dogs show them to be incredibly faithful to their people. They rescue them, listen endlessly to them, adore them, follow them everywhere. Here's an interesting quote I found:

"The one absolutely unselfish friend that humans can have in this selfish world, the one that never deserts them, the one that never proves ungrateful or treacherous is their dog."

~George Graham Vest, Senator of Missouri, 1855

But there is another Friend, even more faithful and dependable than the canine He created… *"there is a friend that sticks closer than a brother."* (Proverbs 18:24). He's always beside us and never lets go of our hand. He leads us through danger and darkness, and He is our constant companion ~ the "Hound of Heaven.**" This Friend is always listening, always ready to forgive. *"Abraham believed God, and it was credited to him as righteousness, and he was called God's friend."* (James 2:23). There are songs we have sung like "What a Friend We Have in Jesus," "He Calls Me Friend" (newer), "I Just Keep Trusting My Lord" (includes the phrase ~ "He's a faithful Friend, such a faithful Friend, I can count on Him to the very end…") This Friend, Jesus, wants to be our BEST Friend. He bore our sins and griefs, takes our pain, heals our illnesses, gives us peace.

I love having friends, and I am blessed to have many. Two of them are the four-legged kind, in fact, I know others (dogs) I can call my friends. But if I had no other friend in the wide world, I know I could count on Jesus to always be there. He said *"I will never leave you nor forsake you."* (Joshua 1:5). There is no sweeter or faithful friend…

JUNE 4

TEARS...

Most of us shed a tear or two almost every day, whether tears of pain, or joy, or frustration, anger, indignation at a wrong done to someone else, relief...tears are meant to cleanse and lubricate our eyes. It's quite an intricate system. We are the only mammals to shed tears of emotion. Many things trigger our tears. I've read a letter with good, or bad, news and cried, I've cried in movies or books that have an especially sad or happy part. There are songs written about tears. It's been said, in a poem or song, I believe, that God saves our tears in a bottle. It's also been said that our tears fill the "crystal sea" in heaven. I haven't found anything talking about this in the Bible, but it's possible. Our tears are important to our Father. Isaiah 25:8 says, *"The Sovereign Lord will wipe away the tears from all faces."* I believe these are the tears of pain, and sorrow, and anguish, because in heaven those things will not exist. But tears are good for the soul. They break down barriers that we have built and give us healing and freedom as well.

Children shed a lot of tears, and we as parents take them into our arms and cuddle them and wipe their tears, kiss their boo-boos and make it all better. I like to picture our heavenly Father doing the same thing. He comforts us by taking us into His big strong arms and speaking peace to us.

Then there is the story of the sinful woman who "anointed" Jesus with her tears... *"When a woman who had lived a sinful life in that town learned that Jesus was eating at the Pharisee's house, she brought an alabaster jar of perfume, and as she stood behind Him at His feet weeping, she began to wet His feet with her tears. Then she wiped them with her hair, kissed them and poured perfume on them."* (Luke 7:37, 38). I'm sure this woman had listened to at least part of Jesus' message that day, and she was very repentant, and her seeking moved her to tears at His presence. Jesus was touched. Of course, Jesus knew that those gathered around were judging the woman as they watched the scene, and He began to teach them about judging, and love. A beautiful demonstration.

And when this life is over, Revelation 21:4 tells us we will go to a place where *"There will be no more death or mourning or crying or pain, for the old order of things has passed away...He will wipe every tear from our eyes."*

JUNE 5

TIME FOR WEDDINGS...

I had not seen my niece in a long time, although we live in the same town. But last night I was delighted when she rang my doorbell to hand-deliver an invitation to her Bridal shower. And to return some books she had borrowed years ago! She is so excited about her shower and upcoming wedding ~ she will be a June Bride. We talked about the theme of her shower, a tea party (she knew I would love that), and that her maid of honor and herself had shopped thrift stores for teacups for each guest. She talked about where her wedding will be, the counseling she and her fiance' have had, the two little flower girls (my 7-year-old granddaughters, who will be perfect since they are both very prissy girls), and how proud of her fiance' she is ~ they have had a long engagement and she has carefully considered this marriage for a couple of years. She seems very level-headed and calm about the whole affair!

The Bible talks about another wedding or two...there was the wedding in Cana where Jesus turned the water into wine, which was Jesus' first recorded miracle. *"...the master of the banquet tasted the water which had been turned into wine...then he called the bridegroom over, and said...you have saved the best until now."* (John 2:9-10). There is the parable of the ten virgins (or brides), waiting for the bridegroom, and half of them were not ready...their lamps had run out of oil but they didn't bother getting more for fear of missing the signal that the bridegroom had come. So they waited with the rest, but when *"the cry rang out: 'Here's the bridegroom! Come out to meet Him!"* (Mt. 25:6), the virgins who ran out of oil begged the others to share, but they couldn't, because they would run out too, if they shared. And of course, while the five foolish virgins were away purchasing more oil, he came and the others went into the wedding feast, *"and the door was shut."* (v.10).

The grandest wedding of all time is coming ~ the wedding between Christ and His church. That is the one I'm looking forward to! *"Let us rejoice and be glad and give Him glory! For the wedding of the Lamb has come, and His bride has made herself ready."* (Rev. 19:7). We are Christ's bride, ladies. We who have been faithful and made ourselves ready, wearing the fine white linens He has given us to wear (v. 8). And the wedding banquet? Oh my goodness...not like ANY church potluck we have ever known. There will be food we've never dreamed about, or even heard of, but we will love each morsel! And although there will be a multitude, this banquet table will stretch all across heaven and there will be room for everyone. I don't want to miss it! Will you be ready? Don't wait until it is too late to prepare, and the gates are shut. The invitation has been sent!

JUNE 6

FRUIT...

"I am the Vine, you are the branches. Whoever remains in Me and I in him will bear much fruit, because without Me you can do nothing. Anyone who does not remain in Me will be thrown out like a branch and wither; people will gather them and throw them into a fire and they will be burned. If you remain in Me and My words remain in you, ask for whatever you want and it will be done for you. By this is My Father glorified, that you bear much fruit and become My disciples." (John 15: 5-8).

Jesus spent a lot of time talking to His disciples about fruit, and the relationship between the vine and the branches. Andrew Murray says, in his book THE TRUE VINE, "There is the lesson of perfect conformity. The branch is exactly like the vine in every aspect ~ the same nature, the same life, the same place, the same work. In all this they are inseparably one. And so the believer needs to know that he is partaker of the divine nature, and has the very nature and spirit of Christ in him, and that his one calling is to yield himself to a perfect conformity to Christ." You notice, he didn't say to strive on our own to become perfect as Christ is, but to yield ourselves to the conformity to Christ. The Father will do it. When we came to Christ, we became part of the True Vine, and essentially our purpose in this is to bear fruit. Our first aim every day should be to know how Christ desires to carry out His purpose in us. So, we must learn how to be branches, hooked up to the nourishment of the main Vine, being filled with His Spirit every day. And we must ask that God Himself show us what may be lacking in the measure or character of the fruit we bear.

This brings us to the fruit...and just what IS the fruit? Galations 5:22 says ... *"the fruit of the Spirit is love, joy, peace, patience, kindness, goodness, faithfulness, gentleness and self-control."* Are we lacking in any one of these portions of the fruit He wants us to bear? The Vinedresser, or Husbandman, our heavenly Father, must cleanse and prune away anything that is not pleasing or that will hinder us from producing the fruit He requires from us. It is usually through affliction that we are brought closer to Him. As Paul recorded God's words, *"My strength is made perfect in weakness."* (2 Cor. 12:9).

My friend, and favorite author, Bodie Thoene said, just recently, "What we do today is not just for this day, but we are meant to bear fruit which will bless and edify generations yet unborn." We are leaving a legacy for our children and our grandchildren, and undoubtedly for others outside our families who rely on us and watch our lives, and who may have no other example than the one which we show them.

Lord, I pray that our fruit-bearing will be pleasing in Your sight, and You will water and nurture it for their sake and for Your glory. God, You are the Lord of our future, and of theirs. I pray each one will grasp that truth, and rely on it throughout their lives, and teach it to their children, generation after generation. Amen.

JUNE 7

AS SHINING STARS...

I love sharing in another person's accomplishments and successes. Last night my second granddaughter, Errin, graduated from high school, with double honors. She was salutatorian of her class, and of course, she gave a brilliant speech. It meant so much to me, I told her, what she said, that at the end of the ceremony, she handed her speech to me. I have carefully folded it and placed it into my journal. Valuable information. Here is a girl who beat the odds that were against her. Her parents were divorced when she was little, and even at that age (6) she began to form bitterness without really knowing it. Do we really know what goes through a little child's mind when their whole world is turned upside down like that? Not unless we've been there ourselves. So, after many years of struggles with depression, anger and hurt, this precious and beautiful girl came forth like a shining star.

Errin had always toiled pitifully in school, so since junior high school, she enrolled in our alternative school program, which is a rescue for many students who can't seem to make it in the public school system. This has been such a successful project here in our city, that Reader's Digest did a story on it several years ago. My oldest daughter is an alumni of our project school, as is our oldest granddaughter. Because of this particular school, and the foresight of the originator and administrator of the school, many kids who would otherwise be on the streets, have a chance to earn a diploma, scholarships, and degrees and certificates of many kinds. These students are not only taught academics, but life skills as well. The classes are small, so the students can get the attention and individual help they need. Each instructor and office staff is gifted with patience and encouragement for the students, some of whom Project is their final hope at gaining an education and getting their diploma. As my granddaughter said in her speech, it is a "saving grace."

So, as many thousands of young people are graduating this week across the nation, whether from high school or college, or vocational school, or kindergarten, we need to remember to pray for them. Each accomplishment is a milestone in their lives. We must remind ourselves to pray for and encourage them every day. It's important. I'm convinced that prayer is what helped Errin to get to this point in her life. There were many times when she wanted to just give up. Paul said to the Philippians in 2:14, *"Do everything without complaining or arguing, so that you may become blameless and pure, children of God without fault in a crooked and depraved generation, in which you* ***shine like stars*** *in the universe."* Well, Errin did her share of complaining and arguing all right, but this girl overcame many difficulties in her life because of the prayers and encouragement of family, pastors, and friends, and came out shining. And she has hope for a bright future.

JUNE 8

GRADUATION DAY...

What a moment! What a thrill! This is the week in our town where three public high schools and at least that many Christian or private schools are holding their graduation ceremonies. It's the commencement exercise where we receive our diploma or degree as a reward for all of our hard work and perseverance. I remember when we attended our first granddaughter's graduation from high school. She was so beautiful and proud, and excited and nervous! And we were proud, too. Some kids breeze through school and others have a real struggle. Jessica has had a bit of a struggle. Her mom and dad were divorced when she was eight and her sister was six. The girls went through some really rough spots. Thank goodness for our big loving and supporting close-knit family, and our alternative high schools who take in these kids who would otherwise fall through the cracks, and believe me, they nurture and love them through it. They don't just learn academics, they learn how to cope with the uncertainties of life. Several of the girls have babies, but there is a wonderful child care class offered, where the students care for the children as they attend the class for credit....the classmates and teachers are the only family some of these students have. We are leaving our kids and grandkids a heritage. And I'm grateful we have a loving heavenly Father to lead and guide us.

Well, life is like this...and the last day we live is our graduation day. We must study and persevere to get ourselves ready for that final commencement exercise. Heaven ~ our reward. Hebrews 12:1 says *"Therefore, since we are surrounded by such a great cloud of witnesses, let us throw off everything that hinders and the sin that so easily entangles, and let us run with perseverance the race marked out for us."*

Just as we cheered for each graduate who walked across the stage, our loved ones and the angels will be rejoicing when we "graduate" into our final home in heaven, on our Graduation Day! "*Rejoice and be glad, for great is your reward in heaven.*" (Matt. 5:12).

JUNE 9

STRENGTH IN MY WEAKNESS...

"My grace is sufficient for you, for my power is made perfect in weakness. Therefore I will boast all the more gladly about my weaknesses, so that Christ's power may rest on me." (2 Corinthians 12:9)

I have heard this verse all my life, but I didn't really understand the true meaning of it until I was well into my adult life. And, of course, the older I get, the weaker I become ~ in my own strength, that is. And the more I learn to rely on God's strength, I have seen so many things come to fruition that never could have been done if I tried to do them on my own, with my own power. A lot of them have to do with relationships. Others are seemingly impossible tasks...you know, the "keep on keeping on" part of everyday life. That's where I am right now. My body is getting frail, and lots of times all I feel like doing it sitting and doing nothing. I can't get motivated on my own. But deep down I know that God will give me the concentration and the might to overcome the "poor me" mentality.

When I was at my worst, physically, I still went to work every day. I was on time, and I completed all my work for the day. Now that I'm retired, I'm keeping even busier. And just recently I began a job I never thought I'd be able to do...of course, it was only my first day as a substitute teacher. And they started me out in a middle school...oh, my, that age can have such attitudes. But looking back now, I can see that the day went very well...and of course the reason for that is that God strengthened me for the task ~ I didn't have much time to think about it ~ one hour after the call, I was on site. But as the classes changed, and a new group of students shuffled in for the hour, I remained friendly throughout the day, even as exhaustion came over me in the afternoon, and I gave praise to my Father for giving me the fortitude to get through it with smiles on my face. *"I can do ALL things through Christ who strengthens me."* (Philippians 4:13). Oh, what a feeling!

JUNE 10

IRONMAN...

Each year our town hosts an Ironman race. This is a grueling undertaking for everyone involved, even the pros. It starts out at 7am with swimming, 2.4 miles, then goes directly into the bicycling portion, 112 miles. After the biking race, the participants will run a 26.2 mile course. You must finish by midnight. Can you even imagine this?! Well, there have been people from all over the world here this week, and some for several weeks, training on the actual course so they can get the feel of it. Hotels are booked solid, and people have even opened their homes, renting spare rooms, or the whole house, to the out-of-towners. It's a huge thing. The community plans for weeks and months. The participants train a lot longer.

This causes me to think about my own race ~ life. Paul talked about this race in Hebrews 12:1 "*...let us run with perseverance the race marked out for us.*" That is the secret. These (Ironman) runners-swimmers-bikers must wear the sleekest clothing so as not to have too much bulk, and allow better speed. And yes, there will be a huge crowd of witnesses and volunteers, helpers on race day, those giving out water, helping with wetsuits, massaging sore muscles, treating medical issues, repairing bicycles, encouraging and cheering… kind of like our real lives. But the finish line is different. The Ironman finish line is somewhere on a street, at an appointed spot and time, and the prize is a trophy, and a great deal of money, if you're up front. Our finish line, as Christians, is heaven. And Paul described our prize here, *"I have fought the good fight, I have finished the race, I have kept the faith. Now there is in store for me the* ***crown of righteousness,*** *which the Lord, the righteous Judge, will award to me on that day ~ and not only to me, but also to all who have longed for His appearing."* (2Tim. 4:7-8). This prize far surpasses any I could win here in any earthly race.

Are you training for this race called life? We cannot expect to make it to the finish line without proper training…Bible study and yes, some memorization (Psalm 119:11) *"I have hidden Your word in my heart that I might not sin against You."* Practicing loving people, especially the unlovely, forgiveness, kindness, encouragement, peacefulness, joyful living…it does take effort and discipline on our part, just like training for an Ironman race or a triathlon…and perseverance. *"But one thing I do: Forgetting what is behind and straining toward what is ahead, I press on toward the goal to win the prize for which God has called me heavenward in Christ Jesus."* (Phil. 4:13) Don't ever give up. It will be worth it!

JUNE 11

PLANTING SEEDS…

"May the words of my mouth and the meditation of my heart be pleasing in Your sight, O Lord, my Rock and my Redeemer." (Psalm 19:14).

I always want to be aware and cognizant of who is around me, hearing my words, seeing my actions. And ultimately the Lord not only hears every word, but knows my every thought. For several years we had foreign exchange students, five girls in all. Their cultures were very different from ours, and that is the reason they came to America, for the experience of a different culture. We learned as much from them as they did from us.

All of our exchange students agreed to attend church with us, nearly every Sunday, and were part of the youth group. Of the five, only one was a Christian before she came here. A few of them would have many questions about our faith, and we'd have some good discussions. One girl let me know that within days after she returned home, she asked Jesus into her heart. Not wanting to pressure her as she expressed she wasn't ready, I had explained salvation in detail in answer to some of her questions during one of our discussions in the few days before she went home. What a blessing to receive that email with the good news.

Yesterday, as I was praying for "my girls," I wondered just who they would continue to hear the message from, if at all, now that they have been gone from our home, some of them for many years. I know of one who has gone as far away from Christianity as she can go. She won't even communicate with me if I mention anything about God, or church, or prayer. But she can't stop me from praying that God will send someone to her who will relate to her and let her know just how lost she is, and how much she needs Him. I wonder about the testimony my life was to each one of them and hope that I did enough, said enough. Then I have to remember that it was my job to only plant the seed. I am not responsible for making sure that seed grows to fruition. That is the Master Gardener's job.

And so, I pray that the "hound of heaven" would pursue those beloved and still unsaved girls, following them around until they will see just how much Jesus loves them, and realize then their deep need for Him. And I have to remember that I did my part in introducing the Savior to them, in planting the seeds, in my words and deeds, and just by how I loved them in my home and with my family. Even if I never know in this life what their spiritual state is, or becomes, I can find hope in the words of Him who pursues them...

"...so is My word that goes out from My mouth. It will not return to me empty, but will accomplish what I desire and achieve the purpose for which I sent it." (Isaiah 55:11).

That gives me hope...

JUNE 12

GOD IN THE WIND...

We have had so much wind in the past three seasons...more than we've ever had. All winter, although we had less snow than anyone else in the nation, the wind blew and the temperatures were sub-freezing, and that made for a miserable winter. We were happy when spring arrived...well, all it did was rain...and blow. More wind, blowing the rain. And less than two weeks ago, we finally received "real" summer weather, and with the warmer temperatures, more wind. Yesterday the wind was so fierce the sky (and my house) was filled with dust and we could not even see the mountains which surround our town on all sides. I am picking up more tree branches and leaves every day. It's incredible. Yet, those same willow trees whose limbs I pick up off the ground, look so beautiful as they flow gently in the breeze.

The wind shows me God's supreme power. He made the wind. And *"the wind blows (breathes) where it wills; and though you hear its sound, but you neither know where it comes from nor where it is going. So it is with everyone who is born of the Spirit."* (John 3:8). The wind can be gentle or the wind can be savage and destructive. I used to be so afraid of the wind. We lived in a house with lots of huge old pine trees in the yard. There were a couple of them which I knew would fall right on my bedroom because of where they were standing and which direction the wind usually blew in from. I couldn't sleep at night in a windstorm. I would go to another part of the house until the wind subsided. We did actually have a couple of the smaller trees fall on the house over time, but they did not cause much damage. Then I gave my fear to God. I began looking up scripture verses on fear, and how God can calm our fears if we trust Him. This was the beginning of my journaling. I would write down the verses, then follow them with prayer on the pages. I can say now that I don't have that same fear of the wind. Oh, I have a respect for it, and an awe. And I always think of God the Creator when the wind is blowing, like He is speaking in the wind.

Winds can also test the strength and depth of the roots of many trees, as well as clearing away dead leaves and branches, making room for new growth. I think the winds of adversity may also be good for us, and it would cause us to put our roots down deeper, sometimes for the purpose of hanging on for dear life. It can also blow away the deadness of sin in our lives and promote new growth in the Spirit. We are sometimes likened to a garden on which His wind blows to spread the fragrance of our lives. It says in the Song of Solomon 4:16, *"Awake, north wind, and come, south wind! Blow on my garden that its fragrance may spread abroad."* I would hope that our own spirit, encouraged by His Spirit, would blow "abroad" and spread to others we meet along the way.

Now, this morning all is calm, there is not even a breeze. And I think life is like that. We cry out to God in the winds and He hears us and brings us through it, and then lets us enjoy the calm and peace. He speaks to me in both places. He's always there.

JUNE 13

COMPANY'S COMING...

Summer is the time for company. Well, we have company all throughout the year, for dinner, overnight, holidays...but this is the season when people travel great distances to spend time with us. Or, we with them. The summer vacation. It's exciting (most of the time) to expect company. Usually it's relatives or friends we haven't seen for a long time, sometimes many years.

I remember as a child, each time my dad was transferred with the Navy, we drove by car and made a vacation out of the move. We stopped along the way and visited friends, or relatives, who lived along our route. What a great time that was. We always looked forward to the visits. Most of the time we kids slept in sleeping bags or on blankets on the floor, but that was part of the adventure. It was so much fun to touch bases with our cousins again.

There are a lot of preparations we make for company ~ cleaning, laundry, extra groceries, planning activities. I am expecting company today. She's a college girl, who was an exchange student from Germany at the same time we had an exchange student staying with us. They became fast friends. And now the friend is coming out west (after spending the year at college in S.C.). I'm anxious to see her and have her in my home, but I've been working hard this week getting ready for her visit.

There is another visitor coming, but not many of us prepare adequately for His arrival. It would help to know when He would arrive, but that's not the deal. *"No one knows the day or the hour, not even the angels, nor the Son, but only the Father."* (Mark 13:32). It won't be like our earthly company who will call ahead of time to let us know when they will arrive so we can plan. In fact, the next verse says, *"Be on guard! Be alert! You do not know when that time will come."* On the day our company is scheduled to arrive, we find ourselves watching out the window, waiting excitedly until they arrive. Our relationship with Jesus should be such that we wait for Him the same way ~ ready, excited. Jesus said in John 9:4, *"As long as it is day we must do the work of Him who sent Me. Night is coming, when no one can work."* There is an old hymn we used to sing in church that said "work for the night is coming when man's work is done." Basically, this means we must ever be working for the kingdom, witnessing, winning souls for Christ, because when that day does come, and He arrives, it will be too late.

God doesn't give us too much work to do…in fact, He is the One who will do it, if we submit to Him and become the willing vessels through which He can work. So, just as we busy ourselves preparing for company, let's remember, every day, that this could be the day Jesus will arrive. There will be no time then to make preparation.

JUNE 14

IN GOD WE TRUST…

"Cast your cares on the Lord and He will sustain you; He will never let the righteous fall." (Psalm 55:22).

"When I am afraid, I will trust in You. In God, whose word I praise, ***in God I trust****; I will not be afraid. What can mortal man do to me?"* (Psalm 56:3-4).

"In God we trust." Our great nation was founded on these words. They have been printed on our money, coins and currency, for many generations. They have been proven to sustain our freedom for years, although it has been threatened now by those who want it taken OFF our money. Even so, it can't stop us from trusting God. Whether or not we have the words on our coins, we can keep them in our hearts, and hopefully will keep trusting God. Who else can we trust?

"Find rest, O my soul, in God alone; my hope comes from Him. He alone is my Rock and my Salvation; He is my Fortress, I will not be shaken. My salvation and my honor depend on God; He is my mighty Rock, my Refuge. ***Trust in Him*** *at all times, O people; pour out your hearts to Him, for God is our Refuge."* (Psalm 62:5-8).

There is so much in God's word of His unfailing love for us, and the hope He alone can give us, even when the earth is shaking and the mountains are crumbling around us. With each crisis or disaster, natural or man-made, that we have experienced, God's love has been shown and proven publicly ~ in the 9-11 nightmare, in Katrina's devastation, our own individual calamities, large or small…many other times throughout history, God has come through for His people. He can be trusted!

People will always let us down, it's human nature. But God can always be trusted! His love will never fail us!

JUNE 15

THANK YOU NOTES...

It is the time of year that a large number of Thank You notes will be written. Graduations and weddings will take place this month and next and some gifts will be frivolous, some useful, and others monetary. Some will be large, and some small. Mother's Day just passed, and my beautiful daughters got together and had pictures taken, by a "professional" and made up a priceless framed collage of the different poses. I will be sending each of them a heartfelt thank you note, even though I told them all in person, with big hugs, how much I loved the gift.

This past weekend we were honored to be invited and flown to the town where our church university is located, because my brother-in-law was receiving an honorary doctorate degree. A past graduate of the school, he has, over the years, done much for the university, as well as creating a foundation that builds seminaries and other colleges around the world, affiliated with our church. He has worked selflessly for many years, and contributed much, not for his own gain or recognition, but to the glory of God. We were flown, hoteled, and fed as the university's guests. And the commencement ceremony included a beautiful presentation of this award with emphasis, by the President of the college, on the fact that this is the highest honor the college bestows on anyone. We were so proud. Between the Baccalaureate and the Commencement exercise, the family was joined by the President, and two other dignitaries, and their wives, at a beautiful luncheon held at a country club in town. There was much sharing around the table ~ our whole family was honored. For this, I want to send a special Thank You note to the University President.

I have mentioned before that I love to write in journals, and if you were to read any one of my journals, you would find that I thank our heavenly Father nearly every day, for *something*. It may be a big, or small request I have been praying for, or it may be just that I am grateful for the life He has given me, the guidance from His word, and the many, many blessings I receive every single day. David's writings were full of thankfulness and praise to God. In Psalm 31:12, *"O Lord, my God, I will give You thanks forever."* And a popular verse, *"Give thanks to the Lord for He is good; His love endures forever."* (Psalm 107:1). And later, in verse 8, *"Let them give thanks to the Lord for His unfailing love and His wonderful deeds for men."* We thank God for giving us victory over sin and death, we thank Him for His leadership, for His light that guides us, for His word, for His indescribable gift of grace. We are admonished to *"give thanks in ALL circumstances, for this is God's will for you in Christ Jesus."* (1 Thess. 5:18). We are to thank Him because He is good. Reason enough. And so I continue to write my thank you notes to God daily. And if I don't feel like I have anything to be thankful for, I think about the fact that I woke up this morning and I can see, and stand. I think about the comfortable bed I just slept in, the abundant food I have to eat, about my wonderful husband and family, and realize just how blessed I really am. How can I not thank Him?

JUNE 16

SICK....

Boy, do I hate being sick. I have been sick for the last three days...thinking it was some kind of food poisoning. Wow. Up all night and sleeping all day ~ something wrong with that picture. No energy, no appetite, but hungry. Knowing there are things I need to get up and do, but can't drag myself up out of bed or off the chair to get it done. Listless. Yucky. I don't get sick very often, but when I do, I think of all the things I could be doing. I hate it.

We can be sin-sick, too. There are many things we could, and should, be doing for the Lord, and we mean to ~ but we don't feel like it. Too many other things get in the way. And, many times we think we are not "pure" enough to come to the Lord. Too many things have happened in our lives, too many attitudes or habits have crept up, and we think we have to clean up our act before He'll look at us. *"But God demonstrates His own love for us in this: while we were still sinners, He died for us."* (Romans 5:8). He didn't say to us, "Clean up nicely and then I'll think about forgiving you," or "If you're serious about this Christianity-thing, you must get rid of all your bad habits." Does the doctor say to us, "Get better, then I will see you?" Of course not! *"It is not the healthy who need a doctor, but the sick. But go and learn what this means: 'I desire mercy, not sacrifice.' For I have not come to call the righteous, but sinners."* (Matthew 9:12-13).

Many of us are under a doctor's care for one reason or another. We want to get better. Jesus wants so much for us to be under His care, His deeply loving care. He wants us to come just as we are, sick in our sin. We *cannot* clean it up ourselves, no matter how hard we try, or how much we concentrate or meditate. We need Him, the Great Physician. Get into His word, it is a healing balm. He said in Exodus 15:26, *"I am the Lord who heals you."* I am so glad He is healing me…it is a process, begun the day I came to Him.

JUNE 17

THE FRAGRANCE OF PRAYER…

I love fragrance! SOME fragrances…that is. I have many scented candles in my home, and I grow flowers, which I cut and bring inside. I love riding my bicycle through the old neighborhoods where the ancient lilacs and syringa are growing, and lots of pine trees…sometimes, I smell a barnyard, and that's OK, too!

I think our prayers are like a sweet fragrance wafting up to God. Fragrances are mentioned throughout the Bible, in the forms of perfumes, oils and incense. In John 12 we read where *"Mary took a bottle of expensive perfume and poured it on Jesus feet…and the house was filled with the fragrance."* This was a beautiful gift. And in Ephesians 5:2 it says "*…Christ loved us and gave Himself up for us as a fragrant offering and sacrifice to God."* And the Psalmist prayed in chapter 141, *"May my prayer be set before You like incense."*

How many times are we given a gift, or receive a letter or phone call from someone with good news, and the message just fills our hearts with warmth and joy? I think this is like a "fragrance." In Philippians 4, Paul called the gifts his friends sent him *"a fragrant offering, an acceptable sacrifice, pleasing to God."*

When we pray, we should examine our thoughts, we should pray wisely. And there is strength in praying with another. There is added joy in secretly praying for someone else, a test of our unselfishness. And prayer brings a calming beauty to our countenance. I heard it said once that "prayer is the highest form of business you could conduct."

When we pray, let's think not only of our needs, or the needs of others, but try to think of how God is accepting our prayer. Is it like a noisy clanging, or a sweet fragrance, rising up to Him?

JUNE 18

JESUS, THE GREAT PHYSICIAN...

"Jesus went through all the towns and villages, teaching in their synagogues, preaching the good news of the kingdom and **healing every disease and sickness**. *When He saw the crowd, He had compassion on them..."* (Matthew 9:35-36). How wonderful to have a Savior who can heal our diseases. He alone is skilled in the art of healing. I have seen His healing many times during my lifetime, and it has been miraculous. I have also seen times when He has chosen not to heal. It's His call. His way is perfect, even though to us it doesn't always seem so and we don't understand His ways.

We have prayed for healing of my husband's heart condition for 12+ years. For the most part his medication keeps him pretty stable and he can function normally. We have also prayed for about six years for healing and relief for my own rheumatoid arthritis pain. At times it's worse than at others, but I'm still aware of it constantly. At times I have gone through the day pretty much pain-free. I'm praising and thanking God for being able to enjoy the freedom from pain, each day and I give Him the glory for those times of relief.

God doesn't always heal our physical pain, but sometimes it's emotional or spiritual pain we bring to Him. He wants us to come to Him with all our wounds, our hurts, resentments, disappointments and bitterness. He wants to cut away the disease and tenderly knit together our relationships, and make us whole. When we are weak, He is strong. He wants to bless us.

Sometimes we suffer and we don't understand why ~ we see no reason for it, we don't understand it. *"But those who suffer He delivers in their suffering; He speaks to them in their affliction."* (Job 36:15). Many times God can get our attention and speak truths to us that we would not hear if our lives were perfect. Lessons are learned. We grow spiritually, closer to Him. We learn to trust Him. And someday our ultimate healing will come when we step over into the place promised to those who have been faithful ~ heaven. *"He will wipe every tear from their eyes. There will be no more death or mourning or crying or pain, for the old order of things has passed away."* (Rev. 21:4). There it is...the supreme healing. He will help me through the painful times here because I know about the reward that awaits me when my suffering is at last ended.

JUNE 19

MY WEAKNESS, HIS STRENGTH...

"He said to me, 'My grace is sufficient for you, for My strength is made perfect in weakness.' Therefore most gladly I will rather boast in my infirmities, that the power of Christ may rest upon me. Therefore I take pleasure in infirmities, in reproaches, in needs, in persecutions, in distresses, for Christ's sake. For when I am weak, then I am strong." (2 Corinthians 12:9-10).

Wow. Can I really say that? *Pleasure* in infirmities? I don't know about you, but it isn't very pleasurable for me to be in arthritic pain all the time. I mean, I didn't ASK for it, for sure, just so it could bless me. But I have been thinking about Paul quite a bit lately. Sure, he was in prison, several times, and beaten, several times ~ probably more times than we know about from scriptures. We know what just ONE injury to our body can do. . . even after much therapy and treatment and medication, it stays with us. I am sure he woke each morning barely able to get up from his sleeping mat, and move his aching body. But in it all, he was able to praise God, go on confidently teaching, and God's glory was shown in his life.

Paul also penned this, in his letter to the Philippians: *"I have learned to be content whatever the circumstances. I know what it is to be in need, and I know what it is to have plenty. I have learned the secret of being content in any and every situation, whether well fed or hungry, whether living in plenty or in want. I can do everything through Him who gives me strength."* (Philippians 4:11-13).

And so, each day I ask the Father in heaven to give me strength for the day, and courage to face whatever He allows in my path. He tells me to *be strong and of good courage*, that *He will supply ALL my needs according to His riches in heaven*, that *He will give me rest,* and that *the kingdom of heaven will be mine.* And He promises me that I will be *more than a conqueror through Him Who loves me*!

I find strength in those words alone. I know when I'm tired He will give me rest, and when I'm afraid He will protect me. He doesn't promise He will take away my pain, but He will be there with me helping me to endure it. And someday, I will know His purpose in it. What can be better than that?

JUNE 20

CHEAP THRILLS...

Also known as...fun things to do that don't cost a lot! For me, they are the simple things that make me happy, that give me joy. Walking around the mall with my daughters and grandchildren...maybe stopping for an ice cream cone, but usually not buying anything else. I am very content to do this on a regular basis. In fact, it was a usual Saturday morning ritual until everyone got so busy this summer...our local theater shows Dollar movies a couple of times a week in the summer months. So, that's something else...

I love riding my bike, and that doesn't cost anything. Well, until recently when I asked permission to feed sugar cubes to my favorite three mules. Still, sugar cubes are relatively cheap, and the thrill I get from having those big lugs nuzzle my hand for that treat through the fence is worth the pennies. Who knew mules could be so selfish, though? Well, I guess lots of people do...One big guy, Snickers, will shove the other two away in order to get ALL the sugar cubes. Last night Henry took all he could take, turned his back on Snickers and began kicking his hind feet at him! And Ajax, well, he just stays away from all the nonsense. Since I can't have horses, but I love them so, I really am delighted to give them treats and rub their noses and necks. I call them "my boys." Cheap thrills.

One of my favorite things is sitting in a quiet place reading a good book, and I usually buy them used, or borrow them, so again, it doesn't cost much. And I lose myself in the stories. And then there's feeding the birds and the squirrels, watching the deer, picking flowers from my own yard, and watching the sun come up...and go down.

There are many things to do for entertainment that don't cost anything...invite friends, or children, over to play board games, attend a community ball game, take some pictures, re-arrange furniture. I know, sometimes we just need to go to a play or movie, or out to dinner, but really, you can find joy in simple things most of the time. It used to amuse me when my kids would whine, "I don't have anything to do!" I would name off a few things, and pretty soon they were happily busy pounding nails into wood scraps on the patio, "making Barbie doll furniture." Wow ~ have we come a long way...or not!

Paul had a few things to say about being content. *"I have learned the secret of being content in any and every situation, whether well fed or hungry, whether living in plenty or in want. I can do everything through Him who gives me strength."* (Philippians 4:12-13). I think that after Paul's conversion, his greatest thrill was to lead people to Jesus. He didn't need the entertainment of the arena, or gambling with the fellas. He said in Hebrews 13:5, *"Keep your lives free from the love of money and be content with what you have…"*I know now that I am retired, I spend a lot less money because I HAVE a lot less money! And it's not important to me. I would sure like to pass these "cheap thrills" along to my grandchildren… actually, they are learning about them already, because I include them!

JUNE 21

THE BIG SKY…

The mystery has been solved. My husband and I were privileged to co-host a "Mystery Tour" last summer with the charter bus company he drives for. And, of course, being a mystery, no one on the tour knew where we would be going, or what we would be doing. (Except the driver, who is the owner of the company). What an adventure. Given clues on our itinerary, we were all invited by the host to guess the destination ~ and, of course, to the delight of our host, no one hit the mark. We headed in a totally different direction than I had guessed when we boarded the bus. And the driver/host kept giving hints, and playing tricks, cleverly traveling different routes, so no one would know exactly. Well, as you may have guessed by my title, we arrived in Montana, also known as "big sky country." And believe me, it is. There is such a huge wilderness area near where we were, just south of Glacier National Park, at Seeley Lake. When we arrived, it was still raining. Our excursion one day took us from overcast to SNOW. Of course, the elevation was about 8,000 feet! The next day was a beautiful sunny day (the only one in the week, actually!). The grounds at the Double Arrow Lodge/Resort are impeccable…a creek, a pond, little log cabins, or larger log lodges, a field with horses, a golf course, snow capped mountains all around, and wildlife abounding. We learned many things by visiting interpretive centers…bears, Lewis & Clark, and most importantly, about each other. It's a 60+ group, with some in their 80's. What a variety of people, lives, interests…it was a fun week. And, the bonus for my husband and me was that we got an all-expense paid vacation out of it.

Some of the people we traveled with know each other, (there was a family of five siblings in their 70's and 80's), and, in fact, have taken other tours together. Paul said in Ephesians 3:6, *"This mystery is that through the gospel the Gentiles are heirs together with Israel, members together of one body, and sharers together in the promise of Jesus Christ."* And so, even though we all came from different walks of life, and different backgrounds, our little bus group were all together as one body on this trip. Even though we were all different, we all had this "mystery" tour in common. And, although it was not sponsored by any church group, most of the people were believers, and I was impressed that there was a common blessing before each meal, offered by our driver, in Jesus' name, and "amened" each time by the group.

Even though there was rain almost every day, I marveled and thanked our Creator when I feasted my eyes on the great beauty of this wilderness, the mountains and plains. Every color of green you can imagine in the forests, brilliant and fresh from the moisture. Our God made that big beautiful sky, and all that is in it! *"The heavens declare the glories of God; the skies proclaim the work of His hands. Day after day they pour forth speech; night after night they display knowledge. There is no speech or language where their voice is not heard."* (Psalm 19:1-3).

Big sky, big world. Big family of God. We are so blessed.

JUNE 22

IT'S STILL RAINING…

Well, except for a day here and there of more pleasant weather, we have had SO much rain this spring. Actually, since fall, and into the winter, as well. A lot! The few nice days have actually been a surprise, because the weather forecast was for rain, rain, and more rain. Of course, it's garage sale season. Until summer temperatures actually arrived, I had mushrooms growing in my lawn. It had to be mowed twice a week, and I'd better do it when the rain stopped, because it would probably be raining again tomorrow, or tonight. But everything is growing so beautiful and lush and green. And even though we've had a lot of rain, we have been fortunate in that we haven't had the terrible flooding they've had in other parts of the country, and the world. And maybe, just maybe, it will cut down on the forest fires we expect each summer.

God sends the rain. It's His way of watering the earth. God sent the biggest rainstorm to the earth in Noah's day. He said to him, *"Seven days from now I will send rain on the earth for forty days and forty nights, and will wipe from the face of the earth every living creature I have made."* (Gen. 7:4). I think that really must have broken God's heart, to destroy everyone and everything He had made by His own hand. But, that was God's judgment for sin. Though we can probably count forty days and forty nights that it has rained here, at least there have been a few breaks, and our storms have not been the magnitude that Noah's storm was. It never let up for forty days. And it flooded the WHOLE earth. I'm pretty sure that won't happen again, for God said after the storm, *"I have set my rainbow in the clouds, and it will be the sign of the covenant between Me and the earth. Whenever I bring clouds over the earth and the rainbow appears in the clouds, I will remember my covenant between Me and you and all living creatures of every kind. Never again will the waters become a flood to destroy all life."* (Gen. 9:13-15). What a promise. And although many do lose their lives in the devastating floods around the world from time to time, the flood of Noah's time will never be seen by mankind again.

On the other hand, there were times when God withheld the rain and the land suffered drought. Usually these were times when He wanted to teach the people a valuable lesson ~ namely, that He was God and in control, and He wanted them to exercise their faith so people would realize that. Sometimes the droughts were in answer to the prayers of a prophet, who wanted to prove to unbelievers that God was Almighty. And we often experience these very dry times in the summer months. Our lives are like this at times. God will seem to rain down His blessings on us regularly and generously, but then at other times, we feel so spiritually dry, we are sure He isn't hearing our prayers or seeing our needs at all. But these are the times when we must trust in Him because He knows what is best for us ~ and He knows what is to come. There is a lesson for us in it all. So, we must be grateful for the rain that follows the sun, for these are times of growing.

JUNE 23

GOD'S UNMERITED FAVOR

Last summer my family members, who had been taking a karate class together for the last year and a half, tested to move up another degree to the next belt color. My daughters and son-in-law have worked very hard with their training.

Since I have rheumatoid arthritis, a lot of the techniques are hard for me, but I went to every class and learned them. So, when it came to the testing, there were some "long forms" and sets that I couldn't remember during the test. There was a class of 32, juniors to adults, 11 of them were our family. I'm guessing the youngest ones were four or five, and the oldest, besides me, were maybe forty. After the testing, the participants had to stand perfectly still in a particular assigned "stance" while the instructors went into another room for maybe 10 to 15 minutes, to discuss the testing. After a few minutes, they called for me (only me) to come into their office. I knew why I was there. I hadn't measured up. I agreed with them when they said they couldn't award my belt because it wouldn't be fair to the students who had practiced and perfected their moves. And I almost did not test because I knew I wasn't ready. So, yes, it was humiliating and embarrassing, but I stood there while the rest went through their individual ceremonies. I got what I deserved. Or, should we say, I didn't get what I didn't deserve!

I got to thinking ~ how different this is from how God treats us. Not that our instructors were mean or acted unfairly…but God's grace is so much more. It's defined as "unmerited favor," or "lenience" or "charity." And here's how it works… *"For it is by GRACE you have been saved, through faith ~ and this is not from yourselves, it is the gift of God ~ not by works so that no one can boast."* (Ephesians 2:8-9). That's the difference. For my own recognition and reward here on earth, I need to work and practice for it to qualify for the prize. But in heaven, in God's eyes, I cannot *qualify* or deserve the indescribable prize I will receive. I only need to be willing to take the gift He offers me. It doesn't make any sense, I know, but that's how much God loves us. He planned on giving us this priceless gift of His love before we were even born.

I may never "qualify" to earn my next degree karate belt, because the advanced techniques of the higher levels are getting more difficult for me and intensify my pain, but I know without a doubt that I have and will continue to receive His divine gift of Grace, unmerited favor, unlike that of any other prize I could receive. And I don't have to earn it. It's free! I'm so glad!

JUNE 24

GOD SPEAKS...

"O God, You are my God, earnestly I seek You; my soul thirsts for You, my body longs for You in a dry and weary land where there is no water." (Psalm 63:1). Do you ever feel like that? Like you are dying of thirst for God's word? I've heard people say "My spirit is so dry right now. God doesn't seem to be answering my prayers." God's word says that only those who *hunger and thirst* after righteousness will receive it. God forces His heavenly manna on no one. Our desire for God's wisdom and the knowledge of His word must supersede everything else. His word is the only thing that will satisfy the gnawing hunger and burning thirst for His answers to our prayers. And His message to us is profound and will be just what we need.

Jeremiah said in vs. 15:16, *"Your words came, and I ate them; they were my joy and my heart's delight, for I bear Your name, O Lord God Almighty."* God personally made sure His word was preserved down through the ages of man. The lessons for living, the history of how He has loved His people down through all generations ~ it's all there in the sacred Book. It's how He speaks to us. And if we don't read it, and study it, how will we know His will for us? David "hid" God's word within his heart ~ *"I have hidden Your word in my heart that I might not sin against You."* (Psalm 119:11). Do you know how to "hide" God's word in your heart? Read it. Memorize it. It sounds daunting, I know, to memorize scripture. But when you read a verse or passage over and over, it begins to "pop" into your mind at the time when you need its encouragement.

"For the word of God is living and active. Sharper that any double-edged sword, it penetrates even to dividing soul and spirit, joints and marrow; it judges the thoughts and attitudes of the heart." (Hebrews 4:12). There is no other book like this Holy Book ~ the Bible. It IS the living word of God Himself. It's how He speaks to us. Oh, and you might hear Him speaking in the wind, the rain, or birdsong... So, next time you feel like you're not hearing from God, open up the Book and look inside. There's a message there for you.

JUNE 25

MY DELIVERER...

"He is my loving God, and my fortress, my stronghold and my Deliverer, my shield in whom I take refuge..." (Psalm 144:2).

Down through the ages, God has delivered His people from all kinds of trouble. In His wisdom and perfect timing, and in ways unknown to us, He has delivered us by His strong and loving hand. We seem to be inundated by troubles, and this week has seen many concerns within one of my ladies' groups. Linda has just been diagnosed with breast cancer. Heather may or may not have cancer, but faces a long haul of medical treatment just the same. My own daughter Bridgette has MRSA, another frightful malady. Judy's daughter-in-law is nearing the birth of her baby boy. Of course, this one will be joyous, but still, it is an emotional event, just the same. There are others, many that we don't know about.

But God is our Deliverer! He led the Israelites through the Red Sea, rescued Noah and his family from the great flood, miraculously helped Gideon win a battle involving scores more soldiers than his own army had. He rescued David from many dangers, Daniel in the lion's den, Paul from prison and death many times, Ruth and Naomi, Moses....and in more modern times, the Jews from the Nazis. Of course, many succumbed to Hitler's devious and evil procedures, but many to the glory of God. Our nation is in danger of changing so much it won't be the same. Have we gone too far to ever turn back now? God is still in the business of performing miracles. Exodus 14:13,14 says, *"Do not be afraid. Stand firm and you will see the deliverance the Lord will bring you today. The Lord will fight for you; you need only be still."* Wow!! What a promise.

In all that we are going through, let us stand firm and be still, and watch God work. He will work in astonishing ways we would never think of. He is our Deliverer!

JUNE 26

OUR IMPOSSIBLE ECONOMY...

I'm not really into politics, but I do know this...the government has really messed up our economy. Of course, this is not really news to anyone. Oh, I know, it's been coming for a long time, and some people's ideas of "fixing" it only make it worse. I am no expert, I'm certainly not an economist, and neither are a lot of people who are in charge of it. I only know that people have suffered because they can't pay for their medical expenses, they are losing their homes that they scraped and saved to keep, car payments are impossible, travel expenses are higher than ever, insurance of every kind is skyrocketing, food and gas and utilities are way out of bounds, even school is more costly these days…and yet, we are still walking around, breathing, living, working…

This isn't the first time we, our nation, have been in dire straits. We, ourselves, may not have experienced it firsthand, but our parents knew the Great Depression, and there is a myriad of books written on the subject, whole series' of novels and history books, relating the desperate circumstances of the people who went through that frightening era. We actually could learn something from that time in history, when people buckled down and helped one another, traded merchandise for services, ("horse-trading," my dad called it), the women did more creative sewing, making clothing out of flour sacks, etc, families grew and shared vegetable gardens, fixed old things instead of buying new…this never hurts. We are so used to having so much handed to us.

In times like these, and at all times, we need to remember that *"with God, nothing is impossible."* (Luke 1:37). He is not broke. "*He owns the cattle on a thousand hills*" (Psalm 50:10), and *"if He cares enough to watch over the little sparrow, or the lilies in the field, why would He ignore our neediness?"* (Matthew 6:26-28). *"Our Father in heaven is truly able to meet all our needs, [ALL of them], according to His glorious riches in Christ Jesus."* (Phil. 4:19). We need to remember to be faithful, even in the midst of our trouble. I know, when we can't even pay our own bills, it's hard to imagine that we would have anything to give. But God said, in Malachi 3:10, *"**Test Me in this**…and see if I will not throw open the floodgates of heaven and pour out so much blessing that you will not have room enough for it."* God promises to take care of us. I have experienced this during the last several years, when things in our lives seem to be falling apart… God has always been faithful, and has always provided for us, when we didn't know from day to day where the resources would come from. Actually, this has been our story for most of our 44 years of marriage! Just as we read of many examples of God's provision for His people in the Scriptures, it can be true for each of us, as well.

JUNE 27

SUFFERING AND TRUSTING...

"Lord, even when I have trouble all around me, You will keep me alive. When my enemies are angry, you will reach down and save me by Your power." (Psalm 138:7). Every one of us has trouble around us, whether we ourselves are suffering, or someone who is close to us...if not now, we have had in the past, or most assuredly, will in the future. It's part of life. Suffering. In our own ladies' group, we have very recently had reports of cancer, financial difficulties, loneliness, relationship problems just to name a few. No one is immune. And we are not alone. Many around us are afflicted and miserable, right now. And many do not have hope. They are desperate. But, *"Those who go to God Most High for safety will be protected by the Almighty. I will say to the Lord, 'You are my place of safety and protection. You are my God and I trust You.'"* (Psalm 91:1-2).

Here is what Max Lucado has to say about suffering: "There is a window in your heart through which you can see God. Once upon a time that window was clear. Your view of God was crisp. You could see God as vividly as you could see a gentle valley or hillside. Then, suddenly, the window cracked. A pebble broke the glass. A pebble of pain. And suddenly God was not so easy to see. The view that had been so crisp had changed. You were puzzled. God wouldn't allow something like this to happen, would He? When you can't see Him, trust Him... Jesus is closer than you've ever dreamed." (from In the Eye of the Storm).

Any suffering we endure here on earth will be worth it when we meet Jesus.

"I leave you peace; My peace I give you. I do not give it to you as the world does. So don't let your hearts be troubled or afraid." (John 14:27). That's the key. The unexplained peace that comes from trusting the Father will carry us through all our suffering here on earth.

JUNE 28

STEPPING OUT OF THE BOAT...

How many times have you walked on water?

*"'**Come**,' He said. Then Peter got down out of the boat, walked on the water, and came toward Jesus. But when he saw the wind, he was afraid, and, beginning to sink, cried*

out, 'Lord, save me!' Immediately Jesus reached out His hand and caught him. ***'You of little faith,'*** *He said,* ***'why did you doubt?'"***(Matthew 14:29-31).

I don't think any of us has really ever been in a boat and looked out onto the water and saw a man coming toward us, in flowing robes, walking on top of the water. However, I was once in a boat much like this fishing boat, on the Sea of Galilee. It was a thrill just to be in the land where Jesus had lived, and to travel the roads He had traveled. We were out in the middle of the lake, and our guide told the captain to turn off the engines. We just sat there, quietly listening to the water lap against the sides of the boat, and the cries of the soaring cormorants. After the crew had demonstrated to us just how the fishermen might have cast their nets over the side, (actually trying BOTH sides when he didn't catch anything the first time!), the guide told us to just sit still and think about what happened here, more than 2000 years ago. As soon as those words left his mouth, I began to weep. I knew that I was very close to the actual spot where Jesus had come to Peter, walking on the water. I can't explain the feeling I had, but it so touched my heart, I couldn't control the tears.

Soon, the motor started up again to move us to the other side, and immediately it began to get stormy on the sea! I couldn't believe the timing. It was almost as if on queue. I smiled to myself, thinking "It's just like God to add in this little detail for the full experience!"

So, again, I ask you, how many times have you walked on the water, as Peter did when Jesus summoned him? Have there been times that you have had your eyes on Him, and trusted Him, but when you began looking around at the storms raging, lost your footing and began to sink? Name anything. A medical test. Financial disaster. The death of a loved one. Unfaithfulness of a spouse. The invasion of your privacy when someone broke in and stole from you. The fear of the wind. Abandonment. There have no doubt been times in your life, as in my own, when you have trusted God and started along your way toward His reaching arms only to find the going got really difficult and you began "sinking," back into that state of worry, not trusting.

The last time Peter and the disciples had seen Jesus, he had shoved them off in their boat, and gone up on a mountainside alone to pray. It doesn't say what He prayed about, specifically, but we do know that He prayed for His disciples, and for us, all Christians, on many occasions. I think He had been praying for His disciples to have an experience that would cause them to see His glory and deepen their faith. They were afraid when they saw Him on the waves, thinking it was an apparition. But when He stepped into the boat with

Peter, the wind immediately died down and it became calm. *"Then those who were in the boat worshiped Him, saying, 'Truly, You are the Son of God.'"* (vs. 33).

What kinds of things, what problems, challenges, and frightening circumstances, are buffeting your boat all around on the stormy sea? Is there something that is causing you to take your eyes off Jesus? The waves in your storm won't seem so high when Jesus is holding you up above them in His great hands. Jesus says, *"Come."* He said that same word to each of the disciples when He called them to follow Him. He repeats that word when we are frightened, and when we are lost and sinking in the mire that can sometimes accompany this life. Step out of the boat and walk to Him. He's holding out His hands to you. As long as you keep your eyes on Him, you won't sink!

JUNE 29

WORKS...

In the second part of James 2 we read about the deeds we do as a result of our faith. A key verse is v.14, which says, *"What good is it, my brothers, if a man claims to have faith, but has no deeds?"* Some religions believe you can earn your way into heaven. Works are good, but they are nothing without faith. Faith just naturally produces good works. Some people are involved in all kinds of things, looking good to their neighbors, families and church. But they're going about it with the wrong attitude. They have their own glory in mind, not God's.

And then there is the passage in Matthew 24, the parable of the sheep and the goats, and Jesus spells it out in verses 34-46. Here's a new take on that passage I heard yesterday...

"I was hungry and you formed a humanities club and you discussed my hunger. Thank you. I was imprisoned and you crept off quietly to your chapel in the cellar to pray for my release. I was naked and in your mind you debated the morality of my appearance. I was sick and you knelt and thanked God for your health. I was homeless and you preached to me of the spiritual shelter of the love of God. I was lonely and you left me alone to pray for me. You seem so holy; so close to God. But I'm still very hungry, and lonely, and cold." From "Listen Christian!" (by Bob Rowland).

So where have our prayers gone? What good have they done? What good does it do for us to come up with answers for those who are suffering, to find prayers in our prayer books to read to them? Oh, our faith may be strong, but what are we doing to help those in trouble, in need? Jesus said, *"I tell you the truth, whatever you did for one of the least of these brothers of mine, you did it for Me."* (Matthew 24:40). Then He goes on to say that if we **don't** do these things for our brother, we will reap eternal punishment (vs. 46). We cannot have faith without it transforming us into someone God can use for His glory.

Is there someone in need you can reach out to today? Some little things we do will only take a few moments of our time, but will make a huge difference and last a lifetime in someone's memory.

JUNE 30

QUILTING...

Wow, I have been learning a new skill…quilting! I think this is right up my alley. For many, many years I have done dressmaking, (although I don't do much sewing anymore), for other people, and when my girls were little, I made all their dresses, all my own clothes in high school and when I was working… did all my girls' wedding dresses and bridesmaids' too. But I have always been fascinated by handmade quilts, the different patterns, and techniques, all the materials, from crazy patchwork to more defined color schemes… And I do have many scraps from all those years of sewing…so, while we were on our mystery trip in Montana, I went to a quilt shop with some of the other ladies, and picked up a book. There were a few quilts in there that looked relatively simple, so I bought the book and just thought I'd "study" it for awhile. When I got home, I discovered while going through my scraps from the past years, that I could make a very coordinated quilt almost entirely with the scraps I had. I only had to buy three more pieces of fabric. I read and studied the pattern I chose, got the proper equipment (most of which I already had), and began my quilt. A LOT of work, first of all cutting all the strips, strategizing ~ which colors in what order. It went together very nicely, and I am pleased and amazed. It turned out to be very beautiful.

I think our lives are kind of like quilts. At times we feel like we are in pieces, and all those pieces don't fit together as we think they should. So many of life's experiences and struggles leave us feeling like we've fallen apart. Sometimes illnesses, heartbreak, other people, and just hard luck take chunks out of us that leave us weak and discouraged. God in His tenderness carefully puts us back together again. Some patterns are more complicated than others, and some cloth is harder to work with, not as pliable or supple. Some of these pieces we would throw away, not wanting to be reminded of what they have meant in our lives. But when God puts those squares and blocks and strips together, they are in perfect order. The colors of our experiences blend together as if He designed it just so. He uses each scrap, each remnant. And the quilt of our lives becomes a beautiful craft indeed.

Just as Psalm 139: 13-14 says, *"For You created my inmost being; you knit me together in my mother's womb. I praise You because I am fearfully and wonderfully made; Your works are wonderful, I know full well,"* we can also know that God didn't stop there. He is in the business of repairing what is broken and torn, strengthening our seams and fitting every piece in place through His mercy and grace. And we are truly His masterpiece, painstakingly and lovingly put together as no other can.

JULY 1

CONFUSED, MUDDLED, JUMBLED-UP...

Things are so mixed up...have you ever noticed that? In the past few years, we have had a very unusual winter, and spring...and so far, summer...the weather has been all wrong for all the seasons. People have had to re-plant their gardens a second and third time, because of cold temperatures in the northwest. We can't count on the Fourth of July being nice. And it's not just the weather. People who are supposed to help you actually make things worse, in government, in banking, in health care. Many are forced to make choices they don't want to make. Mommies have to take a special class to learn how to install a baby seat in their car because they are so complicated. We went through that with my granddaughter a few weeks ago...the safety seats are mandatory, they cost a lot of money, and mothers cannot figure out how to get them in the car properly. It just doesn't make sense. Older retired people who are on fixed incomes (I now understand what that term means!) need medications for various health problems, and end up paying exorbitant prices for those drugs, or for the insurance premiums to cover them! And some of those drugs cost only pennies to manufacture. It's all wrong! My daughter went to apply for a job yesterday, and because a mapping site on the internet told her to turn the opposite direction than she should have, she drove back and forth on that stretch of street for an hour before she actually found the place. Directions mixed up.

But Psalm 18:30 says, *"As for God, His way is perfect."* David said that. His life was certainly mixed up, wasn't it? But he recognized God's way in everything. He was used mightily of God. God's way IS perfect. *"The heavens declare the glory of God, the skies proclaim the work of His hands!"* (Ps. 19:1). They can't help it. *"And God saw all that He had made, and it was very good."* (Gen. 1:31). The universe is still in perfect working order. Then He made man. Oh, don't get me wrong…man was the perfect creation. Intricate in design, a masterpiece, perfectly woven together. But it didn't take us long to mix things up. Eve promptly disobeyed God because she listened to wrong advice. And we have been messing up ever since. The horrific things we do to our bodies, God did not mean for us to do. He gave us everything to sustain us in the way of prime and healthy foods, laws that would keep us out of trouble (if we followed them), and He gave us the perfect example of Love, in His Son, Jesus. And Jesus is never mixed up, although we have mixed Him up in our own minds and hearts and lives. We have confused His word and confounded His laws. Remember, "His way is perfect." And ONLY His way is perfect.

So, what will we do with Jesus? *"If we confess our sins, He is faithful and just to forgive us our sins and purify us from all unrighteousness."* (1 John 1:9). Do you see that? He will purify us, just as we were when He first created us. *"Though our sins are like scarlet, they shall be as white as snow…"* (Is. 1:18). He can do that. He's waiting to right the wrong, to straighten out the mixed up lives we live. Will you let Him?

JULY 2

GOD, PLEASE BLESS AMERICA…

The day our new president stepped into his position of power was the beginning of a new era. Many of us were not happy about the outcome of the last election. But many were. As always. It became our job to pray for the man and his family, for wisdom in the daunting task that was before him. Hebrews 13:17 says, *"Obey your leaders and submit to their authority. They keep watch over you as men who must give an account..."* And again in 1 Timothy 2:1-2, scripture tells us, *"I urge, then, first of all, that requests, prayers, intercession and thanksgiving be made for everyone ~* ***for kings and all those in authority****, that we may live peaceful and quiet lives in all godliness and holiness."* Wow!

I do believe that there have been more prayers for the president during and after the last election than at any other time, and this is good. We need to keep praying, sincerely and genuinely, for the man who has been leading our nation, and for the next president who will lead for the next four years. I admit, I have had fear for our country, but I have to remember, God does not give a spirit of fear, the enemy does. He (Satan) would have us wringing our hands and lamenting that nothing will ever be the same, which we have done. But there is power in prayer. Pray for wisdom, and knowledge of God's word, and that our president's heart will be touched and changed in every church service he attends, every meeting that is begun with prayer, every look at his children, every sunset he sees.

God's ways are not our ways. He said, *"For My thoughts are not your thoughts, neither are your ways My ways," declares the Lord."* (Isaiah 55:8). So, we need to keep praying that God's will be done in this nation. And if this has all come about to cause Christians to pray more fervently, then so be it. And God, please bless America!

JULY 3

GOD'S WORD [NOT VOID]...

"As the rain and the snow come down from heaven, and do not return to it without watering the earth and making it bud and flourish, so that it yields seed for the sower and bread for the eater, so is My Word that goes out from My mouth; it will not return to me empty (or void), but will accomplish what I desire and achieve the purpose for which I sent it." (Isaiah 55:10,11).

Wow! I love this. It tells me that I am simply to speak the Word, share the gospel with others, and live my life in testimony to God's love...(well, that's what I see here...). You've heard the little phrase, "plant the seed and God will water it..." this is where that idea comes from. If we speak the Word, God will be faithful to bring it to fruition. If we share Jesus with another, and they seem not to be interested, or they don't respond to it, we leave them in His capable hands...there may be someone else down the road who will cultivate that little seed, and then someone else who will share again...and finally that person you shared with will "get it." They will grow, and bloom, and all because of a tiny seed. God said His word would *"not return to Him void."* That means the person who is meant to hear it, will hear it.

We sometimes become discouraged because we have shared Christ with someone, and it seems they don't respond or even care. We pray for them for years, and seemingly nothing happens in their heart. Nothing changes in their life. This is when I pray that God will send someone else to them, especially if that person has moved away, or has dropped out of my circle of friends, or family... we may not see the fruit of our sharing, or our prayers, for years, or even our lifetime. But we can trust that God has His eye on them, and He will lead someone to them who will continue caring for them...nurturing and watering their soul. I think we will be pleasantly surprised when we step over into heaven and see those we thought were lost because they didn't respond to the message we gave them...but someone else was able to get through. This does not mean, however, that we are incapable of reaching an individual for Christ, because we may also be used after someone else has planted a seed....

So, don't give up in your witnessing. Cling to the hope that Jesus gives, and the promise of this verse spoken and preserved for us so long ago in the precious Book of God.

I wish all of you a wonderful day of celebration as we commemorate the freedoms we have and the nation we live in that was founded on the principles of this great Book. Be sure to keep our troops and our President in your prayers, and pray earnestly for the elections this fall, that God's anointed person would be appointed to lead our country...

JULY 4

FREEDOM...

"Since therefore, brethren, we have confidence to enter the holy place by the blood of Jesus, by a new and living way which He inaugurated for us through the veil, that is, His flesh, and since we have a greater priest over the house of God, let us draw

near with a sincere heart in full assurance of faith, having our hearts sprinkled clean from an evil conscience and our bodies washed with pure water." (Hebrews 10:19-22).

Jesus' broken body is the New Covenant which has brought together opposites ~ Jew and Gentile, male and female, young and old, rich and poor, black and white. As we look upon His face, He will wash us free from prejudice ~ and give us liberty to love, to forgive, to demonstrate His compassion in our circumstances... and in our world.

As we prepare to celebrate the independence we enjoy in our great nation, let us also celebrate the freedom we have in Christ Jesus. May we observe and honor these freedoms we have every day of the year. We are so blessed!

JULY 5

BARNYARDS AND BARBECUES...

I am so fortunate to live in a part of the country where the air is clear and clean, no smog, no pollution...just fresh mountain air. I love riding my bicycle through our semi-rural neighborhood and enjoy the small farms and acreages with their established gardens and huge ancient trees...and I marvel at how many sights, smells and sounds I can pick out. The wildlife, of course, and not-so-wild life ~ deer, cows, horses, chickens, goats, every kind of bird, dogs & cats, I even saw a moose a few weeks ago. And in the spring and summer the fragrance of the flowers and blooming bushes and trees is most pleasant. If I go in the evening, there are the wonderful smells of barbecues, or other cooking odors wafting from kitchens. Sometimes there is the fragrance of a dryer sheet when someone is doing laundry. Animal sounds are pleasing to me, too...I stopped and petted a sweet mule once, and every time I pass him, I talk to him...he usually brays back at me as I'm going by. Now I take him and his two "brothers" sugar cubes. Dogs that used to bark now are quiet when they hear my voice.

There isn't a lot said in scripture about our five senses...or is there? I wondered, so I looked around...in Mark 12:29, *"**Hear**, O Israel, the Lord our God, the Lord is One."* And in John 20:25, *"Unless I **see** the nail marks in His hands and put my finger where the nails were, and put my hand into His side, I will not* *believe."* (That was Thomas). One of my favorites is Psalm 34:8, *"**Taste** and see that the Lord is good."* In Luke 8:45, *"Who **touched** Me?"* (speaking of the woman who touched the hem of Jesus' garment for healing). And 2 Corinthians 5:2, *"Christ loved us and gave Himself up for us as a **fragrant** offering and sacrifice to God."* There are the five senses. I'm not sure that these are the best examples, but you get the idea.

I am blessed to have very keen senses…extra-good hearing (which is beneficial because my husband is near-deaf), and although I need to keep buying stronger reading glasses, my eyesight is pretty good still…I am very aware of the pain in my body, sometimes my sense of taste is TOO good (!), and I can smell things others can't seem to pick up, sometimes good, sometimes…not so good…but I am very grateful for all my senses, and I never take them for granted. And the fact that God put us all together like He did ~ we are SO intricate ~ is so amazing to me. So, I will continue to enjoy touching, looking, feeling, tasting and sniffing, from barnyards to barbecues, and all in between, being thankful that God made me as He did….and I can enjoy His beautiful creation.

JULY 6

CRUSHED ROSES…

The rose is by far my favorite flower. I've heard it said that the rose is "God's autograph." I have many bushes growing around my home, several different varieties. Ever heard of Rose Petal Jam? This is a wonderful condiment, a special treat, for sure. I think it may have originated in England, but I've also heard India or France. Hardly a summer goes by that I don't make up several batches of this delicacy. I first tasted rose petal jam when a friend bought a jar on her vacation in a hotel tea shop and gave me a taste on a spoon to see if I could identify it. Although I'd never tasted it before, my palate knew immediately what it was, and I began searching for a recipe. I found one online but I was not too satisfied with it, so I have modified it a little, and I love to make it not only for my own use, but to give as a gift. People who taste it are always astonished, as I was at first. I have found that some of my roses have little or no fragrance, which is kind of disappointing when cutting them for a bouquet, but when I *crush* those petals and puree and heat them for jam, the beautiful fragrance then comes out.

There is only one Rose I can find in the Bible, and that is the Rose of Sharon in the Song of Solomon. I know it isn't referring to Jesus, or is it? But it is one of the names commonly used for our Savior. Many songs and poems have been written about the "Rose of Sharon." Sharon is a plain ~ it is one of the largest valley-plains in all of Palestine. Back at the time of Solomon, it was considered a wild, fertile plain known for its floral beauty and majesty. It is fitting that we would use this name in reference to our Savior.

I once saw a sentiment in a greeting card that said "Character, like sweet herbs, gives off its finest fragrance when pressed." I believe that the troubles and the struggles we go through in this life are for a purpose, and are meant to strengthen us, to send off the beautiful fragrance of God's amazing grace. David penned *"The Lord is close to the brokenhearted and saves those who are* ***crushed*** *in spirit."* in Psalm 34:18. He is aware of everything that would come in against us, all the crushing pressures of this life. He knows about the heartaches and strain and stress that we feel.

"But He was pierced for our transgressions, He was ***crushed*** *for our iniquities; the punishment that brought us peace was upon Him, and by His wounds we are healed."* (Isaiah 53:5). Call on Him through your troubles. Your suffering and your prayer is like a sweet fragrance rising up to Him.

JULY 7

THINGS I LOVE...

Singing "How Great Thou Art" at the ocean's edge ~ the color red ~ bird song ~ Christmas ~ a baby's toothless smile ~ sunrises ~ sunsets ~ fresh cut flowers ~ tea ~ a friend's tears ~ the quiet of early morning ~ clouds ~ elderly hands ~ trees ~ stories of healing in the Bible ~ photo albums ~ Easter ~ kittens ~ teaching Sunday school ~ lilac bushes ~ rainbows ~ covered porches ~ mountains ~ a new calendar ~ family ~ answered prayer ~ God's pardon ~ wildlife ~ Thanksgiving ~ the moon and stars ~ birthdays ~ books ~ retirement ~ thunderstorms ~ America ~ health ~ music ~ a walk in the woods ~ swings ~ sleep ~ God's sufficient grace ~ springtime ~ dogs ~ weddings ~ the memory of my mother ~ candlelight ~ prayer ~

freedom ~ God's word ~ Gethsemane ~ friendship ~ snowflakes ~ good food ~ healing ~ laughter ~ eyesight and hearing ~ encouragement ~ geese ~ bright hope ~ eagles' wings ~ peace ~ church ~ doctors and dentists ~ surprises ~ new clean paper ~ mercy ~ water ~ Valentine's Day ~ sunshine ~ home ~ butterflies ~ God's faithfulness ~ footprints ~ riding bicycles ~ company ~ thick green grass ~ jump ropes ~ collecting shells at the beach ~ walking in the Holy Land ~

As you see, I have been counting my blessings and I have SO many things to be thankful for...this list isn't even half of them! I think of new ones each day. It says in James 1:17 *"For every good and perfect gift is from above, coming down from the Father of lights, who does not change like shifting shadows."* When I see or think of these things, I make sure to give God thanks for them all. They are all gifts. How many do we take for granted?

"And I pray that you being rooted and established in love, may have the power together with all the saints, to grasp how wide and how long and how high and how deep is the love of Christ, and to know this love that surpasses knowledge ~ that you may be filled to the measure of all the fullness of God." (Ephesians 3:17-19). Count your blessings! Name them one by one...

JULY 8

REFLECTIONS OF A GARAGE SALE...

My daughters, all three of them, and myself, held a garage sale on Friday and Saturday a few summers ago, and what a lot of work that was, as you all know! And we didn't get rid of some of the larger items we had hoped to, but let me tell you, it was fun, in spite of all the heavy lifting, scooting, carrying ~ sitting! Up early, and to bed early ~ worn out!

My daughters were all here, helping, sitting, visiting, laughing...and the people who came by, the shoppers, were so interesting and nice. An old neighbor from about 34 years ago in a different neighborhood happened to come along and we visited happily, catching up on family news. Another customer, a lady I had graduated from high school with 43 years before, came by, and recognizing each other, we visited for some time.

Some of the patrons didn't speak at all, but quietly, and quickly for some, scanned the merchandise and went on their way. Others stood and visited for the longest time, whether we knew them or not. A sweet lady from Puerto Rico (40 years prior) visited like she was our old friend, while her husband patiently waited in the car…neighbors came over to hang out. We ate donuts for breakfast and McDonald's for lunch, with snacking in between, sharing a pot of coffee. And when it was time to pack up, everyone pitched in and made it easier. I'm not so sure I want to do that again anytime soon, but it was good, and the weather cooperated beautifully.

It gave us, as a family, time to work together, rest together, and just be together ~ this was good. And the neighbors we usually wave at in passing took the time to stop and visit, whether they bought anything or not. In fact, our next door neighbor even brought over some items to add to our sale!

1st Peter 4:9 says *"Offer hospitality to one another without grumbling."* I think hospitality is as important at home as it is to the neighborhood and the community. Garage sales give us an opportunity to practice that!

JULY 9

THE GIFT OF ENCOURAGEMENT…

"Go in peace, and may the God of Israel grant your petition." (I Samuel 1: 17). Eli the priest said this to Hannah, who had been barren, at a time when her heart was very heavy.

How many times have you been discouraged about circumstances that just don't seem to get better? There will always be situations or people who will cause us to feel disheartened and hopeless. We have all been there. We will be there again. David wrote: *"Why so downcast, O my soul? Why so disturbed within me? Put your hope in God, for I will yet praise Him, my Savior and my God."* (Psalm 42:5-6). He was encouraged by the hope he had in the Lord. God lifted Him up and "drew him out of the deep waters." (Ps. 18:16).

Author George M. Adams said "Encouragement is oxygen to the soul." We know our bodies cannot live without oxygen ~ it is vital to our survival. And so, if we live in a downtrodden state day in and day out, our souls do not flourish. Encouragement costs us nothing to give, but it is priceless to that person who receives it. "One word or a pleasing smile is often enough to raise up a saddened and wounded soul." (Therese of Lisienux). On the other hand, a discouraging or harsh word can be devastating. We see this so much in our day, especially in children, when parents are impatient with them and so many times are abusive.

Encouragement is the finest gift we can give, and it should be given often to those we cherish. It is the ability we have to give courage, hope and confidence to another. What an impact this simple gift of encouragement could have on the lives of those we see from day to day. There is energizing power in a simple word of cheer or inspiration. May you and I bless and encourage someone today, just by a kind word, a simple act, a smile, helping with a difficult task, a card in the mail. Simple, but valuable.

JULY 10

MORE ENCOURAGEMENT…

Ran across this wonderful quote about encouragement, so I thought I'd piggyback on my last posting a little…it's good stuff…this one by Nicole Johnson of Women of Faith…

"Encouragement is to a relationship what confetti is to a party. It's light, refreshing, and fun. It's cheer you can throw someone's way. But even deeper, it is the assurance you are there, that you are standing behind them and supporting them. The time it takes to gather little pieces of love, grace, strength, and hope is well worth it when you see what happens as you shower those gifts on someone else."

And from God's word, *"We have different gifts, according to the grace given us. If a man's gift is prophesying, let him use it in proportion to his faith. If it is serving, let him serve; if it is teaching, let him teach;* ***if it is encouraging, let him encourage****; if it is contributing to the needs of others, let him give generously; if it is leadership, let him govern diligently; if it is showing mercy, let him do it cheerfully."* (Romans 12:6-8). You can find a more extensive list of these in I Corinthians 12, the first eleven verses. And some of us will recognize we have more than one gift. They're all from God.

So, you see, in addition to being a gift we can give others, encouragement is a gift given to us by the Holy Spirit in the first place. And if you can't think of anything to say in a given situation where encouragement is needed, try something from God's word: *"All things work together for good to those who love God and are called according to His purpose."* (Romans 8:28).

There is so much we can do to encourage one another, and if you can't think of anything to say, just an arm around the shoulder, or an open ear to listen, is enough to hearten someone during a rough time. A gift in itself.

JULY 11

BABY KITTENS...

My daughter's beloved cat, Chloe, is having her first litter of kittens. Of course, my daughter is more nervous than the cat is. The mama cat will purr through the whole delivery. God made her that way. And by instinct she will clean her babies all off and immediately begin nursing them. These babies will not be able to see or hear for a couple of weeks, since their eyes and ear canals will not open until then. So, they are totally dependent on their mother for care and nurturing. For awhile they will exist only to sleep and eat. And then, what personalities they will develop!

We marvel at the way we are made, *"knit together in our mother's womb... made in the secret place..."* (Psalm 139:13,15), but God also made each animal, each species and type within that species. God has a conversation with Job (38 & following), where He talks about the animals He created... *"Do you know when the mountain goats give birth? Do you watch when the doe bears her fawn? Do you count the months till they bear? Do you know the time they will give birth?"* (39:1-2). God knows when the mother cat is ready to bring forth her litter, when baby birds are ready to peck out of their shell, or the butterfly is prompted to emerge from its cocoon. A mother turtle will lay her eggs in the sand of the beach and when those eggs are ready, they will hatch and all the baby turtles will run to the sea. They already know the way. God's design is amazing. It boggles my mind to think how he must have imagined each creature.

And the animals aren't the only ones He envisioned. Just try to count how many different trees and flowers He made, or identify the song for every bird. I think there are still some sea life that we have never seen or heard of at this point. The seasons, and all the characteristics of each one, and God's masterpiece, Man. Each one unique and yet the same. We all need Him. He made us that way. And when we try to live our life without Him in it, we lose our way, and we lose hope. When a little blind kitten wanders away from the litter and the protection of its mama, she will go after it and lovingly carry it back to the safety of the litter. When we wander away, God comes after us to bring us back into the safety of His shelter. That's why He sent Jesus. Through His death on the Cross and His resurrection, He made it possible for us to have that loving and nurturing relationship with God the Father. It's the only way. *"Jesus answered, 'I am the Way, the Truth, and the Life. No one comes to the Father except through Me.'"* (John 14:6). We are dependent on Him for our care and nurturing, guidance, and rescuing when we have gone astray. Just like baby kittens.

JULY 12

THE HOUSE(S) I GREW UP IN...

We all have memories of the house we grew up in. The street it sat on, the neighbors, the kids we used to play with. We remember the back yard, the gardens and trees, the school it was near. The sounds...faucet dripping, furnace kicking on, a tree branch blowing against the house, and we recall each room and how they were situated. Some of us were fortunate to grow up in one house, in fact, I know adults who still live in the same house their parents raised them in. One of my daughters occupies our old house with her family, so I guess she could qualify...

I lived in many different houses while I was growing up...I remember nine, and there were probably a few more before I was old enough to remember them. I even remember some of the addresses. Since my dad was in the Navy, our houses were in various parts of the country. I loved most of them. My mom always made them feel homey and comfortable. There was a tiny little cracker box house when I was about two, with no lawn, just dirt, then we moved into a real neighborhood on a nice corner lot, and I had a real playhouse of my own. We next lived on an 80-acre farm ~ this was a log cabin that I wish was still there. The rest were pretty much tract homes, in military housing, then the last house my parents bought when my dad retired, again in the woods, but I can draw you a floor plan of each one, even though we spent only a year or two in some of them.

Just like our house(s) all had a living room, bedrooms, kitchen and bath, our lives also have different rooms, used for different purposes. We have places and times of rest, nourishment, fellowship, learning and growth, just as we did in our homes as children. I realize some homes did not have a father, but our heavenly Father wants to be at home in each of our hearts. He will feed us abundantly, speak His love to us, discipline us and teach us His truths, keep us safe, offer grace and healing, keep us warm, and best of all, we can trust Him with our deepest thoughts and secrets. *"If anyone loves Me, he will obey My teaching. My Father will love him, and We will come to him and make Our home with him."* (John 14:23). Our homes are familiar to us. And God can be, too. Why not make Him your Home…your dwelling place?

JULY 13

A SINCERE HEART…

"Let us draw near to God with a sincere heart in full assurance of faith, having our hearts sprinkled to cleanse us from a guilty conscience and having our bodies washed with pure water. Let us hold unswervingly to the hope we profess, for He who promised is faithful. And let us consider how we may spur one another on toward love and good deeds. Let us not give up meeting together, as some are in the habit of doing, but let us encourage one another." (Hebrews 10:22-25).

Here is another song currently being played on Christian radio, by Matthew West, which says in the chorus,

" 'Cause I don't wanna go through the motions
I don't wanna go one more day
without Your all consuming passion inside of me
I don't wanna spend my whole life asking,
"What if I had given everything,
instead of going through the motions?"

This song has been going through my head for two days. The song is "Motions" and it is standing at the #1 position in Christian music right now. It's not one of my favorites, not one that I love to sing over and over again, but the message is rich. I got to thinking about that message of "going through the motions"…am I doing that with my Christian walk? Or am I sincere in my faith. Am I going to have regrets when I stand before the Lord on that Day? Do I "walk the walk and talk the talk," even in my family? Do I volunteer to help those who are needier than I am? Am I faithful in prayer? What about my attitude? Am I judgmental? Hmmm...am I stepping on anyone's toes...?

We need to come before the Lord, "with a sincere heart" and confess where we are falling short. God knows the secrets of our heart. (Ps. 44:10). *"The Lord does not look at the things man looks at. Man looks at the outward appearance, but the Lord looks at the heart."* (1 Samuel 16:7). Let's stop just going through the motions, and ask God to make our hearts sincere, and may we have that wonderful assurance of faith...

JULY 14

HERE AM I LORD, SEND ME...

Did you ever say that, sincerely and solemnly? Isaiah did. God wanted him to go to a people who wouldn't listen, wouldn't see, who had turned their back on Him. He was actually sent to pronounce doom upon them...kind of strange. Truly, Isaiah didn't feel qualified to be used of God, to proclaim any kind of message to the people. But God purified him, on the spot! And he was willing to go ~ he stepped right up! This was a prime example of godly leadership. He said, *"Here am I, send me!"* (Isaiah 6:8). It used to be, when someone was willing to step out and "go" for God, it meant AFRICA! I even heard a humorous little song years ago, penned by missionaries, no doubt, that talked about the mission field, anywhere, "but please don't send me to Africa!"

I know for a fact that just because God calls us to be "missionaries" it doesn't always mean He will send us to Africa. There are so many places and situations where God can use us, whether it be across the globe, or just across town, and if we are willing, whether we think we are qualified or not, then God can do His work through us. You may be used in a soup kitchen somewhere, a jail ministry, a ladies Bible study. You may sit in the church nursery during the service so parents can enjoy worship without the interruption of their little ones. Maybe paint the house of an elderly person, or weed their garden. You may go on a work and witness trip for a couple of weeks to a less fortunate community or country, to build a church, administer medical treatment, or run a vacation Bible school. Or maybe sit with a sick neighbor. Caring for a sister, being Jesus to someone ~ that's what God is "sending" many of us to do. We need to be willing. And, of course, He just may send us to Africa.

Most of the time we think we are not "qualified," or well-versed enough in the scriptures, or trained...God doesn't care. He only wants our willingness. He will actually do the work Himself, if we just offer ourselves as His vessels. His words will speak through our mouths, His actions will take place through our hands. Miracles He performs through ordinary people are most believable. We need to empty ourselves of our selfishness and our pride. Sometimes we feel we are having so many problems coping, God couldn't possibly use us. But as long as our deepest desire is to be used of Him, to make a difference in even one person's life, God can work through us, even in the midst of our own troubles. *"But we have this treasure in jars of clay to show that this all-surpassing power is from God and* ***not from us****."* (2 Corinthians 4:7).

Don't listen to your own self-talk that tells you that you are no good, that there are "better" people who could be used by God. Our Father, the eternal and unchanging Sovereign God of the universe knows us better than we know ourselves. We just need to be willing to let Him mold us as He meant for us to be. He is the Potter, and we are the clay. His plan for us does not depend on our ability to follow through, but on His own power and majesty. Somehow our story fits in. "Here am I, Lord. Send me!"

JULY 15

SERENDIPITY RECIPROCATED...

I love surprises ~ well, nice surprises, that is. Even since I was a young girl, I never wanted to know what any of my presents were until I opened them. I knew many people, including my brothers, who would snoop, and shake, and rattle and squeeze the presents under the Christmas tree to see if they could guess what was inside. I have known some people who have actually unwrapped gifts then re-wrapped them again, just to find out what was in them! I never even wanted to SEE my presents because I wanted to be surprised.

We are surprised in many ways. Maybe a letter will come in the mail. Or we might be the recipient or the winner of a special prize from a contest or a drawing. Some of you may remember when I surprised my cousin, Joni, in a faraway state a couple of years ago by showing up at her house for an event I was invited to, both of us knowing I couldn't simply hop a jet and be present for it. Which is exactly what I did. It was a wishful idea. The planning was almost as much fun as actually pulling it off. Her daughters knew about my plan and went along with the secret. It turned out perfect.

So last year the Women of Faith conference was held in a town close to me, and two of my daughters and I typically attend each year. So on Friday morning there was nothing unusual about my daughters stopping by to pick me up, except for when I opened the back door of the van…and there sat my cousin, Joni!! She had been in town staying with a friend of the family until the appointed time. Needless to say, I was pleasantly surprised. Ecstatic! We shared a wonderful weekend together. She said she "owed" me. Of course, her visit was too short, just a few days together…but what a nice surprise. Everyone in my family, and a lot of people in my church already knew about this visit, but I didn't have a single clue.

"Serendipity" is defined as an *aptitude for making fortunate discoveries accidently*. This has come to my mind often during my life as I have made a certain discovery, or been surprised in a pleasant way. I love the word. It's a little more than a surprise. It has also been defined as a "happy accident." I have learned over the years to thank God for these moments. I'd also like to call them "blessings." Something really pleasant that you are not expecting. And it's fun when someone who has been on the receiving end works to reciprocate in some small, or large, way, as my cousin did.

I think "random acts of kindness" can be included in this idea, as well. Many years ago we were having a really rough time financially (well, we have been there several times, actually). One day we came home and there was a sack of groceries on our porch. Another time there was an unexpected refund check in the mail from an insurance company. Pleasant surprises that we do not expect. Or how about the email my daughter received already the first week of school from one of her son's high school teachers, which said what a pleasure he was to have in class, and what a good student he was? This is a boy in his first year in high school who has really struggled in middle school, and has not had the best of study habits, or attitudes. This was a huge deal. Such a little thing to do, but it made such a difference in my daughter's day.

I have known about Jesus' gift to us since I was a little girl. But what a wonderful surprise to those who have not known about it, when they find out that Jesus, God's own Son, died on the cross for them. For one thing, who would love us enough to do something like that? It's the ultimate of serendipity. It really should not be considered a surprise, when it has been made public in the Book of books down through the ages. But some just do not realize it – until they discover for themselves that it is true.

I love the way God works in our lives. I do believe these little, and big, surprises and blessings are orchestrated by our heavenly Father who knows just what we need to encourage us. When we are losing hope, or when we are lonely, or when we are thinking what we do does not matter to anyone, God comes through with "serendipity." I believe His healing and His provision can fall into this category. When you think about it, I'll bet you could come up with some blessings of your own to thank Him for.

JULY 16

THE AIRPORT...

Yesterday I went to the airport to pick up a friend who was flying in to spend some time with her grandkids. Although she'll be here for two weeks, I may not get to see her if her grandkids keep her busy enough... and there is a brand new days-old great-grandbaby for her to cuddle, too! So, we had plans to spend a few hours together before she drove to their house...

Although I had been notified that her flight would be a little late, I arrived at the airport early, had maybe a ½ hour, to just watch people. There were lots of people leaving, saying goodbye, waving as they headed to the security stations, but there were also a lot of people arriving. The hellos were much different that the goodbyes. I watched their faces. The goodbyes were sometimes tearful, and the hugs lasted a little longer. But, on the other hand, when someone spotted the one(s) they were waiting for, faces broke into big smiles, and there were exclamations, and laughter, and hugs, and pats on the back. I have met many people at the airport over the years. Most of them I knew. Some of them I didn't know...we've had five foreign exchange students, and although we had seen their photos on the paperwork, we still weren't sure exactly what they would look like. And most of the time, their hair was styled differently than in their picture. So, we carried a placard with their name on it to hold up so they would see we were there for them! I know those feelings, both the goodbyes, and the hellos.

I got to thinking of these reunions, meeting the visitors, or the ones coming home after a long absence, and I thought of how heaven would be when we arrive. Certainly there will be loved ones there waiting for us to arrive. I think there will be "great rejoicing" over each one who steps through those pearly gates. It will be the best homecoming ever. Not only will our loved ones be rejoicing that we have arrived, but all the hosts of heaven will be joining in the celebration ~ for EACH one of us! Can you imagine? And the celebration will go on and on. The lost has been found. The prodigals have come home. And we will be right on time…not late, like my friend's flight was yesterday. And best of all, Jesus will be there to greet us… "*Well done, good and faithful servant*." (Mt. 25:21). I can't wait for that arrival!

JULY 17

LASTING FRIENDSHIP….

Friendships come and go, all our lives. And then sometimes they are renewed, as has been the case with some of the women I know. Many friendships are only temporary, but in one way or another, most have made some kind of an impact on our lives. I don't readily remember *all* of my friendships, but I can recall a good number of them. As I have mentioned before, my dad was a military man, and that meant moving around the country often. So, it was difficult for me to make friends. However, I did have one or two good friends at each "port" who touched my life, even as little girls, and then several others who all played or went to school together. As I got older, my friendships became deeper and had more meaning. It was easier to keep in touch through letters, as "pen pals."

The Bible speaks of friendships, too. One of the most popular stories is of Ruth and Naomi. At the death of Naomi's husband and sons, she tearfully dismissed her daughters-in-law to go back to their families. And though they both loved her very much, one went, one stayed. And one of the most beloved quotes in the old testament is what Ruth said to her mother-in-law: "*Where you go I will go, and where you stay, I will stay.Your people will be my people and your God my God.*" (Ruth 1:16). What a beautiful example of faithfulness. Ruth loved her mother-in-law so much, she couldn't imagine life without her. They had formed not only a familial relationship, but a deep and true friendship, as well.

And I think Ruth may have felt some responsibility to take care of Naomi in her old age.

David and Jonathan were also "best friends." David was up-and-coming as future king, and his companion was Jonathan, the son of King Saul. 1 Samuel 18:1 tells us that *"Jonathan became one in spirit with David, and loved him as himself."* They even became "blood brothers" by cutting themselves and mingling their blood. The king, Saul, enjoyed listening to David play his harp, to relax him when he was stressed by his responsibilities. But soon Saul became jealous of David because David was successful in all he did, and Saul sought to kill him. Eventually David had to flee, and Jonathan helped him to get away safely.

Job had some friends, too; Eliphaz, Bildad, and Zophar, and when they heard about Job's troubles, they came to spend time with him. They were so distraught at his suffering, no one spoke for a week, but they sat with him in silence, grieving with him and comforting him. Commendable. When they finally began to speak, they became judgmental and blamed Job's sin for his trouble. They apparently were ignorant of the fact that God Himself had named Job as a most righteous, *"blameless and upright man, like whom there was no one else on the earth."*(1:8). And in the end, God sent these three "friends" packing. And yet, Job prayed for them, even as the Lord sent them away. (Ch. 42).

Other friendships we read about in God's word are Abraham and God, Jesus and Lazarus, Jesus and...US! John quotes Jesus in 15:13, saying *"Greater love has no one than this, that He lay down His life for His friends."* Jesus did that for us! There is a fairly new song entitled, "Jesus, Friend of Sinners," and the chorus says it all...

"Oh Jesus, friend of sinners
Open our eyes to the world at the end of our pointing fingers
Let our hearts be led by mercy
Help us reach with open hearts and open doors
Oh Jesus, friend of sinners, break our hearts for what breaks yours"

I am thankful for the lasting friendships I have. I thoroughly enjoyed meeting my old friend at the airport and spending the afternoon with her before I deposited her at her grandson's home in my town. Nancy and I met in my neighborhood when I had only one baby, and her three boys were very small. We became fast friends, studying God's word together, spending time and sharing almost every day, but after a few years she moved away. Yet we still kept in touch ~ it's been almost 40 years. We are kindred spirits. Her friendship is so uplifting and encouraging to me. And she prays for me often. Many of us have a friend like this. I have a few. I consider myself very blessed.

And I know that no matter what I do, no matter where I go or what I say, Jesus will always be my friend. He loves me with an everlasting, undying love, like no other I could imagine, better than any best friend I could name. He loves me when I'm unlovable, when I've sinned, when I've put Him off, when I turn away. And as I read in Proverbs 18:24, He is a *"friend who sticks closer than a brother"* (or sister!).

JULY 18

MID-SUMMER...

Well, In North Idaho it's usually about this time of the summer when it actually begins getting nice. The constant rains have stopped, the days are warm, the nights clear and cool, flowers are blooming, and some are waning, fruit and vegetables are maturing, and if you don't water enough, some lawns are turning brown. It's this time of the summer when we forget about how disappointed we were to keep waking up to cloudy and rainy days, not too long ago, because the days are now so nice. Kids are suntanned, the beach is crowded with sounds of laughter and splashing, and there are bicycles everywhere. The air is fragrant with mowed lawns, freshly cut alfalfa fields, and barbeques. The campgrounds are full and the highways are cluttered with cars and SUVs heading for vacation destinations. It's a favorite time of year for almost everyone. Carefree, relaxed, with long evenings to enjoy. Seems like it could go on and on…and sometimes we wish it would.

Our lives are a little like that from time to time. There seems to be a long rainy and cloudy season that leaves us a little, or a lot, depressed. But when the sun breaks through, we find ourselves smiling a little more and enjoying the warmth. It seems our troubles have lifted and we can relax some. God's word tells us it won't always be sunshiny. In John 16:33 Jesus said, *"I have told you these things so that in Me you may have peace. In this world you will have trouble. But take heart! I have overcome the world!"* I'm not trying to spread doom and gloom, saying our bliss will not last, but we all know summer will end some day, not too many weeks away, and then will come the rain again, and winter. And we just need to keep in mind that when that happens, we can still enjoy the sunshine of His love, and His peace, and know that the warm days will come again. Actually, it's the warm glow of His love that gets me through the cold dark days that are certain to be coming along sooner than we think. And Jesus has promised that someday *"There will be no more night. They will not need the light of a lamp or the light of the sun, for the Lord God will give them light."* (Rev. 22:5). When we finally make it through this life and are with Him in our heavenly home, it will be mid-summer every day. And just like children, we won't have a care in the world.

JULY 19

GET REAL...

Do you know the difference between what is real, and what is not? We used to be able to tell the difference pretty easily. In fact, pretty much everything WAS real, generations ago. Today many things appear to be the real thing, but they're not, really. For instance, furnishings and surfaces in your home may appear to be wood, or even marble, but are really a substitute, some other material, even plastics, made to only *look* real. I think of the fairly new decking that looks like wood, but is made from ...milk cartons?!

I think about the detriment we cause young girls these days, advertising and flaunting beautiful models, girls they could never be, even air-brushed photographs in teen magazines, making girls feel less important and less valuable because they will never look that way. I heard on the Christian radio station a recent report about a 14-year old girl who was fed up with all the beautiful models in a teenage magazine, she began a petition for that magazine to include at least four (I think) models of "regular"-looking young women per issue that their *normal* audience could identify with. She collected tens of thousands of signatures, and actually traveled to the office of the magazine's editor and presented her petition. She made an impact. They agreed to her request.

Have you looked at the labels on the foods you're eating lately? Do you know what disodium inosinate, silicon dioxide, cellulose gum, sodium stearoyl lactylate, maltodextrin, and sodium caseinate are? I don't either. Those are ingredients listed on a package of sauce mix in my pantry. And I read a report some time ago that all the ingredients listed in margarine make it one molecule away from plastic. Occasionally, you will see something with "natural" ingredients, or flavors in it. I'm convinced that a lot of the foods we eat are not real food at all. In fact, many could be dangerous for us to consume. And yet, we do, every day. How scary. Do you suppose that's why we're sick?

I'm pretty sure that all we read in the newspapers isn't the whole truth. I really hate to be duped, don't you? There is one thing, though, that is really real, one source of information that has stood the test of time. Many people have tried to change it, or prove it wrong, but the Living Word of God cannot be changed or replaced by any other doctrine. II Samuel 22:31 says, *"The word of the Lord is flawless."* That means it's perfect. You can be sure that God means what He says. *"So is My word that goes out from My mouth; it will not return to Me empty, but will accomplish what I desire and achieve the purpose for which I sent it."* (Isaiah 55:11). So, no matter what men do with God's word, it will never be voided. In fact, John 1:1 says, *"In the beginning was the Word, and the Word was with God, and the Word WAS God. He was with God in the beginning."* So, in truth, Jesus is the Word. (vs. 14), *"The Word became flesh and made His dwelling among us."* It's REAL. It's alive. It is true and trustworthy. Everything we ever need to know about life is in God's Word. *"For the Word of God is living and active... Sharper than a double-edged sword..."* (Hebrews 4:12).

Don't be deceived by the lies that society tells us. Be careful what you eat, be careful of what you listen to. And be careful when other doctrines try to tell us "this is the way." For Jesus said, *"I am the way, the truth and the life."* (John 14:6). Get real!

JULY 20

THE BIG RED SUN...

Are you tired of hearing me say, "I love looking at the sky?"...the clouds, rainbows, sunsets, moon and stars, and phenomena such as those circle rainbows, or...a red sun! We had a very wet spring and half of summer, but about the middle of July, it turned hot and the rain stopped. This is the season we worry about forest fires here in North Idaho, because the forests get awfully dry, and though we do have thunderstorms, they do not always produce rain. But the lightning strikes will spark a fire in the dry woods. And, many times the wind knows just when to blow to wreak havoc. Yesterday was cooler because there was a haze that was obscuring the sun, but in the evening, when the sun was beginning to sink in the west…it was awesome to look at (I know, you're not supposed to look directly at the sun!) because it was just a huge red ball in the sky. It brought a lot of people outside to have a look. Everything was bathed in a red glow. It was eerie. It was really beautiful. But we knew…well, those of us who have lived here a long time…that there was a forest fire somewhere causing that smoke haze and the redness in the sun. I heard it was in Canada, and we are close to the Canadian border. So, the fire season has begun. And we pray for rain.

God is so absolutely awesome. Everything that has come from His hand is unbelievable ~ do we even notice it? *"The day is Yours, and Yours also the night; You established the sun and moon. It was You who set all the boundaries of the earth; You made both summer and winter."* (Psalm 74:16-17). Sure, it's easy to believe the creation, the sun and moon, the stars, the wind, thunder and lightning… but did you ever think about the intricacies of the seasons, and which plants grow and bloom at which times, when the wild animals give birth to their young, the "boundaries of the earth?" Job had quite a conversation with God about this…or the other way around, actually. In Job 38, God reminded Job of things we don't even think about…when God marked off the dimensions of the earth, when He fixed limits for the ocean and the tides, ordered the dawn at just the right time. Or what about the beginnings of the bubbling springs, the vast expanses of the universe, where the darkness goes when daylight appears? He talks about the storehouses of snow and hail…did you know there was such a thing?? He tells the lightning where to strike, the ice crystals when to form. He provides prey for the lioness to feed her young, tells the bear when to crawl into his cave and sleep, and signals to the robin when to lay her eggs. Oh, I love reading this passage in Job, actually, the next three or four chapters, too. There is no end to God's awesome power, no end to His creation…it goes on and on. And I love to look at it. His creation always prompts me to praise Him. There is none like Him.

JULY 21

GROWING UP…

Boy, doesn't it seem like the kids just grow like weeds in the summer months? What is it? All that exercise? The sunshine? And, of course, everything grows in the summer…our gardens, the trees, baby animals…I love to watch the deer in our neighborhood. We've had three sets of twin fawns, along with their mothers, roaming our streets and yards. We saw the babies in the spring while they were just hours old, and it's been fun watching them grow. I'm fascinated by them. They don't wander too far from their mamas. And they trust that their mamas are watching out for them. Isn't it amazing how God created everything to give and have new life? And how He sustains it all?

We are like that in our knowledge of His word and in our relationship with the Savior. I Peter 2: 2 says, *"Like newborn babies, crave pure spiritual milk, so that by it you may grow up in your salvation, now that you have tasted that the Lord is good."* All babies need milk in order to grow, and it makes sense that baby Christians also need the milk of God's word to grow and mature. But Paul put it very clearly to the Hebrews when he said, *"We have much to say about this, but it is hard to explain because you are slow to learn."* (is that us sometimes?) Paul goes on… *"In fact, though by this time you ought to be teachers, you need someone to teach you the elementary truths of God's word all over again. You need milk, not solid food! Anyone who lives on milk, being still an infant, is not acquainted with the teaching about righteousness. But solid food is for the mature, who by constant use have trained themselves to distinguish good from evil. Therefore, let us leave the elementary teachings about Christ and go on to maturity…"* (Hebrews 5:11-6:1). So, of course, after we learn the basics, we do need to move on to the meat of the word. And then as we grow and mature, and our faith strengthens, we learn and experience more of God's grace in every situation of our lives.

Are we ready to move on to bigger and better things God's word has promised to us who are faithful? I want to learn all I can, while I can. *"Your word have I hid in my heart that I might not sin against you."* (Psalm 119:11). We must read it and digest it daily!

JULY 22

BLESSINGS OF FAMILY…

Here is a saying worth repeating…I am SO blessed! I never cease to thank God for my wonderful family. I have three grown daughters with families, a married granddaughter, who makes another arm of the family, and an almost 3-year-old great-granddaughter, who is a joy to everyone…and she knows it!

Since our family all live close to us, we do many things together. And one thing we have traditionally done, for forty-plus years, is go camping together on Labor Day weekend, at a State park near us. My own children grew up on this camp trip along with their grandparents, now deceased, but we have carried on the tradition all these years, and they will probably still get together for camp with their families after we are gone. Of course, my husband likes to take (almost) all the conveniences of home, even if we don't have electricity. He brings along plenty of propane bottles so we will have lots of light and be able to cook. And, thankfully, there was not good cell phone reception where we were, so there was a lot of familial interaction. A heap of time spent together. Everyone helped out with meals, babysitting, and dog-walking. And there was a lot of conversation, games, and much good-natured joking.

A weekend trip like this, with family, causes me to reflect on the family I grew up in. We were much the same way. We camped out often, and my parents taught us much about nature and how to get along without all the conveniences ~ my dad was very innovative. He built his own tent trailer of wood, and a very heavy canvas tent, which I sat on the living room floor and sewed together on my machine at his instruction. This was later snapped onto rivets he had installed onto the edges of the trailer. Anything he could do himself, he didn't have to pay someone else to do. My parents also taught us real life lessons, which I have tried to pass along to my own children as they grew up, and now onto our grandchildren. David said in Psalm 71:17-19, *"Since my youth, O God, You have taught me, and to this day I declare your marvelous deeds. Even when I am old and gray, do not forsake me, O God, till I declare Your power to the next generation, Your might to all who are to come. Your righteousness reaches to the skies, O God, You who have done great things. Who, O God, is like You?"* Oh, it goes on, and this passage is rich, talking about how God restores us after we have seen trouble, and how He increases our honor and comforts us. It's one of my favorites. I want my kids and grandkids to know all the wonderful things God has done for our family.

On the first night at camp a couple of years ago, after we had gotten mostly set up, all the tents and awnings, and were sitting around a beautiful campfire, God gave us a display of His power in a beautiful thunderstorm. There were oooh's and awe's, and suddenly, the storm was directly above us, with the thunder and lightning striking at precisely the same second. It was only then that we thought to get up and move our chairs into the "protection" of a big tent where we were to have our meals. Of course, we brought our girls up to not be afraid of storms and instead they all love them, even the little ones. But this one was a little close to home! What a wonderful exhibit of God's might! Job described the thunder in his book, chapter 37, as *"the roar of His voice,""the rumbling from His mouth."* The next morning, I took out my Bible and read this passage to all of the family as they were seated around the fire, eating their breakfast. There was much discussion and contemplation about how thunder and lightning "happens." I think it's pretty complicated, but I know this, *"The heavens declare the glory of God, the skies proclaim the work of His hands!"* (Psalm 19:1). That's good enough for me.

And so...once again I marvel at how blessed I am. I have seen Him work in so many ways, all my life, and I want to be sure my children call this very thing to the attention of their children as well. And in the end, perhaps maybe *"my children will arise and call me blessed!"* (Proverbs 31:28). Because I truly am!

JULY 23

OUR HOPE IN HIM...

Do circumstances sometimes get so bad that you just seem to give up hope? You work and work, and it seems one disaster after another befalls you and you have to start all over again. Or, you, or one of your loved ones, receive a diagnosis of a grave disease, and after much treatment you, or they, don't seem to be getting better. You pray and pray for your children to have a relationship with your Savior, and for years you lovingly counsel them, and keep praying, but it never seems to happen. For three summers my youngest daughter has planted a garden, diligently caring for it and watering and weeding it, but it was the third summer it has barely produced anything worth eating. Yet, she hasn't given up hope ~ she is already planning for next year's garden, strategizing about how she can do it better. My granddaughter has been looking for a job in the medical field since she received her degree five months ago, but she hasn't given up hope because her family won't let her! We keep encouraging her.

God doesn't want us to give up hope, especially when we come to the point where everything seems so ~ hopeless. God is the restorer of our hope. He is the Master Builder of our lives, He has the original plan and as the shepherd said, *"He restores my soul."* (Psalm 23:3). God restores our energy, our vigor, and our hope. He makes us new.

Many times a person will give up hope in a marriage that seems to be dying, or in a job where they feel they are going nowhere. One is ill, and has gone to many doctors for a cure and nothing seems to work...they feel like giving up. A young mother, discouraged because she can't keep up with the housework gives up hope on ever having a clean house. And so on. God never promised us that this life would be easy ~ we live in a fallen world. But we can have the hope He gives for eternal life. We must be diligent in seeking after Him and pray for the *"Spirit of wisdom and revelation so that we may know Him better. May the eyes of our hearts be enlightened in order that we may know the* ***hope*** *to which He has called us, the riches of His glorious inheritance in the saints and His incomparable great power for us who believe."* (Ephesians 1:17-19 ~ my paraphrase).

It's easy for us to look around and see the devastation in our country and our government, in our world, and to want to give up hope and walk away. But our God, because of His unfailing love for us, is a God of hope. That familiar verse in Isaiah 40:31 says, *"but those who* ***hope*** *in the Lord will renew their strength. They will soar on wings as eagles; they will run and not grow weary, they will walk and not be faint."* Paul had a lot to say about Hope...that it will not disappoint us, that we can be joyful in hope, the scriptures will give us hope, God will fill us with hope, hope goes well with faith and love, hope inspires endurance. We cannot live without hope. It's so plain to see.

"We have this ***hope*** *(in Christ) as an anchor for the soul, firm and secure."* (Hebrews 6:19). "*Christ in us IS the* ***hope*** *of glory."* (Col. 1:27). Don't ever give up hope. Ask God for it and it will be renewed in you.

JULY 24

IN DEFENSE OF MODERN WORSHIP MUSIC...

I have to admit, many years ago, when our church first added drums to hymns, my eyebrows went up. There was some muttering in the following Sundays, until we got used to it. I've been listening to Christian radio for a long time, so the "new" worship music doesn't bother me at all. There is much of it I love. Unlike some who only hear the beat, or the voices, I listen to the words. The messages are exactly what we need to hear. The other day I wrote about praying the music. It's an easy thing to do. There are usually several comments about the "new music," and one idea expressed was that though the old hymns are about God, many of the new songs are about "me." I don't see that.

Indulge me to include just a few phrases from the modern music I listen to...all of a sudden I am unaware of these afflictions eclipsed by glory ~ it's all about You ~ my hope is in You Lord and my heart cries glory hallelujah ~ lost are saved, find their way at the sound of Your great name ~ worthy is the Lamb slain for us, Son of God & Man ~ Redeemer, my Healer ~ Jesus, You are my reward, You're all I'm living for ~ my heart will sing no other name, Jesus ~ I'm running to Your arms, the riches of Your love will always be enough ~ Light of the world ~ I just might bend but I won't break as long as I can see Your face ~ O glorious day ~ sing, sing, sing & make music with the heavens, grateful that You hear us when we shout Your praise, lift high the name of Jesus...

Well, these are just random phrases I wrote down today while listening in. We need to remember that when hymns are about God, they are also about the struggles the writers were going through. Paul's and David's writings and songs were about "me," about the struggles they were going through, the failures and pain, but they still pointed to God's strength, hope, love, mercy. They talked about miracles, about faith. Their messages were about God ~ and to God. And the modern music really is no different. It addresses our modern day struggles and crises, and the answers to which only come from our Savior. They clearly point to God's redemptive love. I agree, some of it is not my style, as it is not your choice either, but still the message is the same. The Word says to *"make a joyful noise"* and Psalm 98 addresses this: ***"Sing to the Lord a new song..."*** and throughout the rest of this chapter it mentions many different instruments, as well as singing and dancing, clapping ~ joy. God just wants us to worship Him, from our heart. Little children are so good at this ~ they are uninhibited in their worship!

I don't think God wants us to argue about what the best worship music is, and I'm not trying to take sides. But I wanted to express my feelings about giving ALL worship music as a sweet offering to God. It all blesses Him. Most songwriters get their lyrics directly from Scripture, or their own experience which brought them to seek God. Many times I have been driving and a song will play that moves me to tears. Not every song will be meaningful for every heart. But no matter what kind of praise music you listen to, always keep a song in your heart. Always allow yourself to be inspired. And look for the prayer in the song.

JULY 25

PAPER DOLLS...

Remember those? When I was a young girl, I always had to have a new book of paper dolls, my favorite thing to own. I was very happy cutting them out and I even designed their clothes when I was bored. I especially loved tearing out the page in my mom's McCall's Magazine with Betsy McCall and her clothes for that month. That one was special. I was probably more excited for the magazine to arrive than my mom was! I think my favorite part of paper dolls was cutting them out ~ I had super good cutting skills! And we didn't have punch-out ones then. I loved the old fashioned southern belle dolls with their huge flowing skirts and tiny waists, and the glamorous movie star ones, and even the little girl dolls. The paper-doll designers sure have an imagination. They've covered everything, even cartoon characters.

When we began to have granddaughters added to our family, I found a set of extra heavy cardboard dolls that had magnetized clothes and wooden stands. No more little folding tabs to tear or accidentally cut off. I still have a set of magnetic snowmen dolls for the refrigerator. During the holidays, I stick them all on the fridge and when any little girl passes by, they can interchange the clothes, hats and boots on two or three snow ladies. I've even seen them sitting on the floor in front of the fridge dressing them.

For the last 8-9 years I have had a new collection of paper dolls I've been saving up for my younger granddaughters, until they were "old enough" to responsibly cut them out. These were in Mary Engelbreit's Home Companion magazines, which I received for about two years several years ago. These pages are nice, heavier paper and I ripped them out each month and put them away in a nice little box that looks like a suitcase. My granddaughters are now 9 years old, and would you believe, I just remembered about the paper dolls this year! I got them out, gave them scissors, and they were so excited! They just cut and visited...it was so cute. They kept commenting on how much they liked them and how much fun it was to cut them out. And they are the kind with the fold-over tabs on the shoulders...something "new?" These even come with accessories, hats, skates, a scooter, and a puppy!

It's not that I'm thinking of myself as a paper doll, or a puppet in God's hands, but I do know He has quite an imagination and an awesome sense of creativity when it comes to making people. He lovingly created me in that secret place. (Psalm 139:13-14). Evidence that He designed each one of us specially, to be like no other. It's amazing to me that of the over 6 billion people on the globe, no two are exactly alike. No assembly line or printing press reproductions. God's resources and inspiration never run out. *"And even the very hairs of your head are all numbered."* (Matthew 10:30). And God doesn't just put us together haphazardly then send us on our way...He keeps His eye on us and knows us through and through...and *"the Lord knows even our thoughts."* (Psalm 94:11). How can He keep track of who's who? Oh, He knows us, and He never loses track of our lives. He sees us when we sometimes feel crumpled up and ripped, and thrown aside, like a well-used paper doll. He knows our every hurt, hears each prayer we pray to Him, either in agony of pain, or in moments of praise and thanksgiving.

And unlike little girls who eventually grow tired and bored with paper dolls, discarding or putting them aside for more "grown-up" activities, God never sets us aside. I like how Jesus' words are recorded in John 6:37, *"All that the Father giveth Me shall come to Me; and him that cometh to Me* ***I will in no wise cast out****."*(That's King James Version). And He promised to *"never leave nor forsake"* us. (Hebrews 13:5). I love that my Creator has followed me from day one and is still very aware of what's going on in my life, even in my old age. He will never cast me aside, even when I no longer feel "useful." I am His masterpiece.

JULY 26

PRAYING FROM THE SONGS...

I have a friend who is publishing a devotional book called "Praying Today's Psalms," which I love to do. There are so many things in the Psalms to pray for. I think God likes it when we pray His word back to Him.

I love to listen to the Christian radio station in our area all day long, when I'm at home and in the car. It has been so easy to pray for young people who were once in my Sunday School class, and are now grown and in high school, or college, and facing struggles in their lives, many because of the choices they have made. I'm inspired when I hear almost every song played. For instance, "I Praise You in This Storm" prompts me to pray that they will learn to praise God in all the storms in their life right now. "I Will Follow" causes me to pray that they will listen and hear God's voice, and that they will turn and follow Him. There's a new song called "Suitcases" and talks about all the baggage we carry around with us ~ when I hear this song, I pray that my young struggling friends will learn to cast all their cares on Jesus. Another new one, "Blessings," says that sometimes the trials of this life are God's mercies in disguise, and that our healing may come through our disappointments and tears. So, I pray that they will learn to lean on Jesus during these hard times and know that He is there.

You can listen to almost any song, and pray a prayer for someone, or yourself, from the lyrics. It seems that since I discovered this, I can be in an "attitude of prayer" throughout the day. 1 Thessalonians 5:17 says to *"pray without ceasing."* I think this is what it means. I feel like that's what I have been doing for the past few days. You may have CDs of certain favorite artists and you can do the same with those songs. They all carry a message of God's love and redemption. When I hear "I Am Free," a style of song I don't particularly like, but the message is wonderful, I pray for my young friends to feel that freedom that God's forgiveness gives. "Lead Me to the Cross" ~ self-explanatory. "You Are God Alone" ~ I pray that they will realize there are no other gods, and since before time began our God is unshakeable, unchangeable, and unstoppable, and He's on the throne. Well, you get the idea.

What an adventure, to pray the Christian songs as they come out of my radio. These prayers can be for anyone. What one song won't cover, another will. When you hear a Christian song on the radio, ask God to bring someone to mind who needs that message, and pray those lyrics for that person. And realize what a privilege prayer is.

JULY 27

MORE ON JOB...

Job suffered innumerable losses ~ his home, his family, his cattle, his possessions. All because Satan thought he could sway him away from God. The enemy of our souls didn't think there was anyone on earth who would stay faithful to the Almighty through such affliction as he could administer. And God gave him permission to do so! I don't think Job knew of this plan, let alone asked what he thought of it...if that were the case, he could have known it was a test of his faith, and made himself ready for the onslaught. Instead, he was stricken with all kinds of hardships, immediately, one right after another. The devil didn't waste any time trying to destroy Job. He took everything. He inflicted sickness on his body. Oh, Job grieved and lamented, but he didn't despair...he knew everything he had was a blessing from God. Even his wife told him to *"curse God and die."* To this, Job answered, *"Shall we accept good from God, and not trouble?"* (2:10).

As things went from bad to worse, Job cursed the day he was born. His friends came to console him, offer advice, prophesy. *"For He wounds, but He also binds up; He injures, but His hands also heal."* (5:18). And then Job went through a time of trying to figure out what he did to make God give him this misery. Again his friends tried to convince him of his righteousness and blamelessness in God's eyes. They tried to encourage him. And Job confirmed His power. But he was overwhelmed with suffering. Then Job practiced what he would say to God. And once more, his friends counseled him... *"Can you fathom the mysteries of God? Can you probe the limits of the Almighty? They are higher than the heavens ~ what can you do?"* (11:7-8). But, then they began to blame him, saying he had sinned to warrant all this suffering. They talk down to him. Who needs friends like that? Finally, Job tells his friends to be quiet, and he says, *"Though He slay me, yet will I hope in him."* (13:15). Job never gave up on God. And this is what God knew, that no matter what ~ He could depend on Job to be faithful. God was his Redeemer, and Job knew it!

Soon his "friends" became pious and judgmental, and downright rude to Job. Job was growing stronger in his resolve... *"when He has tested me, I will come forth as pure gold. My feet have closely followed His steps; I have kept to His way without turning aside."* (23:10-11). Sometimes our friends mean well, and try to give us advice while we are going through rough times, but God is who we need to pour our hearts out to. God will never give us bad advice. He will never mock us, nor lead us astray. We may never go through times as hard as Job did, but we will suffer, and have hardships. Many voices will offer advice. God wants us to know He will be there with us through them all...He is testing us, and if we lean on Him and do not turn away from Him, we will *"come forth as pure gold."* Job's story goes on. Maybe I'll save the rest for next time. Just know that God sees you in your suffering. He sees me. We just need to take His outstretched hand.

JULY 28

JOB...HIS FRIENDS VS. GOD...

After Job was afflicted, his friends showed up and sat with him, silently, for seven days. No one said anything. Would have seemed a little uncomfortable.

I think they were overwhelmed at the gravity of his troubles. At the end of the seven days, Job spoke at last. Then the others spoke, and all gave their impressions of what had happened. Most of them came to the conclusion that Job had sinned, and that he wasn't as righteous as he had made everyone think he was, or all these terrible things would not have happened to him. They were sure of it. When the youngest, Elihu, finally spoke up, his words were accusatory. And, it seems to me, he was very arrogant. Oh, he defended God's motives, and His Mighty-ness, but he talked down to Job… *"Pay attention, Job…and listen to me, be silent, and I will teach you wisdom."* (33:31,33). How dare he. As if Job wasn't already wiser than this young one. Elihu went on about the attributes of God, he talked about where his own knowledge came from, he seemed to have all the answers. He accused Job of "empty talk," and said "*God would not take His eyes off the righteous.*" (36:7). I don't know this, but it is my thinking that this "counseling" from his friends may have lasted for several weeks, even longer…

And finally God speaks, out of a storm, after listening to the bantering back and forth amongst the men, listing all His own attributes and describing many of His wonders, including the dinosaurs, dragons, and sea monsters. This is where He spoke of all creation, the sea, the animals, the gases and vapors which come together to make rain and snow and ice. What a wonderful depiction of everything He created, even stuff we seldom think about, the "*cords that hold Orion together*," the timing of sunrises and sunsets, the ocean tides, how the clouds are formed, when the baby animals are born… (chapters 38-41). The Lord then dismissed the "friends" who have tried to lead Job astray, but not before He pronounced sentence upon them, and demanded that they offer gifts and sacrifices to Job, (Ch. 42). He said, *"You have not spoken of Me what is right, as my servant Job has,"* (v. 8), and then God insisted that Job *pray* for his friends before they went on their way. Wow. And God accepted Job's prayer for his friends. They were exonerated. I'm sure they had plenty to talk about amongst themselves as they went their way.

And of course, the best part of the story was that God made Job prosperous again, giving him twice as much as he had before in the way of cattle and land, and children. He was faithful to God during all his distress. All his brothers and sisters, and old friends celebrated with him again, comforting him and giving him gifts and money. And, after God had blessed him, Job lived another 140 years. I don't know how old he was when all his trouble came, but he had to be up in years if he had seven children, and he had been considered *"the greatest man among all the people of the East."* (1:3). Quite a story. I have learned so much from Job. And it's true, when we suffer, not all our friends will give us good advice. Oh, they're well-meaning, no doubt, but they usually don't know all the circumstances. I think of Joni Earekson Tada, and her story of when she was first injured. Her friends from her church came to her, as she lay face down in a Stryker frame, paralyzed for life, and told her she must have sinned for this to have happened to her, and not have God heal her. Later in her life, she has shared that if this accident hadn't happened, she would not have the ministry she has today, would not be able to help so many people as she does, all as a result of her injury. She is such a blessing to others. What a testimony to God's grace!

I doubt many of us will have to suffer as Job did, with as much loss as he endured, and ill health on top of everything else, but when we do have hard times, and we will, we must remember that God sees us right where we are. And we must not be discouraged when well-meaning friends come to us with all kinds of advice that will throw us off…just remember that God will never leave us. He is aware of our state every day, every minute. And we can say with Job, *"I know that my Redeemer lives, and that in the end He will stand upon the earth…I myself will see Him with my own eyes….!"* (19:25,27).

JULY 29

ANTICIPATION…

That can mean a lot of things. It usually means we know of something that is coming…a certain package, a special date, a new baby, company, Christmas… but it's hard to wait. Sometimes we anticipate a less positive outcome; or just knowing a task is coming due gives us cause to work to get it done on time or even earlier than needed. Or we expect a bill we will owe, so we can plan for it…so many meanings for a word. Medical tests usually don't produce instant results, and sometimes it's 2-3 days, or more, before we have an answer. Anticipation. I have a few favorite authors, who write books in succession that I like to read, and I don't want to miss a single one in their series, so I always find out when the release date is for a given new book, and write it on my calendar so I can be sure to obtain it the day it is released. There are two I'm waiting for right now, one is coming in the mail. So, of course, I have been anxiously watching my mailbox. Whatever it is ~ we wait.

There used to be a cute commercial for ketchup that showed a child holding a ketchup bottle upside down, waiting for the S-L-O-W liquid to pour out on the hamburger. This was before the advent of plastic squeeze bottles, and all we had were glass bottles. Of course, the song "Anticipation" was playing in the background, and they were advertising the benefit of nice, thick, rich ketchup. Kids are fun to watch when they are waiting for something, or someone, important. So are animals, when it's time for dinner. It seems their whole body quivers as you're fixing their food.

What are you waiting for? We wait every day ~ in traffic, in line at the bank or the grocery store, in the kitchen, standing in front of the oven which will soon yield a tray of delicious-smelling cookies…or, at the mailbox, or the doctor's office…

Psalm 27:14 says, *"Wait for the Lord; be strong and take heart and wait for the Lord."* Christians right now are in a heightened state of anticipation…the problems we read and hear about in our government could bring bad results, and many wait for the Lord to come and take us away from it all! And I'm pretty sure whatever we expect to happen, is going to happen. But, *"The Lord is my light and my salvation; whom shall I fear? The Lord is the stronghold of my life, of whom shall I be afraid?"* (Psalm 27:1). So we wait, anticipating that wonderful promised land we will see if we don't give up. That is one prize we know will come to us, no matter how long we wait for it! Soon we will hear that unmistakable trumpet, and see Jesus split the sky, and there He will be with ten thousand angels, the biggest choir we have ever heard, and in a split-second we will rise and meet Him in the air. Sounds spectacular, doesn't it? It will be worth all the anticipation!

JULY 30

OUR NEEDINESS…

Is that even a word? Yes, it is…I looked it up after it popped into my head. My friend, Webster, says it means "the quality or state of being needy; poverty; indigence; want." Neediness. It's all around us. I have it. You might look at me and think, "*she's* needy?" How can she be needy ~ she's in good health, she has clothes to wear and food to eat, and can even go out to lunch occasionally, she has a pretty nice house and a car that runs, lots of friends and a loving family. You call that needy? We should remember that things are not always what they seem on the outside. *"Man looks at the outward appearance, but the Lord looks at the heart."* (1 Sam. 16:7). Well, it's not that I'm trying to LOOK like someone I'm not, or pull the wool over someone's eyes or deceive them...but the state of someone's life is not always as it appears. That's where first impressions come in...we may look at someone and see that she looks and seems to "have it all together." But what we do not see are the struggles she has every day, financially, health-wise, relationally, or the deep fears she has for her family and their well-being. She may be too embarrassed or ashamed to tell anyone just how dire her circumstances are.

There is another kind of neediness, and that's the spiritual kind. On the other side of *"I can do all things through Christ who strengthens me"* (Philippians 4:13), is *"...apart from Me, you can do nothing."* (Jesus' own words in John 15:5). So, outside of Christ there is really nothing we can do on our own. Oh, we can go to work and make a living, we have talents and abilities (that God gave us), we can grow our own food, harvest it, chew it and swallow it so that it will nourish our bodies, but that doesn't nourish our souls. We have no hope but Jesus. We cannot love or receive love without His love. We cannot bear fruit without His Spirit living in us. Without Him we despair in all we attempt to do.

It may seem to us that the Godless get ahead ~ but God's word says in Proverbs 24:19, *"Do not fret because of evil men or be envious of the wicked, for the evil man has no future hope, and the lamp of the wicked will be snuffed out."* Wow! And God is watching, ladies. It may not seem so in our government, in our workplaces, our homes, and sadly, even in our churches, as those who strive to get ahead will beat us down to do so. Just remember that *"Your Father knows what you need before you even ask,"* (Matthew 6:8), and His grace is there for the asking. I need what He has to give me, every day. I need His Spirit in me to guide me, I need His forgiveness so I can in turn forgive others, I need His strength when mine is gone. *"For He will deliver the needy who cry out, the afflicted who have no one to help."* (Psalm 72:12). I love to hear the stories of desperation turned to triumph, sadness turned to joy, poverty turned to riches, all at His loving hand. Oh, the big miracles are sensational to see and to hear about, but those little miracles that would otherwise go unnoticed, except by those who experience them...priceless. And I have experienced many of those little miracles, and...a few big ones too. God knows how needy I am, and how frail

I am without His strength. And nothing is too difficult for Him. Nothing. We are rich in His Spirit, and in His love.

JULY 31

PLANS AND PURPOSES...

Almost everything we do in life requires some kind of plan, and some determination to carry it out. A builder cannot just begin sawing and nailing some boards together without specific and detailed plans. The plans need to be studied and materials and supplies ordered and delivered, right down to the finishing with cabinets, carpeting and paint. A banquet needs to be planned by the chef ~ what foods are needed, and preparation time calculated, in order for everything to be ready at the appointed time. And a teacher needs to have a lesson plan in order to teach students in a manner so they will learn what is required. And in order for a vacation to be enjoyable, there must be a plan, an itinerary so that the travelers aren't wandering aimlessly.

Do you sometimes feel that you are wandering aimlessly through life? That occasionally you have no clue what is expected of you, or even what you expect of yourself? I, for one, need to have a list of things I need to get done each day – I can't stand just floundering through my day. I keep a big calendar on my desk to write tasks on. Each day I wake up with purpose...I must have gotten that from my mother. She was a great organizer. Had calendars, address books, recipes, plans, and kept track of everything. I never wake up in the morning wondering what I'm going to do that day. Any project I do needs a plan. Sometimes those plans become altered by someone else's needs, but nevertheless...

I wonder how long God planned our earth and the inhabitants in it before He actually began His Creation? My Bible says that God's Spirit was hovering over the waters after He had created the heavens and the earth. Every part of the Creation is terribly intricate, and I know it couldn't have just "happened." Look at the flowers, and how the petals all meet in the middle, how they open up as they bloom, and then as the seeds fall to the ground after the blossom is spent, dead, and re-grow the next summer. And what about the silly giraffe? Do you know that when he lowers his neck to take a drink out of a pond or river, his brain would explode from the rush of blood that would speed down his neck if he didn't have a special "trap-door" that would let only a little blood trickle in at a time, much like a brain shunt works in someone with hydrocephalus? What about the bumble bee, whose body is too big and bulky for his tiny wings, but God designed him in such a special way that aerodynamically his flight is delightful.

I am in awe at His plan, His creation. And though it may take us a long time to realize it, sometimes a lifetime, God has a plan for each one of us. " *'For I know the plans I have for you,' declares the Lord, 'plans to prosper you and not to harm you, plans to give you a hope and a future.'* " (Jeremiah 29:11). He goes on to say in the next verse, *"Then you will call upon Me and come and pray to Me, and I will listen to you. You will seek Me and find Me when you seek Me with all your heart."* Sometimes we don't realize God even has a plan for us until we do seek Him with all our heart. He created each one of us with a specific purpose, and has given us each special gifts and abilities, so that we may make a difference in our lives, and in someone else's life. God's purpose for us is eternal, not just something that will burn out when we wear out, or at the end of our life. It will be carried out through all generations, and even until the end of time.

"So do not be ashamed to testify about our Lord...but join with me in suffering for the gospel, by the power of God, who has saved us and called us to a holy life ~ not because of anything we have done, but because of ***His own purpose*** *and grace."* (2 Tim. 1:8-9).

AUGUST 1

TRAVELING...

One of my favorite trips, a few years ago...for eight days, my husband and I got away on our Goldwing motorcycle with some friends and traveled to Yellowstone, and other points...camping in KOAs...taking in the sights and smells of the great outdoors.

I got to thinking about modes of travel ~ there are SO many...the most common now is just to get in the car and go. And now that gas is so high priced, our motorcycle is more appealing than ever. Airfare, train and boat travel costs have gone up because of the fuel prices. But, what about the days when there was no gas, because there were no vehicles. It was either horse-power, (or camel-power), or man-power...and I really believe people went places out of necessity, rather than pleasure. How many vacations do you read about in the Bible? True, there were the feast celebrations, to which people excitedly traveled out of religious obligation, but there weren't many leisurely trips just for the relaxation and sight-seeing aspect.

Jesus' parents were traveling, but only because they were ordered to by the King, for his own benefit. I don't believe they would have taken this long trek in Mary's condition, in the winter, just for the pleasure of seeing the king or the city. The shepherds were traveling during that time, too, because they were instructed to follow the star. And the wise men were on an even longer journey in anticipation of worshipping the Christ child and presenting Him with their gifts. In all of these, walking was the manner of getting there. We all know it isn't very comfortable walking any distance in sandals, and yet, these walked miles, days, months and longer, across the hard, rocky and dirty terrain in mean sandals.

I think how easy we have it nowadays. Many of us walk for exercise, in comfortable shoes made just for walking. But for the most part, travel is easy and fast. My favorite part of traveling is meeting people…it says in Job 31:32 *"but no stranger had to spend the night in the street, for my door was always open to the traveler."* The Bible doesn't have a lot to say about the traveler, but I love those "friends we haven't met yet," the ones who open their hearts and homes to you while traveling. I hope that, as summer is waning, you and I will have the chance to "open our door to a stranger." We have no idea what a blessing that could be. I made two new friends this summer simply by having them in my home when they needed a place to stay. It's about reaching out.

AUGUST 2

TURN THE OTHER CHEEK…

I don't know what their conversation was about this morning, but I received a text message from my daughter saying that her little girl, Kadee, who's 5, informed her that *"turn the other cheek"* is not in her Bible. Well, of course, that is cute, but it makes me wonder what they were talking about. No doubt, her older brother was picking on her, or visa versa! And it prompted me to think about this phrase, *"turn the other cheek."*

It was spoken by Jesus, in the sermon on the mount, In Matthew 5, right along with *"love your enemies," "go the extra mile," "pray for those who persecute you..."* all that goes against our nature. Does it mean that we must allow ourselves to be defenseless victims of every thief or attacker that may come along? No, this does not mean that we should stand by and let thieves and criminals walk all over us and steal our goods. Of course, we want to protect our possessions. But why should we *"turn the other cheek"* toward those who are persecuting us because of our religious beliefs? They are unfriendly to us because they don't yet have "ears to hear."

Consider this: *"And the Lord's servant must not be quarrelsome but kindly to every one, an apt teacher, forbearing, correcting his opponents with gentleness. God may perhaps grant that they will repent and come to know the truth, and they may escape from the snare of the devil, after being captured by him to do his will."* (2 Timothy 2:24-26 RSV)

A thief is totally aware of what he's doing when he is breaking in to your home or car, stealing your property. But, someone who attacks you because of your Christianity at times is not aware of what he's doing. His or her time of understanding of God's Truth, and choosing whether or not to obey it, has not yet come. Right now, you have an *enormous advantage* over that individual. And who knows but that someday that persecutor may just turn out to be a good friend? Look at Paul, and how brutally he persecuted Christians...until God got hold of his soul. He became one of the most celebrated Christians in the Bible. His life and his example can be solid proof that sometimes our worst enemy can become the best friend. We must be patient and forgiving, and God will do the rest.

Jesus said, *"Father, forgive them for they know not what they do."* He was speaking of the very men who were killing him. (Luke 23:34). I guess this is what He meant by *"turn the other cheek."* Now I'll be anxious to know what Kadee's story is!

AUGUST 3

THE LORD SINGS....

"The Lord, your God, is in your midst, a warrior who gives victory; He will rejoice over you with gladness, He will renew you in His love; He will exult over you with loud singing." (Zephaniah 3:17).

This is so like God. It's His nature. He's our cheerleader. We have all rejoiced over our own children, sometimes more than others…like when they accomplished something great, like walking, finally being potty-trained, learning to read, getting that first home run or goal, passing a hard test in school ~ or life…or we remember when our parents exulted over us, sometimes just because we were *theirs*. I looked up the word "exult" in my "Book of Webster" and it's defined as: "to leap for joy; to rejoice greatly; be jubilant."

We don't have to do something great for our heavenly Father to exult over us. He rejoices just because we are His. The first time I saw this concept of God "singing over me" was in a song "The Voice of Truth" by the group Casting Crowns, and one particular line *"I will soar with the wings of eagles when I stop and listen to the sound of Jesus singing over me"* gripped me…Jesus singing over me? I hadn't ever thought of that before. What a picture! All because He is pleased merely with who I am…and not necessarily with what I've done.

So who are we to think less of ourselves than God does? God made us ~ and He loves us just the way we are, warts and all. He expresses it in His tender care, in the gift of His Son, and in our adoption into His family as His true children. He wants to remove our sorrow and give us honor and praise…this may not happen in our lifetime, but most certainly on the other side! He loves us with an everlasting love, and He is *singing* over us. I love that!

AUGUST 4

OAKS OF RIGHTEOUSNESS…

How could you not notice the mighty oak tree? It's stately in its ancient splendor, strong and beautiful. Its hard wood is of the strongest found, its branches are broad, giving shelter and shade. Its "fruit," the acorn, feeds wild animals. Birds build their nests in the branches. The oak is the subject of many poems and songs, stories about strength, and yet, it can be humbly brought down in a severe windstorm. Sometimes a tiny worm works its way into the trunk, and over time devours the inside of that mighty tree until the beautiful hard wood rots, its core is empty and its strength is gone.

I was reading in Isaiah the other day and ran across this passage (61:1-3): *"The Spirit of the Sovereign Lord is on me because the Lord has anointed me to preach good news to the poor. He has sent me to bind up the brokenhearted, to proclaim freedom for the captives and release from darkness for prisoners, to proclaim the year of the Lord's favor and the day of vengeance of our God, to comfort all who mourn, and provide for those who grieve in Zion ~ to bestow on them a crown of beauty instead of ashes, the oil of gladness instead of mourning, and a garment of praise instead of a spirit of despair. They will be called* ***oaks of righteousness****, a planting of the Lord for the display of His splendor."* At first, while I was reading that, I thought this was referring to Jesus ~ that these things were His job...but, He actually gives us the power, in His name, to perform them, and in this we will be giving glory to Him. We are *"a planting of the Lord for the display of His splendor!"* Our lives should glorify Him ~ we were created for that very purpose.

Like the mighty oak tree, we sometimes allow a tiny "worm," a worm of doubt and discouragement, unbelief and hopelessness, to work its way into our very core and destroy us, to bring us down in the strong winds and storms of life. If we do not draw our nourishment from the Father, and His word, the very River of Life, we will become hollow and diseased, like that massive trunk of the oak, still looking good and healthy on the outside, but rotting away on the inside, unable to stand in life's toughest storms.

His Word can strengthen us, help us to stand firm and provide comfort and shelter for those who are not so strong. And like Paul we can say *"I can do everything through Him who gives me strength."* (Phil. 4:13). Let's be the oaks of righteousness planted by the Lord for His glory and splendor!

AUGUST 5

KIDS BELIEVE IT...

Little kids are so cute...they will believe almost anything you tell them. My friend once planted spaghetti with her little grandchildren. They were scheduled for a visit, so she crunched up some uncooked spaghetti, and when they arrived, she took them out to her flower beds to plant some spaghetti. Of course, they were excited! She watched them squat down in the dirt, poking holes with their little fingers, then let them sprinkle the spaghetti "seeds" into the dirt and cover them up. They carefully watered the spot and went back inside. A week or so later, on their next visit, they went out to check on the seeds, and to their astonishment, there were some little spaghettis growing! Within a few weeks time, they had grown to full height, and my friend allowed the children to "pick" them, then went inside and cooked them. They were proud of the spaghetti they had "planted."

And naturally, most kids believe in Santa Claus until they learn otherwise. And reindeer that fly, and the Easter Bunny. How about the Tooth Fairy? Children believe that characters in their books are real, and that teddy bears can talk. Why wouldn't they? Those are tangible things they can see, and in their very young manner of reasoning, it's all true.

Children also believe such outlandish things as a garden snake that talks, a fish big enough to swallow a man whole, huge stone walls of a city falling down when men blew their trumpets, a little boy killing a giant with a small rock, a boat big enough to hold all those animals, a baby born in a manger who would grow up to be a king, a little boy's small lunch feeding a whole field full of people, a man who could walk on water and heal sick people, and come back from the dead…they believe it all. Why can't we? Children accept the Bible at face value and if you read something to them from the pages of this holy book, they believe it, and sometimes they grow up to trust it, rely on its promises, count on its truths. Why is it so hard for us as adults? Do the cares of life just crowd in and take over our thoughts and beliefs? Maybe we still believe there are monsters in the closets. Perhaps now that we are older and more "intelligent" those things we thought true as kids seem too unbelievable. But in Proverbs 30:5 it says, *"Every word of God is flawless."* And in 2 Peter 1:19, *"And we have the word of the prophets made more certain, and you will do well to pay attention to it."* God's word is a record of real things that happened to real people. And if we pay attention, we will see those same things happening in our own lives and of those around us, even now.

God's word was given to us to guide us and encourage us. It's a lamp to our feet, it cheers us up, it gives us life. Little children have no trouble believing it. *"Then little children were brought to Jesus for Him to place His hands on them and pray for them. But the disciples rebuked those who brought them. Jesus said, 'Let the little children come to Me, and do not hinder them, for the kingdom of heaven belongs to such as these.'"*(Matthew 19:13-14). Are we leading our children and our grandchildren to Jesus and teaching them about Him? God has given us an awesome responsibility. Believe it.

AUGUST 6

TRUST...

I am a stamper. I love making my own greeting cards, and I have many (probably too many) stamps. Some are fun and silly and cute, others are beautiful, whimsical, sensible. I have one sentiment stamp that says, "All I have seen teaches me to trust the Creator for all I have not seen." ~ Ralph Waldo Emerson. That salutation has been used in many different types of cards ~ sympathy, encouragement, thank you, even birthday.

This greeting always reminds me of Hebrews 11:1, *"Now faith is being sure of what we hope for and certain of what we do not see."* Basically, it says the same thing. Whether we want to or not, we trust in a lot of things we don't see. We trust that when we start driving across a bridge, we will safely make it to the other side. We trust that at the end of a work period we will receive a paycheck. When we are young, we trust our parents to mean what they say, and that they will take care of our needs. We trust God ~ for everything we cannot see.

I heard someone say the other day that she "wished she knew where the road of her life was going to end up."This is the kind of statement that prompts me to encourage one to trust the Father, the only One who does know where that road will lead. Realistically, we wouldn't *want* to know what lies ahead. If I had known ahead of time all the experiences and crises I would be going through in my life, I wouldn't have wanted to go there. I would have been filled with a sense of dread and doom every waking moment. The future is not for us to know. I basically told my friend this. And that if we keep our hand in the hand of the Master, He would never lead us astray, and if we somehow got into trouble, He would get us through it…if we but trust Him. Trusting Him is the opposite of worry. And we are admonished not to worry ~ again, in God's word. Jesus said, *"Therefore I tell you, do not worry about your life, what you will eat or drink, or about your body, what you will wear."* (Matthew 6:25). What a great manual for life He has given us.

David warned us, *"Do not put your trust in princes, in mortal men, who cannot save…"* (Psalm 146:3). Isaiah says, *"those who trust in idols, who say to images, 'you are our gods,' will be turned back in utter shame."* (Is. 42:17). And Jeremiah (7:4) tells us, *"Do not trust in deceptive words…"* We are told throughout the Word not to trust in riches or wealth (our bank accounts), in ourselves (our own understanding), in the multitudes (just because 'everyone is doing it'), in stongholds (our borders, our unlocked, or locked, homes)…

Not only can we trust in our heavenly Father to do what He says He will do…we can trust in His NAME. *"My Father will give you whatever you ask in My Name."* (John 16:23). There is no other name…where is your trust?

AUGUST 7

SEEKING MEN'S PRAISE...

"But because of the Pharisees they would not confess their faith for fear they would be put out of the synagogue; for they loved praise from men more than praise from God." (John 12:42-43). I don't know for sure that the Jews purposely rejected Jesus, or their faith, but they were afraid of what others would think of them. They were so pious. People "looked up to them." They were *leaders*.

I know that because of who our peers are, sometimes we are embarrassed to identify with Christ. Not children ~ they are very uninhibited as far as their faith in Jesus goes. But teenagers, on the other hand, although some of them are head over heels about Jesus, others believe that their friends will not think they're "cool" if they are Jesus-followers. In the '60s a group of young people in the hippie world were called "Jesus Freaks." The term was used loosely and "its usage broadened to describe a Christian subculture throughout the hippie and back-to-the-land movements that focused on universal love and pacifism, and relished the radical nature of Jesus' message." There have been songs and books written on the subject of "Jesus freaks." The message was spread by some through the distribution of "Good News for Modern Man," a paraphrase of the New Testament.

But there is another Book written (and many, many songs) that explains a different relationship with Jesus. A necessary relationship, not one in name only. The true nature of that relationship is that *"I have been crucified with Christ and I no longer live, but Christ lives in me. The life I live in the body, I live by faith in the Son of God, who loved me and gave Himself for me."* (Galatians 2:20). This is what it takes. Sticking like glue to Jesus. No turning back. But so many times, though we are Christians, we still want men's praise. We care what others think of us. We want recognition for things we do, in the name of Jesus. We want people to notice when we give, to whom, and how much. We want acclaim and applause for our performances. We speak eloquently when we pray so people around us will be impressed. We want our works to be well-known. There is nothing wrong with those things we do, the giving, speaking, writing, singing, but if we are doing it "as unto the Lord" and still expecting commendations and compliments, then we are definitely doing these deeds for the wrong purposes. No matter how many people are helped through our various "ministries" in different areas, God sees it as "filthy rags" if it is not done for *His* glory. The Father wants us to be willing to do everything for Him, even if it is in our own closet where no one will ever see or know. God will see.

Paul asked, *"Am I now trying to win the approval of men, or of God? Or am I trying to please men? If I were still trying to please men, I would not be a servant of Christ."* (Galatians 1:10). Paul had to learn this, as we do. It's not wrong for people to compliment us on our song, or a painting we did, giving to the poor, volunteering our time, or a book we wrote, but if that is the approval we are expectantly looking for, then it is done in vain. *"And whatever you do, do it all for the glory of God."* (I Cor. 10:31).

AUGUST 8

INSPIRATION...

OK, so when you spend a weekend with Nicole C. Mullen, Shiela Walsh, Luci Swindoll, Nicole Johnson, Lisa Harper, Marcus Buckingham, Mary Mary, Karen James, Andy Andrews, Amy Grant, and Mary Graham...and about 14,000+ women who are on fire and energized by the Holy Spirit, how can one NOT be inspired. I'm talking about Women of Faith conferences that have been going on all over America for 15+ years. It's not merely being with other women in a spiritual and uplifting setting, listening to messages and songs; but each one of the speakers and musicians makes you feel a PART of what they are doing...who they are. We sometimes tend to put famous people, especially famous Christian people, on a pedestal and look at them as if they have it all together. But I assure you, these women (and men), bared their very souls, and I am sure there was not one woman or teenager in that whole arena who did not identify in at least one way, with what was being shared so openly and poignantly.

I felt the music, I felt the tears in the sharing of their hearts. The scriptures were opened up in unique ways, through word and through song. There were happy talks, instructional and informational talks, and very sad ones. But every one of them spoke of Victory as they came through their personal heartache. Every one of them inspired me to want to serve Him better. These women are not afraid or too proud to share their deepest thoughts with a room full of "girlfriends" whom they've never met. These women are genuine and real. And ordinary, like us. They just said "yes" to God.

The theme of one particular conference was "Imagine," and they key scripture verse is Ephesians 3:20: *"He is able to do immeasurably more than all we ask or* ***imagine****, according to the power that is at work within us."* More than our wildest dreams, even. We learned how important it is to trust God. Sheila said, "Christ comes not to get us out of our difficulties, but to live in us through them." She shares lessons she's learned in her own life. Luci talks about how living life is an adventure, and shares how we can "savor each moment, let go of regrets, and embrace our dreams." Nicole is a dramatist who writes and acts out very real and close-to-home scenarios that we all identify with, some humorous, others absolutely heart-wrenching. All of them point to Christ who ultimately can make the changes in our lives we so desperately need and desire.

And, of course, there is the shopping! So many BOOKS, bags, DVDs and music CDs, coffee mugs, T-shirts, jewelry ~ all meant to inspire us after the weekend is over. But when the women gather together for a meal, or in a hotel room, the sharing takes place. Two of my daughters and two very close friends shared a hotel room, and we shared meals with each other, and these were perfect times to encourage and motivate one another to trust more, to study His word, and basically to not give up in the hardships we all go through. We can have an encounter with Jesus every day. He can prompt us and liberate us so that we can live and love without fear. He'll help us fulfill our dreams and inspire us to never give up. *"Let us not become weary in doing good, for at the proper time we will reap a harvest if we do not give up."* (Gal. 6:9). That's inspiration!

AUGUST 9

SEARCHING...

It seems like I am always searching for something. I generally have a pretty good idea where the item is, but it's usually in the last place I look ~ naturally.

I used to get a kick out of my kids when they would ask me where their stuff was… "Mom, where are my brown shoes?" They had looked "everywhere." Well, of course, they had gone into their room and just scanned the area, didn't see it, then gave up. I would tell them to pick something up ~ it might be under some clothes or bedding. My husband is kind of like that too. He doesn't really think of lifting something up to look under it, but will just scan the area, like the kids did. I know better. When I'm looking for a certain article, I lift, open, and move other items. I looked two days for some baby pictures this weekend. Almost ready to give up, I spotted some more boxes in the basement I hadn't looked in yet. Sure enough, just what I was looking for.

We search for a lot of things…lost pets, a new outfit, an address, a special gift, that perfect pair of shoes, a missing item ~ sheep, money…answers to life's tough questions. In our day of modern technology, searching for things is a bit easier than it used to be. We can just log onto the internet and find all kinds of items to purchase, especially the hard-to-find and vintage objects. And there is a world of information at our fingertips, answers to many questions. Some of us search all our lives for purpose and life's meaning. God's word says, as for wisdom, we are to *"look for it as for silver, and search for it as for hidden treasure, then you will understand the fear of the Lord, and find the knowledge of God."* (Proverbs 2:4-5).

Sometimes, we are actually searching for God, without even knowing it…we search for Him in money, in possessions, in relationships and jobs, looking for fulfillment. King David told his son, Solomon, in 1 Chronicles 28:9, as he was giving him the plans for the temple, which the Lord had given to David, *"And you, my son Solomon, acknowledge the God of your father, and serve Him with wholehearted devotion and with a willing mind, for the Lord searches every heart and understands every motive behind the thoughts. If you seek Him, He will be found by you…"*

Okay, so the Lord searches our heart, but where should we search for Him? Not in all the things mentioned above, but in His word, in His beautiful Creation. No matter where we are, we can find God. *"But if from there you seek the Lord your God, you will find Him if you search for Him with all your heart and with all your soul."* (Deut. 4:29). It's not hard. He's not hiding from us. He's right out in the open, right beside us. We just need to reach out and take His hand. Invite Him into our heart. He is always with us and He has promised to *"never leave us nor forsake us."* (Deut. 31:6).

AUGUST 10

THE LITTLE RED CHAIR....

My daughter, Bridgette, has always wanted a red rocking chair on her porch. It's just a little porch, not one of those massive covered porches with the railing, but, nevertheless, a porch, with just enough room in the corner for a chair. A rocking chair. All around our town I see houses with those nice big white rocking chairs on the porches…it's the rage now, I guess…but she's wanted one for awhile. And I have been watching garage sales and thrift stores for something I could refinish for her for an anniversary gift. For about a year. Of course, finding an already red one would be best., but…

Today is their 14th anniversary, and they have been on a trip in the Virgin Islands. Last week I found the chair. I decided to dedicate part of a day to hitting one thrift store after another until I found something that would work. I started at the first one, an antiques/thrift store, and was going to work my way up the street ~ there must be 12 of these stores on this one stretch, and others elsewhere. I went in to the first place, and lo and behold, there sat the cutest little rocking chair ~ not a child's size but not a giant size either…it is Mama Bear size. Perfect. All brown and chipped, but nice and sturdy, not wobbly. I bargained with the guy who came down $6 more, and brought it home. I went to the home improvement store, picked up a can of spray-on stripper, (guaranteed easy), and came home to get my little chair ready for it's new coat of brick red paint. Why do people love stripping and refinishing furniture so much? That stripping job just about did me in…of course, I have arthritis and had to rest my hands often. What a mess…but I got it done.

I asked my husband if he would sand it for me with his trusty power sander, and last night he got right on it. Now it is ready to paint. Our kids got home a couple nights ago, and when I showed my daughter the chair, she was delighted. Of course, it isn't red yet, but I can picture how it's going to look later today when I get the paint and change its looks and give it new life! While I was watching my husband sanding, smoothing out all the rough spots and some of the old paint that didn't come off, running his hand over the surface to make sure it was smooth enough…I got to thinking about how we are like that chair. I don't know how old the chair is, but I know they don't make them like that anymore. I don't have any idea where it came from, who all sat on it, and where it was stashed when it was no longer useful. I know we feel like that sometimes. We are roughed up, our finish is peeling and chipped, and we feel like we've been put off into a corner somewhere, even covered with a sheet because we are no longer attractive.

But Christ came along to give us new life...to sand down all those rough spots and scratches, peel away all the old dirty stains, clean us up. *"Therefore, if anyone is in Christ, he is a new creation; the old has gone, the new has come!"* (2 Cor. 5:17). We don't have to be cleaned up first in order to come to Christ. He loves to do the refinishing Himself! And the thing is...He doesn't just stop when we are looking good...He keeps polishing and sanding and fixing us when we get banged up in the process of this life. *"He has made everything beautiful in its time."* (Ecc. 3:11).

AUGUST 11

PRAYING FOR THE FORGOTTEN...

The other day I was writing a prayer in my journal, and I asked God to bring to my mind someone who needed my prayers ~ someone I hadn't thought of in a long time. And as I was writing that down, the name of a friend I haven't heard from in awhile "popped" into my head. I almost dismissed it, since I wasn't even finished writing down the thought. But then, God gently nudged me, and I thought that this is the person I should pray for that day. And even though we may not know what their need is ~ and it could be immediate ~ we can still pray something like this:

"Lord, thank You for bringing Marie to my mind. I believe You have made me aware that she needs prayer right now, for whatever reason. And so, at 6:10 am, I lift Marie up to Your throne and ask You to surround her with your holy angels, and Your own holy Spirit. If she is in danger, protect her and keep her safe. If she is sick, give her Your healing touch. If her heart is breaking, give her comfort and peace as You hold her in Your arms. And if she is frightened, give her courage and the assurance of Your hope."

I think it is important for us to pray for one another, and, of course, we do every day. But there are some who have no one praying for them. No one. An old classmate, the clerk at the grocery store, that homeless woman sitting in the corner. Ask God to bring a name to your mind, and don't hesitate to lift them to Him in prayer when He does. Even if we are not aware of their need,

God knows it. James 5:16 says *"...pray for each other...the prayer of a righteous (wo)man is powerful and effective."*

So whether you are awakened in the middle of the night with someone heavy on your heart, or if their name is just a fleeting thought in your consciousness, say a prayer for them. Yours may be the only prayer uttered for that person.

AUGUST 12

BLESS ME, INDEED...

"Jabez called on the God of Israel, saying, 'Oh, that you would bless me indeed and enlarge my territory, that Your hand be with me, and You would keep me from evil, that I may not cause pain.' And God granted him what he requested." (1 Chron. 4:10 NKJV).

When I first heard this prayer, I thought it was kind of selfish and daring to pray so boldly. In a world where we should be praying for others, here is Jabez asking for blessings for himself. But I believe everything is in the Bible for our knowledge and instruction. As far as I know, Jabez is not mentioned anywhere else in the whole Bible. The name isn't even listed in my concordance or helps. But God must have thought it was important for us to know about him. This verse shows up right in the middle of long lists of genealogy ~ pages of them! So, what does it mean to us? I know of some people who pray this little prayer every single day.

My translation (NIV) says that Jabez *"cried out to the Lord."* We don't know what his circumstances were, if he was in trouble, or in danger, or what, but the verse before that mentions he was more honorable than his brothers. I'm not even sure it says who his brothers were. This verse seems to be out of place with no story around it. But he cried out, and that means to me he was in some kind of agony, either physical or spiritual. He wanted a miracle. He wanted to claim a blessing that God had reserved for him. He could have been asking for a new beginning. But there seems to be an urgency in his prayer. I believe he wanted exactly what God wanted for him, no more and no less. And he wasn't asking for what he could obtain for himself, but for the limitless resources of the Father.

Jesus promised, *"Ask and it will be given to you."* (Matthew 7:7). Maybe we aren't supposed to ask for "things" but simply for God's blessing. A lot of His blessing! And as for "enlarging our territory," I think that includes all that we are responsible for. You say ~ "oh, I don't need any more responsibilities!" But what about your business? Or your circle of influence? As more children and grandchildren are born into your family, I think this would count as "territory." Maybe God will give us more opportunity to impact others' lives for His glory. Maybe He will grow your ministry, whatever that may be. I feel like that when I consider how many devotionals I have shared with the women in my groups. Some have been entertaining, some haven't had much impact, but others may have just hit the spot, even for one person. That's up to God. So when I asked Him to show me how He could use me, I believe this is how He "enlarged my territory."

Such a little verse, seemingly unimportant, often unnoticed, but we can glean much blessing from asking God the same thing, by praying the same prayer, *"Lord, bless me indeed!"* He will give us opportunities to share His love, and He'll bring people into our paths that need to hear His message in the way we can tell them, or show them. He will give us the resources and the strength to accomplish this. Ask everyday for His touch and His blessing.

AUGUST 13

TAKE YOUR VITAMINS...?

Humans have not always taken vitamins for their health. The first vitamin tablets were available in pharmacies and grocery stores in the mid-1930's. They were meant to supplement our diet with nutrients we may have been missing by foods we were not consuming. These multivitamins were actually made from compressed fruit and vegetables, dried foods and concentrates. Within the next decade synthetics were made available. Now vitamins are available to different categories of the population; children, prenatal, iron-deficient, body-building, over 50 or "mature," or stressed. They come in liquid form, tablets and powders. There are huge tablets or tiny pills. Some are designated to strengthen our bones, lubricate our joints, nourish our brain or our liver. Some actually promise to make our hair grow. I just wonder if we would need all the vitamins of we ate the foods God gave us in the first place. In fact, some of the foods we eat are not even really food. Are they healthy?

But what about our spiritual health? Do we take spiritual vitamins? You could look at God's Word as just that – vitamins for our souls and spirits. *"Do not be wise in your own eyes; fear the Lord and shun evil. This will bring health to your body and nourishment to your bones."* (Proverbs 3:8). One day the disciples urged Jesus to eat something and He replied, *"I have food to eat that you know nothing about…My food is to do the will of Him who sent me, and to finish His work."* (John 4:32, 34). Later Jesus said, *"Do not work for food that spoils, but food that endures to eternal life, which the Son of Man will give you."* (John 6:27). So, just as our bodies need the vitamins we take daily as supplements, or better yet, by eating the proper foods, our spirit needs the nourishment of God's word ~ daily. If we neglect our vitamins over a period of time, we will begin to feel sluggish and weak. The same is true with God's word, our spiritual vitamin. We need a healthy daily dose of God's promises, of His expressions of undying love, His wisdom in our troubles. We should not only read it, but we should incorporate its Truth into our lives. Nourish our souls. We need to devour it, just as we devour some favorite foods.

As humans, we need the vitamins and minerals that are contained in the foods we eat. Babies begin with milk, or a prepared formula, which has been fortified with the vitamins they need in order to grow and develop properly. And when we are grown, we need more serious foods, such as meat and potatoes, salads and veggies, daily bread. Paul said to the Hebrews, *"Anyone who lives on milk, being still an infant, is not acquainted with the teaching about righteousness. But solid food is for the mature, who by constant use have trained themselves to distinguish good from evil."* (Hebrews 5:13-14). The more we consume God's word, the more mature we become, and the stronger we can be against the wiles of the enemy, who wants us weak and powerless.

Are you taking your vitamins? We need them daily.

AUGUST 14

DISTRACTIONS…

Well, it just dawned on me that it is time to write a devotional, and I have been distracted by a new quilt I'm working on. It's made of cut-out hearts appliqued to large squares, and I am hand-stitching all around each heart. It is addicting. Quiet and relaxing. I'm on my last heart, then I can begin the assembly of the rest of the pieces. I had been so intent on working on my quilt squares, so distracted from anything else, I had forgotten that I need to stop and write. By the way, I did put my last heart down, mid-stitching, to get this done!

In our busy lives, it is so easy to become distracted, isn't it? I usually have a pretty good idea of what I want to accomplish in a day. Some days are busier than others, and some of that busy-ness distracts from important things we should be doing. I think TV and electronics are major distractions today, especially among our children and teens. It's so easy to become mesmerized by those boxes, large and small, that we sometimes do not get around to important chores and tasks. I keep a large write-on calendar on my desk so I can see tasks and appointments for each day, at a glance. I try to keep busy, but I try to also take time for relaxation as well. Quilting has become a form of relaxation for me, just like curling up with a good book. Or riding my bicycle.

When Jesus came to the house of Mary and Martha to have dinner and fellowship, Mary was all over that. She sat at Jesus' feet listening intently to Him speaking and teaching. *"But Martha was distracted by all the preparations that had to be made."* (Luke 10:40). She was making the meal, making sure things were picked up and the house was presentable…this was *Jesus* after all! And when the Israelites were wandering in the wilderness for so many years, they became distracted by their own discomfort and expectations that were not fulfilled. Never mind that God told them what they needed to do (obey Him) and they would be there by now.

How many things take your attention away from those more important tasks, problems, responsibilities and relationships? We are bombarded by so many urgent messages that want us to drop everything and pay attention to them. But, even though they seem urgent, how many are really *important?* When you settle down to read your Bible and pray in quiet, does the phone ring? Do the kids begin fighting or needing your attention? The dog wants a walk? Do you let your mind wander to the many things you will need to take care of today, or right this moment? Does your stomach growl? I'm not suggesting everyone needs to get up at the crack of dawn in order to have a quiet time with God, but I get up at 5:am (or before) every morning while my household, and my whole neighborhood for that matter, is likely still asleep. I write a lot of my devotions, scripture, prayers, song lyrics, in my journals as my prayer and praise time to my Father. There is hardly ever a phone call or a knock on the door at that time of day. Even the dog and cat are still sleeping. It's a very nice way to start the day. *"In the morning, O Lord, You hear my voice; in the morning I lay my requests before You and wait in expectation."* (Psalm 5:3). Late evenings are almost impossible for a quiet time with God. For one thing, we are tired from the events and work of the day, and many things are going through our heads. How many of us has fallen asleep while praying in bed?

Let's not allow the things of the world, and the cares and worries that will still be there in a few minutes, become a distraction from our prayer time. The enemy himself designs distractions on purpose because he does not want us to spend time in the Word and much less communing with the Almighty God. Our Heavenly Father is never distracted when He hears us calling His name.

AUGUST 15

GOD'S ECLIPSE...

There is a song on the radio these days...by now most of you know how I am influenced and inspired by not only Christian music, but the words to many of these songs, for most of them come from scripture. The song is entitled "How He Loves" and although I don't care too much for the artist's voice, the words are wonderful...the first verse goes like this:

"He is jealous for me,
Loves like a hurricane, I am a tree,
Bending beneath the weight of his wind and mercy.
When all of a sudden,
I am unaware of these afflictions eclipsed by glory,
And I realize just how beautiful You are,
And how great Your affections are for me."

The phrase that first popped out to me is "these afflictions *eclipsed* by glory." Do you see that? I started to examine the rest of the verse, and it's so true. We are like a tree and sometimes the wind and storms blow all around us, bending us until we think we will break in half. We have all seen an eclipse, whether solar or lunar, where one of the planets, the sun or the moon, is covered over by the other, at times where we cannot even see it for a short while. Webster defines eclipse as "a temporary obscurity or dulling; to overshadow; outshine." And when we look at God's glory, it will indeed obscure, or outshine, life's problems. Our struggles may seem so overwhelming, but when we remember Who He is, they are overshadowed by His great strength and mercy.

We can hardly *"grasp how wide, and long, and high, and deep is the love of Christ…it surpasses knowledge…"* (Ephesians 3:18, 19). So even though He sends the storms and the winds of life, always remember His love is far greater than any of our struggles. And if we look for His glory in it all, it will outshine the troubles we have. He calls us to trust Him. He is holding out His hand.

AUGUST 16

THINK ON SUCH THINGS…

"Finally, [sisters], whatever is true, whatever is noble, whatever is right, whatever is pure, whatever is lovely, whatever is admirable ~ if anything is excellent or praiseworthy ~ think on such things…And the God of peace will be with you." (Philippians 4:8-9). Paul spoke these words to the church in Philippi…good advice. He also interjected, *"Whatever you have learned or received or heard from me, or seen in me ~ put it into practice."* (vs 9a). I don't think he meant to say here that he was the only expert who had all the answers, and everyone must do as he said. But God Himself personally gave Paul instruction…Paul was so tuned into the Father, that he really *was* the expert of the day in the fairly new concept of Christianity…and God sent him to tell others about the unbelievable joy they could have in following the Master. He made such an impact on the people in many churches and towns, that the religious rulers in those towns wanted to kill him, and they punished him for preaching these things. But Paul did not give up. God had given him an assignment and he carried it through, even though he was sick, beaten and locked up frequently.

The words of Paul that we read today are inspired by the Holy Spirit. These are not just his ideas because they sound good, and heaven knows, they are really hard to follow sometimes. This teaching is truly the best, but not the easiest, guideline for our lives. But sometimes, in fact often ~ daily, even ~ the negative creeps in. We cannot let it fill our minds with dread and doom. This is easier said than done. Everywhere we look, TV, newspapers, the internet, bad things are happening, events and situations that would take away our hope. Let's pray that this admonition from Paul, to *"think on such things,"* would become a natural part of our being…if we spend time in the Bible, God's word, these "things" will come to the forefront in our minds, and things of the world will diminish. So many concerns that have been looming in our thoughts will begin to fade in the light and the glory of His word.

So, we should indeed fix our minds on the truth, everything that is worthy of our respect, and all thoughts that will measure up to God's model of ethics and honor. Busy ourselves with wholesome activities, and be morally pure. Avoid evil, and cleave to things of spiritual beauty. Concentrate on the positive. Stay away from anything short of moral virtue and quality. And in praising God, be aware of those things He Himself may in turn praise you for.

Paul did not have a Bible to show to the people. He had to bring to mind all the things God had personally taught him, so he could convey them to the people. These were new ideas to most of them. But in living in the way he presented to them, he told them that they would experience the *"God of peace"* in their lives. We are to meditate on these truths day and night. David said, *"Oh, how I love Your law! I meditate on it all day long."* (Psalm 119:97).

AUGUST 17

VIOLATED!

Sunday morning, our garage was boldly broken into. At 3:45 am I awoke to the sound of the garage door being opened. Thinking it was my husband doing something out there, I opened the door a crack and peeked out...saw someone in his car rummaging around, then suddenly, after someone shined a flashlight in my face, two people in black took off running. I found my husband in his recliner and called to him that someone had broken into the car...he was up in a flash, took off in his car to see if he could find them while I called the police. After he came back, the police came, took a report, and left. Not 20 minutes later, we heard sirens, and in a matter of moments, five police units were stopped in front of our next door neighbor's house. They had a guy in custody, but not until both the man and the woman had fought and wrestled with the young man they found in their motorhome closet, again, inside the garage! We were missing an item from my husband's car, but the neighbors had the guy. A few hours later, we got word that the police had arrested three more burglars, all in this one group. 2 of them were women. And I found out later in the afternoon, the two who ran from our garage were the women! The police found a getaway truck around the corner filled with stolen goods of all kinds. Not exactly the way I wanted to start my day, and certainly spend my Sunday. I was still shaking when I drove to church, 5 hours later.

Many of the neighbors have been talking since the break-ins, appalled that people think they have the RIGHT to break in to someone else's property and mess with and help themselves to our stuff. What a violation! What an invasion of privacy. But you know, this is what the enemy of God does all the time. He sees that we are going along, right in step with our Father, but he cannot stand for us to be happy, or close to God. He'll do everything he can to steal our joy. But our real joy is not in things. *"Do not store up for yourselves treasures on earth, where moth and rust destroy, and where thieves break in and steal. But store up for yourselves treasures in heaven, where moth and rust do not destroy, and where thieves do not break in and steal. For where your treasure is, there your heart will be also."* (Matthew 6:19-21). These are Jesus' own words, and who would know better than He? True, we all have a lot of stuff. It happens. It accumulates in our homes, sometimes on purpose, sometimes without our even realizing it. But it's just "stuff."

God gave us commandments, one of which is *"Thou shalt not steal."* (Exodus 20:15). The commandments were not just suggestions, or good ideas that would make our lives easier, but God COMMANDED us to obey them. Apparently we don't realize that. There is a penalty for the crime. But sometimes, the thieves don't get caught. They have no regard for the laws or rules of the land. They just go on helping themselves. So what this recent incident has done in our neighborhood is to make the citizens more aware of how lax we have been in locking up our homes. Of course, the thieves have ways of getting in anywhere if they really want to. But locking more doors, and windows, maybe even investing in an alarm system, may help deter a potential robber, especially if they are nervous and in a hurry…nothing is absolutely foolproof, but we all do want to be safer. And we have to make a conscious effort to safeguard our homes and lives.

I am convinced that God had His angels protecting all of us. I love what Psalm 91 says, *"If you make the Most High your dwelling ~ even the Lord, who is my refuge ~ then no harm will befall you, no disaster will come to your tent. For He will command His angels concerning you to guard you in all your ways; they will lift you up in their hands, so that you will not strike your foot against a stone."* (vs. 9-12). What a promise! Our robberies could have turned out a lot worse than they did. But God kept us safe in the midst of the battle…again!

AUGUST 18

SECURITY...

Well, yesterday we had a security/alarm system installed in our house. We've never had one, in 42 years, but since Sunday's break-in, we have gotten very serious about our safety and security. Oh, we lock our doors at night, and when we're gone, but in very hot weather, we've been known to leave windows open. We have even taken off on a 30-minute walk, or a bike ride during the day, leaving our garage door open. The kids and grandkids know the combination to our garage door opener and that's how they get in when we aren't home. We have felt pretty secure, and the neighborhood we live in is nice and safe...until now. Because of someone else's greed, and their boldness, and total disregard for another's property, our lives have changed in an instant. Not just ours, but all the neighbors, as well. Security has been on everyone's lips all week, since the break-ins. They are even talking about having a neighborhood meeting in order to make everyone else aware, and exchange phone numbers, and do introductions of those who may not know each other.

I suppose we will feel more secure after the alarm system is activated. But God's word says, in Deuteronomy 33:12,*"Let the beloved of the Lord rest secure in Him, for He shields him all day long, and the one the Lord loves rests between His shoulders."* And in Proverbs 14:26, *"He who fears the Lord has a secure fortress..."* Does this mean that we don't really have to do anything in order to keep ourselves safe from harm, because God promises to protect us? No. We need to be sensible, of course. We live in an evil world, and sin and destruction is all around us. There are people who want what we have, at any cost. And just because we have a security system is no guarantee we will never suffer loss. The innocent are the ones who suffer. But I can still say *"I will lie down and sleep in peace for You alone, O Lord, make me dwell in safety."* (Psalm 4:8). Not because of a new alarm system, but because the God of the universe has His eyes on me at all times. And as long as my mind is on Him, He will give me peace. (ref. Isaiah 26:3).

So, we have been talking to our kids and grandkids about safety, not leaving purses or keys in the car, even in the garage, locking doors at night, even the back door which is behind a fence...we are very fortunate this incident didn't turn out worse than it did... *"The angel of the Lord encamps around those who fear Him, and He delivers them."* (Psalm 34:7). We are secure in Him. We are so blessed!

AUGUST 19

JARS OF CLAY...

"But we have this treasure in jars of clay to show that this all-surpassing power is from God and not from us. We are hard pressed on every side, but not crushed; perplexed, but not in despair; persecuted, but not abandoned; struck down but not destroyed." (2 Cor. 4:7-9).

I have been sick now for fifteen days. I have always had plenty of energy, and strength to do all I need to do ~ housework, mow the lawn, walk the dog...I must have taken these things for granted...they're certainly not getting done now. The longer I am sick, the more I'm aware of the frailty of my human frame. I'm still the same person God made me ~ bones, skin, hair ~ I still have need of food and water and air. But I am just an earthen vessel. I have no power in myself. I need Him. And He has promised me that His power will be shown in my weakness.

Did you ever walk through a pottery shop or display, and notice the seemingly like pieces, but then realize none of them is exactly like the other? You could purchase a set of "matching" dishes, and they would not be uniform. Potters are fascinating to watch. They take a chunk of smooth wet mud, place it on a wheel, and begin turning it, shaping the piece, usually a vase or a pot, with their hands as it turns faster and faster. If it doesn't seem to be turning out like the potter wishes, he will slow the wheel and let the mud crumble, re-wet it, form it back into a chunk, and start over again. Each piece is made individually, one at a time. Then, when it is the desired shape, the potter puts it into a very hot oven (kiln), where it will harden and strengthen under the intense heat. Then it may be painted with designs of the potter's choice, and then glazed.

There is a little story, which I cannot find right now, about a woman who walked down a road with two clay pots hanging from a yoke across her shoulders. When she reached the well, she filled both pots, and walked back home. But one of them had a crack in it, and was near empty when she got home.

After a few weeks, she began to notice flowers growing along the side of the road where the pot dripped the water day after day.

I think I am on the mend, finally, but I want to be sure that my cracked pot can be used as a vessel for whatever God wants to put in it. And if it trickles out, then hopefully others will be touched by my life, by the love that God has shown me. But sometimes God chooses to just pour it all out. After all, this vessel is made of clay as well, and will someday decay and crumble. I want it to be used to the full.

AUGUST 20

DISAPPOINTMENT...

Every one of us has been disappointed in something, in someone, or many things, in our life. Oh, gosh ~ where does it start? When we were children, and we were disappointed when the gift wasn't exactly what we were wishing for. Or a promise was broken. We plant some seeds in the garden, and they don't grow. The item we ordered has been discontinued. The child we have raised has gone astray. The lottery ticket we purchased wasn't a winner. (Hmmm...). We spend hours on a painting, or a craft project, and it doesn't turn out like we had pictured it. Some things just don't happen as we had hoped and anticipated. Are our expectations too high?

We do have a right to expect good behavior in our children, if we have *"trained them up in the way they should go."* (Prov. 22:6). We expect our employees to meet certain criteria and ethics in their work for us. We trust that we will be treated with respect by those in businesses that we must frequent, ie. the bank, the grocery store, the schools our children attend. But if that banker has had a bad day, or that grocery store clerk just found out her husband wanted a divorce, or the school teacher has wrongly accused our child of an act...it's easy for us to become very disappointed.

At times, dare I say, I'm sure some of us have even been disappointed in God. We expect that if we pray, He should indeed answer our prayers! Did He not say, *"Ask and it will be given to you; seek and you will find; knock and it will be opened to you?"* (Matthew 7:7). Our heavenly Father does not play with us... whatever He withholds from us, things or situations we ask Him for, it is truly for our own good. Only God can see what the future holds for each of us and answering one of our prayers in the way WE want it done, could be dangerous, or devastating, to our lives or to our spirit. He will answer every prayer we pray, either later, or in a different and unexpected way, but He will always answer. He does not ignore our heart's cries. He has our best interest in His heart of hearts.

People and things, circumstances and mistakes will disappoint us, but Jesus gives us hope if we trust Him. *"And hope does not disappoint us, because God has poured out His love into our hearts by the Holy Spirit, whom He has given us."* (Romans 5:5). *He will make all things beautiful in His time.* (Ecc. 3:11). And His timing is perfect.

AUGUST 21

TALENTS AND GIFTS...

Do you have talents? I'll bet you do. Oh, you may say, "I can't play a musical instrument"...or "I can't paint"...or "sing." Many people do have talents we can see. There are artists, decorators, musicians, woodworkers or glassblowers all around us. Just go to a crafts fair sometime and see the many things people can do. Sometimes we are envious of them ~ we wish we could grow flowers like that, or build furniture, or write a book. Photography is another skill I am in awe of...many times you have to be in the right place at the right time to capture an unforgettable shot.

I have found out, just in the last few months, that I have a talent for quilting. I have sewn all my life, since I was in Jr. High School and have made many types of clothing, both for myself and for my friends, then later for my children. Never in all those years, though, did I make a quilt. I always wanted to, I have always admired them, but didn't take the steps to learn how. Two summers ago, I was looking through a quilt book, and got the bug. Some of the patterns looked pretty easy, so I tried one. I took my time and "studied" the instructions, and strategized, and took the plunge. I had made a beautiful quilt in five weeks, from start to finish. Six months later I had finished my fifth quilt. I just can't stop! I would have to say I have discovered I have a talent for quilting, and I love it. And now at the two-year mark, I can show you 17 (maybe 18) quilts I have made. I have kept two, and the rest have been gifts.

Scripture talks about spiritual gifts. In Romans 12:6-8, Paul speaks of our God-given gifts: *prophesy, serving, teaching, encouraging, contributions, leadership, mercy*...we all have at least one. There are classes we can take, or books we can read to figure out which one we have, but I think if we just examine our lives, it will be revealed to us...shouldn't be hard to interpret. Do you teach Sunday school? How about sending a card to someone who is sick or feeling discouraged? What about a few extra dollars in the plate when a special offering is called for to help another church family? Visiting someone who is lonely? Even caring for an abandoned pet...where do you think these "feelings" of compassion and mercy and generosity come from? These are gifts from God.

Ephesians 2:8 says, *"For it is by grace you have been saved, through faith ~ and this not from yourselves, it is the gift of God ~ not by works, so that no one can boast."* We need to be very careful when we are fulfilling any of these gifts that we don't call attention to ourselves for the glory that someone may give us, but that we would do for others naturally, without desiring recognition. At times we may not even realize we are teaching, or giving, or encouraging because it is spontaneous or instinctive, it is part of our makeup. It's how God made us, individually. It's the best part of His gift to us. But the greatest gift He has given is that of eternal life. *"For God so loved the world that He gave His one and only Son, that whoever believes in Him shall not perish but have eternal life."* (John 3:16). Nothing compares to that Gift.

AUGUST 22

BOOKS...

I love books. I loved books in high school...well, even younger than that, and I was always reading something. Granted, many of them were assignments in English class, but nevertheless, my teachers had a way of making me appreciate the written word. I don't think I have read so much in my whole life, though, as I have read in the last 6-8 years. It may be because of the point where I am in my life ~ my children are all grown and have their own families, and I have more leisure time. I love historical novels, and as much as I hated history in high school, I find myself devouring anything that is about the Revolutionary war, Civil war, World Wars I and II, and most of the books I read include the saga of a family, real or fictional, during those times. I'm learning so much, not just about the politics of those times (which I don't care for at all), but of the way the people lived, the hardships they had, the houses they dwelt in and the mode of transportation. Certainly none of the conveniences we have nowadays.

I have even enjoyed the very thick book of love letters between Winston and Clementine Churchill ~ these are very entertaining, show a lot of their personalities, and contain so much detail about the real feelings and concerns of two popular people during the two World Wars.

And to me, the people in these books are not just characters on the pages or someone's imagination, they were, and are, real people, with needs, who were in love, who had impossible illnesses, and fears, and much hardship ~ well, some of them. There were the well-to-do families who lived in mansions on plantations in the South, or Tudors and manors in Europe. I read a series about Scotland, where the farmer tenants of rocky pastures and crude little mud and straw "homes" were suddenly evicted from the land by the landlord who, on a whim, decided to use his land for other purposes. So, these poor people were driven from their homes with their meager belongings, with no place to go. Many of them starved or became ill and died along the way to… where? Can you imagine?

These stories prompt me to look at similar accounts in God's Book, the Bible. I find stories of wars, famine, illnesses, wanderings, love and marriage, birth and death ~ nothing much has changed. God is just as real today as He was in all those times we read about in His word, or in novels. And all the better if those novels I read are written by Christian authors, who can show how the faith the people had in God got them through the roughest of times. The troubles we have today are not exclusive to the present, but have been in existence since the beginning of time. And principal in all these stories is how God led the people, how he taught them and cared for them. We see how He was present in every situation. Many did not realize this, and did not believe He was sovereign, but much praise was on the lips and in the hearts of those He delivered from their troubles, however large or small they were. He's the same today. God never changes. *"I, the Lord, do not change."*(Mal. 3:6). And Paul, speaking to the Romans (15:4), said "*For everything that was written in the past was written to teach us, so that through endurance and the encouragement of the Scriptures we might have hope.*"

Who is going to read my story? When I am gone will someone look at the life I lived and see evidence that God was leading me? Will they see how, when life was tough, I believed and had faith in my Maker, to get me through the storms? Will my experiences give someone else hope? *"Let this be written for a future generation, that a people not yet created may praise the Lord."* (Psalm 102:18).

AUGUST 23

CAST YOUR CARES...

"Cast your cares on the Lord and He will sustain you; He will never let the righteous fall." (Psalm 55:22). How many times have we read that verse, and others similar, in the Scriptures? What exactly does it mean? It certainly doesn't mean to *reluctantly* hand them over to Him, but then closing our hands before He takes them away.

Mr. Webster defines "cast" as: *"to propel with haste or violence; throw, fling, hurl, project, direct..."* those are just a few ~ this is quite a long entry in the dictionary. I like to think of a fly fisherman standing knee- or hip-deep in the river, pulling back his pole and casting, or flinging, his line as far out into the water as it will go. This takes practice, as I've seen fishermen at sporting goods stores, trying a pole outside in a little pond provided for that purpose. I've seen them in their yards, drilling to get it just right. Casting. Casting. Over and over again. I don't think God meant for us to save up all our troubles and throw them into His lap all at once, although that wouldn't be a problem for Him. That would mean we would have to carry them all on our own shoulders until the load got so heavy ~ how could we possibly "cast" that kind of a load? We need to treat our distresses as if they were a hot potato, getting them out of our hands as quickly as possible. I believe David was in the habit of casting his anxieties on his heavenly Father daily, if not hourly. We see much evidence of that in the book of Psalms. And we see God's answers, as well. It doesn't do us any good to hold on to them for any length of time. And we shouldn't expect Him to play some kind of tug-of-war with our cares. We either give them to Him, or struggle with them ourselves, suffering under the burden.

So many times, we either don't think of giving them to God, or we imagine that we can just handle them ourselves. We might think they are not important enough to bother God with. Or, we are too proud. And before we know it they have piled up and become overwhelming. This causes much stress on our minds and our bodies, and we become ill, literally. Worries and troubles often do lead to dire health issues. Oh, I'm not saying we should not *be concerned* about what is going on in our lives. We are responsible for many things ~ our families, providing care and nurturing, and well-being for our children, earning a living, providing for the needs of our families…watering our lawns, picking up our garbage, and changing the oil in our vehicles…but there are worries that we have no control over…but God does. These are what He wants us to *relinquish* to Him. He insists that we surrender our situation just as it stands, without first trying to "clean it up" or rectify the details. And often we need to simply agree with God to resign ourselves to whatever our circumstances are, and not to pray for God to change things. We need to give up our own will and trust God for a better purpose than we can imagine. And sometimes this will be in desperation! It's a very hard thing to give up something that has been a part of us for so long…but many times, when we open our hands and give up, God gives it back, or something much better. Oh, we want to give God a little of what we're holding in our hands, but not all of it. What happens if we don't get it back? I believe God will always replace what we've given up with something much better. But we must trust Him. *"And my God will meet ALL your needs according to His glorious riches in Christ Jesus."* (Phil. 4:19). What have we got to lose?

AUGUST 24

FRIENDS IN DANGEROUS PLACES…

"Then Jesus said to his disciples: 'Nation will rise against nation, and kingdom against kingdom. There will be great earthquakes, famines and pestilences in various places, and fearful events and great signs from heaven.'" (Luke 21:10-11).

We have seen much evidence of this pledge lately. There has always been war, and we have known loved ones and friends who have been involved or touched by the terror of war. Even the warfare that hasn't taken place in our time, we have read horrendous things about. We see men and women in uniform everywhere we go, as a reminder of those who are fighting for our freedoms. Pray for them.

In our mailboxes we receive fliers and advertisements, and letters pleading for financial help to feed thousands of hungry children all over the world. There are teams of missionaries and individuals who go into diverse places to tell lost people who have never heard, about Jesus, in their own languages. Pray for them.

And just recently, still so fresh in our memory, there is the devastating earthquake in Japan and the unbelievably frightening tsunami that has destroyed the homes and livelihood and identity of thousands upon thousands. And the nightmare continued with innumerable aftershocks. Whole families have been lost. And something we have not experienced in many, many years, the danger of widespread radiation from the damaged nuclear plants there. The effects from this disaster can literally send contamination all over the globe. This kind of devastation is something I only remember reading about in comic books and seeing in old science fiction movies when I was a child. And yet, here we are in the midst of a very real nightmare.

Of course, we should, and do, pray for these people, the victims of this earthquake, as we have for the others ~ for Haiti, the terror of 9-11 in New York City, the bombing in Oklahoma City, hurricane devastation in New Orleans, and recently this summer, the horrendous wildfires in Colorado Springs. And there have been so many other catastrophes. I have friends and relatives, as I'm sure some of you do, who were in the path of the tsunami, and fortunately they have escaped harm. As unbelievable as these tragedies look to us, it's still hard for us to even imagine what those people are going through. They are so lost and confused. They must feel like they have no hope. My prayer for them is that they will see Jesus in the midst of their troubles. Already they have been astonished at the number of people from other countries who have just shown up and started working, digging, searching, helping. Offerings are pouring in from different organizations. Mercy and compassion is going out to the victims through those who are volunteering. These are God-given attributes. I pray that the people of Japan have seen God's compassion in the people who helped... *"But because of His great love for us, God, who is rich in mercy, made us alive with Christ..."* (Ephesians 2:4). May they trust the people who have been sent to help, and in turn, find their way to trust our heavenly Father as well.

AUGUST 25

THE RIPPLE EFFECT...

When I was very young, I enjoyed dropping a stone into a pond from a little walk bridge, or even into a mud puddle. In fact, I'd be happy with a bucket to drop a little pebble into, just to watch the ripples. I can't tell you the last time I did that. I would watch the ripples until they disappeared and the water stilled. I would try to count them. I was mesmerized.

As I grew older, I heard the term "ripple effect" applied to many different things. It made sense. One thing affected something, and then in turn, something else, and so on. I even thought of that in the days following the Japan earthquake and the ensuing tsunami ~ certainly the ripple effect in enormous proportions. It seems that everything we do can have this ripple effect. Gosh, if we make a dish someone likes, they ask for the recipe, make it, and someone else asks them for the recipe. And so on. With the insecure economy, if consumers spend less, then the suppliers and their employees come away with reduced revenue and incomes. The ripple effect.

I once heard a story about a man who was mad at his wife and went out and kicked the dog, who then chased the cat, etc...I don't remember all the sequence, but you get my point. Even at school, one kid will bully another, and that child who was bullied sometimes turns around and bullies another...

In Exodus 20:5 God said, *"I, the Lord your God, am a jealous God, punishing the children for the sin of the fathers to the third and fourth generation of those who hate me."* We have seen this very thing as crime grows, and as a pattern has been discovered in criminals' families. And we know if a grandparent was an alcoholic, it's very likely the parent will be, and the child will have tendencies in this direction as well. I have seen this sad truth myself in several families. Sexual sin does the same thing...think about it. It can ruin (and has) many lives. But then God said, in verse 6, *"...but showing love to a thousand generations of those who love Me and keep My commandments."* This passage is repeated in Deuteronomy 5. This is the good news, as a strong Christian legacy is passed down from generation to generation. Just as talents and skills, characteristics, personalities, good habits, go beyond a single generation, so do bad habits, laziness, anger...unless we break the cycle. Violence and hatred can, and does, have a real effect on our families, on society…and so can love and kindness. I have seen reports of this very effect from Japan, where people are showing this wonderful, giving sort of kindness to one another in the midst of their turmoil. How can we do any less? Let's change the pattern.

AUGUST 26

OUR INHERITANCE…

When I was very young, I used to think of an "inheritance" as piles of gold ~ lots of money…a nice big bank account. My dictionary defines "inheritance" as follows: "something inherited or to be inherited; legacy; bequest; ownership by virtue of birthright; right to inherit; any blessing or possession coming as a gift…" And here's what God's word has to say about inheritance ~ "*…give thanks to the Father who has qualified you to share in the inheritance of the saints in the kingdom of light.*" (Col. 1:12). Inheritance can be something physical, material, or spiritual, even character can be passed along from parents to children.

My husband is a builder by trade. But in the last 6 years or so, because of the economy, he has not built a single house. But he does have the last spec home he built still for sale, and we have lost a lot of money on that house, paying a considerable amount of interest on the construction loan each month for the last six years. This is a beautiful home, and fortunately it is rented at the moment. He could have just let it go back to the bank, except for one item… my inheritance, the house and land left to me by my parents, is collateral on that spec home loan. If we lose the home, we lose my parents' place too. This endeavor to hold onto the house for sale, trying desperately to sell it, has cost us everything ~ well, our own kids' inheritance, at least!

But God has been so good to us, supplying every need. He has given my husband work in a field he never dreamed he would be working, charter bus driving. He loves meeting the people, and of course, operating that huge piece of machinery, and seeing many varied parts of our country. And we are just now coming to the agreement that we can lose both of those houses and still have so much. One of my siblings has not been in favor of "selling my inheritance" because we have talked about doing that too, to pay the bank loan down. This sibling really does not understand the implications of trying to hold on too tightly. I have been thinking about this, and I truly feel I'm okay with losing it. I have wonderful memories of times in our family home. My children and the older grandchildren have recollections of Christmases and tree-hunting, summer exploring, wildlife and visits in the huge country kitchen. And I have inherited so much more from my parents than just an old house on some property in the woods. They taught us about Jesus, and gave us love and understanding, and prayer. We are now making memories in our own home for the grandchildren, and since they all live very close, they drop in often. Jesus Himself said, *"But store up for yourselves treasures in heaven, where moth and rust do not destroy, and where thieves do not break in and steal. For where your treasure is, there your heart will be also."* (Matthew 6:20-21).

Colossians 3:24 says, *"Whatever you do, work at it with all your heart, as working for the Lord, not for men, since you know that you will receive an inheritance from the Lord as a reward."* The inheritance we receive here on earth is only temporary, and usually we will pay taxes on it. But the inheritance we receive from the Lord is eternal. It will *"never perish, spoil or fade ~ it is kept in heaven for us!"* (1 Peter 1:4). So, even though I may lose my earthly inheritance, I know my inheritance in heaven is kept safe and will be more than I could ever dream or imagine!

AUGUST 27

IF IT'S NOT ONE THING...

We all know the rest of that sentence...."it's something else!" Or, "when it rains, it pours." This simply means there are too many things going on, or going wrong, at once. And when someone quotes this famous idiom, it doesn't mean a lot of *good* things are happening. For mothers of small children, one is usually crying and needs attention, while at the same time the other is getting into some kind of trouble. And to make matters worse, the doorbell just happens to ring, and then the phone. And, of course, the pot on the stove decides now is a good time to boil over! Seriously, this has happened to me. Moms are pretty busy, and a lot of their busyness is from re-doing something they've already done because someone is UN-doing it! Seems like this kind of work never ends.

If you're a professional, and you are working on a project, someone may bring in yet another assignment for you to work on, and of course, it's more important than the last one. Homeowners know about this kind of frustration, too...something in the house goes haywire, the TV, refrigerator or washer, and while you're trying to figure out how to get that fixed, something else happens, like a flashing light on the car's dash, a broken pipe, flooding the basement, or the paycheck that didn't arrive on time. But, unquestionably, the bills still arrive on time. Murphy's Law says, "If anything can go wrong, it will," and it's usually just when you think you have a problem solved or under control... some are just little irritations, others are bigger problems which will make a huge impact on our day, or our life.

It seems that Paul had this kind of thing happen to him a lot. If it wasn't enough to be struck blind while he was merrily going about his business, he was "taken captive" if you will, and told in no uncertain terms how his life was going to change. He was told where he was to go, to whom he was to speak, and what he was to do. For a headstrong guy like Paul, this was quite a rude awakening. But the thing is, Paul was very willing ~ he was a believer from the get-go. And he learned so much from being an obedient follower instead of a villainous pursuer. And where did it get him? Well, it seemed the more he did the things Jesus asked him to do, or that he was prompted by the Spirit of God to perform, the more trouble he ended up having. His reputation was attacked, and he was threatened ~ a lot of it being political. Eventually, Paul ended up being beaten, threatened, and thrown into prison, where he penned in a letter, *"I have been crucified with Christ, and I no longer live but Christ lives in me. The life I live in the body, I live by faith in the Son of God, who loved me and gave Himself for me."* (Galatians 2:20). But through all his trials, Paul remained faithful and is one of the greatest teachers we have of God's grace.

Another example to us is God's servant, Job. Oh, I love Job! Here's a man who truly did not deserve all that befell him ~ you can read yourself that Satan did a number on him, and why? Because he was the most righteous and upright man on earth, and Satan wanted to prove to God that Job would turn his back on Him in troubled times. *"The Lord said to Satan, 'Have you considered my servant Job? There is no one on earth like him: he is blameless and upright, a man who fears God and shuns evil."* (Job 1:8). Satan said, "we'll see about that." [my paraphrase!]. So, everything that could happen to anyone, happened to Job. His wife died, and all his children, and his cattle, and his servants were all taken away from him, as well as his stuff. The messengers just kept coming, one by one, without a rest in between, with yet more bad news. In all of this, Job did not waver from his faith in God – *"The Lord gave and the Lord has taken away; may the name of the Lord be praised."* (1:21). As time went on, more calamity came upon Job in the form of sickness, pain and despair. It was so bad, Job cursed the day he was born. But he did not curse God. His so-called friends gave him bad advice, and criticized him, and he answered, *"Though He slay me, yet will I hope in Him."* (13:15). Job had a conversation with God, and all his "friends" were cursed and sent away. He came to the conclusion that *"when He has tested me, I will come forth as gold."* (23:10).

We all have days when everything just keeps piling up and we never seem to get through all that is waiting for our attention. Just when we get a few tasks completed, two or three more appear that are even more urgent. So when it seems that you just can't handle one more thing, say with Job, *"I know that my Redeemer lives, and that in the end He will stand upon the earth."* (19:25). And at that time, nothing else will matter. God is faithful.

AUGUST 28

LOVE LETTERS...

Do you remember receiving a love letter, or several of them, from your first boyfriend? A secret admirer? How about the man who would become your husband? If you're like me, or any of the girls I grew up with, those letters were sacred. They would be read and re-read many times, tied up together in a beautiful bundle with a blue ribbon or stashed away in a secret treasure box. Hidden away, because they were for our eyes only! And in our heart of hearts, we believed every word.

Sometimes, what was said to us in those love letters came true ~ sometimes it didn't. The words contained on those pages would make our hearts soar, or they would break our loving hearts into a million pieces. You may have even written love letters to your children. I have, and sometimes I still do. There are books containing the love letters of famous people ~ Winston Churchill and his dearly loved Clementine...some of these are very amusing...and touching. I even have a comical book called "Cat Love Letters!" I'm not sure too many love letters, or any kind of letters, are sent anymore. In this age of email and cell phone texting, it's just faster to say what we wish to say electronically.

Love letters. Did you know God wrote us love letters? His word, the Bible, is full of His love letters to us. Granted, there is a lot of history in that big book, and a lot of family names that might not be of interest to us. But the whole book is full of incredible stories of God's love for His creation ~ us. He tells us that He knows where we are every moment, He knows everything about us. He actually made us in *His own image*, and in Him we are who we are. He loves to give us gifts... *"And it is My desire to lavish my love on you simply because you are My child and I am your Father."* (1 John 3:1). God, our Father, promises to provide for our every need, and has filled our future with hope. *"His love is everlasting."* (Jeremiah 31:3). He thinks about us all the time. *"You are My treasured possession."* (Exodus 19:5). He is our greatest Encourager. He's our Comforter. And the ultimate expression of His love for us was His death on the Cross. (1 John 4:10). His letters to us should be read and re-read. They should be passed down to our children. They are sacred.

I'm not sure the writers of any of those love letters in our youth could promise or follow through with the kind of love Jesus has shown us, and wants to show us. In fact, there is **no greater love** than that of our Savior. And I sort of feel like my writings in my journals are my love letters to God. What a love affair we have! It's out of this world!

AUGUST 29

WE ARE ONE...

"Like pilgrims of promise we march side by side, from every nation and every tribe, out of the darkness and into the Light we have come...the Word of the Lord is a lamp to our feet, it calls us to follow the path that it leads, to live set apart for the whole world to see ~ we are one. United in holiness, children of righteousness, washed in the blood of the Lamb...we are one, brothers and sisters we stand side by side as one, this glorious church in the image of Christ as one, a people of mercy telling the story, unto the cross we come...together we stand as one." (Dave Clark, from 'One').

This is a song from a short musical our church presented awhile back; actually, it was written for our denomination's 100th year celebration (Nazarene), and hundreds of churches across the nation and the world will be presenting this mini-cantata to their congregations. I'm so glad to have been a part of my church since my husband's and my first date, to church, in 1966. It's been fun collecting memorabilia for a display in our church foyer, and reminiscing ...

Every time I sing or read these words, "we are one," I think of my groups of women, studying, praying and encouraging together, in person, and online, and how, although we all come from different walks of life, live in different parts of the country, and the world, we have a myriad of challenges and situations among us, our stories are diverse, and we are at various stages in our walk with Christ, still, **we are one** in Him. A lot of us don't even know each other personally, but we have a bond in that we are all needy, we share an unbroken unity, all of us struggle with one thing or another, and we are here to help each other with our prayers and encouragement. We are one. This is a safe place. And God Himself is here within our group(s), transforming us. I believe He has blessed us ~ I know, I have received many, many blessings from words shared, words of comfort and teaching, and love. Prayer. And hope. We are one.

"Therefore, as God's chosen people, holy and dearly loved, clothe yourselves with compassion, kindness, humility, gentleness and patience. Bear with each other and forgive whatever grievances you may have against one another. Forgive as the Lord forgave you. ***And over all these virtues put on love, which binds them all together in perfect unity."***(Colossians 3:12-14).

AUGUST 30

ANNIVERSARIES...

We've had 44. Just celebrated that one today. Quite a feat in this day and age. Oh, it hasn't been easy ~ making a marriage work is a tough business. And unfortunately, it isn't a 50/50 proposition, as we often hear it referred to.

My husband is a romantic. He is always looking for unusual ways to surprise me. A celebration I wouldn't think of, or figure out until the end. Last time was a regular date, which we don't have many of. Well, we've had a lot going on in our lives lately. But it was a special evening, starting out with dinner at a nice restaurant, the same restaurant where we had dinner on our wedding night, with 25 white roses in a vase on the table, which he had delivered himself earlier. Then we saw a movie. Flowers, dinner, and a movie. It was a special night. I felt special. I have always asked God to make me into the wife and mother He designed me to be.

And repeating what I have shared a few times before, here is the woman I have always striven to be...the "Proverbs 31 Woman:"

"She is clothed with strength and dignity…She speaks with wisdom, and faithful instruction is on her tongue. She watches over the affairs of her household and does not eat the bread of idleness. Her children arise and call her blessed; ***her husband also, and he praises her;*** *'Many women do noble things, but you surpass them all.' Charm is deceptive, and beauty is fleeting; but a woman who fears the Lord is to be praised. Give her the reward she has earned…"* (Proverbs 31: 25-31).

I know I will never really reach this goal, or attain the reward until I meet Jesus face to face, but the little, and big, acknowledgments here and there along the way build my confidence and make me want to serve my Lord even more diligently. Just like marriage, it is hard, and sometimes we want to give up, but perseverance will pay off in the long run. Our children need to see that in their parents.

AUGUST 31

STAND AT THE CROSSROADS…

Crossroad…we know this is where two roads intersect each other. Webster further defines it "at the point where one must choose between different courses of actions."

We come to many crossroads throughout our lifetime, even daily…physical crossroads when we are traveling, and at times, we really don't know which way to turn. Thank goodness for GPS! There are crossroads that involve situations in our lives and we must make a decision. Decisions about relocating, or choosing another job, to sell or not to sell, what college to go to. Whenever **change** comes into our lives, which is constantly, really, we face a crossroad. Our country is at a crossroad right now, and we all feel the stress from the leadership situation…

"This is what the LORD says, 'Stand at the crossroads and look; ask for the ancient paths, ask where the good way is and ***walk in it****, and you will find rest for your souls.'"* (Jeremiah 6:16). The problem here was that the people blatantly refused to follow God's leading. Israel had forsaken God. Jeremiah agonized and begged them repeatedly to turn from their idol worship and back to God. He would make His promises good.

God promises to prosper us, to turn our mourning to gladness, to forgive our wickedness, and to bring health and healing. But we must trust Him, and take that good path. He will lead us and bless us if we put our confidence in Him.

"Obey Me, and I will be your God and you will be My people. Walk in all the ways I command you, that it may go well with you." (Jeremiah 7:23).

Heavenly Father, You know we want to follow the right path You have shown us, but life is so hard and the crossroads are so confusing sometimes. Cause us to put our trust in You, knowing that You will never lead us astray. You have great plans for us, *"plans to give us a hope and a future,"* (Jer. 29:11) but we must put our hand into Yours and walk with you, all the way. Thank You for Your faithfulness.

SEPTEMBER 1

THE GARDENS...

Many of us are preparing to reap the rewards of our gardens. And others are not so fortunate, depending on where you live and what the weather has been like. It has been a difficult year in most places. There have been such extreme weather conditions pretty much everywhere. Where I live, in northern Idaho, the winter was hard, the spring was ridiculously wet and soggy, and so was summer, up to a few weeks ago, when the temperatures turned to HOT and not a drop of rain has fallen. Some gardens across America are thriving, and others are parched from the drought.

I haven't planted a garden for many years, but I do enjoy the fresh vegetables friends pass on to me. I know quite a few people who have flourishing gardens, and in our area we even have some "community gardens" where volunteers come in to plant a donated portion of land, weed, water, and harvest, and these gardens serve those who need help with groceries...sort of like a food bank. And I have a friend in Texas who always plants a beautiful garden each year, and does a lot of canning, then shares pictures of everything on her blog. Last year, the pictures made me want to cry. All her hard work was all burned up ~ a month of temperatures over 100 degrees, and no rain. She tried so hard.

The Garden of Eden was perfect. There were no weeds, it required no care, not even watering, because of the way the Lord designed the earth, and the garden was like a rain forest, watering itself. There were also several rivers flowing in and around the garden and every kind of produce grew there to nourish the first couple, Adam and Eve. And the wonderful thing about this garden was, they never had to harvest and "put up" food for the winter. Every day there was fresh food, no matter what time of the year it was. There were no jars to sterilize, no root cellar to keep stocked, no freezer bags to buy. It was the perfect garden, the perfect life. They didn't even need to grow alfalfa for the horses and other livestock because the animals were cared for as well ~ plenty of foliage for them, every day.

But now we have only a few short months in which to plant, grow and harvest, and there is a lot of work in between, because of the curse God pronounced, *"Cursed is the ground because of you; through painful toil you will eat of it all the days of your life. It will produce thorns and thistles for you and you will eat the plants of the field by the sweat of your brow…"* (Genesis 3:17-18). God's word talks of another "harvest," that of human souls. Jesus said, *"I tell you, open your eyes and look at the fields! They are ripe for harvest. Even now the reaper draws his wages, even now he harvests the crop for* ***eternal life****…"* (John 4:35-36). He is speaking very clearly here of the lost souls who are everywhere, all around us, even in our own families. The Revelator speaks about the "harvest of the earth," referring to the time of Christ's Second Coming. (Revelation 14:15).

Paul said to the Galatians (6:9) *"Let us not become weary in doing good, for at the proper time we will reap a harvest if we do not give up."* Just as in raising and growing a garden of vegetables for our body's use, we need to be diligent in our work of sustaining and caring for it, and the same holds true for nurturing the garden of souls all around us, sowing the seeds of God's word, growing them and preparing them for the final harvest of the righteous. I think that time is getting very close.

SEPTEMBER 2

ENDINGS…

Everything has a beginning, and everything has an end. Right now, we are experiencing the end of summer. The long, hot, sunny days are shortening, and there is a chill in the air. Evening comes a lot earlier now, and morning a little later, or so it seems. Vacations are drawing to a close as the children prepare to return to school ~ another beginning. People with fireplaces and wood stoves are putting away firewood for the winter, others are harvesting gardens and canning or freezing their produce for winter enjoyment and sustenance. Gardening and yard work will end soon. Our entire family ends summer as we have for the past 40+ years, with a huge camping trip to the same State park nearby. We just ended one month, and began another, and so it goes.

Everything ends. A good book, a movie, a game, a job, sometimes, sadly, a friendship or a marriage relationship. And ultimately, life ends. This was not God's plan in the beginning, when He created all the world and everything in it, including His masterpiece, man. He created us perfect, in His own image to live and have fellowship with Him forever. But we messed up somewhere along the way...in the garden, to be exact. Isn't it interesting that it was the Tree of Life which caused man to experience spiritual death? *"He has made everything beautiful in its time. He has also set eternity in the hearts of men; yet they cannot fathom what God has done from beginning to end."* (Ecclesiastes 3:11). Eternity? So ~ He *did* create us to live forever. Webster defines **eternity** as: "continuance without end; infinite time; time without beginning or end;" oh, and how about this one... "*the endless time after death*." And so, although it seems our lives end at a certain point, which only the Maker knows, it actually continues, only in a different realm than we're used to. So...it's really a beginning...of eternity!

And here's the simple formula for that un-ending life ~ *"And this is the testimony: God has given us eternal life, and this life is in His Son. He who has the Son has life; he who does not have the Son of God does not have life."* (I John 5:11-12). It is ours for the taking. It's His gift to us. A very extravagant gift, but specially ordered just for us. Will you take it and enjoy eternal life with God? Or refuse it and spend eternity in darkness and pain? The choice is up to us. And by the way, that Tree of Life is still there in the garden and will be waiting for us to enjoy its fruit in heaven. *"To him who overcomes, I will give the right to eat from the Tree of Life, which is in the paradise of God."* (Jesus speaking in Revelation 2:7). And there will be no end to the joy we will experience. No end.

SEPTEMBER 3

THE PEOPLE IN OUR LIVES...

It's been a rainy day, the house is quiet, and I've been sitting here perusing a book my daughter gave me for Christmas last year called "Mom, Tell Me

Your Story." It is a form of journal, and it asks various questions about my childhood, schools, friends, growing up, meeting my husband, our marriage, how I felt about this or that...it's one of many out there that are designed to record family history and heritage. As I have written answers to the questions (I've spent all year doing this), I also rummaged through a box of old photos ~ found a lot of old school friends among the snapshots. Some I don't even remember their names, but I know that in some way they touched my life, even if only for that school year. I found photos of myself, and my husband, when we were dating, of family members, my "little" brothers, my grandchildren when they were tiny...even pets we have had through my growing up years.

I found a picture of my third grade school teacher, Mrs. Driessen, from right here in my hometown. It was on a Christmas card that she had sent me after I was an adult. She was 82 years old in the picture, but didn't look any different than when she was my beloved teacher. She died when she was 95, about 12 or so years ago. She remained my friend after I moved away, faithfully answering my letters, and then when my family came back to town, we resumed our friendship. I've never known anyone like her. She had pure white hair, always. And a broad smile that would crinkle up her eyes. And I'll never forget her laugh. She encouraged me, and she loved me. What a role model for a shy third-grader. I remember wishing she could be my teacher for each subsequent year.

There were many others. My doctor whom I had seen since I was three, who treated all the illnesses of our family, and who delivered my own babies. He and his wife, also a doctor, had been friends of my parents, and so we knew them all our lives. There are a couple of Sunday School teachers and Pastors I remember, who were infinitely wise and caring. Neighbors in some of the places we lived while my dad was in the military, who would treat us and care for us like their own children. And there were my many "best" friends. Then, of course, there were my parents, whose faith shone in every circumstance. We glean a little information, a little style, a little of a lot of things from the collection of people we've known throughout our lives. I thank God for them all. Some of them I had forgotten about. Sometimes an incident, or some little phrase, or a place, will trigger a memory of someone I hadn't thought about in a long time. When their names come to my mind, I whisper a prayer for them. Perhaps I will never know what their situation is, and most probably I will never see them again, but still, I wonder who else would be praying for them at that moment.

I try to think about how many peoples' lives Jesus impacted, and in only three short years. He readily befriended them, He rebuked some, He healed many, He restored life to some, He taught them all. He was, and is, *the Way, the Truth and the Life* to all. He was Brother, Son, Friend, Confidant, Judge, Healer, Teacher. Though He was only on earth thirty-three years, His Spirit lives on, in and through all of us who accept that friendship. I like to think that the spirit of many of the people in my life still lives on in me, a little here and a little there, even if I have not seen them for 30, 40, or 50 years. We all have the capability to impact someone else's life, to make a difference. It blows me away when I try to remember everyone I have encountered throughout my lifetime, friends, employers, co-workers, and in some small way, or a big way, they have made a difference in who I am. Most memories of "my people" are good memories, but a few are not. I will dwell on the good ones. But a thought has come to me...Christ died for ALL men, even those who have hurt me in some way. Are they less deserving of my prayers?

And of all the people who have been in my life at one time or another, my family are the ones who have been with me all my life. What a heritage I have. I hope to pass that along to all those who come after me...

SEPTEMBER 4

MORNING STAR...

A few years ago we were camping over Labor Day weekend, and as usual, I got up WAY early in the morning to traipse down to the restroom. Of course, anytime I get up in the night while camping, I *always* have to look up at the sky. The stars are SO brilliant when you're out away from the lights of the city. This particular morning, though, I noticed the most beautiful bright star, even though the dawn sky was lightening. I couldn't take my eyes off it, even while I was walking! I'm sure I had seen it sometimes before, but not this bright.

When I got home, I emailed my friends who know a lot about stars, and learned that morning star is Venus (meaning "Splendor"). A planet! I haven't been much into stars all my life, which stars are which, except of course, the big dipper. Everyone knows that one! Then the words of a song came to my mind "He's the Lily of the Valley, the Bright and Morning Star..." Jesus is the bright herald that darkness is past and the eternal day where God alone reigns is dawning. Jesus wants us to welcome Him into our hearts, our secret places, and let His light shine on us so that when He comes in fullness of glory there will be no place in us to make us ashamed. He made that possible by His death on the cross, and His resurrection.

"And so we have the prophetic word made more sure, to which you do well to pay attention, as to a lamp shining in a dark place, until the day dawns and the ***Morning Star*** *arises in your hearts."* (II Peter 1:19). So look up! See the beautiful works of God's hands, and rejoice! He brought the Light into the world, and we can let that light shine through us to others who are in the darkness.

SEPTEMBER 5

FIRST DAY OF SCHOOL...

"This is the day that the Lord has made, let us rejoice and be glad in it." (Psalm 118:24).

Today is the first day of school in our town. Kids have been living in anticipation for weeks, shopping for school supplies, new clothes, some of them excited and some filled with dread. My daughter actually did a joyous dance yesterday when she remembered that school starts today! She has two children, the older boy very compliant and not much trouble at all...but on the other end of the spectrum, a VERY strong-willed first grade daughter. Last year she went to kindergarten for half-days, but this year it will be all day. My daughter is rejoicing, for she has finally earned the full day to herself. I think she will kiss the school bus this morning!! Of course, she will be thinking about them all day, wondering how they're doing, how they like their teachers, if they're making new friends...

What is it about the first day of school? It can be a little scary, or a lot, facing a new classroom, new teacher, new kids, a new routine. Some will cry, some will be nervous and have upset tummies. But after a few days of settling in, they'll be back in the swing of things. Many will feel like Daniel in the lion's den. As parents, we hope and pray that our child will make the right choices, that their minds will be fresh and receptive to the lessons they are taught. My daughter and her husband will pray with their children this morning as they send them off to school, committing them to the Lord, and to someone else who will be teaching and disciplining them every day, all day. They have done their best to *"Train a child in the way he should go, and when he is old he will not depart from it."* (Proverbs 22:6).

And what about us? It may not be the first day of anything for many of us, and yet, we will face unknown situations, problems and joys today, or this week, as well. *"Commit your way to the Lord; trust in Him and He will do this: He will make your righteousness shine like the dawn, the justice of your cause like the noonday sun."* (Psalm 37:5,6). Commit. The children are making a commitment for nine months. We must commit our whole lives to Him, in order to lead them. Pray for your children and your grandchildren, and other kids you know as well. Pray for their protection. Some may have no one else to pray for them. They are facing such "lions" as we have never had to face in school. Let's remember them all year long, and not only on the first day of school.

SEPTEMBER 6

THE BIG YELLOW SCHOOL BUS...

Three of my grandchildren ride the same school bus, and they live in my neighborhood (yes, I'm blessed!). Morning and afternoon, their bus, #29, drives on the street behind my house, so that all I have to do is stand in my sliding glass door and we can wave at each other as the bus goes by. It is so cute to see these little first-grade and third-grade hands waving in the bus windows. Sometimes other kids wave too. I love it. And I know it will make memories for my grandchildren as they grow up. My daughter is so happy to see the bus coming along, she named it "Sunshine!" Even her children, and others, now refer to the bus as "Sunshine." But now, whenever my daughter calls her little girl "Sunshine," she adamantly answers, "I'm not a bus!" This morning, as I watched bus #29 go by, I got to thinking about what a wonderful thing it would be to pray for all of those children on the bus, and other school buses as I see them on the roads.

2 Thessalonians 1:11 says, *"With this in mind, we constantly pray for you, that our God may count you worthy of His calling, and that by His power He may fulfill every good purpose of yours and every good act prompted by your faith."* Now, why wouldn't that be an excellent prayer to pray for those children? I wonder how many diverse backgrounds those children are coming from...what kind of parents they have, did they get breakfast, or do they have enough money

for lunch? How many are foster children, facing the unknown every day, how many are in physical pain, or emotional pain? And let's face it, children are cruel, and they can discern whether or not a child is "underprivileged" and will often treat them as such. I also wonder how many children have anyone praying for them, a parent, grandparent or Sunday School teacher? Is there a child on Bus #29 who has *no one* praying for them? How sad and unfortunate. *"Jesus said, 'Let the little children come to me, and do not hinder them, for the kingdom of heaven belongs to such as these. I tell you the truth, anyone who will not receive the kingdom of God like a little child will never enter it.' And He took the children in His arms, put His hands on them, and blessed them."* (Mark 10:14-16).

So, I have a challenge for you…whenever you see "Sunshine" the school bus, any school bus for that matter, pray for those children who are passengers. Pray for their safety, their health and well-being, pray that someone will tell them about Jesus. And the same for those you see walking along the sidewalk or street with their backpacks, alone or with friends, or riding their bicycles…some of them truly do look forlorn, and may have very good cause for it. Maybe their parents yelled at them as they were leaving the house this morning. Pray for their home life, the love of their parents, and the innocent fun of childhood. Pray these prayers for teenagers, too ~ *especially* teenagers! Not all of them are receiving the love, nurturing and teaching at home that they need. God commanded us to pray for one another ~ this means children too! And children "get it!" Jesus said, *"I praise You Father, Lord of heaven and earth, because You have hidden these things from the wise and learned,* ***and revealed them to little children****. Yes, Father, for this was Your good pleasure."* (Luke 10:21).

SEPTEMBER 7

ASAPH WHO???

"For I envied the arrogant when I saw the prosperity of the wicked…when I tried to understand all this, it was too painful for me, till I entered the sanctuary of God; then I understood their final destiny." (Psalm 73:3, 17). I have received so much encouragement from this verse over the years, when things are just not going right. This particular Psalm could even be part of the book of Lamentations, since it is filled with discouragement and deep despair. Just thinking about his

problems caused Asaph much pain, and he became dangerously anxious and bitter.

Asaph is known for a few Psalms he wrote (12 of them), in Book III of the Psalms. He was David's music director, as well as a priest from the tribe of Levi, in the tabernacle. His position as director of music carried over into Solomon's reign as well, assisted by his brother, Zechariah. He was very close to David. In some of Asaph's Psalms, 75 & 82, we can see his disillusionment with Solomon, whom he greatly admired, and he even thought he could have been the Messiah. 76 & 80 reflect Asaph's pain during the division of Solomon's kingdom. 74 & 79 reveal his distress at the invasion of the king of Egypt, and 73 shows the bitterness at his family's, and Zechariah's murders at the hands of Solomon and the Egyptians. And when he was an old man, near a hundred years of age, he surveyed the wreckage of his hopes and the deep disappointment he had in his heart. Solomon had not been who Asaph always believed he was ~ he came to reveal his wickedness in many ways.

Through it all, Asaph finds just how faithful God is, and what a strong tower of hope He is to those who love Him as God revealed His truths to him.

I think any of us could look at our lives and see disappointment and disillusionment as we think on those experiences that brought us so deeply into despair. Just this week my husband was scheduled to undergo a surgical procedure in his heart to put it back into rhythm. He had the same procedure done 15 months ago, and it didn't work. The cardiologist was confident it would work a second time. So, on the appointed day we showed up very early at the hospital and he was prepped, but there was a complication which showed up in some of the tests. The cardiologist was hesitant to go ahead with the surgery until he found the root of the problem, and consulted with two other doctors. Consequently, he cancelled the surgery on the spot until he could determine what the problem was. What a letdown in all of our emotions. He ordered a CT scan, since we were already in the hospital, and when that report came back he was relieved, and so were we, that it was kidney stones ~ many of them, in both kidneys. But all passable! It could have been a worse problem. And the procedure has been rescheduled for a later date.

This week's inconvenience is just another in a string of "bad luck" our family has had in the past month. We could easily become discouraged and distressed at the obstacles and heartaches that have been placed before us. But God's faithfulness is higher than the heavens and He knows just what we need to move through the roadblocks and delays. It's always a learning process.

Just as Asaph found peace in the presence of God, so can we, no matter what we are going through. I know that whenever there is a delay in our plans, it usually turns out for the better in the long run. And as defined in another Lamentation, this of Jeremiah (3:21-23), *"Yet this I call to mind, and therefore I have hope: Because of the Lord's great love we are not consumed, for His compassions never fail. They are new every morning; great is Your faithfulness."* Just remember, we all go through hard times and as long as we trust in Him, the same Lord who brought Asaph through his deep despair, we can experience that peace and joy that eventually he knew.

SEPTEMBER 8

CLOUDS...

Well, here it is, the end of summer, and yesterday's clouds brought much needed rain. When it's been hot, I welcome the clouds to cool things off a bit. But now, at this time of year, we will begin seeing a lot of clouds, and they really do affect some people's moods. And then the term "cloudy" defines things like fog, darkness, hazy, unclear...and they usually promise a storm. And we know life is full of storms, as well as sunshine. But there are other clouds, the beautiful white fluffy clouds that seem to add a certain breathtaking beauty to the blue sky, and cause artists and photographers to want to capture the beauty of the sunset, each one different from the last.

God's word says, *"At that time they will see the Son of Man coming in a cloud with power and great glory."* (Luke 21:27). And in Daniel 7:13, *"In my vision at night I looked, and there before me was One like a Son of Man, coming with the clouds of heaven."*

Do you ever sit and just look up at the sky and study the clouds? When I was a child one of my favorite things was to lay on the grass and stare up at the sky, and try to make out forms in the clouds ~ a sheep, a teddy bear, a hand... and now I always notice the sky, especially if there are clouds illuminated by the sun, and when there are rays falling down from the clouds, I always think "it looks like what I'll see when Jesus comes." Of course, I have NO idea how breathtaking and marvelous it will be ~ our finite minds cannot fathom the beauty of the coming Christ! But my Bible says that ALL will see Him when He comes in the clouds. And to make it even more spectacular, He will be bringing with Him thousands of angels in a choir like we have never heard on this earth! And then the best part, *"those who are still alive and are left will be caught up together with them in the clouds to meet the Lord in the air."* (IThess. 4:17). What a trip!!

So remember when you see clouds, there is sunshine on the other side... and one day soon we will welcome the magnificent clouds that will bring the King of Kings, and Lord of Lords, our Redeemer!

SEPTEMBER 9

THE LUNCHBOX...

Remember the old metal lunchboxes we used to carry to school with Superman, Roy Rogers, Mickey Mouse, Popeye, Zorro, and other characters on the sides? They usually came with a matching Thermos inside to carry milk or juice. For awhile I had to carry a plain brown paper sack, but when I graduated up to my first real lunchbox, I was so proud of it, and to this day, I cannot tell you what character it had on it...in fact, I think it was just a solid dark blue color. Our mother would lovingly pack us a sandwich, carefully cut in half, cookies, or if we were lucky, a Twinkie or Hostess Snowball, an apple or grapes, maybe some chips or crackers, a couple of carrot sticks... quite a lunch. And then at the end of the day, I would carefully fold my school papers and lay them inside my now empty lunchbox and bring them home. I'm pretty sure we didn't have backpacks in the '50's, or if we did, I didn't have one. By the end of the school year, those lunchboxes were pretty banged up, with dents in the corners, or in one of the sides, paint peeling off, and the lid wouldn't stay latched. Sometimes the lowly lunchbox would be used to stand or sit on, adding to its damage. We would beg Mom to let us use them for treasures in the summertime, marbles, little cars, a rock collection, paper dolls...hoping to get a new lunchbox for the next school year.

Sometimes there would be a child at school who didn't have a lunch, and instead of letting him or her go hungry, I would share a ½ sandwich, or some raisins with them. My Mom never *said* to do this, I just naturally felt bad for a child with no lunch. And the schools didn't have the free lunch program for needy children like they do today.

There was a little boy, a very long time ago, who shared his lunch, not just with another child, but with thousands of people. It was designed by God alone that this boy was in the right place at the right time. How would the disciples have found a child with a lunch in a crowd of five thousand, all crammed together on a small hillside? I still marvel at this story. Jesus had been preaching for hours, and it was evening. *"Then Jesus went up to a mountainside and sat down with His disciples.When He looked up and saw a great crowd coming toward Him, He said to Philip, 'Where shall we buy bread for these people to eat?'...Philip answered Him 'Eight months' wages would not buy enough bread for each one to have a bite!' Another disciple, Andrew, said, 'Here is a boy with five small barley loaves and two fish, but how far would they go among so many?' Jesus said, 'Have the people sit down.' ... Jesus took the loaves, gave thanks, and distributed to all those people as much as they wanted."* (John 6:3-13). Wow. I still don't get it. And the fact that they collected twelve baskets of leftovers after the people had eaten their fill, astounds me. Can you imagine the story that little boy had to tell his mother when he arrived home that night? Do you ever wonder who that little boy grew up to be? There is quite a lesson here...when our resources are woefully inadequate, we bring them to God and place them in His hands, who blesses them and multiplies them before our eyes. I have seen this happen, just in this last year!

In our day of food banks, soup kitchens, free lunch for needy school kids, food stamps...there are many ways to feed the hungry. Sometimes our church will do a "food pounding" in which they collect food for a certain family who has fallen on hard times. But Jesus said, *"Do not work for food that spoils, but for food that endures to eternal life, which the Son of Man will give you."* (John 6:27). He still wants us to share with those who have less than we do, but when we do that, let's remember to share the gospel, the real food, Jesus Christ Himself. As we nourish another's body, or other various needs, let's also nourish their soul...

SEPTEMBER 10

CHEERING YOUR TEAM ON...

I pass by one of our local high schools every day, and many times there is a full stadium of cheering fans. Of course, now it's football season. And there are some teams still playing soccer. We live just within a couple of blocks from the school, so in the evening we can actually hear the cheering and announcing from our house. So much enthusiasm!

Some living rooms and family rooms are alive with this same enthusiasm during various sports seasons, as teams square off for the World Series, and later in the winter it will be the Super Bowl. Some fans like to watch golf, or tennis…even bowling. And of course, the Winter Olympics are popular. Oh, and we could get into car racing, or horse racing. No matter what it is, we are there to cheer on our favorite team. The ones I love are the little kids. My grandchildren are involved in a kids' flag football program, and cheerleading, and one is in cross-country, all in elementary school. They are so cute as they are learning their sport.

This life we are living is somewhat like a sport, in that we must practice our skills to do our best, and hopefully we have people on the sidelines to encourage us and cheer us on. Paul told the Philippians in 3:13: *"Forgetting what is behind and straining toward what is ahead, I press on toward the goal to win the prize for which God has called me heavenward in Christ Jesus."* We are called to persevere. If the teams we watch did not stick to a game plan, or persevere in the game, and in their practice times, they would fall apart and it would be impossible to even come close to winning. It is the same with life ~ we will run into hard places, but we still cannot give up or we'll never break through the barriers. It takes hard work to win the trophy.

Paul also said to the Hebrews, *"Therefore, since we are surrounded by such a great cloud of witnesses, let us throw off everything that hinders and the sin that so easily entangles, and let us run with perseverance the race marked out for us. Let us fix our eyes on Jesus, the author and perfecter of our faith…"* (12:1-2). I believe this "cloud of witnesses" are the saints and angels who have gone before us, and are cheering us into heaven, into the very presence of God Almighty. I can picture them high-fiving us all the way in through the pearly gates. And our biggest cheer-leader of all, Jesus, who will present our crown. Our trophy.

SEPTEMBER 11

ALARMS…

Alarms are devices, or situations, that are designed to get our attention quickly. I don't like them. Most of us don't. When I was in school, the fire drills we had scared me. And I think the more sophisticated the systems become, the louder the alarms. I hate setting an alarm clock, because I usually end up waking up several times in the night, checking the time to see if it should be going off ~ why do we do that? Thankfully, I don't usually have trouble waking up on time, or early. Alarm clocks are interesting, aren't they? Radios have them, so you can wake up to whatever kind of music you want. Some alarm clocks are the old-fashioned kind that you wind up with a key on the back, and they actually have a ringing sound, usually loud. My favorite, simply because I love to hear the ticking sound. The alarm clock that puts me to sleep! But I never set it to wake up.

My daughter had an alarm clock when she was in school that was a chicken, and at the appointed time he would sing this really annoying little song, flap his wings wildly, then crow! Needless to say, she gave that away after awhile. Some have soft little beeping sounds, and you can even set your wristwatch and cell phone to sound an alarm of your choice.

Our bodies have alarms as well, to let us know when something is wrong. Different symptoms alert us to an illness or condition that we should have checked by the doctor. A toothache tells us we have a cavity, or some nerve problem that will require some treatment. Blood tests show when there is an infection in our body and we need antibiotics. An X-ray, or scan will show what we cannot see – a broken bone, or a tumor.

This morning I was awakened at 4:30 by an alarm I did not want to hear – our home security system! After our break-in last summer, we had the system installed and every once in awhile, someone (usually my husband) will open the door without remembering to disarm the system. While I leapt out of bed at the sound of the siren so loud within the walls of my home, heart beating fast, my husband was calmly walking around the kitchen. He didn't have his hearing aids and truly didn't hear the alarm! We got it shut off, the alarm center called to see if we were OK, and he was off on his trip, and I went back to bed. And of course, after that "rude awakening" I couldn't fall asleep again.

God has given us many warnings in His word, about the way we should live, and how to watch for the Day of His coming. *"You will hear of wars and rumors of wars…nation will rise against nation, and kingdom against kingdom. There will be famines and earthquakes in various places…"* (Matthew 24:7). [Not to mention floods, tornadoes, terrorism, economic collapse…] And following, in vs. 30-31, *"At that time the sign of the Son of Man will appear in the sky…they will see the Son of Man coming on the clouds of the sky, with power and great glory. And He will send His angels with* ***a loud trumpet call****, and they will gather His elect…"* I think this trumpet will be the loudest alarm we have ever heard, for everyone on earth (and under it) will hear its blare.

For years the alarms have been going off. Generation after generation have been warned that we must walk in the way Christ showed us. I want to be ready when that holy trumpet sounds the alarm and the Lord of All calls my name.

SEPTEMBER 12

GOD'S COUNTRY…

I have heard many places called "God's Country." I would be biased if I were to say one place is more beautiful than another…it's also said that "beauty is in the eye of the beholder." So, I'll just describe what my Labor Day Camping Weekend was like. There is a place in North Idaho, the historical 4,000-acre Farragut State Park, only about 20-25 minutes from home, that has been used as a Navy base, and is situated beside the largest lake in Idaho. Pend Oreille Lake is deep enough that the Navy still does submarine testing here. The area that housed the base in the 1940s has been turned into many campgrounds and day-use areas. Covered with pine and other trees, it's a haven for deer, mountain goats, lynx, many types of birds and small critters, and bears. In the wee hours, you can even hear the coyote choirs as you are lying in your tent. Sometimes they're nearby, and other times they echo from across the vast lake. They always bring a smile to my face, even in the middle of the night when the song wakes me, because I know they are praising God in the way they were created to.

On the "outside," the end-of-summer temperatures hovered in the 90s all weekend, but where we were nestled in the trees, around our campfire, it was at least 10-15 degrees cooler. And, here's the heavenly part…our entire family was with us ~ kids, grandkids and our great-granddaughter, and we even brought an extra friend of our grandson's. Camping in this place has been a family tradition for over 40 years. We cooked all our meals in camp, there was a playground very near our campsite, and dogs were allowed. (And I might add here, our dogs were very well behaved!). There are many trails for riding bicycles or walking, planned activities and programs, such as hikes and movies in the outdoor amphitheatre about nature, and the stars ~ oh my goodness, the stars were so brilliant and every night sky was crystal clear. God's country, indeed!

It is hard for me to imagine that anyone could not believe this was all hand-crafted by a loving and brilliant and powerful Creator-God. The beautiful mountains, deep blue lakes, wildlife, the twinkling stars, vegetation and wildflowers could not have been the idea of a mere human, or have happened by chance. And the small children in our family are learning this truth as well. We did, however, see several satellites while gazing up at the sky each night, and I imagined the pictures they were seeing!

"The earth is the Lord's, and everything in it, the world, and all who live in it; for He founded it upon the seas, and established it upon the waters." (Psalm 24:1-2). Yes, it is unmistakably God's country!

SEPTEMBER 13

HIS EYE IS ON THE SPARROW...

"Look at the birds of the air. They do not sow, nor reap, nor gather into barns, and yet your heavenly Father feeds them. Are you not worth much more than they?" (Matthew 6:26).

This week I rescued a little sparrow. What a feeling! I heard him hit the sliding glass door, and I quickly checked the porch, and he was lying on his side, right next to my Springer Spaniel, who was looking down at him. I told Stormy "no-no" and gently picked up the bird. His little eyes were blinking, although he didn't appear to be breathing ~ sometimes they will pant. The air was knocked out of him. He laid on his side in my hand and I gently stroked his feathers with my finger, and talked quietly to him, (is that like being a "bird-whisperer?") then I turned him over and stroked the other side. ~ wondering all the time where I should put him that would be safe from the dogs. I decided to take him into the front yard ~ but the cat! Well, she's old, no claws, and usually sleeps under the bushes just near the house, so I wasn't too worried about her. Just as I went through the gate, the sparrow popped up onto his feet, still in the palm of my hand. I still stroked the feathers on his back, and as I bent over to put him on the grass under a bush, he fluttered into the bush!

What a relief…then as I stooped to take a look at him, he hopped onto another branch. He was revived!

I immediately thought of how God rescues us and holds us in the palm of His great and mighty hand, gently speaking His unfailing love to our hearts. My mother's very favorite song was "His Eye is on the Sparrow" sung by Mahalia Jackson. *"Why should I feel discouraged, why should the shadows come, why should my heart be lonely, and long for heaven and home, when Jesus is my portion? My constant friend is He…* ***His eye is on the sparrow, and I know He watches me…"***

My favorite authors, Bodie and Brock Thoene, speak in some of their books about a small band of cast-off boys in Jerusalem in Jesus' time called the "Sparrows." They are homeless boys, for one reason or another, some very little, and they live in a quarry and take care of each other. And God takes care of them. In their travels to and fro, three of them somehow end up with a humble shepherd who cares for them, and the littlest boy finds a little sparrow who becomes his pet and stays with him. It's a heart-warming portion of the story. How like Jesus! Caring for us and loving us and yet… *"Are not two sparrows sold for a penny? Yet not one of them will fall to the ground outside of your Father's care. And even the very hairs on your head are numbered. So don't be afraid; you are worth more than many sparrows."* (Matthew 10:29-31).

Just know that when your heart is troubled, whenever you are tempted, when clouds arise, when your hope dies, you can draw closer to Him and He'll set you free from the cares. *"His eye is on the sparrow, and I KNOW He watches me."*

SEPTEMBER 14

PENCILS…

I love pencils. Almost as much as I love paper. My penmanship seems to be better with a pencil than with a pen for some reason, so it is more pleasing for me to use lead. A ballpoint pen seems to get away from me at times, but I can at least erase a pencil. I write in all my journals with a mechanical pencil. Of course, if I'm writing a letter, a real letter on stationery, I use a pen. Just seems more proper and attractive … looks nicer.

All pencils are not created equal, however. There is hard lead and soft lead, and I like mine somewhere in between. When you think about it there are art pencils (have you seen the beautiful pencil sketchings of Jesus?), there are those big fat carpenter's pencils, colored pencils, and eyebrow pencils.

I think of another journal that couldn't have been that easy to write. David's. First of all, the "paper" he used to records his thoughts and prayers and songs had to be difficult to produce. Papyrus or parchment, and sometimes even pounded animal skins, must have been tough to write on. And he would have had to use just the right kind of "ink" so that his writings would not run and bleed, but could be preserved, as they were. Usually the writing surface of the papyrus, or skins, was irregular and it was difficult to form the characters and words. Then there was the storage of such material. It had to be handled very carefully so as not to crack. It was very fragile and susceptible to moisture and dryness. So, many scrolls were kept and stored in clay jars with lids.

Well, back to David's writings…he spilled his heart in his journals. He showed his love, his fears, gave instruction to his fellows (and to us), wrote prayers, and his praise to God Almighty. I'm so glad his writings were preserved! I wonder if he would have written even more if he'd had pencils. I have gleaned so much from David's compositions. Many other books in the Bible talk about David, and we see a lot of his life in them ~ how he grew, what he accomplished, and what he didn't…but in the Psalms we see David's heart, and we learn that he was very aware of the condition of his heart…he was called, by Samuel, at the time he was anointed, (1 Sam. 13:14), *"a man after God's own heart."* In his journal, he asked God to *"create a pure heart"* in him (Ps. 51:10), he recognized he needed a *"broken and contrite heart"*(51:17), in 86:11, he asked for *"an undivided heart,"* he acknowledged his *"heart is steadfast"* (108:1), and he knew that God could *"know my heart"* (139:23). I often write these same kinds of prayers in my own journal. It seems that when I am writing, I can focus better on what is in my heart, and on what God is saying to me in His word. I'm so glad for David's example.

Guess I'd better go now, and sharpen my pencils!

SEPTEMBER 15

WORD PROCESSING…

In this day and age of computers, word processors are an essential piece of equipment, "software." Word processors will let you fix mistakes in typing as you go along without having to re-type a whole document, or letter. You can delete, insert, file and store anything if you have the right computer program. It will correct spelling and grammar for us, and even come up with words we cannot think of. Gone are the days of typewriter erasers and white-out correction fluid.

But Man has been processing words since the beginning of time. Our brains are very intricate word processors. Adam and Eve didn't have to take any language lessons in order to understand God when He spoke to them. I don't think it took a lot of processing when He told them the rules of the Garden, either. And when they had sinned, they knew it immediately. God came along momentarily, and there was more word processing going on as He expelled them from their home, forever.

The most fascinating word processing for me is to watch a baby learn and work out words in their young minds. They learn so fast. First they experiment with different sounds they make in place of words…sounds for "hungry," for "wet," and for "tired." Then comes the baby talk. And I think before this even begins, they start to understand what mother means by the loving tone of her voice, and then the association of certain repeated words, with actions. Babies communicate with each other in their own language, and it's so cute to watch. The fun part is when they start trying out real words and can actually communicate with adults. They don't always pronounce words correctly, but we can pretty much guess what they're saying.

My two-year-old great granddaughter gets to come to my house every Thursday for a break from her daycare. Last week she pointed to my cookie jar and said "pookie?" When I finally figured out what she was saying, I offered her a chocolate chip cookie and she refused it. The week before there had been some orange Jell-o sugar cookies in there and they are her favorite. So, today when she came, we made her orange "pookies." Her mama wasn't even aware she was saying this word, so I sent her home with a bag of pookies ~ yes, that name is probably going to stick. She knew exactly what she was asking for!

We process words every day, either in our reading of books, or correspondence, listening to a news report on the TV or radio, or just conversing with another human being. Even the dog knows what we're saying most of the time! When I read my Bible, I am processing what God is trying to tell me through His word. His teaching and the examples of stories of godly men and women all throughout time, are showing me just how I should live. Not only do I process His words with my mind, but I process them in my heart. But why does it take us so long to process the Almighty's words? We can read instructions for a certain project and get it done; we can read a novel and know exactly what the story line and plot is; we can be touched by the words of a song that are meaningful. But sometimes it takes a whole lifetime to process what our heavenly Father wants to say to us, communicating His unending love for us, giving us the formula for abundant living.

In Deuteronomy 8:3 we are told that *"man does not live on bread alone, but on every word that comes from the mouth of the Lord."* And a few chapters before that He gives us the words that we are to live by, and that have lasted down through the ages, ten words. Ten Commandments. They are simple. But not so easy to follow. And men are trying to do away with these words. Can't we see that not following them has caused so much trouble in the world we live in? David said, *"Your word is a lamp unto my feet and a light unto my path."* (Psalm 119:105). And Solomon declared that *"Every word of God is flawless..."* So why do we think we have to change it? God's words are the answers to the life we're living. They are written in stone. We make it too difficult to process His laws. But His ways are best. The Bible is our handbook for life, our instruction manual. If we follow it, we'll get it right.

SEPTEMBER 16

ADJUSTMENTS...

Oh, dear...I just got new glasses yesterday. I haven't worn glasses much of late, except for reading glasses, which I take off and put on about 50 times a day. Not exaggerating. I used to have bifocals, years ago, but this time I opted for (or, more accurately, I let them talk me into) "progressive" trifocals. Sounded good. I would be able to see clearly no matter what the distance...as long as I bob my head up and down and look straight ahead through the center of the lenses at all times! So, everything is still as fuzzy as they were before I got the new glasses! But they told me my eyes would adjust and I'd get used to them in about a week and a half. I guess I thought that by wearing them the entire day, I would be used to them by evening. I was wrong. So, I'll wait a couple of weeks and then go back and see what can be done.

Adjustments are a part of our every day life. Not just in new glasses, but almost anything we do. When we are in school, we have to adjust to a new classroom, teacher and classmates each year. When the statement is billed incorrectly, we, or the store or the bank, have to make adjustments in our account. When we double a recipe, there are adjustments in the amounts of ingredients. We sometimes have to compromise, come to a settlement or an arrangement that will satisfy all parties involved. If we lose, or gain weight, adjustments have to be made to our wardrobe. Or, our diet! Oh, and what about going to the chiropractor?

So, how about our faith? We talked quite a bit in our Bible study this week about Romans 12:1 & 2… *"Therefore I urge you, [sisters], in view of God's mercy, to offer your bodies as living sacrifices, holy and pleasing to God ~ this is your spiritual act of worship. Do not conform any longer to the pattern of this world,* ***but be transformed by the renewing of your mind.*** *Then you will be able to test and approve what God's will is ~ His good, pleasing and perfect will."* Sounds like quite an "adjustment" for a lot of us. It's so easy to go along with what everyone else is doing, and no one even notices. That's just it. Many times, and in numerous situations we act no different from anyone else, Christian or non-Christian. So how will they know we ARE different? Do we have fear? Let Him replace it with faith. Or worry? Prayer calms. Or how about inferiority? Our heavenly Father will give us self-acceptance. And forgiveness and love will replace our anger and bitterness. And here's how: *"If we confess our sins, He is faithful and just to forgive us our sins and purify us from all unrighteousness."* (1 John 1:9). He already paid the price. He made the adjustment!

SEPTEMBER 17

BROTHERLY (OR SISTERLY) LOVE…

This past week I had the honor and the pleasure of finishing a quilt for a friend which her beloved grandmother had begun many years ago. The grandmother had lovingly and painstakingly sewn pieces to make flowers-in-vases all over this quilt top, but never finished it. My friend carried it around the country with her long after her grandmother had passed away, but never had or took the time to finish it. Knowing that I had learned to quilt, just last summer, mind you, she considered me the "expert" and asked me to finish it. I fell in love with quilting during the construction of my very first quilt, not quite nine months before this writing. And since then, to this writing, I have made nine quilts. So, I said yes, I would finish it for her. She didn't care what fabrics I used. My friend would let me choose, she just wanted it completed. I went shopping for some borders and backing that would coordinate with the colors used, and started to work. I was pleased with how it turned out, but I was not prepared for her reaction when I delivered it yesterday. She LOVED it ~ she loved the fabrics I used, and my special signature touch of buttons. It was worth it just to see her face and feel her joy. I'm not sure, but I may have been more blessed, just seeing her happiness.

There are so many little things we could do for one another, simple things, to cause blessing and joy in someone's life. I have some neighbors who are always sneaking fertilizer on my grass when they do their own lawn, or tying up one of my trees so it grows up straight. We even had a couple of grown willow trees which were getting out of control, and they volunteered to cut them down, remove the roots, and cut the trunks up into fireplace lengths for my daughters' stoves. They spray and prune my little apple tree year after year without even being asked, and will not let me pay for the solution. I can never thank them enough. God blesses the little acts of kindness we do without being asked, but just out of the benevolence of our hearts.

The Word says, *"Be devoted to one another in brotherly love. Honor one another above yourselves."* (Romans 12:10). I love when someone will try and help a friend secretly, without seeking any recognition…sometimes people in our church will hear of a need another person has, and will contribute financially, anonymously. This is such a humbling blessing for the recipient. And a blessing as well, for the giver. The food pounding is another way to show this brotherly love, and these can be anonymous gifts, too. Jesus said, in Mathew 6:4, *"But when you give to the needy, do not let your left hand know what your right hand is doing, so that your giving may be in secret. Then your Father, who sees what is done in secret, will reward you."* We had a program in our church for the ladies for many years called "Secret Sisters," and for a year you would have a sister who would remember your birthday, send encouraging notes, surprise you with a gift now and then, and pray for you. That was my favorite part, knowing that someone was praying for me and not needing to know who she was.

I remember the thrill I used to get as a child on the first day of May, May Day, when we would quietly place a basket of flowers onto the porch of a neighbor, ring the doorbell, then run and hide, listening for their gasp of surprise when they opened the door and found our gift. Do children still do that? I have been the recipient of a surprise like that from my grandchildren a few times, but I'm not sure it is a practice anymore. One of our local Christian radio stations sponsors a fun day of paying for the car behind you in what is called the "Drive Through Difference." You simply pull up to the window of a drive through lunch place, or coffee stand, and pay for the person who will follow you. It's a surprise when they come to the window and find that someone they don't even know has paid for their order.

When was the last time someone secretly gifted you, or you gifted someone else? It is such a blessing, both for the giver and the receiver. And it does wonders to build our faith.

SEPTEMBER 18

THE TERRIBLE TWOS...

Unless you've had, or known, a two-year old, it's hard to imagine how frustrating it can be to train this little one. When a child is a baby, it's pretty easy...you just feed them, change them, rock them and watch them grow... but when they grow, and become more and more independent, testing authority, wanting to have their own way, trying to express themselves with words they're learning but not getting them quite right, it gets really baffling. They repeat a word over and over again, and you keep interpreting it incorrectly, and they try again, thinking they are pronouncing it right...they try to show you what they are talking about by dragging you to the kitchen, or the bookshelf, or wherever.

My little great-granddaughter, Brooklynne, is 2-1/2 and speaks very well, but once in awhile she mixes up a word and we have to play the little game of guess and repeat. I watch her one day a week to save our granddaughter a little in daycare expenses. This week she was asking for "sacks" and I couldn't understand so she took me into the kitchen and opened the pantry, pointing up to a shelf she couldn't reach, vehemently repeating "sacks!" Oooohhh...I finally got it! She wanted *fruit* snacks! Bless her heart, it had to be as frustrating for her as it was for me. Raising kids, teaching them, nurturing them, isn't for cowards. And if they don't get what they want when they ask for it, there could very well be some drama.

I think at times we can be just like the two-year old when we are talking with our heavenly Father. Jesus did say, *"And I will do whatever you ask in My name, so that the Son may bring glory to the Father. You may ask Me for anything in My name, and I will do it."* (John 14:13-14). But how many times do we really ask for something that would truly bring glory to the Father? We whine, and beg for things that are unimportant, things that we think we need, or at least surely want, things that we believe will make our lives easier and happier, more fulfilled. Many times (a LOT of the time) our prayers are selfish. We beat our fists on the floor, we stomp our feet. But… *"Your Father knows what you* ***need*** *before you ask Him."* (Matthew 6:8). How many times do we pray for patience, and then what happens? God lets trials come into our lives, because it is through trials that we *learn* patience. We pray for healing, for financial help, for obedient children, for a good job, loving family and friends ~ never for hardship. Who would actually *ask* for such a thing? Paul said we should *"give thanks in* ***all*** *circumstances…"* (1 Thess. 5:18). Would that mean in the hard times, too?

There is a song recently being played on Christian radio, which includes the following chorus:

"Bring me joy, bring me peace
Bring the chance to be free
Bring me anything that brings You glory
And I know there'll be days
When this life brings me pain
But if that's what it takes to praise You
Jesus, bring the rain."

I think it's not until we grow up that we realize we are not always going to get our way, and as we mature in our Christian faith, we become more accepting of that fact. I wonder how God views us as we rant and complain when things in our lives don't go right? Is it like the parent of the two-year old who has to be the disciplinarian, calling for time out, or taking away privileges? Take a look at the Israelites who just didn't get it. God sent plague after plague to get their attention, and still the tantrums came, loud and clear. I think of Jonah, who refused to do what God asked him to do, and ended up as dinner for a fish. But the second time God asked him, he obeyed. Some of us learn quicker than others. There is much in the book of Proverbs about discipline. We hate the discipline, but that's what it takes for us to see that God's ways are best. He alone knows our future. We can trust Him with it. He is the One who knows what the good is that can come from trouble. So let's continue to praise Him, even in the storms and pain of life and remember that *"God inhabits our praise."* (Psalm 22:3).

SEPTEMBER 19

NOT SO SILENT NIGHT SOUNDS...

Last night I felt a headache coming on, and since it was a little early to go to bed, I took advantage of the beautiful warm evening just to sit alone on my front porch, feet up, with a cup of tea. Ahh...it was nice and quiet, and peaceful. Or was it? As I sat there, looking out at nothing in particular, enjoying all the brilliant green in the grass and trees, I began to hear the sounds. Although the birds were almost silent by this time, there was still one or two sending out last-minute night messages before darkness closed in. I heard a quiet rushing sound, like sprinklers somewhere, the sound of tires on the pavement as a car slipped quietly by. A dog barked in the distance. Children were finishing up an outdoor game a few streets over and their squeals were diminishing. Crickets. A man's laughter a few houses down. A chain and tags jingling as someone walked a dog. Windchimes. Leaves rustling in the quaking aspen across the street. Beautiful "quiet" night sounds.

I began to think how blessed I am not to live in the city where the night sounds are horns honking, tires squealing, sirens blaring, people yelling ~ how can anyone sleep with all that noise?

But then I began to think about some of the other night sounds...a mother quietly weeping as she prays at the bedside of a sick child, the chaos of a house on fire in the night, sirens, loud trucks, people screaming, the violent cracking of thunder in a storm, the deafening wind of hurricane and tornado, the terrifying sounds of a busy hospital emergency room.

We call on God through the many noises...whether to thank Him for the peace, and quietness of a tranquil evening, or to cry out to Him in our pain and fear. He hears us every time, even through the deafening noise around us. *"This is the confidence we have in approaching God: that if we ask anything according to His will, He hears us. And if we know that He hears us ~ whatever we ask ~ we know that we have what we asked of Him."* (1 John 5:14). It doesn't matter how much noise there is...God can hear our faintest cry, even if we don't make a sound. He knows and understands our fear, our sorrow, our uncertainty, and our pain.

And sometimes, if we're real quiet, even amid the chaos, we can hear His still, small voice, *"Be still and know that I am God."* (Psalm 46:10). Even if our circumstances seem far beyond our control, nothing is impossible for Him. He hears us. And He will give us peace.

SEPTEMBER 20

MOTOR SKILLS...

A few weeks ago, I dug a bunch of empty thread spools out of the trash next to my sewing machine. I have been doing so much quilting this past year, that I've emptied a lot of spools. I put them in a basket, thinking my little two-year-old great granddaughter would like to play with them, stack them and rattle them around. My husband suggested I give her a shoelace and show her how to thread it through the hole on the spool. It took once. Those little fingers were steady as she skillfully threaded the end of the shoelace through each hole, pulling it out through the other end, collecting many spools on her string. I was amazed that such a young child could "get it" so quickly. That is now one of her favorite toys when she comes to my house. I told her mom and grandma about what she's doing, and they were pretty surprised, too. She does very well at a lot of things, fitting and putting and pushing and pulling and turning.

So, why am I so astonished? Most every child learns these tasks sooner or later. It just seems to me that she is so young. And her mind is so sharp. We don't usually ever have to show her something twice. But then, when I read in God's word about how He created us, individually, to be exactly who we are, I shouldn't be surprised. *"For You created my inmost being; You knit me together in my mother's womb. I praise You because I am fearfully and wonderfully made..."* (Psalm 139:13...). This is the part that is so astounding to me...that God was able to make so many billions of people, all different, and keep track of who they are, where they go, and what they will grow up to be.

We all have those God-given motor skills ~ anything we do with our hands, God enables us to do ~ playing the piano, watchmaking, typing, sewing, gardening, painting. Not only the things we are able to do with our hands, but our feet as well ~ dancing, running, etc. Every muscle and tendon in our bodies works together to perform those many tasks. He created us with many diverse abilities, every one as individual as each person. I'm in awe whenever I think about it!

I look at my little great granddaughter as she plays, or as she's napping, and I wonder what is going through her little mind. I marvel to imagine who she will be when she is grown up. I pray for her and her parents daily that they would raise her in the wisdom of the Lord, and that she would have every opportunity to learn just what it is that God is preparing her for. I know God has given her those excellent motor skills and dexterity. And I am so blessed to have a part in her development, once a week...on Thursday.

SEPTEMBER 21

MORNING COFFEE...

Some people have to have their morning coffee in order to even wake up. Two of these people are my daughters. In fact, many people need to have that coffee all throughout the day to keep going! Can't make it through the day without it. And there are coffee stands all over town, on almost every corner, and in nearly every major bookstore, with all varieties and strengths of the caffeined elixir. I once saw a cute cartoon with a woman sitting at the kitchen table, rollers in her hair, bags under her eyes, dressed in her bathrobe, with a fresh, steaming cup of coffee sitting there in front of her...the next frame shows her lifting the cup to her lips...and the next ~ she's bright-eyed, makeup on, hair fixed, and dressed! All from that first sip. A miracle tonic.

I kind of feel this way about Jesus. I must spend time with Him first thing in the morning ~ the perfect, and essential way to start my day. *"The Lord is my strength....the Lord gives strength to His people..."* (Psalm 28:7 & 29:11). In fact, I can't get all the way through the day without talking to Him often and seeing, or hearing, what He has to say to me. I need to have that strength renewed as I go through my day. *"Show me Your ways, O Lord, teach me Your paths; guide me in Your truth and teach me, for You are God my Savior."* (Psalm 25:4-5). If I don't continue to commune with Him all day, other influences may come in and pressure me into an attitude or an action that may not glorify God. *"These commandments that I give you today are to be upon your hearts. Impress them on your children. Talk about them when you sit at home and when you walk along the road, when you lie down and when you rise up."* (Deut. 6:6-7).

So, when you fix that first cup of coffee in the morning, take it with you to your quiet place and enjoy some blessed fellowship with the Lord. He will tell you *"great and unsearchable things you do not know."* (Jer. 33:3b).

SEPTEMBER 22

SEASONS...

Fall is here! Can you feel it in the air? Although the days are still sunny and warm, for the most part, the nights and mornings are very cool and crisp. This morning we saw FROST on some rooftops in our neighborhood while we were walking early. I love the seasons God has designed...each one is beautiful in its own way. I love Winter, because as the snow covers the earth's scars and gives new birth to nature, it reminds me of God's forgiveness washing us "whiter than snow." And the sweaters I love to wear in winter remind me of God's warmth as He wraps His arms around me. Spring is a promise of new life, as the plants and trees begin to bud, faithfully, on schedule, and the flowers that have been resting under the ground, seemingly dead, burst forth into the spring sun. Just like the New Life we receive when we trust in Jesus. And Summer – ah, Summer! Such an active time, warm and restful, unless we try to pack too much into our long days! It's a time when the trees and flowers are at their fullest and most colorful, when gardens are growing...and children are growing!

But Fall...the time when I enjoy God's Paintbrush the most. Just take a walk in the woods and see the beautiful colors ~ the leaves turning every color, carpeting the ground, the bright orange-yellow of the tamarack. The sunsets are out of this world, literally! Sometimes I wish I could capture the scene in my mind, then quickly paint it, just as God has, but I don't have that talent!

God designed each season so brilliantly! And just as the seasons change throughout the year, so do the seasons of our lives. The more years that pass by cause me to look back to the changing of the seasons...when I was young and carefree, when I married and the children came along there were more cares and concerns, and watching them grow, their own seasons changing, rather quickly I might add, and now that our children are all grown, we are watching our grandchildren grow up, and a little peace has returned to our household, and we are slowing down. In fact, watching the energy in my grandchildren makes me tired! But what I see is that God has been with me through every season of my life. Sometimes I didn't see Him or feel Him, but He was (and is) always there.

"To everything there is a season,
a time for every purpose under the sun.
A time to be born and a time to die;
a time to plant and a time to pluck up that which is planted;
a time to kill and a time to heal ...
a time to weep and a time to laugh;
a time to mourn and a time to dance ...
a time to embrace and a time to refrain from embracing;
a time to lose and a time to seek;
a time to rend and a time to sew;
a time to keep silent and a time to speak;
a time to love and a time to hate;
a time for war and a time for peace."
(Ecclesiastes 3:1-8)

In the seasons of your life, just know that God is always there ~ He designed them for His great purposes. Enjoy them!

SEPTEMBER 23

MY BLESSED LITTLE APPLE TREE...

About nine years ago I purchased a very little apple tree from my neighbor's garage sale. It's true. One of their apple trees died and without the other one knowing it, the husband and the wife each bought a tree to replace it. So, I bought the "extra" one for $7.00. I have always wanted an apple tree. In fact, not too long after we had our third daughter, I bought one at the nursery and planted it in the corner of a garden spot in the back yard. After a few days of watering and nurturing it, I went out to find the entire tree had been chewed off by our dog! We had a lot to learn.

So, I brought the little garage sale tree home and planted it on the edge of our front yard and watered it. I asked God to bless this little tree. It grew, and by the third year I picked five beautiful apples from it! The next year there were over a hundred. Then 300. I get so excited when I see the blossoms each spring, then the tiny little apples sprouting on the branches. One Sunday afternoon, my grandchildren came over to pick apples. Midway through summer they begin asking me if it's time yet, because they check them out all summer, and watch them grow. So between the two 9-year-olds, the 12-year old, and the 2-year old, they picked 9 ice cream buckets of apples, and piled them high. I picked two more buckets full for myself, and that wasn't even half of the tree. I always tell the next door neighbors they can have apples from their side of the tree because they are faithful to spray it for bugs, and prune it. It's what they do. I don't mind sharing at all. Seems like a fair trade!

But the best part about this annual event is that my grandchildren will have great memories of being able to personally pick their own apples from Grandma's apple tree. Their moms will make apple pies and applesauce from them, and they'll snack on a few of them, dipping slices in caramel or peanut butter. There are so many different varieties of apples and they are grown all over the world. They are grown in cultivated orchards, and in the wild. Have you noticed that each apple, when cut open crosswise, will reveal a perfect "star" in the center by God's design? And, of course, they are highly nutritional.

We often depict the forbidden fruit that Adam and Eve ate as an apple. Scripture doesn't really say what kind of fruit it was, only that God told them not to eat it. I don't think it would have mattered what type of fruit the Lord named, it only mattered that they were disobedient.

So, did God bless my tree? I like to believe He did. He certainly blesses me with the nice crops year after year. I am happy. The only verse in the Bible I can find about apples is Proverbs 25:11: *"A word aptly spoken is like apples of gold in settings of silver."* My mom used to have a little book titled "Apples of Gold" and although I regret that I cannot find that book, a description of it would be "a sprightly collection of hundreds of famous, amusing, serious, and inspirational sayings on such subjects as Love, Joy, Peace, Long Suffering, Gentleness, Goodness, and Faith." I'm going to have to look harder for it. But wait…in Zechariah 2:8 we read that God considers Zion *"the apple of His eye,"* and gives warning to anyone who would come against her. And still there are countries who are trying to overtake Israel, and Jerusalem. They must not take God's warnings seriously.

Whether you grow apples, or buy them at the market, eat them whole, or cook them in a pie, cover them with caramel, or bob for them in a tub, know that they are one of God's finest creations ~ so good for us, enjoyable, and can give you cause for a party!

SEPTEMBER 24

GOD'S WAY....

I dreamed a song last night and woke up with it on my mind ~ "God will make a way where there seems to be no way, He works in ways we cannot see, He will make a way for me..." Only it was the rendition by the Brooklyn Tabernacle Choir that I was hearing. I may have shared this story before, but when my grandson David was born, he had many problems and was flown within the hour by helicopter to a neighboring bigger hospital that had a good NICU (neo-natal intensive care unit). Of course, my youngest daughter, who had had no problems with her pregnancy, had to stay in our hospital while her baby was taken away. It was the hardest thing I ever experienced. We stayed with her, while my son-in-law and his parents went to the other hospital to be with David. My son-in-law had prayed while in the shower that morning before they went to the hospital, that God's angels would watch over David as he made his way into the world. He had a strong sense of the presence of Jesus, and the words, "no, I Myself will be with him" were spoken to his heart. The night before, they had both prayed that God would be in this birth, and gave David, hands down, "even to the point of death" to the Lord's keeping. What faith!! And now, they weren't sure what God had in mind.

On the way back from the NICU that evening, as they were turning off the freeway, the Bible book store's sign came into view and on it was this: *"As for God, His way is perfect."* (from Psalm 18:30, and 2 Sam 22:31). My son-in-law was blown away by this loud and clear message from God to his heart, and couldn't wait to share it with my daughter. We were there in her room when he came, and were all rejoicing with him at God's clear message. She spent a difficult night, hearing all the babies crying in other rooms, but was released the next morning and we all headed to the NICU at the other hospital, where David spent three weeks after surgery to correct his problems. Without going into detail, it was major. And this little boy would go on to experience more problems, having been diagnosed with hydrocephalus a few months later with consequent surgeries through his nine years. Yes, this is some miracle boy!

God has been faithful. We have all learned so much. And my daughter and son-in-law have had opportunities to speak to other parents and grandparents whose children are in the same situation, to encourage them and share their faith.

Jesus said, "*I am the Way, the Truth and the Life...*" (John 14:6). And Proverbs 14:12 says, "*There is a way that seems right to a man, but in the end it leads to death.*" Many times, most times, really, we can't see ahead or know the consequence of our actions and our choices. And many times we have to call on God to bail us out of trouble. Trusting in His way does not necessarily keep us from having troubles, but trusting and following His way will assure us of life eternal after the cares of this world are behind us.

David is now twelve, and as he grows he will need more surgeries to replace or repair the shunt implanted in his brain. We all know this. But we also know that God is in control of this precious boy's life, and our own lives. God admonishes us, "*Whether you turn to the right or to the left, your ears will hear a voice behind you, saying, 'This is the way; walk in it.'*" (Isaiah 30:21). That is good advice.

SEPTEMBER 25

HOLY GROUND...

"*God called to him from within the [burning] bush, 'Moses! Moses!' And Moses said, 'Here I am.' 'Do not come any closer,' God said, 'Take off your sandals, for the place where you are standing is holy ground.'*" (Exodus 3:4-5). This was kind of a surprise visit from God as Moses was going about his daily work out there on the mountainside, tending the sheep of his father-in-law. His attention was first piqued by an angel, and as he crept closer, Almighty God spoke to him from the bush. This isn't the only holy place recorded for us ~ how about when Zachariah's name was drawn for his once-in-a-lifetime turn to burn incense in the holy of holies, behind the curtain. What an exciting time for him, and he received a wonderful and miraculous revelation while there, when an angel of the Lord appeared to him with the message that he would father a son ~ a very important son ~ in his old age.

Other places considered holy ground are Mount Sinai, where Moses received the Ten Commandments from God Himself, the place in the Garden where Jesus prayed and wept, and sweat great drops of blood, the manger ~ the birthplace of our Lord, and Golgotha, the hill where the Cross stood. Many places where miracles occurred can be regarded as "holy ground" to us.

But do we think about standing on holy ground in our daily lives, our everyday busyness, our idleness? There is a beautiful song titled "We Are Standing on Holy Ground," with very moving melody and lyrics. They speak of sensing God's presence, of His love abounding and angels all around. Of finding sweet peace at His feet, and joy where He abides. I was surprised to find a rendition of this song by Barbra Streisand, and it is incredibly beautiful. I truly believe that anywhere we stand, where we call upon the name of the Lord, can be considered holy ground. Think of it! Whether it's in our church, or a cozy little empty chapel, out on a mountaintop, rocking a fussing baby in the middle of the night, in traffic on the freeway, or in your favorite chair, or one beside a hospital bed ~ wherever we summon the Presence of God is considered holy ground, and we must figuratively "remove our sandals." We must be ready to hear the still, small voice of God speaking to us. *"Come, let us bow down in worship, let us kneel before the Lord our Maker, for He is our God..."* (Psalm 95:6-7).

SEPTEMBER 26

CARRY ME...

We spend our lives carrying...things, children...burdens...some of us carry loads way too heavy for us. Whenever I go grocery shopping, I try to carry all the sacks of groceries in at once, because I don't want to make another trip out to the car. I'm silly that way. It hurts my back, and my arm bones. And sometimes, if no one is home to help me, I end up carrying the boxes of Christmas decorations up from the basement, wishing I had an elevator! It's because I'm anxious to get the job done. If you're a mom, you've carried babies, diaper bags, purse, blankies ~ all at once, sometimes. And the older they get, the heavier children are, but we carry them anyway, because sometimes it's faster than waiting for them to catch up. And because they ask us to carry them.

We carry firewood, lumber, cats and dogs, too many hangers laden with clothes, vacuum cleaners, suitcases, and many items we just should not be carrying. The burdens we carry are, many times, the memories of past failures. We've been wounded in the battle of life and sometimes we feel like we just cannot go on. In the '60s there was a song entitled, "He Ain't Heavy, He's My Brother." It was about war, of course, and soldiers carrying fellow troops who had been wounded. No matter what their color or creed, a man just could not leave one to die on the battlefield. They were brothers because they were fighting and working side by side for the same cause. The bled the same color of blood, their hearts broke in the same ways.

Isaiah 46:4 says, *"I am He, I am He who will sustain you. I have made you and I will carry you."* We sometimes have deep hurts and heavy burdens that we think we will never be able to stand up under, but Jesus said, *"For My yoke is easy and My burden is light."* (Matthew 11:30). We are invited to *"Cast our cares upon Him, for He cares for us."* (1 Peter 5:7). We do not have to carry our hardships alone, though many of us try. And if He has to, Jesus will carry US. We have all seen the poem "Footprints" in which the author talks of walking along in the sand with two sets of footprints, Jesus and me, and then life seems to get really hard, and for awhile we see only one set of prints. We worry that maybe we have been left alone during that difficult period, but Jesus assures us that when we saw only one set of prints, that's when He was carrying us. Jesus will carry us through the sand, through the river, through the storm, up the mountains ~ have you ever carried any considerable load UP a mountain? For me, that is impossible. But Jesus carries us anywhere He needs us to go, because He loves us. He knows there are deep and difficult places that we just cannot get through on our own. He is our burden-bearer. That's what He went to the cross for. And incidentally, He carried that heavy cross Himself, for our sakes.

SEPTEMBER 27

BIBLE STUDY...

We had a fantastic Bible study this week...quite a bit of discussion about the prodigal son, his father, and his brother. A real eye-opener, for sure. I love Bible studies. I have learned so much, whether it's been a book of the Bible, or another book, with references to scripture throughout. I have led many Bible study groups, but this one I am attending is under the leadership of another woman, a very dedicated lady who loves Jesus, and loves talking about Him.

The Bible, God's holy word, is a wealth of information, history, letters, poetry…all meant to teach us about God. I've read somewhere that the Bible isn't just a book, it's a complete library. All the writings in the Bible speak of God, His nature, His love, His sovereignty. We learn of the people who followed Him from the beginning of time, the experiences they encountered, and how God worked in each situation. We read of the many laws that were put into place and the customs, and how people's sins were atoned for. Numerous celebrations and rituals are carried over into the New Testament, but when Jesus comes on the scene as a human baby, and then dies a real death on the Cross, to rise again as He promised, we find that we no longer have laws for our redemption ~ only Jesus. Then we learn of His tender love, His mercy, grace and compassion.

And all the writings of generations in between the beginning and the end of this holy book tell us so much about ourselves and of God. As God gave Moses the Ten Commandments, Moses proclaimed to the people, *"Hear, O Israel, the decrees and laws I declare in your hearing today. Learn them, and be sure to follow them."* (Deut. 5:1). So, why was that so hard? The Lord went on to give the Laws, in detail so we could understand them, but how soon we forget. How soon we begin to complain that it's too hard, or it's old-fashioned. There was more…much more. Moses told the people to "take care" to follow **all** the commands, decrees and laws… *"If you pay attention to these laws and are careful to follow them, then the Lord your God will keep His covenant of love with you as He swore to your forefathers. He will love you and bless you and increase your numbers."* (Deut. 7:11-13). Now, Adam and Eve only had ONE law to pay attention to in the garden…they were free to do anything else, but that one forbidden thing. And yet, what did they do? They chose to eat of the tree they were instructed *not* to approach. There were plenty of other trees. Their needs were substantially provided for.

It is not hard for some of us to keep the Ten Commandments, except for maybe one or two. But I'm sure God meant for us to keep ALL of them. In Chapter 5, vs 32-33 of Deuteronomy, Moses said, "…*Do not turn aside to the right or to the left.Walk in all the way that the Lord your God has commanded you."*We are implored to *"impress them on your children, talk about them when you sit at home and when you walk along the road, when you lie down and when you get up."* (6:7). Sounds like Bible study to me.

Now, if some of you have a hard time studying the Bible, join a group, pick up a study guide, or a book ~ some of them have questions you can answer by looking up scriptures. There are online Bible studies as well. And once you get into the habit of regular study, you will be amazed at the world of knowledge in the library called the Bible. And, of course, start out by asking God to reveal His instruction and His precious promises to you. He will.

SEPTEMBER 28

JIGSAW PUZZLES...

I like them ~ jigsaw puzzles. All my growing up years my dad had one going on a table in the corner, or the basement, or somewhere. In fact, puzzle-making was sometimes a family activity. As he grew older, in his retirement years, he really liked the more challenging kind (aren't they all?), so each year for Christmas I would search for a really unusual one ~ penny candy, a needle in a haystack, chocolate chip cookies, dalmations (we're talking LOTS of dalmations), jars of pasta. We used to have a book store in our mall that sold unusual puzzles. I always tried to outdo the last one each year. Then I found a 3-D model of the White House...he built it in a day. Not much of a challenge, I guess. It was amazing.

The rest of my family doesn't care for them much, although the younger ones would spend a few minutes at Grandpa's puzzle table trying to place a few pieces. I'm not sure what has happened to all of his puzzles. Maybe my siblings ended up with some of them. And I haven't worked one in years.

My friend just happened to mention the other day that she was doing a jigsaw puzzle online! I didn't even know there was such a thing! Well, what ISN'T there online, for that matter? So, I found a site and tried one. And then I tried another one. One thing about online puzzles...the pieces don't fall on the floor and go missing, or get vacuumed.

Sometimes I feel like my life is a great big puzzle. I have felt so many times that there are pieces missing and I just can't get it together. I work on trying to at least get my borders together, but then someone bumps into me and pieces fall out. It's frustrating. Sometimes I feel like just breaking it all apart, giving up and putting it all back into the box. It isn't turning out like the picture. I once read a story about a little girl who kept talking to her daddy while he was reading the paper and so he tore a magazine picture page in pieces and told her to go put it back together again. It was a landscape picture, or something.

When she was able to complete it quicker than he'd expected, he asked her how she did that. She said, "well Daddy, there was a picture of Jesus on the back and I just put that together." Wow! Gave that Daddy something to think about.

We have a Father who will put all the pieces of our lives back together. After all, He designed the picture in the first place. David knew that... *"For You created my inmost being; You knit me together in my mother's womb..."* (Psalm 139:13-16). I know I've used this passage many times, but it means so much to me. Especially when I feel like my life is "falling apart." And the promise in Romans 8:28 gets me through these times, *"And we know that in all things God works for the good of those who love Him, who have been called according to His purpose."*

God is standing there with His hands open waiting for us to bring our brokenness to Him. I believe He is poring over the pieces of our life and gently putting them into their proper place. Sometimes He doesn't "fix" it immediately, but when we place our lives in His hands, He lovingly heals our broken hearts and gives us strength to handle the difficulties. And when He comes for us, our puzzle will be completed. He is our only Hope.

SEPTEMBER 29

LIGHT IN THE DARKNESS...

This morning I woke up at my regular time, but it is SO dark, and the rain makes it intensely dreary...it seems now that fall is in full swing, there is a lot of darkness in our days. I thought about how DARK it is...and I went around my house lighting a few candles, because I hate turning on a bunch of lights early in the morning. It's surprising how a few tiny flames will add light and warmth to a room. And the little song I learned as a child in Sunday school rang through my mind as I was lighting my candles ~ "This little light of mine, I'm gonna let it shine..."

And then I got to thinking how, no matter how dark and dreary it is, my spirit is far from gloomy, because Jesus is the Light of my soul. I found that David felt the same way ~ he wrote *"You, O Lord, keep my lamp burning; my God turns my darkness into light."* (Psalm 18:28). And again, in Psalm 27:1, *"The Lord is my Light and my Salvation, whom shall I fear?"* Still later, he said, *"You are resplendent with Light, more majestic than the mountains..."* (Psalm 76:4). I love that word "resplendent" ~ you could also say "full of spendor, shining brightly, *dazzling*!" In the gospels we find that Jesus is the Light of the world, the true Light that shines in darkness.

We really have no idea just how dazzling Jesus' light will be when we see Him face to face ~ we've never seen anything as glorious or brilliant in our lifetime. We could light all the candles we have, turn on all the lights in our house, open all the windows so the sun shines in, and we wouldn't even come close to the Light that Jesus' love gives. And the best part is that He lights us up from the inside out. I pray that others will see that Light in me today and every day, even on the darkest and most dismal days that are ahead.

SEPTEMBER 30

BRIGHT HOPE...

The last few days in North Idaho we have had some beautiful sunshine, after close to a week of rainy and dreary days. And not only that, we have been able to see the beautiful brightness of the full moon at night and early in the morning. I know more bad weather is on the way, and it will even get worse, but whenever the sun shines through, it lifts my spirits, and I am reminded of the bright hope we have in Jesus. I feel like our country is also going through some "bad weather" and it'll be getting worse, as we face more of the economic crisis and other unknown circumstances in anticipation of the "changing of the guards" in our government.

No matter how dismal the weather is, or gloomy the outlook seems for the future of our country, we must keep our eyes on the Son, our Bright Hope for tomorrow. I found this in 2 Chronicles 20:17 ~ *"Take up your positions; stand firm and see the deliverance of the Lord... Do not be afraid; do not be discouraged. Go out to face them tomorrow"* [and tomorrow, and tomorrow] *"and the Lord will be with you."* These were words from the Lord to Jehoshaphat as he was preparing to fight a battle the next day. He won, because he kept his eyes on the source of Bright Hope.

Let the bright rays of Jesus love warm you and give you that hope, that unshakable confidence that God will fulfill His promises to us who believe Him. As the hymn "Great is Thy Faithfulness" says, "strength for today and bright hope for tomorrow, blessings all mine and ten thousand beside ~ great is Thy faithfulness!"

OCTOBER 1

THE EMPTY PAGE...

I sat before my computer today facing an empty page, ready to be filled with words. Now, an empty page can be in a notebook, a journal, or even a calendar. And, in this day and age, the computer. These pages don't fill themselves as we stare at them. We have to deliberately begin writing, or typing. To me, an empty page is an invitation to say something. A book to be written, a song to be composed, a letter to send. So much that is written is a reflection of what is in the heart. Poetry is an expression of one's deep feelings, and some of it is musical, some is light and refreshing, and some is dark and disturbing. I don't write poetry. Nor music. But I do love writing letters, and I admit I don't do that enough anymore. Does anyone, now in this day of email and texting? Our messages can be sent instantly, instead of waiting days for a letter to arrive, as we did in the not-to-distant past.

I used to collect beautiful stationery. I loved writing on it, and I imagined the joy the receiver would feel when she, or he, opened my letter and read my thoughts and news. I still have quite a stash of nice letter paper and I try to write a letter every now and then to someone special who I feel could use an encouraging word. There have been times when I have written a letter full of my deepest feelings that was composed mainly to get something upsetting off my chest, and never meant to be read. Sometimes this can help us when we have a great burden. We have things we may want to say to another person, but to blurt them out would hurt feelings, so we can say them in a letter, then throw the letter away. I have found that this usually lessens the burden.

I love reading. One book after another. And I can appreciate how difficult it is sometimes for the author to get the points in order to follow a story line. I have never written a book, but I sure enjoy reading them. I love historical novels. And I learn so much. There is one book that is like no other. The author is the specialist, the Master, of every subject, every chapter. It is full of history, the kind we don't find in regular history books or historical novels. It is the history of God's love from the very beginning of time. The ultimate Love

Story. The Bible…it contains stories of the first day of time, many stories of war, of rescue and redemption, and beautiful poetry. But they are not made up stories, out of someone's imagination. They speak of Truth, and of never-ending Love. God has told us, through the Living Word, *"I have loved you with an everlasting love. I have drawn you with loving kindness."* (Jer. 31:3). All through time He has been trying to get His people to believe that, through His timeless letter to us. Those pages of old have been filled up with ancient words that are just as meaningful today as they were thousands of years ago.

When we finish reading an exceptionally good book, do we just put it away, or do we pass it along to someone else to enjoy as well? Do we recommend the author to others? What about the Bible, this archaic collection for today's seeker? The truths between its covers, the message and the instruction, never change, all throughout time. Let's dust it off and fill the empty pages of our hearts with the amazing love found therein. *"All Scripture is God-breathed and is useful for teaching, rebuking, correcting and training in righteousness, so that the [woman] of God may be thoroughly equipped for every good work."* (2 Timothy 3:16). Not to mention the comfort, peace and joy we receive from God's own words.

OCTOBER 2

GRUMBLING…

I don't suppose many of us are given to grumbling and complaining…really? I know it has been my prayer many times that God would help me to be grateful and thankful, and that I wouldn't complain so much. I'm in the middle of such a prayer right now, today. In James 5:8-9, it says, *"Be patient and stand firm, because the Lord's coming is near. Don't grumble against each other, brothers, or you will be judged."* The little sub-title in this passage in my Bible is "Patience in Suffering."

Sometimes we think it's okay to grumble, or complain, especially if we believe it is warranted. We complain about the way someone treated us or a loved one, when we didn't deserve it. We complain about the government and those running it. We grumble about the weather, or about how much work we have to do that no one else seems to help with. Students squawk about how much homework they have. We lament the fact that we don't have a job, or not the one we want. I complain about the rain because it causes me to have more pain and stiffness than I do on sunny days!

Well, God's word says, *"Give thanks in all circumstances, for this is God's will for you in Christ Jesus."* (1 Thess. 5:18). I believe it means that we should give thanks to Him IN all our troubles, not necessarily FOR them. We will always have troubles and challenges. Jesus said we would; *"In this world you will have trouble. But take heart! I have overcome the world!"* (John 16:33). To me, this means Jesus has overcome every type of hardship or trouble that we will ever face. It doesn't mean that we should just sit on our hands and not do anything, because we know Jesus will take care of it all. God gave us certain talents, skills, and abilities, and He told us that we must work hard. He knows the effort we put forth, if we do. And He in turn works through us.

God also works through our attitude. If we have a thankful heart, not complaining, or grumbling, though we may have enough to mutter about, He will show it to others. And really what we are showing other people by NOT complaining, is God's own Spirit, His own Nature, in us. And it can be catching. Have you ever noticed when two or more people gather and at least one of them is complaining, pretty soon the others will be adding their negative comments as well? People have been complaining since the beginning of time ~ I think of the Israelites after they were rescued from the Egyptians. It wasn't enough that they were liberated from slavery through the love and obedience of one man, but when they spent too much time on the desert, they began to whine about the food, how long it was taking, the rules ~ and look how long it ultimately took them to get to the Promised Land! Oh, that's a whole different story…

We just need to learn to be thankful that God is aware of our situation, and He is in supreme control. He wants us to praise Him. And although that may seem hard at times, especially when our circumstances are extreme and seem to take away all hope, just remember that our heavenly Father's love is eternal and he will strengthen us for the battle, whether it is financial, relational, health-wise, or spiritual.

O, Lord, take away my complaining spirit and help me to concentrate on Your many blessings, which are much more than anything I could grumble about. Give me a thankful heart for the life You have given me. Amen.

OCTOBER 3

THE DEBT IS PAID...

Remember toll booths? Usually a road or bridge where there was a fee collected for the use in order to pay for taxes or construction of said bridge or road. In fact, I guess there are still some of these in existence. My husband actually crossed a toll bridge the other day crossing a river separating two states. A very old and narrow one ~ a little precarious in a big bus. We lived on the east coast when I was a teenager, and there were no such things as "freeways." They were "turnpikes" and there was a charge for using them. And there was no other way you could go, usually. It was the main thoroughfare. So, the charge per car was either 10-cents or 25-cents. It was not unusual to get to the toll booth and learn that the car before you had paid your toll, and the toll master would just wave you through.

We have all heard stories of people in line at the grocery store who discovered they did not have quite enough funds for the total grocery bill, and some kind soul behind them offered to pay the difference. Or, what our local Christian radio station does a few times a year, "The Drive-Thru Difference," when patrons go to McDonald's or Starbucks (or a similar place), order their drink or food, and pay for the person behind them as well.

I have a friend whose husband was a pastor, and years ago he died while waiting for a heart transplant. When it came to tax time a few months later, an IRS agent came to their house and told my friend his taxes had been forgiven and she wouldn't have to pay anything. That, I know, is just about unheard of.

We all have debts, some of us more than others. Wouldn't we love it if someone would come along and cancel that debt? Actually, we all have had a huge debt that we will never be able to pay, but Someone did come along and pay it for us. It is that debt of sin that has followed us all our lives. When Jesus agreed to go to the Cross and die a horrible death, He was thinking of only us, and He did it in love. That was the plan from the beginning of time. Not for just one, or a few, but for the whole human race. *"When they came to the place called the Skull, there they crucified Him, along with the criminals ~ one on His right, the other on His left. Jesus said, 'Father, forgive them, for they do not know what they are doing.'"* (Luke 23:33-34). And there it is. The debt we would never be able to pay has been erased in that single act of love and grace. *"But because of His great love for us, God, who is rich in mercy, made us alive with Christ even when we were dead in transgressions ~ it is by grace you have been saved."* (Ephesians 2:5).

OCTOBER 4

CASUALTIES OF WAR....

There always have and always will be wars. It's a given. As long as people disobey God and turn away from Him, we cannot have peace. Literally millions of people have lost their lives throughout all time due to the brutality of war and the selfishness of man. Often, God was the initiator of conflict, such as the war between the Amalekites and the Israelites, in Exodus 17. And in Numbers, 31:2, *"The Lord said to Moses, 'Take vengeance on the Midianites for the Israelites. After that you will be gathered to your people.'"* We remember the battle of Jericho, in Joshua 6, when the Lord told Joshua to have his people march around the city for six days, then on the seventh day the priests sounded their trumpets, and the people shouted, and the walls fell inward...only God could have orchestrated something of this magnitude. Amazing! Another astounding story is the day the Lord gave the Amorites over to the Israelites, but to do that, He stilled the sun and the moon for one full day so His people could win the battle. *"The sun stopped in the middle of the sky and delayed going down about a full day..."* (Joshua 10). Many kings were killed in the wars of the Bible, as well as innocent women and children, and livestock. But I don't think war in Bible times was really any more brutal than it is now.

There are many battles listed in our history books: Ticonderoga, Bunker Hill, Civil War, Revolutionary War, World Wars I & II, Vietnam, Korean, Desert Storm, and you could certainly call 9-11 war, as well, one that is still going on. Many, many brave individuals have lost their lives. This has hit close to home in our town recently.

In recent weeks two young men from our city were killed in Iraq. It was a shock to those who knew them. Within the week they flew their bodies home, and honored them in an impressive procession from the airport, through town to the funeral home. The next day they held a beautiful military memorial service at one of our high schools that was attended by countless friends, classmates and loved ones. Even people who didn't know them came to show honor. These services were followed by individual funeral services. My two granddaughters, and grandson went to school with one of the young men, Nick, so this was an emotional time for them. In fact, a very sobering thought is that my grandson was in basic training for the National Guard with Nick, and had he not been medically discharged the year previous, he would have been in that same truck with those soldiers who were killed. That's a very hard thing to think about. And yet, this scene is being replayed every day in almost every city in America. Fallen soldiers coming home ~ saying goodbye. Children without daddies. Widows too young.

The Bible speaks of yet another war, the war to end all wars, the Battle of Armageddon. We read about it in Revelation 16. The final battle in which Christ will return to earth to defeat Satan once and for all, and establish His kingdom on earth for His millennial reign. Some of the trials we go through as individuals, as corporations, as a nation, have been loosely referred to as the "Battle of Armageddon." None of these will compare, actually. God's fury will be unleashed as never before, and Satan will be cast into the lake of fire, his final resting place! He and his evil angels will be the biggest casualties of this war. This war is unequaled from the beginning of the world. I can't even imagine it, can you?

Just know that when you go through trials and battles, as we do every day, in some way, God is in control of the outcome. He is the Most Executive Commander-in-Chief. He has fought the battles for us for centuries, and will continue until the end of the age. We don't know when that final battle will happen, but we can trust that if we are followers of our Lord and King, Jesus, we will be saved from it and reign with Him forever.

Oh, and next time you see a soldier, whether you know him or not, tell him thank you for his part in defending our freedom.

OCTOBER 5

HOPE...

My hope is built on nothing less than Jesus' blood and righteousness ~ My hope is in you, Lord ~ Walk on, walk on, with hope in your heart ~ I've got hope like a river ~ Precious name, oh how sweet, hope of earth and joy of heaven ~ *For I have put my hope in Your word ~ who put their hope in His unfailing love ~ plans to give you a hope and a future ~ be joyful in hope ~ Christ in you, the hope of glory*...these are phrases from songs, and snippets of scripture that contain the word "hope," as you can see. I woke up this morning with the first song going through my mind ~ it would not leave me alone. Not one of the newer choruses either, but an old hymn. Maybe the Lord knew I needed hope for myself, and to share, today.

We hope many things. We hope it won't rain, we hope we'll have enough money for the rent, we hope the car will start, that we'll get the job, and that our kids will turn out okay. We have hope for the future, for our children's future. Hope is what gets us through the day, or the week. Or the hour. When things in life get really difficult, when disease wracks our body, when the check didn't come in, or the house deal fell through, when there doesn't seem to be enough food in the refrigerator, it's easy to get discouraged and to lose hope.

This is where Jesus comes in. He came into the world for this very purpose ~ to give us Hope. His death and resurrection gave us hope for eternal life. That's hard for me to grasp ~ eternal life. I know it means we'll live in heaven with Him forever, and ever. But, when I try to think about what that means, exactly, it's hard to fathom. Only a loving and sovereign God could provide that. Even if things don't improve in our situation, if we never get that raise, or if our children follow their own dreams and aspirations, no matter how far off from the dreams we have for them, we can still hope in the Lord. As Paul told the Hebrews (6:19), *"We have this hope as an anchor for the soul, firm and secure."* We hope in many things, but sometimes those things let us down. Hope in things, in money, in the government, will always let us down. The hope that Jesus gives will never fail us. *"Let your unfailing love surround us, Lord, for our hope is in you alone."* (Psalm 33:22).

OCTOBER 6

READ THE INSTRUCTIONS...

I'm working on another quilt, but this one is the most difficult one I've made so far...it came in a kit, with the patterns and instructions in a magazine. There are multiple techniques, at least three of which I've never done, and there is some quilting language I've never heard (or read) before, let alone know the meaning of. Much of the difficulty was that I couldn't find the continuation of the instructions in the magazine. I was really frustrated. I am making the quilt for a friend, and I was even considering talking to an expert for some advice on how to put it together. I read and re-read what instructions I could find, when finally….after three or four pages of advertisements, I found the continuation of the instructions. And then it began to make sense! I might add, the quilt is turning out beautifully, although I did make a few modifications. I can imagine what a mess that quilt could have been if I didn't find, or bother to read, the rest of the instructions.

Did you know that God's word is the instruction manual for our lives? Every story, every book, contains a lesson for us to learn. There are instructions on how to teach our children, how to tithe, how to bless others, how to forgive, how to worship, how to prosper…but we cannot just read them… we must follow them. Proverbs 8:33 advises us, *"Listen to my instruction and be wise; do not ignore it."* I wonder what my quilt would look like if I read the instructions but didn't do what they said, or ignored certain parts. Or if I didn't read them at all and just tried to muddle through on my own? (Actually, a few times I felt like putting it down and forgetting it!) We know what happens when we try to muddle through this life on our own. We've all done it. Sometimes we still do. God has all the answers, for everything. He's written them all down and preserved them for us, because they are so important.

When we are guilty, hopeless, worried, suffering, when we have doubts about whether we are doing life right, when we are angry, frightened, despairing…God teaches us to have courage, faith, hope. His instructions include, of course, His love, His mercy, faithfulness, comfort, blessing, and power. The Bible used to be the only textbook children used in school, and they grew up knowing God's truth. But when "they" took the Bible out of the schools, it seems that our society began to deteriorate. You all know what I mean. All you have to do is read the newspaper or listen to the news to hear of the terror, the wars, the famines, governmental collapse, around the world. Sin. I wonder if we had kept teaching from God's word all these years if our world, or our society would be in the dire straits we are in now?

We are simply not reading God's Instruction Manual. It's like an ongoing college course in life. As long as I have been reading the Bible, I'm amazed at the new things I am still learning, about God's love and provision for me. As Paul wrote in 1 Timothy 3:14-15, "*…I am writing you these instructions so that, if I am delayed (in coming to you), you will know how people ought to conduct themselves in God's household, which is the church of the living God, the pillar and foundation of* *the truth."*That, dear sisters, is why we must read the Word. Our daily news is evidence that people are NOT reading His word.

David said, in the very beginning of his book of Psalms, *"Blessed is the man, [or woman] who does not walk in the counsel of the wicked or stand in the way of sinners...but his* ***delight is in the law of the Lord, and on His law he meditates day and night****."* (Psalm 1:1-2). That's the secret. Everyday brings another set of problems, of questions, different from the day before, or some of the same. If we only read the word and set it aside, soon we forget what it said, or we don't even think about it. I am convinced that God wants us to meditate, somewhere in His word, daily. That is how He speaks to us.

OCTOBER 7

WONDERS WITHOUT NUMBER...

"He performs wonders that cannot be fathomed, miracles that cannot be counted." (Job 5:9). Have you ever tried to "count your blessings?" Like the little chorus goes, "name them one by one." I've tried to list them from time to time, and it's just impossible. Just when I think I've gotten a complete list of my blessings, there are more that come to my mind. I think we have blessings and miracles every day that we are not even aware of. The poignant words of Eliphaz, Job's friend, are so true ~ His wonders are without number! Many of them are named ~ the healing of the sick, raising of the dead, rain upon the earth, the safety in His hands, feeding the birds, His voice in the thunder, new life that blooms in the spring, angels, the snowflake, a bubbling spring, the birth of a baby, the majesty of the horse, love, a diamond or precious gem contained in a brown and dirty rock, grace, shooting stars, forgiveness, eyesight and hearing, the rainbow, music, oh my goodness...it goes on and on. No wonder His works are said to be countless.

God names but a few Himself, in a discourse with Job after his little pity party. You'll find quite a list in Job 38, 39, 40 & 41. I love these chapters. Especially when Job says to the Almighty God, *"I am unworthy ~ how can I reply to you? I put my hand over my mouth!"* (40:4). How many times do we have to say that to our heavenly Father? We see His miracles every day ~ I've seen quite a few this month alone ~ and yet, we keep complaining. It's a miracle when someone gives their heart to Jesus. It's a blessing when the check arrives just in time. Sometimes food will appear on our doorstep mysteriously when we don't know where the next meal will come from. And just yesterday I heard of a dear friend who has come through months of sickening chemo therapy, and now has been declared "cancer-free" ~ that is a miracle. And God is doing far more than we can even imagine "behind the scenes." There are wonders He is performing that we will never know about in our lifetime.

Many of these marvelous things we take for granted ~ fresh drinking water, clean air, our health, the privilege of worship, talents and skills we use every day, a car that starts without trouble, the way God created bees to make honey and the perfect form of the beehive. It's unbelievable and overwhelming when I try to think about all God does daily in my own life.

The very fact that God poured out His own Spirit on us is a wonder. And that He would actually die a grisly death on a cross for each one of us ~ wonder of wonders! That in itself is a mystery ~ we will never know the full impact of the burden He bore at Calvary until we are walking with Him in heaven...which is another marvel. We can read the details about heaven in God's word, but we really have no idea...I know the Bible says we will be singing and praising God with the angels for eternity, but I think my mouth will be hanging open in awe for about the first thousand years or so! We will be seeing the numberless wonders from the other side.

"Oh the depths of the riches of the wisdom and knowledge of God! How unsearchable His judgments, His footsteps cannot be traced!" (Romans 11:33).

OCTOBER 8

SCRAMBLED EGGS...

Made myself a scrambled egg sandwich for my dinner last night. I don't eat a lot of meat, so once in awhile I'll opt for eggs...this just sounded good. Eggs are such good food. The question has always been asked, "what came first, the chicken or the egg?" I think it kind of a no-brainer...you can't have the egg *without* the chicken...

Eggs are important. They are needed in many recipes to hold things together, you can prepare them many different ways ~ I use them a lot for breakfast, hard-boil them for egg salad or deviled, they make my pancakes fluffier, and did you ever try to make an angel food cake without eggs? We've done omelets quite often, for dinner. It's quick and easy, and quite filling, after you add all the cheese and veggies, and other things. The egg is a symbol of Easter, as well, because it denotes new life.

Did you ever try to explain the Trinity to a child? We've had many discussions like this in my Sunday school class of 1st and 2nd graders. Of course, the conversation begins with God the Father, God the Son, and God the Holy Spirit...and we take off from there. They always ask, "how can one person be three people?" I tell them I am a mother, a sister and a daughter...that makes me three people, but the same person. They think about that for a few minutes, and then we start talking about the egg. We name all the parts, well the shell, the white and the yolk. They all have a purpose. Individually they can be used for different things. And they are very delicious if scrambled all together (minus the shell, of course!). But, it's kind of like God. One God, but three parts. So we talk about the purpose of each of those parts, and they are fine with that. It's believable to them.

Actually, it's astounding to think of the Trinity. The thing that's different from the egg, is that God the Father is fully God...and God the Son, Jesus, is fully God, and so is the Holy Spirit. God. They were all together at the Creation of the world. Genesis 1:26 ~ "Then God said, *'Let Us make man in Our image, in Our likeness...'* " Who did we think He was talking to there? In Deuteronomy 6:4 we read, *"Hear O Israel, the Lord our God, the Lord is One."* And in 1st Corinthians 8:4, *"...There is no God but One."* God thought of everything, didn't He? He, God the Creator, made the whole earth and everything in it, then He sent Jesus, God the Son, to be humbly born so He could grow to be the Sacrifice for our sin, and God the Holy Spirit is here to give us peace, and comfort, and guidance ~ but they're all God. One God. Not three individual gods.

I love the picture Matthew gives us in 3:16-17: *"As soon as Jesus was baptized, He went up out of the water. At that moment heaven was opened and he [John] saw the Spirit of God descending like a dove and lighting on Him [Jesus]. And a voice from heaven said, 'This is My Son, whom I love; with Him I am well pleased.'"* So, here we actually see all three "Persons" of God together at the same time. That's a beautiful image, isn't it? And unlike my sandwich, this image is not scrambled in any way!

OCTOBER 9

FASHION TRENDS...

I'm sure you're just like me, marveling at all the different fashion trends through the years, and that when the designers seem to run out of ideas, they bring old styles back again, changing them ever so slightly, and we go through the gamut of vogue once again. Some styles we probably will not see again, such as the long flowing robes the women (and men) wore in Bible times. They're not practical for our lifestyle today. And there were different styles for the sects of people, like the peasants, or the royalty who lived in palaces… the latter seemed to be a little skimpier for women, at least from the pictures we've seen, and the men showed their legs too, and bared their chests.

I don't know when each fashion type evolved into another, or when men actually began wearing trousers instead of robes and skirts, (the Scottish men still wear kilts). But I do know there are some styles I would not want to have repeated…for one, the colonial days, with the many full skirts and petticoats, and the laced corsets which were cinched up so tightly the women seriously suffered many health problems, including trouble in childbirth, for the sake of having a perfect waistline. There were no easy slip-on shoes ~ they were laced-up boots that must have taken forever to get on, and off. And hats ~ one to match every dress.

I think the more popular styles to be repeated are anything from the 1920's to the present. For awhile the women wore the shorter dresses with big shoulder pads, from shapeless to shapely, then the skirts got longer, and shorter again, and bell-bottoms and tight-legged pants have traded places several times. And though men's fashion changes aren't as drastic as women's, suit lapels and neckties have gone from wide to narrow and in between several times. Same with shoe styles, from pointed, to rounded to squared toes… and at this point, I don't think blue-jeans will ever go out of style, and frankly, jeans have to be my very favorite piece of clothing ever. And hats are in fashion once again.

Remember, God was the first designer of any type of clothing. In the beginning, there was no such thing, until Adam and Eve sinned and realized they were naked. God has designed attire He would like for us to wear, always. And it doesn't ever go out of style. In Ephesians 6 we are instructed to *"Stand firm then, with the belt of truth buckled around your waist, the breastplate of righteousness in place, feet fitted with readiness that comes from the gospel of peace…the shield of faith…the helmet of salvation, and the sword of the Spirit ~ on all occasions."* (vs. 14-16). I think He means that this is the ensemble we should wear to everything…*all occasions*…every day. Of course, Christians should dress modestly, that goes without saying, nothing too suggestive or revealing. Jesus reminded us, *"Consider how the lilies of the field grow. They do not labor or spin. Yet, I tell you, not even Solomon is all his splendor was dressed as one of these. If that is how God clothes the grass of the field…how much more will He clothe you, O you of little faith?"* (Luke

12:27-28). God's Book has guidelines for every detail of our life. What fashion will you be wearing this year? Who will be your Designer?

OCTOBER 10

THE VALUE OF OLD FRIENDS...

I am blessed with friends I have had for a very long time. Yesterday I had lunch with an old girlfriend. We actually were hired together for the same company over 28 years ago. We didn't know each other before that, but we became fast friends rather quickly. We saw each other through many, many things as we raised our children into and through the teen years, saw them married, and rejoiced with each other when our first, and subsequent, grandchildren were born, prayed, and still do, for each other. We even retired together.

I have another long-time friend that I haven't lost touch with since I went to high school, my sophomore and junior years, on the east coast. We were best friends, and we even made clothes alike in our home economics class. I loved her handwriting so much, I imitated it. I have not spent time with her all these years, although I did visit her in California when her husband was stationed there with the military. That was in the '60's. We used to write letters every couple of weeks, for many years, until email came on the scene. We still send birthday cards. This is one friend I wish were closer to me, physically, because she has had lung cancer, and then later, it was determined she needed a lung transplant. She has been on a list for over seven years. I send her messages often, encouraging her, and assuring her that I am praying for her. What I would love to do is sit with her, and wrap my arms around her. But our email messages will have to suffice.

Friendships are important. I cherish mine. True friends will be there for you when the going gets tough. It says in the Bible that Jesus is a *friend of sinners*. (Matthew 11:19). It says, too, that *"Abraham believed God and it was credited to him as righteousness, and he was called God's friend."* (James 2:23). One of the Proverbs, 18:24, reads *"A man of many companions may come to ruin, but there is a friend who sticks closer than a brother."*

Have you ever felt abandoned by your friends? Well, Jesus will never abandon you...He said, *"I will never leave you; I will never forsake you."* (Hebrews 13:5). You can count on Him to always be there, no matter who else walks away. He is that friend who sticks closer than a brother.

OCTOBER 11

WHO'S IN CHARGE HERE?

Did you ever walk into a room, or into a business for that matter, where everything was chaos, and you wondered, "Who's in charge here?" I know there have been classrooms where the teacher has stepped out of the room for a moment and complete bedlam breaks out. Kids are throwing erasers and pencils, spit-wads, and there is much yelling and screaming...why do they dare to do that, when the teacher, or the principal, could walk into the room at any second and catch them all in the act? And I have actually walked into a business, where the employees are standing around, telling jokes, eating snacks, not really noticing that there is a customer, seemingly without any management or supervision, and I have certainly wondered, "who's in charge here?" We really have shown that we cannot self-manage without getting off track. We need guidance, we need a plan, no matter how old or experienced we think we are. We may even BE the manager, or the parent, or the teacher, but we still need guidance.

I guess that I had enough training and guidance at home that I was somewhat bewildered by these scenes, especially in school. I wouldn't think of throwing an eraser, in fact, I was the one who just sat in my seat while the rest of the classroom was in pandemonium, really afraid for what would happen when the teacher walked back into the room. And when I worked, I was afraid NOT to spend idle moments dusting something, cleaning a window, or filing a pile of papers. I was taught to always be busy, and responsible, in my schooling, and in my work. I didn't want to suffer the consequences of loafing and wasting time.

I wonder if God looks down at us from on high and waits for just the right moment to walk into the room, as we are dallying, wasting valuable time that could be used doing something for Him. A lot of people do not realize He really is in charge...of the whole universe. Who do we think keeps the stars and planets on course, and sends the rain and snow to the earth? Who do we think sends the thunder and lightning, or causes the new buds to form on the trees and flower seeds to burst up out of the dirt in the bright sunlight? These things just happen year after year, day after day, like clockwork...the seasons change, baby wild animals are born, the sparrows get fed. And many of us just take it for granted that the world will go on and on, just like it always has. And it seems that nothing man does, or does not do, makes a difference in the functions of nature. Read some astonishing facts in Job, chapters 38 and following to the end of the book...

But God had a purpose in creating all He created. He wanted someone to fellowship with Him. He wanted us to enjoy His world, and gave us but a few rules to follow so we would be successful. Just like children need teachers and parents, and employees need bosses, we as God's creation, also need Him to guide and lead us. He has given us everything we have, the whole world to enjoy. He will manage our day if we give it to Him. He is ultimately in charge anyway. And *"His way is perfect."* (Psalm 18:30). It always has been. Sometimes we think our way is better, or that God is not working fast enough, or not answering how we expected, so we tend to take matters into our own hands, and this causes us more trouble. We create our own "storms" so to speak.

"By faith we understand that the universe was formed at God's command..." (Hebrews 11:3). If God were not in charge, if He did not take control of this earth and of the heavens that He had created, we would not have such a place to live in and enjoy. If we trusted in chance, or a big explosion, nothing would work, nature would not be dependable. I believe we can make a difference in our world, in our society, in our families and our circle of friends and co-workers, if we put our trust in the Maker, the Creator of heaven and earth, the Designer of our lives. And He wants us to depend on Him. He is the One in charge. And He has given us the instruction Book. We need to actually read it. Then we will see that we cannot do it better than He, no matter how much we'd like to be in charge.

OCTOBER 12

WILDERNESS...

Has God ever led you into the wilderness, and then seemingly just left you there? The scriptures have quite a bit to say about the wilderness...of course, we all know the story of Moses leading the Israelites through the wilderness on their way to the land God promised them, a land flowing with milk and honey. (Exodus). It wasn't supposed to take them forty years, but because of their disobedience, He couldn't let them in to their "reward." God showed them so many things of Himself along the way, so many miracles, He fed and clothed them, and still they balked and complained.

In 1 Kings 17, we read the account of Elijah, *"Then the word of the Lord came to Elijah : Leave here, turn eastward and hide in the Kerith Ravine, east of the Jordan. You will drink from the brook, and I have ordered ravens to feed you there."* It doesn't say how long he was out there, but the scripture says, *"**some time later** the brook dried up because there had been no rain in the land…"* (vs. 7) So from there the Lord sent him on to another assignment.

Then what about John the Baptist? His birth was miraculous, since his parents were aged, but God had a very special plan for him. He hung around in the desert, eating locusts and wild honey, and must have looked pretty scary, in his camel's hair clothes, and dreadlocks. But God had a place for him ~ *"A voice of one calling out in the desert (wilderness), 'Prepare the way for the Lord, make straight paths for Him.'"* (Matthew 3:3). Yet, even in the wilderness, people were drawn to John, confessing their sins, and being baptized by him.

Jesus Himself was sent to the wilderness, for forty days and forty nights. He fasted that whole time. Satan had been waiting very close by. I can see him rubbing his hands together, chuckling and saying, "Here's my chance to finally get Him alone." And, oh, he did tempt Jesus. He knew He was hungry, so tempted Him to turn stones into bread. He could have. Satan also wanted Him to prove He was the Christ by throwing Himself off a high pinnacle so angels could swoop down and rescue Him. He also tried to "give" Him all the kingdoms of the earth. Jesus finally sent him away, saying, *"It is written, 'Do not put the Lord your God to the test,'* and *'worship the Lord your God and serve Him only.'"* (Matthew 4).

The Apostle John was banished to the Island of Patmos to write down all that God would show him, the book of Revelation. *"Write on a scroll what you see and send it to the seven churches: to Ephesus, Smyrna, Pergamum, Thyatira, Sardis, Philadelphia, and Laodicea."* (Rev. 1:11). I don't know how long John was exiled, or how long it took him to write every incredible detail of the visions he was shown, but if he was to write it on a scroll, long-hand, I would imagine it would take quite awhile, months at the very least. My thought is more like *years.* John's head must have been spinning at what he saw.

SO, for the last almost two weeks I have felt like I am in the wilderness. I've been ill with something mysterious that apparently must run its course, and so I stay at home with my Powerade drinks, bullion, rice cakes and bananas, my book, a lot of time on the couch. I have been missing my exercise classes, my Bible studies, and even had to have my daughter do some shopping for me. I have prayed for healing. I have prayed that God would teach me whatever lesson He wants me to learn here. But a few days ago it dawned on me that I should just praise Him. I know we need to praise Him in any circumstance. *"Give thanks in ALL circumstances, for this is God's will for you in Christ Jesus."* (1 Thess. 5:18). So, I praise Him for WHO He is, for all that He has done, for all that He knows, for the wonderful way He has created me, and I praise Him that He WILL heal me. In His time. He wants me to just "be still and know" that He is God. His love for me is unfailing. There is nothing I am suffering that He doesn't know about. And so, I praise Him in my wilderness.

OCTOBER 13

HAVING A LITTLE FUN...

When was the last time you spent a few minutes doing something fun and carefree? It seems our lives are so busy and full ~ we're raising and caring for our families, working hard at our careers, carrying the weight of the world around on our shoulders. And our concerns are very real, and they do require a lot of our time and concern. Every day there is something that comes up, or continues from the day before, that just consumes our thoughts, our energy, and our time. Have fun? I do know what it's like to carry burdens, to wring our hands with worry. About finances, children, illnesses...I have been there plenty of times.

My Bible says we should *"Cast your cares on the Lord, and He will sustain you; He will never let the righteous fall."* (Psalm 55:22). This doesn't mean we should sheepishly and hesitantly hand our cares and worries to Him ~ it means to fling, hurl, throw or heave them onto Him! As in casting your line when you're fishing. Or casting the nets over the side of the boat as the fishermen did on the Sea of Galilee...I have seen these nets. You can't possibly get them in the water by just dropping them over the side. They're huge, and heavy. "Cast your cares..."

Childhood is, or it should be, a time of fun and carefree days. Mine was. What would happen if you took a few minutes out of your busy day...*just a few minutes*...and played like a child? How many times have you stood in the window and watched your children or grandchildren draw hopscotches in the driveway with sidewalk chalk? Remember doing that as a little girl? Why not join them now? Use your imagination. We all have a little bit of child in us still.

I like to ride my bicycle ~ the same kind I had as a seven-year-old child, a 1955 Schwinn Cruiser. I don't ride for sport or competition, only for relaxation and exercise. One time I stopped at the school playground near my home, parked my bike, and sat on a swing. Then I began swinging…oh, what a feeling! Take a walk and pick some flowers. Blow bubbles and listen to the little children giggle as they try to catch them. I also play Bunco once a month with eleven other women, two of them are my daughter and granddaughter. We laugh and visit ~ it's fun to hang around with others who are laughing, even if only for a little while. It's refreshing, and good for you.

Life is full of very heavy and serious things. There is always war. There are always financial woes and illnesses. But a little laughter, a few moments of lightheartedness, will do wonders. I'm sure it's okay with God if we laugh… He invented laughter. Look up how many verses you can find with the words "joy," and "rejoice," in them. In Proverbs (17:22) we see that *"A cheerful heart is good medicine."* And in Job 8:21, *"He will yet fill your mouth with laughter and your lips with shouts of joy."* (This was in the midst of Job's suffering, by the way). And we all know Ecclesiastes 3:4 ~ *"There is a time to weep and a time to laugh."* Lighten your day and lift your spirits, and those of the people around you, by learning and taking the time to relax, even if just for a few minutes each day. Especially when times are hard. *"Rejoice in the Lord always, I will say it again: Rejoice!"* (Philippians 4:4).

OCTOBER 14

SOMEONE LIKE MOSES…

I pray often for our leaders and for our nation, and recently I have been praying more earnestly that God will heal America. But it has to start with individuals. So I pray for myself, that God will give me grace and wisdom for each day, and understanding. *"I gain understanding from Your precepts… Your Word is a lamp to my feet and a light for my path. I have taken an oath and confirmed it, that I will follow Your righteous laws."* (Psalm 119:104-106). That last part isn't quoted often, but look how important it is. We must stay true to our covenant with God, to follow Him.

And we must pray for our President, and for his staff, even if we don't like him. (I saw this on a church sign a few weeks ago!). Much of our leadership is evil, I believe, and power-hungry, full of pride. And influential. David prayed for another king at another time, *"May his days be few and may another take his place of leadership."* (Psalm 109:8). I know people who have joked about this verse, but there it is. And David was serious. There was evil leadership in the country then, as there has been many times since. But we must remember, nothing is too difficult for God. He can change hearts. I believe this is God's judgment that we're going through right now, for turning away from Him as a nation. We need to pray that God will raise up godly men and women to the leadership of America. He can hold us up and help us to endure, and to make a difference.

If we all strive to make a difference in our own circles, all across this great land, and stand firm for God's truths, asking for wisdom, strength and endurance, I think we could help America survive. As Moses spoke to the people he was leading, *"Do not be afraid. Stand firm and you will see the deliverance the Lord will bring you today."* (Exodus 14:13). God brought water from a rock because of Moses' faith. He turned a river into blood, and then fresh again. He parted the sea and delivered His people from the enemy. He gave Moses the words when he could not speak. God is our Redeemer. He saved the Israelites from the yoke of the Egyptians. *"I will free you from being slaves to them, and I will redeem you with an outstretched arm and with mighty acts of judgment. I will take you as My own people, and I will be your God."* (Ex. 6:6-7). What a promise! Do we believe it for America?

We are like the Israelites who wandered in the wilderness. So many have lost our way. God alone can bring us out safely, help us and guide us. He will feed us His manna from heaven. Sometimes we do not hear His voice, and we find no comfort. But He is there. He was there in the wilderness, He was there when Moses was placed in the river in a basket. Let us hold on to God's promise of redemption. When we are beaten and bleeding, He will keep our hands grasped in His. We will know that there is a purpose in our sufferings and when we *"have endured a little while"* His glory will break through and we'll know He has been there all the time. *"My grace is sufficient for you, for My power is made perfect in weakness."* (2 Corinthians 12:9).

We are so weak, Lord, as individuals, as a nation. Bring us back to You. Let Your glory pass by us as we stand barefoot on Holy ground. Amen.

OCTOBER 15

RANDOM ACTS...

A random act can be anything, really. It is usually something done without planning, or careful choice, and without regard for the consequences.

That's how the dictionary defines it. Frequently we hear of "random acts of kindness" and we are encouraged to practice these. Not bad advice, really, to treat people with kindness, and when they least expect it but need it the most. Ideally we could do something extra nice in turn for someone who has not been very pleasant or agreeable toward us. A person who seems to be grumpy most of the time might have good reason, such as some underlying problems or a frightening illness no one else knows about. For instance, an elderly person, or shut-in may be just very lonely, and their whole outlook may be changed by a visit, a card, or a phone call. Maybe the gift of a pie, or help with gardening, or grocery shopping. A bouquet of flowers. And sometimes, you may wish to do something nice without the person ever knowing about it.

Many times, though, a random act may be one of violence.

I once read a story about some delinquent boys who were joyriding and broke into a car, found a credit card, and used it to buy all sorts of things. They bought some DVDs, a frozen turkey (!?), among other items. Driving down the highway, one of the boys threw the turkey out the window at a passing car (a random act), and it crashed through the person's windshield, smashing the driver's face, breaking bones and destroying the woman's entire facial structure, and her trachea. The boy who threw the turkey was caught, and many months later, following many surgeries to restore her face, the woman met the boy face-to-face in a courtroom. The woman actually embraced the remorseful, weeping boy who did the deed, and forgave him on the spot, bringing tears to the eyes of the judge and attorneys. A random act of violence had been redeemed by mercy and kindness. Almost unheard of. I think she was instrumental in reducing his sentence, as well. And he joined forces with her to go around and speak to high school groups!

We know of another undeserved act of kindness that wasn't exactly random…a Man who chose to die a horrible death on a cross for someone else's sinful actions…mine and yours. This act of mercy, grace and love, however, was well thought out, and although we do not deserve the compassion that was shown to us, Jesus went to the cross willingly. This was why He came in the first place. He did no wrong to deserve this sentence of death, yet He *died* for us, for the wrong we have done. No act of charity or mercy will ever equal what Jesus did for us. Before He even knew us. *"But God demonstrates His own love for us in this: while we were still sinners, Christ died for us."* (Romans 5:8).

Next time you are compelled to do something nice for someone, whether they deserve it or not, do it. Without even thinking about it. Even if it's a smile. You never know how badly someone may need it just at that moment.

OCTOBER 16

WINGS OF ANGELS...

I have never actually seen an angel. Well, not that I know of. The Bible says that we may have *"entertained angels without knowing it..."* when we entertain strangers. (Hebrews 13:2). We hear many stories of how a "person" carried someone from a terrible accident, or was there just when needed, comforting, helping, but then "disappeared." "Angels are creatures of good, spirits of love, and messengers of the Savior Jesus Christ. At times there is identification of individual angelic messengers: Gabriel, Michael, Raphael, Uriel, and Satan/ Lucifer."

God's angels are beautiful creatures, or at least, the pictures and illustrations we have seen of them. Many people have reported seeing an angel, or angels, in times of crisis or deep turmoil. Their massive pure white wings are the most impressive part of this picture. Wings are fascinating. I'm sure we have all watched birds in flight, all kinds, from the tiny hummer to the impressive eagle with the six-foot plus wing-span. God has designed the wings aerodynamically so the birds can dip and soar accordingly. If geese, or another large breed of birds, fly low enough, you can actually hear the rush of their wings as they are flapping. A wing is such an intricate and delicate arrangement of bones and feathers, strategically placed, together with muscles used to move the wings up and down perfectly, and seemingly effortlessly, the air resistance giving the uplift with the flexing of the "wrist" or gliding with wings outstretched.

Angels' wings are not mentioned often in the Bible, but we do read about the seraphs in Isaiah 6:2 and following, who are of the highest order of angels, each having six wings. Angels appear to be like human beings, as far as their form, but I've often wondered how their wings could be attached. *"And God made man a little lower than the angels."* (Hebrews 2:7). Such a mystery.

There are some references to Jesus in the Bible as having wings, although I have never seen a painting or portrayal of Him with wings. In David's prayer of

Psalm 17, he asks the Lord to *"hide me in the shadow ofYour wings."* (vs. 8b). And in 91:4, he speaks of the Most High who will *"cover you with His feathers, and under His wings you will find refuge."* Malachi 4:2 refers to the *"Sun of righteousness rising with healing in His wings."* And in Luke 13:34, Jesus' own words, *"O Jerusalem....how often I have longed to gather your children together, as a hen gathers her chicks under her wings..."*

There are songs that sing of angels' wings ~ "with peaceful wings unfurled," "the rush of angels' wings," and "when I sing redemption's story, the angels will fold their wings." The angels do, and will, sing praises and worship God, but unlike us, grace and redemption are something the angels know nothing about ~ we alone experience God's great gift of salvation. They have to fold their wings and be silent ~ they cannot sing that song. Nor can they imagine the love that flows from being wrapped in the protective wings of the Most High Angel, full of flaming beauty and awesome power to overcome our adversaries. *"Behold, I am going to send an Angel before you to guard you along the way, and to bring you into the place which I have prepared. Be on your guard before Him and obey His voice."* (Exodus 23:20-21).

OCTOBER 17

IT'S SO DARK...

I love the fall. But one thing I don't like is the intense darkness. After just having set our clocks back for Daylight Savings Time, I see that it does *seem* light a little earlier in the morning. But, then by 4:30 in the afternoon, it is as dark as night. So, where is the daylight savings? If one works, there is no daylight at all, and for the children in school, there is not a lot of time to play after arriving home. The nights are so long. I know this is the time of year when many people suffer from a despondency, or melancholy from lack of light. I like the soft light and the coziness of flickering candles. But, yes, this time of year it is very dreary outside.

We have had some beautiful autumn days, however. The leaves changed slowly on the trees this year, and in fact, some of them are still green. Because of the shortness of daylight, I am confident they, too, will be turning and dropping soon. The bright colors of trees also add a little glow to otherwise dismal days. Especially if their leaves are illuminated by a nearby streetlight.

We know that the Bible describes darkness as merely the absence of light. I don't have a very scientific mind, but I do know where the Light comes from. *"You are my lamp, O Lord; the Lord turns my darkness into light."* (2 Samuel 22:29). There are many things that can cause darkness in our lives, besides nightfall, or the absence of natural light in fall and winter months. David mentions *"pestilence in the darkness, and plague that destroys at midday."*(Psalm 91:6). Wickedness and sin bring on darkness in our souls. Lengthy illnesses will cause our spirit to darken as well. The joy and health seems absent from our eyes. And there is a sadness which is caused by many things…loss, financial troubles, death. Jesus said, *"Your eye is the lamp of your body."* He also went on to say, *"See to it, then, that the light within you is not darkness. Therefore if your whole body is full of light, and no part of it is dark, it will be completely lighted, as when the light of a lamp shines on you."* (Luke11:34-36).

So, is it possible for us to be in turmoil, suffering illness or sadness, loneliness and fear, and still be full of light? Jesus said it, so it must be so. I have read many accounts of people who have gone through that "long, dark night of the soul" and are still able to stand in the Light, because they have kept their eyes on the Source of Light. Peter wrote, *"But you are a chosen people, a royal priesthood, a holy nation, a people belonging to God, that you may declare the praises of Him who called you out of darkness into His wonderful light."* (1 Peter 2:9). Sometimes the darkness is caused by not knowing, we are "in the dark," as we put it. But God has given us a clear message that Jesus is the Light of the world. (John 8:12).

Is it dark where you are? I have a picture in my mind of opening up my Bible on my desk and suddenly light bursts out of the pages. Actually, that really is what happens! His word is full of Light. We don't have to walk in the cold shadows but can bathe ourselves in the warmth of His light.

OCTOBER 18

THE PHOTO ALBUM…

We all have at least one. I dare say, most of us have many of them. You remember the photo albums "of old," the ones our parents put together, full of black and white, and sepia pictures of people we can't identify? I am in possession of several of those, retrieved from my parents' home a few years ago. Collecting photos has changed a lot over the years. From the black pages holding pictures on with those little corners you had to lick and press to keep in place, bound by cords tied through punched holes to hold the front and back covers together, to the elegant art of scrapbooking many of us now engage in, the intent and result is the same...to capture special moments and people, and preserve them for future generations. I think we have become better at identifying the subjects of our albums these days. We categorize them too...the wedding album, the first baby album (and subsequent babies after that), the vacation album, the school days album. And then, there's the refrigerator...but that's another subject!!

My daughter is a scrapbooker, although she will insist she's not. But she has put together the most beautiful scrapbooks of her children, their vacations, their family, complete with momentos, beautiful themed background papers, journaling, and clever stickers and stamps to decorate the pages. They are delightful to look at, and will make wonderful memories for her children as they grow older. They take time, but the finished product is well worth the effort.

Did you know that God made a beautiful picture album for us? The Bible isn't just a book of stories about people who lived before us, and their experiences that will hopefully teach us how to live as we should. But it's full of pictures, and you can see them as you read the accounts of those who walked with God. I'm a visual reader, so when I'm reading, I can picture the scene and see myself right there in the story. God's word is like that...if you look closely, you can see Adam and Eve in that beautiful garden, you can see the exquisite coat of Joseph's in a rainbow of colors. See that picture of the Israelites crossing the Red Sea on dry ground, while their enemies are in hot pursuit as the waters close in on them? Then there's the one of Moses, standing on the mountain receiving the first Book of the Law from our heavenly Father. And look at all the work Noah is doing on the ark, measuring and hammering exactly as God instructed, then gathering all the beautiful animals as assigned. And how about young David as he stands next to his giant trophy, Goliath? That's quite a picture. There's so much more, but turning lots of pages ahead, we see a special star and a holy Baby, then a young Boy teaching the teachers in the temple. One of my favorites is of the crowd sitting on the sloping grassy hillside beside the Sea of Galilee, listening intently to the beloved Teacher for hours on end. I see sheep with their adored Shepherd, and best friends gathered for a meal...the picture of a boat in a storm, and that of a crude cross... and an empty tomb. When I turn to the last few pages, I see the beautiful likeness of a King riding in the clouds on an elegant white horse with flowing mane, and then many, many people, a family reunion, gathered at a long table enjoying a fabulous banquet.

What do you see when you look at God's picture album? Do you see yourself in His family? *"Only be careful and watch yourselves closely, so that you do not forget the things your eyes have seen or let them slip from your heart as long as you live. Teach them to your children and to their children after them."* (Deut. 4:9). Our Father has preserved these pictures for us to share with our own families. But unlike our earthly photo albums, these pictures will not fade, or fall out of the book, or become lost. And each one is identified ~ we will never have to wonder who our Lord is talking about. Every one pertains to us. This is our Family album, filled with the Father's love. When was the last time you sat down and turned the pages?

OCTOBER 19

IDOLS THEN AND NOW...

All through time man has worshipped idols. And all through time, even before time began, God has been there. He has shown His glory, His power and His love ~ none of which any other god or idol even has to give. *"No one is like You, O Lord; You are great, and Your name is mighty in power. Who should not revere You, O King of the nations? This is Your due."* (Jeremiah 10:6-7). Did you catch that? *"This is your due?"* Doesn't this mean we are obliged to worship and praise Him, the God of the Universe, the Creator of everything? Yes, I believe our praise IS due Him. Not only for what He has done, but simply for Who He is. And yet, all down through the ages, man has worshipped other things, both created and man-made. Men have worshipped rainbows, the sun, or the moon. We have bowed down to the rain, the buffalo, graven images of invented "important" gods, made of wood, stone, metal or glass. Deaf and dumb.

Jeremiah said, *"But the Lord is the true God. He is the living God, the eternal King."* (10:10). Much evidence abounds in our universe, if you don't want to take Jeremiah's word for it. Much of it we have worshipped...the sky (our space programs, for example), the rain or snow, fire, certain animals and birds, science and medicine…oh, I'm not saying we should not explore and study these things, but to make them our gods, or use them as idols, is futile. God has given humans intelligence and a bit of creativity, to do and learn many things, but we need to recognize that these are indeed God-given. We rely on paper or plastic (money), electronics, empty promises. When things are going well, we give ourselves the glory and the credit for our lifestyles, our businesses and our relationships. But we don't recognize that we are nothing without God. There are many people who seem to be successful in all they do, busily working for yet a higher rung on the corporate ladder. But David warned in Psalm 93, *"The senseless man does not know, fools do not understand, that though the wicked spring up like grass and all evildoers flourish, they will be forever destroyed."* (v. 6-7). It is sometimes discouraging to us to see the unfair and wicked get ahead, while we struggle and don't seem to make headway. Yet, *"how great are Your works, O Lord, how profound Your thoughts!"* (v.5). He will bless and provide for us who remain faithful.

The huge difference between our Creator God and all other gods people can conjure up is that our God made the ultimate sacrifice, and paid for our sins with His own Son's precious blood. Every drop. No other god can offer redemption and forgiveness. He alone deserves our praise and our devotion.

OCTOBER 20

THINGS THAT ANNOY…

I am a person who really tries to look at the positive side of life. I try to give people the benefit of the doubt. Be encouraging. Look on the bright side. But, there are things that really annoy me, and usually they're unimportant, like…a scratchy radio, cold feet, mosquitoes, not being able to reach the high cupboards, unidentified sounds under the hood, crows, telemarketers, weeds, late mail, slow computer, ants, lukewarm tea, being late, people who run red lights, pain, bills…oh, the list goes on. You have them too. Annoyances.

I am wondering how the plagues in the Bible were considered. Did Pharaoh see them as a threat? Was he fearful of them? Or were they simply annoyances? What about the thorn in Paul's flesh? Job's "friends?" How did Goliath first see the boy David? Was Moses annoyed with the disobedience of the Israelites? I really don't know how he, or God, put up with their attitudes for forty years. How does God put up with our sin?

Paul admonished the Philippians to keep their hearts and minds in Christ Jesus. He said in 4:11-13, *"I have learned to be content whatever the circumstances. I know what it is to be in need, and I know what it is to have plenty. I have learned the secret of being content in any and every situation, whether well-fed or hungry, whether living in plenty or in want. I can do everything through Him who gives me strength."*

Let's not be complainers. We will be tempted to say or think, "if only…" It's not easy to "be content in all circumstances," or even few circumstances. Many things will continue to annoy or irritate us, but let's remember that God wants us to be thankful in everything, and nothing on earth will satisfy our deepest wants and desires. Except Him.

OCTOBER 21

THE CAT ON MY LAP...

We have always had cats, usually two at a time. Well, we're down to one now, and I think, at this time in our lives, this will be the end of the line for us. The cat we have is a classic tabby named Theodora, "Teddy" for short. She's my daughter's cat. In fact, most of the cats we've had have belonged to one or the other of my girls, and ended up unwanted for one reason or another. Teddy is getting quite persnickety in her old age of 15. She has pretty much picked me out as her only friend these days (I feed her). In fact, she usually hides when someone else is in the house. I don't really care to have her sitting on my lap because she leaves little tufts of her hair everywhere. And she's pretty scroungey. But she comes back time and time again. It makes her happy. And she doesn't waste any time when I go to my chair.

How much our heavenly Father is like this. Not the cat, but the Lap. We call Him "Abba" which is a good word for "Daddy." *"And by Him we cry 'Abba, Father.' The Spirit Himself testifies with our spirit that we are God's children."* (Romans 8:15, 16). I think of the beautiful pictures I've seen of Jesus sitting with several little children on his lap. The pictures are always pleasant, and the children look well-cared-for and happy. He blesses them all. But in reality, others may be sitting on His lap, receiving His love and nurturing, and instruction and comfort, who are less than desirable. They may be unclean or downright filthy. Yet, I know He accepts them onto His lap because that's just His nature. *"As a father has compassion on his children, so the Lord has compassion on those who fear Him."* (Psalm 103:13). We can come to Him whenever we need His arms around us, whenever we need our tears kissed away. Sometimes we do not have time to get cleaned up before we come to the Father. We are desperately needy for His consolation, for His arms around us. He doesn't cringe when He touches our dirty face, tracing our tears. His heart is full of compassion and a deeper love than we can ever imagine, and His arms are ever open to us. Sometimes we come timidly, and other times we run to Him, terrified of the things life has handed us. And we don't have to save that time with Him just for when we are destitute. We can come to Him any time, just to love Him and thank Him for being our "Daddy." Like my cat, He wants us to jump up on His lap the first chance we get. There is always room for one more on His huge lap.

OCTOBER 22

HINDRANCES...

Did you ever have a really good plan and work very hard at trying to get all the details together, but some little thing hindered you? Frustrating, isn't it? Something or someone will restrain us, or get in the way of our progress, sometimes deliberately, and other times they don't realize they are holding us back. Many situations may get in our way to prevent us from getting the job done. Sometimes I plan my whole day, or a big part of it, to work outside in the yard. There is always something that needs to be done. But then it rains. And then later, I'm out of the mood. Or there is a task or job I've been trying to get done, but there are too many interruptions. This happened a lot when my children were little.

Lots of times, at least in the few recent years, we have had plans of travel, or remodeling, or some purchase, but then the economy doesn't cooperate. Lots of things take money, but we are short on funds. So, these circumstances hold us back from what we want to do, what we had planned for so carefully.

Hindrances may even be of our own making ~ like fear. Nothing that we can see is holding us back, but we are afraid to go, or try, or do.

The disciples tried to discourage the children from seeing Jesus, but Jesus said, *"Let the little children come to me and do not hinder them."* (Matthew 19:14).

Paul spoke to the Corinthians (chapter 9) about "putting up with anything rather than hinder the gospel of Christ." So, what I'm reading here is that, no matter what comes our way, we should not complain about it because if we did, people around us would not see Jesus in us? That's how I'm seeing it. Ouch!

Then, to the ones who have done the hindering, Jesus warned: *"Woe to you experts in the law, because you have taken away the key to knowledge. You yourselves have not entered and you have hindered those who were entering."* (Luke 11:2). Wow! I think here the teachers of the law in the synagogue were endeavoring to prevent the people from understanding the Scriptures that would lead them to the Messiah. They wanted the knowledge, but the scribes would not let them hear it. Jesus promised great trouble and sorrow to those who were holding them back. It is a great sin to deliberately keep people in ignorance when it comes to spiritual matters.

And finally, Paul admonishes us, as he was addressing the Hebrews, to *"throw off everything that hinders and the sin that so easily entangles, and run with perseverance the race marked out for us."* (12:1). There are numerous "things" that keep us from doing what WE want to do, all those special events and plans. But the important thing to contemplate is, what is holding us back from becoming all that God wants us to be, giving glory to His name? Why is it so hard? What's hindering you? What hinders me?

OCTOBER 23

IT'S GETTING COLD...

It's been such a beautiful fall, getting cooler and crisper gradually, a little rain, and lots of sun still, but there is a chill in the air. I have unpacked all my sweaters and heavier clothes and put away the tank tops, shorts and light skirts for the coming winter. I love this time of year. And soon it will be downright cold...where I live, freezing! I am thankful for a warm comfortable home and cozy blankets. Football fans will be wrapping up in their blankets sipping hot chocolate as they sit out on the cold bleachers cheering on their teams. Soon, there will be bonfires of leaves that have been raked up into oversized piles. Before long the beautiful trees will be bare and dead-looking as freezing temperatures dip and the snow piles up. Cold.

But we have many ways of keeping warm. Wonderful hot drinks such as the aforementioned hot chocolate, hot spiced teas, pumpkin and eggnog lattes ('tis the season!), there are fireplaces that will be blazing, warm thick socks and mittens, mufflers and caps. There is the warmth of friendships, and those we love. Car heaters take the place of the air conditioning. Some music warms our very souls.

I love to think of God's love as being a true feeling of warmth. His arms wrapped around me, His unfailing love protecting me from the chill of gloom, His gentle words guiding me through the uncertainty of the storm. It cannot get cold enough that the warmth of His Spirit will not penetrate the chill of our disobedience, or of the evil lurking. *"But because of His great love for us, God, who is rich in mercy, made us alive with Christ even when we were dead in transgressions ~ it is by grace you have been saved."* (Ephesians 2:4-5). I can't think of anything that warms my soul and spirit more than the knowledge of God's gift of mercy and grace to me when my heart was cold. He came looking for me when I was wandering in the storm. *"He got up and rebuked the wind and the raging waters, and the storm was stilled, and all was calm."* (Luke 8:24). I love the fact that I can be friends with a God like that. The fire of His love warms me through and through, and gives me hope.

OCTOBER 24

RECIPES...

My granddaughter recently honored me by asking for old tried and true recipes I use, most of which were handed down to me by my own mother, her great-grandmother. And some of these beloved recipes came to her from *her* mother, my grandmother. I love this. Along with some recipes come favorite traditions. One of them is a Scripture Cake and the ingredients are listed by scripture verse and you have to look each one up in the Bible, for instance, 2 Cups Jeremiah 6:20...which translates to sugar (called sweet cane in scripture). My mom always made this cake at Christmas as a birthday cake for Jesus, and the children would gather around to blow out the candles and sing Happy Birthday to Jesus.

Recipes are important because some things don't turn out if the recipe is wrong...like jam or candy. They have to be followed exactly. There was a cake my three girls loved to have me make for their birthdays, year after year, we called the "princess cake." It was an angel food cake with white fluffy frosting, with the pastel Smarties all stuck in it, and when we could still buy them, the tiny silver balls sprinkled across the top. Very easy to make! Not sure where the name "princess" came from, but we have always called it that.

There are millions of recipes for this and that, and even some that are not for food items at all, but for happiness, or something such as that, and include ingredients like 1 Cup of patience, 1 heart full of love, a dash of laughter…sprinkle with kindness, etc. And some people have secret recipes they will not share with anyone. Restaurants typically do. But recently there have been websites that carry these "secret" recipes of famous restaurants. So much for secret recipes! Myself, I love to share my recipes…it's a compliment when someone asks.

God's word has the ultimate recipe for life. Actually, the Bible IS the recipe for life. We must follow it exactly. Deuteronomy 11:1 says, *"Love the LORD your God and keep His requirements, His decrees, His laws and His commands always."* And then of course, He gave us the Ten Commandments. Many think these are Ten Suggestions and treat them as such. But God called them *Commands.* A "command" is an order, given with absolute authority. Our lives just do not work as they should if we don't follow the whole recipe.

Lots of times I've tried to make a dish without following the recipe exactly, and though it sometimes works and tastes okay, if there is a missing ingredient, or a poor substitute, it's just not the same.

Jesus said, *"I am the Way, the Truth and the Life. No one comes to the Father except through me."* (John 14:6). The recipe for life is not complete without Jesus.

OCTOBER 25

TOMORROW…

We all have days when we really hope and pray that tomorrow will be better. But, what if it isn't? What if we don't even have tomorrow? I've been reading a little book by Emilie Barnes called "My Cup Overflows" and one of the stories she tells is that she was praying for a daughter who had gone astray, hurting her whole family. She began praying that she would get back on track, of course ~ we would want that, right? A friend told her about a book, "Praying God's Will For My Daughter," and she began reading and praying the scriptures in this book for her every day, expecting a change soon. She tells how she began and ended the book several times, until finally, she herself was the one who began to change. She had begun to hear God tell *her* to trust Him, and to *thank* Him. And then He wanted *her* to ask her daughter's forgiveness. God revealed to her that her anger and her own attitude regarding her daughter's waywardness was actually holding back a change in her daughter. God seemed to tell her *"I want you to thank Me today for what I will do tomorrow."* I love that! That is faith!

We have been going through a really rough time for the last few months… actually, years. This is a particularly bad year, though. And we are right smack in the middle of another crisis…but I have already found myself thanking God for the answer we don't know is coming. Oh, I know *some* answer is coming, but probably not the one we expect. It's okay. God knows what is best. Many times we pray for God to change another person, or a situation. He can do it. We know He can do anything. But, in the end, if we are faithful with our prayer and praise, we are the ones who end up changing. And our outlook becomes transformed. Each day, and each step, if we are faithful to be in His word, He will pour some of His heart into ours. He will restore us. Sometimes it will take days, sometimes months. And believe it or not, we can stay faithful in our prayers and see the changes come about even years later. It all comes down to unwavering trust in Him, forgiveness, and thankfulness.

David must have felt like this at times, for he said in Psalm 13: *"How long, O Lord? Will You forget me forever? How long will You hide Your face from me? How long must I wrestle with my thoughts, and every day have sorrow in my heart?…But I trust in Your unfailing love; my heart rejoices in Your salvation. I will sing to the Lord, for He has been good to me."*

We don't know what tomorrow will bring, but God does, and He wants to bless all our tomorrows. My own crisis isn't turning out how we wanted it to, but we are beginning to see, after six years of struggling with it, that the solution that is coming is for the best. It's something we never considered, but God knew about it from the beginning. I am not surprised…only thankful!

OCTOBER 26

WHEN TRAGEDY STRIKES…

I think it's safe to say we have all experienced some kind of tragedy in our lifetime. Just in the last decade or so we have seen some major catastrophes, which have been mentioned here before ~ 9-11 for one, before that the Oklahoma City bombing, the Challenger space shuttle, Littleton Colorado… in this last year we've watched news coverage on the Chile mine cave-in, which could have been devastating, but the miners were rescued in the 11th hour. Many mine cave-in rescues are not as successful. We have seen and heard about the Japan earthquake which sent tsunami literally all around the world. And just recently we watched and prayed as the people on the east coast experienced a rare earthquake and a few days later, hurricane Irene. Wildfires abound in the summer months, as well, causing people to evacuate their homes, and many losing everything. And of course, there is the tragedy of war.

Tragedy affects all of us, whether it's personal and individual, or within our family unit, our town, our country. Every culture experiences tragedy of some kind. It's part of life. This week we had a devastating accident in which a family's car rolled down an embankment and into the lake. The mother and father were able to get out of the vehicle, but they could not get the doors open to rescue their precious children, a 5-year old boy, and a little girl who had just turned one last week. The boy perished, and the baby is in intensive care, in critical condition in the children's hospital nearby. These parents are devastated to say the least, as is their entire family. Our community is shocked and saddened, and standing by in prayer. And I know this young mother will carry the guilt of this little boy's death all her life, as she was driving the car at the time. I don't know them personally, but I just can't get them off my mind, and pray for them often throughout the day, and wonder how that baby girl is doing, and her parents?

God is the only One who can truly give comfort in a time like this. We read of many tragedies in the Bible, some were unnecessary, but people were disobedient. Others were righted by a heavenly Father who wants to draw us closer to Him. He uses His people to do this, when we console and comfort one another. *"Praise be to the God and Father of our Lord Jesus Christ, the Father of compassion and the God of all comfort, who comforts us in all our troubles, so that we can comfort those in any trouble with the comfort we ourselves have received from God."* (2 Corinthians 1:4).

We don't know why these things happen to people, or why so many things happen all at once, but we do know that God is sovereign and He is in control. Sometimes even the most menial tasks are huge when we are wounded or ravaged by disaster. But how can we not trust Him when tragedy strikes? Ask Him to give you a heart of compassion so you can comfort someone who is in need of it. And never stop praying for each other.

OCTOBER 27

THE GIFT BAG...

When did this start? It used to be that every present, birthday, Christmas, wedding, was enclosed in a nice box of a suitable size, and wrapped in beautiful paper, harmonious to the occasion. Then, once in awhile, a present would show up in a clever gift bag, stuffed with tissue paper. Suddenly, the gift bag became more and more popular (because a lot of people simply don't *like* wrapping gifts) and now that's just about all you see. Gift bags come in every conceivable size, color, holiday, themes from Bug's Life, camping, seashore, floral, Strawberry Shortcake…well, you've seen them. I like gift bags. I don't lament the fact that paper-wrapped boxes are going by the wayside. It's what's inside that counts, really, isn't it?

Of course, some gifts are impossible to wrap, no matter what you try. I once got a car for Christmas, and it was backed into my garage with a huge red ribbon across the windshield. Bicycles, jungle-Jims, and lawnmowers are difficult to hide behind paper.

What is the greatest gift you ever received? A diamond ring? A puppy? A new set of dinnerware? A special book? Try asking a kid. You'll get a myriad of answers, and sometimes from the same kid! I mentioned previously that we used to have a "Secret Sister" program at our church where the ladies would gift one another, anonymously, with little trinkets and cards and pray for her daily. I have to say, I really preferred being on the giving end, although I did receive some very nice and meaningful gifts. There is something about giving that causes us to feel warm all over. I think random acts of kindness would qualify here, too.

I wonder how God felt when He gave us His only Son as the greatest Gift of all? I actually think it was agonizing, especially in light of the reason He sacrificed His greatest possession. And it wasn't because we were being rewarded for something special we did. Oh, no. It was because of our sin, and that there was no other way for us to be forgiven, to be saved from eternal darkness. The Father and the Son were in on this together, from the beginning. Jesus didn't go kicking and screaming to the Cross…He went willingly. He did ask that if there was any other way, God would find it. But, He made sure His Father knew He was willing to go, if it was His will. I cannot even imagine the agony both Father and Son must have gone through. God gave us His own Son, the most extravagant gift, because of love. *"For God so loved the world that He gave His only begotten Son, that whosoever would believe in Him would not perish but have eternal life."* (John 3:16). So familiar, but just think about it. Could you give up your only child for someone, even one, who did not deserve such a gift? And yet, God the Father saw a dying world with no chance of reconciliation, unless...

We haven't earned it because we are nice, or we are born into a good family, or we have lots of money. We cannot even obtain eternal life through our own parents who may be pastors, or Sunday school teachers, or doctors or nurses. No, *"For it is by grace that you have been saved, through faith ~ and this not from yourselves, it is the* ***gift of God*** *~ not by works, so that no one can boast."* (Ephesians 2:8-9). It does not come to us in a pretty or delicate gift bag, wrapped up in coordinating tissue paper, but in an agonizing, blood-covered and horrendous package. A rugged Cross. It was the only way. The *"good and perfect gift, from above, coming down from the Father of heavenly lights..."* (James 1:17). We can't earn it, but we do have to open our hand, and our heart, and receive it. And then be sure to say "thank You!"

OCTOBER 28

MAGAZINE RACKS...

We have a few magazine racks in our home...one in the living room, in the bedroom, and in the bathroom. Well...don't you have one in there too? I try to keep the bathroom rack stocked with a variety ~ home decorating, hunting, food (!?), a few children's books, and a devotional book or two. Let me tell you, this stash gets pretty neglected. Some of those magazines are pretty old ~ like years! And dusty. Ugh!

It's kinda like that at the doctor's office, too. Outdated and well-perused magazines, puzzles all done, coupons, recipes, and articles ripped out...but there is usually a variety for all tastes and interests while we wait. There have been a few times when I have even asked if I could take a magazine with me, and bring it back next time I come in! (And, yes, I have brought it back, unless they just tell me not to worry about it!).

Reading materials. They are everywhere we go. People stand in grocery lines and read magazines, tabloids and booklets. They pick up the newest advertiser or real estate listing booklets. There are cushy chairs in book stores, along with a coffee nook, so we can be comfortable while we read. We want to keep up with the latest issue of a favorite author.

There is one Book that is never outdated. And though it is the oldest book ever, its contents never go out of style. Valuable information, right up-to-date for today. It gives us direction, wisdom, confidence, comfort. Love. But sometimes, sadly, it collects dust.

Wisdom from Joshua 1:8 tells us, *"Do not let this Book of Law depart from your mouth; meditate on it day and night, so that you may be careful to do everything written in it. Then you will be prosperous and successful."* There's John's account of the miracles Jesus did, in John 20:31, *"But these are written that you may believe that Jesus is the Christ, the Son of God, and that by believing you may have life in His name."*

Unlike old books, some of which are classics and may even go into a second or third printing, and after time will fall apart, turn to dust, and be forgotten, the Bible has survived since it was written, first painstakingly copied and the scrolls stored in clay pots, then as it became a printed book, has been translated, revised and re-printed down through the ages. It contains important information. Some Bibles have been discovered and preserved as far back as the 4th century and are kept safe in museums. You will find a large family Bible on the coffee table in many homes, or a small purse or pocket-size for convenience in carrying. The Bible can now be downloaded into Kindle, or the fancy smart phones, and other modern technological devices which I know nothing about! You can read the Bible on your computer screen. And listen to it on CDs.

Unlike other books or magazines, the Bible is the Holy Word of the Living God. And we have not yet had the freedom or privilege to read it taken from us. But just in case, let us proclaim, like David, *"I have hidden Your word in my heart that I might not sin against You."* (Psalm 119:11).

OCTOBER 29

WHEN EVERYTHING'S GONE WRONG...

What a week! Made a bank deposit last week, then got a letter a few days later from the bank saying that one of the checks I listed on the back of the deposit slip wasn't included. So, they deducted that amount from my deposit. They didn't add the checks when I sent them through the tube in an envelope? They gave me a receipt for the whole amount, however. So, the next day I went to the bank and told the "senior personal banker," who looked to be 17, exactly step by step how I KNEW the check was in the envelope with the rest, and he said this kind of thing was very rare, but assured me they'd do a search, and I should hear from someone within a day or two. I made sure he knew the check HAD to be in the bank somewhere. So, this morning I called (four days later) to follow up and he said, "Oh, they found the check and added it back in ~ the next day!" And yet, I hadn't heard that. I am just shaking my head...

I tried making a mortgage payment over the phone yesterday, and when the automated voice came on telling me the company had been taken over by another, and I didn't have the right account number (but a new one had been assigned to me!) and gave me the new phone number I could call...I knew it was not going to be a good day.

So, later yesterday morning, I called the hospital about a bill I don't think we owe, left over from the therapies my husband went to after his stroke, and after obtaining all my information confirming I was who I said I was, the billing agent told me she couldn't access that information for me because of the privacy act. I argued with her that I was indeed his wife, I am the one who drove him to therapy three times a week, and I am the one who wrote the checks for each co-payment. And, that in fact, I have been his wife for almost 44 years. Yet she wouldn't give me any information without his signature stating I could have access to it. I am ashamed to say, the volume in my voice went up and I wasn't talking in a very nice tone. So within 30 minutes of hanging up from that call, I called back, hoping to get the same woman on the phone (which I didn't), but the one who answered looked up the account number so she could see who processed the first call and was very gracious to accept my apology and said she would be sure the agent got my message. And she was astonished I called back with an apology.

Last night my husband called me from another town (he'd been driving a charter bus and had to stop to stay the night), saying that he threw his back out loading/unloading luggage. He didn't know what to do, but was in very much pain. I suggested a hot, then cold, shower, and maybe someone from the hotel could drive him to an Urgent Care for some muscle relaxers, so he could at least drive the bus home in the morning...and he has more trips scheduled for the next few days!

Does it seem sometimes like the trouble never ends? We just get through one crisis, and another occurs? God's word must have something to say about this…

Jesus Himself said, "*…In this world you will have trouble. But take heart, I have overcome the world.*" (John 16:33). There are many examples of people throughout time who have had troubles of some sort, some of them more than their share. Moses lamented to the Lord about the Israelites, for *years*. Jonah got himself into trouble and God had to bail him out ~ literally. With Job, it was one unbelievable thing after another, with no break in between. And there are many more…Joseph, Paul, Judas, even Jesus. There was a song several years ago, "Through it All" with a line that said, "if we'd never had a problem, we wouldn't know that God could solve them, we wouldn't know what faith in His word could do." That's true, isn't it? If we just went along day by day without any hardships at all, why would we need God? Our afflictions are a reminder that we do need Him, every day.

I realized that people are watching how I handle the troubles that come my way. Sometimes I realize that too late, like when I yelled at the lady on the phone who was only doing her job. It was the Holy Spirit who was prompting me to call back and apologize. And the woman who answered was so gracious, I knew it was the right thing to do. God cares about what we care about. No one promised our lives would be trouble-free, but our heavenly Father assures us that He will be right there to pick us up when we fall down, to forgive us when we do or say the wrong thing ~ even if it's *just* an attitude!

Paul asks us, *"Who shall separate us from the love of Christ? Shall trouble, or hardship, or persecution, famine, nakedness, danger, or sword?…No, in all these things we are more than conquerors through Him who loved us."* (Romans 8:35, 37). Wow. We CAN get through our hardships. Tomorrow is another day. And Jesus will be right there beside us, "through it all." *"The Lord is a refuge for the oppressed, a stronghold in times of trouble."* (Psalm 9:9).

OCTOBER 30

TEAPOTS AND TREASURES…

Well, some teapots ARE treasures. I have quite a large collection, and some of them are quite unique. One in particular is from Jericho, Israel, and has the design of a mosaic floor (from the Church of the Loaves & Fishes) on it. I have two others that were wedding presents (almost 44 years ago), and at the time I wasn't using teapots but put them away in a cupboard anyway. My thought was, "someday when I'm old, I'll probably use them!" Seriously. I really thought that. Well, now I am, and I do!

I sold tea and teaware for a few years, and I learned a lot about tea, teapots, infusers, the origin of "high teas" and many other things. One thing I appreciate about tea is how healthy it is, and in fact some teas are used for medicinal purposes. Isn't it wonderful how the Creator furnished us with natural remedies for many of our illnesses? There is one tea grown in South Africa so high in anti-oxidants it fights free radicals, lowers blood pressure, soothes stomach pains, aids in weight loss, and even calms colicky babies, among other things.

Teapots we use are made of ceramic, china, metals, or blown glass. Earlier teapots were made of a red clay found in England, and in the 17th century were unglazed. These teapots, called the Brown Betty, are still being made in the same place, and are popular because they hold in the heat much longer. Many of us simply fill a cup with hot water, or heat it in our microwaves, and drop in a teabag. Of course, the best teas are loose teas, made with water brought just to boiling, and brewed in a pre-warmed teapot. It can be enjoyed with ceremony, with a friend or alone. I love having a cup of tea early in the morning when I am studying God's word. I truly treasure these times. My "cuppa" creates an atmosphere of relaxation, and makes me thankful for the quiet moments, for many things ~ life, family, health, abundance.

Webster defines "treasure" as: "any person or thing that is considered very valuable; to value greatly; cherish; accumulated or stored wealth in the form of money, precious metals, jewels, etc." God's word says, in Matthew 6:19, *"Do not store up for yourselves treasures on earth, where moth and rust destroy, and where thieves break in and steal. But store up for yourselves treasures in heaven…for where your treasure is, there your heart will be also."* You see, my treasure in my early-morning ceremony of tea and scripture isn't the tea itself, or the pot or cup, but my time with the Lord and the truths I learn from Him during my reading and prayer time. This is most valuable. Paul had it right when he wrote his letter to the Colossians: *"…that they may be encouraged in heart, and united in love, so that they may have the* ***full riches*** *of complete understanding in order that they may know the mystery of God, namely Christ, in whom are hidden* ***all the treasures*** *of wisdom and knowledge."* (2:2-3). How else am I going to discover this "mystery" unless I dig deeply into His word? And hide it in my heart…

And so, I cherish my quiet time, my cup, or pot, of tea, and give thanks every morning for the treasures I can call mine, realizing that they could be taken from me at any moment ~ my precious family, enough food to eat, a bed to sleep in, a church to worship in, and the living Word of my God, written and preserved just for me, to teach me, and affirm God's never-ending love for me. That's the treasure!

OCTOBER 31

BE STILL AND KNOW…

"Be still and know that I am God; I will be exalted among the nations, I will be exalted in the earth." (Psalm 46:10). David was saying here that no matter what was happening all around, in the face of wars and desolations, and trouble of every kind, God's people could know that God is God. There are times when we may wonder where God is, or if He's paying attention. We cry out to Him, demanding that He answers us, inquiring why we have to go through the fiery trials, sometimes daily. We rant and rave, don't we? We question and doubt. We are so caught up in our troubles. But God says, *"Be still and know…"* He says, "Listen…" There are certain answers to our problems that we wish for. But God alone knows what is the best for us. *"His ways are not our ways."* (Isaiah 55:8). *"Be still…"*

Can you hear a butterfly as it flits by? Can you hear the sound of the snowflakes as they gently fall? Has your gaze fallen on a deer as it stands quietly in a field, or have you stood beside the ocean and watched the waves flow in and out, rushing with enough force that no one could hear you if you spoke? Do you think of God at these moments? This time has also been called "spiritual serenity." Are you listening? Psalm 48:9 says, *"Within Your temple, O God, we meditate on Your unfailing love."* And later, David prays, *"Let me understand the teaching of Your precepts, then I will meditate on Your wonders."* (Psalm 119:27).

At times, we may not think that God is answering our prayers quickly enough. Our trouble seems to be an emergency, at least to us. We do all we can to fix the problem. But I think God wants us just to drop our hands, relax, and listen to His still, small voice. We are sometimes too frantically running around looking for the solutions, when He already has the resolution at hand. Do we say to Him, "Lord, I know You are in control…" but then try to take control of the situation ourselves?

I love to have my "quiet time" each morning when I can open God's word and focus on what He has to say to me. This is a time when I can "be still" and listen for His voice. I love reading in the Psalms, if you haven't figured that out by now! I love David's heart as He seeks to *know* God. *"I have hidden Your word in my heart...Give me understanding... How I love Your law! I meditate on it all day long...I have more insight than my teachers, for I meditate on Your statutes...I gain understanding from Your precepts...Great peace have they who love Your law, and nothing can make them stumble."* (Selected verses from Psalm 119). We find David pleading with God many times, but we also see him pondering, being still, being quiet, meditating on what God would say to him.

OK, you say, but how can I "hear" God in the clatter and rush of everyday life? If I try to get some time alone early in the day, something, or someone, always comes up to get my attention. Your quiet time doesn't necessarily have to be in the morning. I find I can enjoy a quiet time while I'm sitting in my back yard listening to the cheerful language of the many birds who come to feed on my fence. Even with the traffic going by on a main street so close to my home, I can concentrate on God's creation. I can sense God's presence even while planting flowers and bulbs. The secret is to *still our hearts*. There may be much turmoil in our day, and many demands on our time, but with the peace that God gives, "the peace that passes understanding," we can be still. We can know that He is God in, and of, all things. It is not a self-made confidence, but a peace that is ours because of what we know about God.

"May the words of my mouth and the meditation of my heart be pleasing in Your sight, O Lord, my Rock and my Redeemer." (Psalm 19:14). There are many things that we could meditate on, worry about, allow to consume our thoughts and emotions, but we will find a calming presence when we bring God's word to mind. What better way to "be still?"

NOVEMBER 1

DARKNESS...

I am typically up real early in the morning, around 5am, sometimes earlier. This is a good time for me to have devotions and Bible study, the quietest time of day. This morning it just seemed to be so much darker than usual. We had a beautiful clear sunny day yesterday, and so it just seems very dark, in contrast. I went to the window several times, expecting it to lighten up a little, but it remained dark. Just a few minutes ago, I began to hear a cheerful voice, that of a happy robin, welcoming the dawn. So, I know it is coming…light.

Jesus said, *"I am the Light of the world. Whoever follows me will never walk in darkness, but will have the Light of life."* (John 8:12). But sometimes the darkness is all-consuming. We cannot find our way through it. It may be actual darkness, in the middle of the night, or it may be the darkness in our soul that seems to consume our thoughts. Either way, it is the absence of light. It can be frightening. We cannot find our way. But Jesus has been there. He has brought the Light into our darkness. And He wants us to be light in a dark world as well. He said, *"In the same way let your light shine before men that they may see your good deeds and praise your Father in heaven."* (Matthew 5:16).

Of course, the enemy of our soul would have us stay in darkness, and not find our way to Christ, or Life everlasting. He confuses our mind and lies to us. Too often we believe him, and he goes away very satisfied leaving us in turmoil. But Jesus has overcome the world, He has triumphed over all difficulties and has overwhelmed Satan, who would try to lead us away from Him, and He gives us a reason to rejoice! *"In the world you will have trouble, but take heart! I have overcome the world!"* (John 16:33). So when it seems too dark to find our own way, let's just slip our hand into the nail-scarred hand of Jesus, and He will lovingly lead us through.

NOVEMBER 2

UNANSWERED PRAYER?

"Evening, morning and noon I cry out in distress and He hears my voice." (Psalm 55:17). But why, we ask, doesn't God answer? We pray, we cry out, "without ceasing" but it seems that nothing is changed ~ in our situation, in our health, our relationships…we wonder, why does God only answer some prayers, and not others? We alternate between hope and despair.

Unquestionably, God's will is sovereign, and this is true with our prayers as well. I've heard it said that "God answers every prayer, sometimes it's yes, sometimes no, and sometimes ~ wait." Just because our prayer is not answered in the way we think it should be, or how we believe is best for those involved, doesn't mean our faith is not strong enough or that we have failed somehow. Many times our prayers are selfish, even though we are praying for others, and for noble things, like the salvation or healing of a loved one. Did you ever think of what would happen if ALL our prayers were answered? There are some of our prayers God doesn't answer for our own good. And do you think sometimes our prayers might be answered at someone else's expense? Like, we win, but they lose?

Pastor Jerry Sittser says, in Today's Christian magazine: "Strange as it may sound, we need unanswered prayer. It is God's gift to us because it protects us from ourselves. If all our prayers were answered, we would only abuse the power. We would use prayer to change the world to our liking, and it would become hell on earth. Like spoiled children with too many toys and too much money, we would only grab for more. We would pray for victory at the expense of others; we would be intoxicated by power. We would hurt other people and exalt ourselves."

I admit, I've never thought of it in this way before. Oh, I know God has His reasons for not answering our prayers as we pray them. *"His ways are not our ways."* (Isaiah 55:8). We have no idea what is around the next corner or down the road. We don't even know if we'll have tomorrow. So, in some ways, unanswered prayer is for our protection. It can transform our lives, for even though we may feel disillusioned because of past prayers left unanswered, or seemingly so, they also prepare us, just as the refiner's fire, for the answered prayers yet to come.

"I waited patiently for the Lord; He turned to me and heard my cry." (Psalm 40:1). He does hear us. Let's learn to trust Him for the answers. His ways are best.

NOVEMBER 3

THE QUILT...

Well, I've done something I never thought I would EVER do...I designed a quilt pattern. I've been quilting less than two years, but have made about 16 in that time. I guess some of them have been my own design, but this one is different. When I was in Israel in January, I took a picture of an ancient mosaic floor, beautifully preserved after excavation, and my first thought at seeing that little floor, which was about 5 or 6 feet square, was what a beautiful quilt that would make. Of course, it was constructed with tiny half-inch tiles, and it was very faded, but it has the most interesting collection of shapes: squares, triangles, and parallelograms, as well as a huge Gordian (Celtic) interwoven knot dead-center. And though the colors were muted, I determined that it was done in blues, creams, rusts, golds, with some black...as were a lot of the mosaic floors in Israel.

I looked at my picture many times, wondering if I could pull it off. I studied it, tried to think how I would design the pieces so they would fit together, and then, wondered how in the world I would actually sew it together without instructions! One day, I decided to bite the bullet and try to draw the pieces. The knot was the most difficult, and I looked for a pattern in dozens of quilting books in all our fabric stores, and online, but didn't find the exact shape I needed. And the measurements had me stumped. Finally, I got out my pencil, a ruler, and some paper and began to draw lines. It became very frustrating. Ultimately I should have gotten down on the floor on that ancient mosaic with a measuring tape and gotten all the correct sizes of the shapes, but it was not allowed! I began cutting out the pieces, all I thought I would need, then made markings on each one as to how many I would need of that particular piece, allowing for the seams on each piece, and sort of laid them out on the table to see how they would fit together. I was too nervous to purchase fabric until I had it just right. This is where I dragged my feet.

Suddenly, an idea came to me that I would take the picture and all my pieces to my brother, who is an engineer, and could put my design on his computer so that all the pieces would be precision-sized and sure to fit together. Oddly enough, my center knot came together the easiest. I ended up using a cup and a bowl to get the right angles of the curves I needed! My brother worked on the pieces in his spare time for a few weeks, and finally gave me the computer-generated pieces so I could get started. Unbelievably, only two of my original pieces were ½-inch off on one side! I shopped for the fabrics I wanted (be assured I did not sew together tiny little squares of material to get the mosaic effect, but I bought fabric of prints that *looked* like a mosaic design!). That was the fun part. Oh, now I was anxious to get started. But of course, since this was not a pattern I acquired from someone else, or a book, I had no idea of how much fabric I needed in each color. (I did buy a little too much, but better than not enough).

Do you see how much work it is to design, or create something? We have architects who design many huge buildings, bridges, city parks, monuments, and they all take careful planning, and sometimes an idea comes together only after several people are involved in the brainstorming. There are fashion designers, landscapers, and chefs, who are always striving for just the right lines, styles, or cuisine. A lot of planning and work goes into just about everything we have ~ the homes we live in, the cars we drive, the clothes we wear, the dinners we serve. And it all takes time.

I love that God, in His infinite wisdom, created the whole world and everything in it, in just six days, including a man and a woman. Every plant, every type of food, each animal and insect, the landscape of the Garden, the hours in the day, seasons throughout the year, the rain and snow, moon, sun and stars, the rainbow. And each one of His created items serves a purpose, and has characteristics that no other has. He could have had billions of years to sit at His drafting table with pencil and paper and design each of these intricate objects, erasing and starting over, as we do. But my Bible says He spoke it all into being. *"And God said, 'Let there be light...Let the land produce vegetation...and living creatures...and God saw that it was good.'"* (Genesis 1). God spoke it all into being.

"Then God said, 'Let us make man in our image'...so God created man..." (vs 26-27). Now, God and His Son could have discussed what the man should look like, how he should function, and think, and live, but God just ~ spoke it! We have no idea how He did this, but the fact is, He did. Instantly. He is God, after all. It's interesting to me that when mankind is reproduced, He designed that process to take a certain amount of time for the growth and development of the human body, a baby. The plants that grow to produce our food and the flora we enjoy, take time; the same with the animals. And all of these, from humans to plant life, need nurturing in order to grow. He thought of everything, but it was all put in place at the beginning.

So, back to my quilt. I think God gave us imagination and creativity, each of us in her own way. Some are musical, others have talents in crafts, teaching, wisdom, nurturing ~ and each of us is created in His image. I am trying to create a quilt in the image of a floor I saw in another country. It's a lot of work, and taking me a long time. God knew just who He wanted me to be, and put into my being all I would need to become that person, from the beginning. I am so thankful, because I know His eyes are on me at all times. I am His creation. He cares so much how I turn out!

NOVEMBER 4

GOT TIME?

Oh, this is a big item! We are always talking about time. There are songs written about time…we complain we don't have enough time, or we have too much time on our hands…we have quiet time, time out, daylight savings time, time off, time keepers and Daytimers… but do we remember that God is the Creator of time, and that we all have exactly the same amount of it ~ every day? Jesus said, *"Who of you by worrying, can add a single hour to his life?"* (Mt. 6:27).

Ecclesiastes chapter 3 talks about the seasons…

"To every thing there is a season, and a time to every purpose under the heaven" (vs. 1). I love this passage. And of course, the tune to the popular 60's song "Turn, Turn, Turn" is going through my mind as I'm writing this.

How do we spend our time? Our day, our week…our year? The Word also tells us that *"the time is short."* (1 Cor. 7:29). And oh, my ~ look at this warning from Jeremiah… *"A curse on him who is lax in doing the Lord's work!"* (vs. 48:10).

So, how we spend our time, the 24 hours each day that we are given as a gift, and each minute is critical. I'm not saying that we must wear ourselves out doing God's work 24-7. But we must always be ready to do what He calls us to do, to look for and be available and prepared for opportunities to glorify Him. Yes, we must rest, as well. But even in our rest, we can be in an attitude of prayer, we can be involved in meaningful and helpful conversation. God just doesn't want us to be lazy or idle when there is opportunity to serve Him… Jesus said, in His great prayer before His arrest, *"Father, the time has come. Glorify Your Son, that Your Son may glorify You."* (John 17:1). There is coming a day when time will be no more. Let's use what time we have with utmost wisdom.

NOVEMBER 5

WHERE ARE THE RIGHTEOUS?

"The Lord said (to Abraham), 'If I find fifty righteous people in the city of Sodom, I will spare the whole place for their sake.'" (Genesis 18:26). God had had it with the people of Sodom. It was filled with wickedness. The people had given in to

their sinful desires and their sin had become grievous to the Lord. It broke His heart. He planned to destroy the whole city. Can you imagine it? An entire city wiped out because of their sinful practices.

So Abraham began to beg of God that He would spare them. God gave a number ~ fifty. If He could see that there were at least fifty people who were righteous and God-fearing, He would not destroy it. Abraham somehow knew there weren't that many. He began bargaining with God, back and forth with the numbers, until they came to only ten. God agreed that if there were even TEN righteous people in the whole city of Sodom He would not destroy them. A sad commentary, indeed.

I have often thought of this story while praying for America. "Surely Lord, there MUST be fifty righteous people in America that you would spare her!" Of course, there are many more people in America than there were in Sodom in those days…I think. So, to even things out a bit, maybe we could plead that the Lord could find a mere fifty-*thousand* righteous men in America. I know there are Christians in every town who are praying for our nation. But the men and women who are running our country and our government seem to be far from fit…and certainly not righteous. Where are these Christians? Are we on our knees pleading for America, as Abraham appealed to God, to save us?

It's sobering to think that God could wipe out our beloved nation just as He did Sodom… *"Then the Lord rained down burning sulfur on Sodom and Gomorrah ~ from the Lord out of the heavens. Thus, He overthrew those cities and the entire plain, including all those living in the cities ~ and also the vegetation in the land."* This isn't beyond imagination. He did it. He kept His word. Why do we think that we should be spared? We, as a nation, have reached rock bottom, and only God can pull us out of the pit. I continue to pray for America, that God will have mercy, send us new leaders, and bless us once again. What happened to Sodom could certainly happen to us. Let's turn America around before it's too late for us!

NOVEMBER 6

THE PRIVILEGE OF PRAYER…

Do you look at prayer as drudgery, or as a joy? How many times have you promised someone you'd be praying for them, then forget and never do? Is it the first thing you want to do each morning, or does your day get started and run away from you before you get a chance to stop and pray? I have always known I needed to pray, I should pray…but it's something I had to learn to do. God's word tells us to pray for one another. There are many examples of Jesus' praying, and He even prayed for us! In fact, He gave us the prime example of how we should pray in the Lord's Prayer. (Matthew 6:9-13).

There are many types of prayer we utter throughout the day…prayers of thanks, prayers for healing, emergency prayers for protection, prayers for a loved one…the Word also tells us that we should "*pray and not give up.*" (Luke 18:1). We sometimes offer up a quick and hurried prayer as we're rushing off to our day, or as we fall into bed at night, realizing we haven't prayed all day… other times we agonize in prayer, not even knowing the right words to say… *"In the same way the Spirit helps us in our weakness. We do not know what we ought to pray for, but the Spirit Himself intercedes for us with groans that words cannot express."* (Romans 8:26). What a beautiful picture this is… He takes on our own agony (once again) even as we are praying.

There was a song a few years ago titled "Somebody's Praying Me Through" and the words made an impact on me, especially where it says, *"Pressing over me like a big blue sky, I know someone has me on their heart tonight, that's why I know it's gonna be alright, 'cause somebody's praying me through…It may be my mother, it might be my dad,* ***or an old friend I've forgot I had****, but whoever it is I'm so glad, somebody's praying me through…"* Because of these words, I began praying for an old friend from school now and then, or someone I haven't thought of in years, and especially when I wake up in the night with someone's name or face on my mind, or if their name just "pops into my head" during the day, I know I should pray for that person. So many times we wonder, "hmm, where did THAT come from" but dismiss it and think nothing more of it. It could be a very important prompting from the Holy Spirit that the person needs prayer right at that very moment. How exciting to hear later of an answer that came just at the time we were praying. Or, we may never know…but what a simple and loving thing to do, to pray for the person on the spot. What a privilege! And here's a sobering thought…we may be the only person praying for that one. I am so blessed to know that many are praying for me, and have been throughout my lifetime.

Don't miss it! This wonderful privilege of prayer. The opportunity to call on the Maker of the Universe, boldly, to access His great mercy and grace to us…

NOVEMBER 7

JEALOUSY…

My favorite dictionary writer, Noah Webster, defines jealous as: "watchful in guarding or keeping; resentful suspicions of a rival or rival's influence; demanding exclusive loyalty; resentfully envious."

From the time we are little and we first realize someone has something we don't, we are jealous of them and want what they have. This could be a toy, a spoon, a bottle…then in the teen years, it seems to escalate when we become jealous of friends ~ we want *our* best friend all to ourselves and to not share her with anyone else. This is also when we notice other girls' clothes, and the fact that some dress nicer than we do; they are able to buy the best name brands. Or, they get the cuter boyfriends. Or better grades. Then, as we "mature" we become envious of others' cars, the job they were able to secure, their talents, the perfect husband and home. It's when "keeping up with the Joneses" comes into play.

God said, in Exodus 20:5: *"You shall not bow down to them [meaning other gods or idols] or worship them; for I, the Lord your God, am a jealous God…"* Do the things we are jealous of become gods to us? God tells us not to be jealous, yet…this is a perfect example of the definitions "watchful or guarding or keeping" and "demanding exclusive loyalty." God does demand our loyalty if we are to be called His children. And He watches over us constantly, protecting from the evil one. Here's a thought I found yesterday…

Are violets jealous of gardenias?
Do maple trees compete with eucalyptus trees,
or redwoods with oak trees?
What do they know of jealousy or competition?
We are all magnificent expressions
of God's exquisite garden.
We are extraordinary
just the way we are.
© 2009 by Fanny Levin

"I will give thanks to Thee, for I am fearfully and wonderfully made; Wonderful are Thy works, And my soul knows it very well." ~ Psalm 139:14

Our life is a gift from God. He placed us right where we are, in the family we're in, the economic situation we're in, the home, job, health situation, for His purposes and to glorify Him.

Lord, help us to realize just how special we are in Your eyes, and not to feel any less because someone else appears better in *our* eyes!

NOVEMBER 8

TEDDY BEARS...

They are soft, cuddly, and comforting. Most children have one, or two... Teddy bears are the perfect gift for a baby shower, or a sick child. It really doesn't matter how many they own, a Teddy bear is always a welcome gift.

Hospitals seem to have plenty to go around in their pediatrics wards. When my grandson, David, was born, he was air-lifted to the medical center in a neighboring town that had an exceptional NICU (neonatal intensive care unit), and the helicopter crew gave him a Teddy bear... I think these were the cute "skinny" ones supplied by the Hershey & Target companies. David was newborn, and really didn't know he received a Teddy bear, until later, and now that he is 12, he still considers that bear a special friend.

When I became a grandmother for the first time, 22 years ago, I began collecting Teddy bears. At first, I bought one just to have at our house "for the grandkids." Somehow, I accumulated many more, and even collected the Cherished Teddies line ~ the last of those I purchased was a set of the Nativity bears. And of course, I put these out for the grandkids, and they like to re-arrange them when they are in my home around the holidays. I even found a Teddy bear full of rice and/or barley which you can put into the microwave to heat up for warmth. Sometimes I warm him up for the kids to sleep with when they spend the night. And there are the books about bears, too, the ever-popular Three Bears, and one of my very favorites, Corduroy. We even have a Christmas book about gingerbread bears! And songs have been written about them.

What an invention, the Teddy bear. It began when President Theodore Roosevelt was on a bear-hunting expedition, but refused to shoot a bear that had been trapped, and this bear was later referred to as "Teddy's bear." A cartoon was drawn of the event, and soon after, someone began making toy bears, here, as well as in Germany, in the early 1900's. They became popular very quickly, with women and children. Who knew? Now we find them literally everywhere. Some dressed, some with bows. My daughter makes jointed bears out of pretty calico fabric or children's prints or flannel for every baby she knows being born to friends or family. They are treasured gifts. Little girls love to invite them to their tea parties, read to them, and pull them in wagons.

But no matter how cuddly they are, or how much we can talk to them and tell them our troubles, which children tend to do ~ as they are actually wonderful playmates for lonely children ~ we have a Comforter who truly does hear our woes, and who really does care. I Timothy 5:7 says, *"Cast all your anxiety on Him because He cares for you."* And in Psalm 55:22, *"Cast your cares on the Lord and He will sustain you; He will never let the righteous fall."* Jesus cares for us so much, that He took the punishment for our sins and gave His life ~ because He loves us. And He is available to anyone and everyone. It doesn't matter if a person is homeless, or has everything they will ever want. Jesus is for everyone. He is there when you are sick, or lonely, or just need someone to talk to. He will hear your secrets, and dry your tears. Snuggle up on His great lap and He will wrap His arms around you, any time of the day or night, no matter where you are.

NOVEMBER 9

INTO THE STORM...

How many of us would go rushing headlong right into a storm? Well, I guess there ARE people called "storm chasers" who are fascinated with storms, especially tornadoes, who follow them around on purpose, either out of curiosity, or for educational and tracking purposes. But it's not a "normal" thing to want to do. In fact, when a storm is coming, we usually try to take cover quickly, if we are able to, and if we receive ample warning.

But sometimes the storms of life catch us unaware ~ they come upon us suddenly. Often we bring them upon ourselves, and others happen because of some outside influence. Nevertheless, they cause us turmoil. Matthew 8: 23-27 tells a story about *Jesus and His disciples who had gone out in a boat on the Sea of Galilee, when suddenly a severe storm came up and threatened to capsize their boat. The disciples cried for Jesus to save them, and He commanded the winds to still, and all was calm. He chided them for their lack of faith.* [My paraphrase]. Some of the storms we face could be disease, death, loss of employment, loneliness, accidents, catastrophe, loss of our life savings…we sometimes ask, in dire circumstances, why this has happened to us? Or to someone else. If we have been walking with God, leading a good life, we wonder how God could have allowed this "storm" to happen to us, or to them? When these storms of life come crashing down around us, it is very frightful and painful. But what can we do to fight off these winds of adversity, to keep afloat through the troubling waves. We need to do what the disciples did that day, to call out to Jesus to save us.

Sometimes Jesus does send us right into the storms of life ~ we will never know why, and in our limited minds we cannot reason how this could be good for us. But as the darkness closes in around us in the midst of the storm, where do we look for shelter? Whom do we reach out to? Whom do we call upon? Jesus. He will help us soar above the storm. Sometimes He seems silent as our storm rages on, and it may seem that He is unaware of our crisis. But, know that He IS aware. He is much more powerful than the raging wind and rain. His disciples asked each other, *"What kind of man is this? Even the winds and the waves obey Him!"*(Matt. 8:27). We have no reason to fear the storms that come to us, some more severe than others. As long as we are walking with Him, He will strengthen us and He will deliver us from the storm of death and hell. He did that already with His precious life's blood. We can weather all the storms of life by holding onto His mighty hand. God is the faithful anchor of our souls. Our lives are held by Him with an unbreakable chain secured to the heart of God. He will hold us on the raging waters of our life and lift us with His love. *"He reached down from on high and took hold of me; He drew me out of deep waters."* (Psalm 18:16).

NOVEMBER 10

THE ANGELS WATCHING OVER US…

It's winter, and when you live in the mountains, there are always mountain passes to drive over to get from one place to another. In winter months, these passes, most of them, are invariably covered with snow and ice. Although they are well-maintained for traffic, sometimes the snowfall just gets ahead of equipment and they can't keep up.

This weekend my son-in-law and a friend had to make a "quick" trip to southern Idaho to pick up the personal effects of the friend's deceased son, who was attending college there. One of the best routes is through Oregon, over the Blue Mountains. They had to stay on the north end of the pass overnight because the highway had been closed, but were able to continue on their way the next morning. They could see why the pass was closed...there were accidents all over the place, including some jack-knifed semi trucks, one hanging over the edge near the river, and sadly, a U-Haul truck carrying a family's household possessions, flipped and torn open, spewing all their belongings everywhere. The boys made it to Boise okay, but on the way back, later that afternoon, the same stretch of road was covered (again, or still) with many accidents, one of which they almost became involved in. Although it wasn't snowing at the time, the highway was covered with black ice.

I had been praying for a safe trip, knowing they would not have the best of road conditions. Also, this weekend, my husband made a charter bus trip to Seattle, which involved driving over Snoqualmie Pass, another one notorious for horrible conditions in the winter. Just the day before it had been closed to traffic. Very frustrating for commuters who are already there and have to sit in their cars and wait for them to open it up again. Still, I was praying. My husband called when they arrived near Seattle, and said they had made it over the pass with no trouble ~ the road was bare and wet. Wow! (I always tell him my prayers work)!

God's word says, in Psalm 91:11-12, *"For He will command His angels concerning you in all your ways; they will lift you up in their hands, so that you will not strike your foot against a stone."* And then in verse 14, *"'Because he loves Me,' says the Lord, 'I will rescue him; I will protect him, for he acknowledges My name.'"* I am convinced that God's heavenly angels are protecting us, hovering over us as we go along our way. Oh, but we do need to use common sense, for sure, in our travels.

God's angels have been watching over us since the beginning of time, almost...in Exodus 23:20 He told the Israelites, *"See, I am sending an angel ahead of you to guard you along the way and to bring you to the place I have prepared."* And David, while singing praises to the Lord for His goodness, declared, *"The angel of the Lord encamps around those who fear Him, and He delivers them."* (Psalm 34:7).

It isn't that God is too busy, or not capable of watching over all of us at once, but there have always been angels, all throughout time. God's Messengers. I think God just wants to keep them busy!

NOVEMBER 11

KEEP MY FOOT FROM SLIPPING...

"My help comes from the Lord, the Maker of heaven and earth. He will not let your foot slip ~ He who watches over you will not slumber..." (Psalm 121:2-3). God keeps us out of harm's way daily. If we are tuned in to Him, He will guide our steps, our words, our actions. They say that when a farmer plows his field, he should focus on a point in the distance as he's pushing his plow. If his eyes veer off from that point, his rows will become crooked. I think it's the same for us, as we walk this path called life. If we focus on God and His word, we will be able to stay on the straight and narrow. If we are distracted, we may end up in all different directions and lose our way, or stumble off the path, and sometimes into the ditch.

This morning as I was walking my dog, before dawn, of course, I noticed how very slick the sidewalks and roads were. They looked almost dry, but had a thin coating of sheer ice over them (frozen fog, I suspect). Instead of turning around and going back (because I didn't want to disappoint my dog, for goodness sake!) we walked our mile, Dog just prancing along, me gingerly taking baby steps. I found myself praying along the way "Lord, please don't let my feet slip on this ice, because I really can't afford to break something!" Well, here I was asking Him to protect me on a path I shouldn't have been walking on anyway. How presumptuous of me. But my Father heard and honored my prayer anyway, and we made it home safely. And, yes, I did thank Him for keeping His hand on me the whole way.

I know that when David wrote this prayer, this Psalm, he was used to walking and hiking the hills in Israel, which consist of very uneven ground, and covered with many rocks and boulders. I visited Israel 12 years ago and again recently, and this was one of the things I noticed about the countryside ~ it's covered with rocks, many the size of baseballs, basketballs and bigger. How hard it must have been to walk that terrain in sandals, or even barefoot. And although most of the mountains where sheep are tended do not seem that steep, still, if one were to step wrong, or slip, he could cause great injury to a foot, leg or ankle. David knew that God was watching over him, and keeping him safe as he tended his sheep on those rugged hillsides. And I knew that God was watching over me this morning as I was walking on the ice. I normally don't put myself in danger of falling like that. Usually I turn around and go back in the house. But, the dog…she was so happy to be going for her morning walk. I probably could have thrown her ball a few times in the street in front of the house, then gone back in. (I'll think of that tomorrow!). But God knows I am a human, and don't always make the right decisions.

So, as I was walking, the words to a song by Aaron Shust were going through my mind…the lyrics, in part: "You watch over me in the darkest valleys, you watch over me when the night seems long. You help me to see the way before me, You watch over me, You watch over me…always faithful to be leading, at this moment interceding for Your children. Though I've wandered astray from your infinite ways, You've never left me alone ~ You watch over me…" God honors our prayers, and He will keep our foot from slipping if we keep our focus on Him. Oh, I know, the pressures and frustrations of life, the pain and sorrow, crowd in on us, when nights are long…but His eyes are on us…always.

NOVEMBER 12

OUR UNCHANGING GOD…

"I the Lord do not change." (Malachi 3:6). There we have it, straight from the Lord's own mouth. And again, from James (1:17) *"Every good and perfect gift is from above, coming down from the Father of heavenly lights, who does not change like shifting shadows."*

Aren't you glad that we can put our trust in God's word, and that it is dependable and eternal? Constant. Imperishable. Unfailing. Like His love for us. His word will never change to fit in with man's plans or desires. It's the same yesterday, today and forever. His Holy Living Word is like no other book on the face of the earth. God has never changed His mind or His thoughts on what is contained therein. There has never been an updated version of His word or His laws. Oh, men have tried to adjust or modify the meaning of the

Bible by writing their own books with the Truth slightly twisted. (Not talking about the different translations here, which are still the Holy Bible intact).

But, I believe sinful and greedy and proud men (and women) feel that the laws and the direction from the Bible do not fit in with their chosen lifestyles, so they try to change it so it's more comfortable for them. They may even try to add ideas from other religions, making sure there is just enough scripture to make it seem believable. They are too proud to bow down to a holy God.

We can depend on God to be the one who loves us, even when we are unlovely. His way is gentle, yet He has a way of burning inside of us until our thoughts and motives are pure. And He will not let us go until the work of the cross is finished in us. *"All Your words are true; all Your righteous laws are eternal."* (Psalm 119:160). The words that were spoken or written to the ancients, through a burning bush, from a mountain top, through a donkey, and to a bunch of awe-struck shepherds on a hillside, still ring true today and are just as powerful and life-changing as they were long ago. Life-changing for us from a never-changing Savior.

NOVEMBER 13

ARE YOU SATISFIED?

In our society today it seems that the more we have, the more we want... of everything ~ money, time, clothes & shoes, electronics, vehicles, food... you name it, we want it. We "collect" everything. Don't you sometimes wish for the simplicity of the "old days" when children actually made up games to play ~ outside? And recipes were simple and nourishing dishes we could make with our stove, not needing all the new modern equipment (which didn't exist then, anyway!). We spent our evenings reading books or playing board games with our families. We mended our clothes rather than throwing them away or donating them to charity so we could buy more. I've even heard of women who made clothes out of flour sacks – imagine! And if we had more than we could use, we gave it away to those more needy than we were.

Well, I do like the variety we have these days, but it's really hard to keep up with the Joneses, if that's what we're trying to do. I know for me, it's impossible, even if I were trying. For one thing, I wouldn't have room in my house or garage to actually store all that "stuff!" And I wonder where in God's word it says that we should strive to have what everyone else has...I haven't found it. But I did find this, written by that wise man of old, Solomon...a prayer to his heavenly Father, *"Keep falsehood and lies far from me;* ***give me neither poverty nor riches, but give me only my daily bread****. Otherwise, I may have too much and disown you and say, 'Who is the Lord?' Or I may become poor and steal, and so dishonor the name of my God."* (Proverbs 30:8-9). Yes, I really believe that could happen. We would have so much and be so comfortable with our luxuries, we might come to feel we did it all ourselves, and that we don't need God. I'm not against people working hard to have the necessities of life ~ the Bible teaches we should do that. But the Word also says, "*You shall not covet."* (Exodus 20:17) It goes on to say exactly what things we should not covet. It's quite a list.

I'm a big one on counting my blessings. I may look at someone who is very healthy and wish I could be like them ~ pain-free without taking meds, and able to move about better, but then I'll see someone who cannot move much at all and is suffering much greater pain than I, and I have to be thankful for the health that I do have. I can say with Paul, *"for I have learned to be content whatever the circumstances. I know what it is to be in need, and I know what it is to have plenty. I have learned the secret of being content in any and every situation, whether well-fed or hungry, whether living in plenty or in want. I can do everything through Him who gives me strength."* (Philippians 4:11-13). It is the secret to living a satisfied life...living so close to our heavenly Father that we will give Him the glory for everything we have. He wants to bless us, and He already knows what we need before we ask Him. And to ask Him is to glorify Him.

NOVEMBER 14

SEND ME, LORD...

"Then I heard the voice of the Lord saying, 'Whom shall I send? And who will go for us?' And I said, 'Here am I, send me!' " (Isaiah 6:8). Have you ever said that? "Lord, send me?" It's kind of scary. You wonder what you would be committing to... spending your life as a missionary, leaving your family and friends for some faraway place. Do you realize the Lord doesn't actually have to SEND us somewhere, to some remote part of the earth, in order to serve Him and be used by Him for His purposes? God touched Isaiah of old, and cleansed him from his sin, and then sent him to repeat His words to the people. Isaiah was

willing. Now, God probably won't use an angel with a hot coal to touch and purify your tongue so you can speak for Him. He uses our willingness and obedience in ways we would never think of. He uses us just the way we are.

Four years ago, I asked God (several times) to show me how He could use me. I didn't once think that He would send me to Africa. But when the call came for me to take part in moderating an online group for women, it didn't take me long to tell God, "yes!" After all, I had been praying about that, and I knew that although I would have to write devotionals each week, if it was something God was leading me to do, then He would be the One to do it. I would just be His "vessel." I didn't question this "appointment" or doubt whether I was "qualified" to do it or not. Actually, I was not qualified, and I'm still not, but God qualifies us when He calls us to do something outside our realm of expertise. God will not ask us to do something, or go somewhere, that He will not empower us to do. I know this. The words I write for this women's group are not my words, but spoken through me from God's great heart. He is aware of a woman, or women, who will need to read the specific message of the day.

We can all be used by God for His high purposes. He speaks His communication to those who will listen, those who are on the same level of *neediness*. I marvel at the words that flow into the posts as His great plan unfolds into our lives and hearts. Our lives are an offering. This group of women is our mission field, everyone we meet is needy. Our own story is part of God's plan. Many times we'll have failures, and setbacks, and we can't imagine how God could use us as we are. But God, in His great mercy, redeems our brokenness and puts us back together again. When you say, "here I am, Lord send me," His plan will develop and He will reveal clearly what it is He wants you to do for Him. And we will not be alone ~ He will be right by our side as He "commissions" us to go forth and do His work. There is nothing more rewarding than knowing you are valuable and useful to the God of the universe. He will restore our confidence, and faith in Him by working His wonders through ordinary people like you and me.

NOVEMBER 15

THE DESK...

I recently, re-acquired a small student desk ~ it was the desk I had in my room since my childhood. Just a little desk with four drawers on one side. I don't even know where it came from originally, just that I always remember it in my room, no matter where we lived. It was my desk. I did my homework, read, studied and wrote letters while sitting at that desk. The drawers held my possessions ~ collections of pens & pencils, bottles of glue, stationery and letters received. When it was moved into my sewing room a few weeks ago to take the place of a small, narrow, not very functional, table, which I have sewn on for over 40 years, I pulled out a drawer to see my middle brother's name penciled in and the date he claimed it ~ 1968. The year I got married. He also inherited my room, and the desk stayed there until we moved it out a few years ago when my dad could no longer live alone, and we emptied the house. The desk then went to my young granddaughter, who now has inherited another grandmother's desk. So, my little desk has come full circle now. It will be more serviceable than the simple table I've used all these years.

Oh, we have several desks in our home...my husband, years ago, bought a big oak roll-top desk, and when we bought our first computer, we needed the classic computer desk, with the compartments for printer and paper, etc. We also have a small antique secretary-type desk that belonged to my husband when he was in school, where we store crayons and paper for the grandchildren. And, a little one-piece steel and wood children's school desk I noticed on the sidewalk in front of an antique store years ago.

The desk, in some form, has been in existence almost since the beginning of time, I think. At least, from Bible times. Whether it was an ornate desk or just a large table, the scribes needed someplace to write out the many scrolls we've found over time. I'm sure the ancient astrologers needed a place to spread out their charts as they watched the stars and planets each night. Then when printing shops, libraries and post offices came into being, the desks were specially designed to hold many drawers for filing and storage. Some desks were "standing" desks, like a podium. Now, you can get just about any type of desk, for any need or profession.

I've just been wondering what kind of "desk" God Almighty will use to display the huge books into which all of mankind and all our deeds have been recorded, since the Creation. (Revelation 20:12), *"And I saw the dead, great and small, standing before the throne, and the books were opened. Another book was opened, which is the book of life."* I believe this will be our "roll call."

I ran across the title of a book, "Your Desk, God's Altar," which, I believe (since I haven't read it) is an encouragement for women in the workplace to be able to look away from business to the cross. Its aim is to encourage us in our work with an eternal perspective. I thought about this for a time.

What kind of work do we undertake at our desks? Is it frivolous? Serious? Do we read, write, play games, pay bills and correspond? I do all of those. And sometimes I eat my lunch there. But, sitting at my desk in the early morning light, with a hot cup of tea, and reading God's word is how I like to start my day.

You may not have a desk. Maybe you have a favorite chair in which to curl up and enjoy a book. (I have one of those, too!). Or perhaps you pay your bills at the kitchen table. Not many of us write real letters anymore in this day of email, texting and Facebook, so our laptop is used for communication. Some people who commute use their car's dashboard or front seat, or the trunk as their desk. I've seen these ~ not very conducive to keeping it all organized! I was always fascinated by the teacher's desk. *Usually* very organized, equipped with clever little containers for pens, pencils, chalks, interesting books ~ always a dictionary! My mom had a built-in desk that took up a whole corner, surrounded by bookshelves to the ceiling. It was her haven. She loved writing letters, reading, keeping the books, and she was created to be organized.

Well, I think I'll go putter at my new, old, desk which has now come home to me. It looks good with my sewing machine sitting on top if it! I have all kinds of little sewing notions to put away into the drawers! A place for everything and everything in its place!

NOVEMBER 16

GOD NEVER MEANT....

In the beginning, God created a perfect world. *"God saw all that He had made, and it was very good."* (Genesis 1:31). And He created man in the perfect image of Himself, and placed him, and a perfect woman, in a perfect garden. (Genesis 2). He gave only one restriction. Just one. And suddenly the Creator's flawless, immaculate world became tarnished. The beautiful Garden had become infected with sin and the Father had to turn the man and the woman out. He had to. They had broken fellowship with Him. They had everything they could ever dream of or wish for. What a life! The impeccable home, delicious food ~ all they desired. And fellowship with the Living God.

The Creator never meant for man to sin, to turn his back on Him, or doubt Him. He never meant for the man and the woman to suffer as they did because of their act of disobedience. He had given them a warning. They didn't believe it. Are we like that? Of course we are. We are descendants of Adam and Eve, whether we like it or not. We inherited their bent to sinning.

God never intended nations to be at war with one another. He never meant for illnesses to strike this human race. He never purposed divorce to happen, or for children to be homeless. He created us perfect. He made the marriage relationship to be honorable. Sin ushered in deceit, disillusionment, doubt, selfishness and bitterness. Just look what we have done to His perfect world.

And then He provided a way to get around all that, to put it all behind us. He sent Jesus. Because of His great love for us, He paid the extravagant price so that we could be healed, and so we could forgive. After all, He forgave us when He went to the Cross. And just as Joseph said to his brothers when he was nearing the end of his life, for all the things they had done to him, *"You meant evil against me* ***but God meant it for good****..."* (Genesis 50:20). Satan will throw everything he can into our path, into our face, into our comfortable lives, to trip us up in our walk of faith, and yes, bad things will happen to us, no matter how closely we walk with the Father. Job is an example of this. Being righteous is no guarantee we will not have trouble. But God is there to lift us up and stand us firmly on solid ground again. *"He makes everything beautiful in its time."* (Ecc. 3:11). And His name is glorified in it.

NOVEMBER 17

LOOKING BACK...

Looking back is just something we do...automatically. When I was growing up my dad was a Navy man, and we got transferred a lot, which meant moving across the country. And when we'd pull out from our house, our street, our town, my friends, I would always look out the back window of the car with tears in my eyes, watching the familiar disappear. Reminiscing is another form of looking back...we think of how things used to be, how our lives were, collectively, when times were a lot simpler. Prices were lower, quality was higher, merchandise lasted longer. Most of us have good memories of our childhood, and we find ourselves sharing these memories with others, and it warms our hearts to think of past events and talk about them. We also find ourselves looking back behind us when we are walking on a dark street ~ hoping no one is following ... personally, I try to stay away from these kinds of situations. These are the kinds of scenes you see in movies. And then, usually around New Year's, newspapers will take a look back at all the biggest stories of the year. And I sometimes take a look at my high school yearbooks familiarizing myself with a person I'm remembering.

I love historical novels. Since I wasn't there, it is interesting to me to look back at times when life was simpler, and the people actually had more time for each other. Some of their struggles I can identify with, others I couldn't imagine going through!

Often, we look back with regret...we are sorry for things we have done in our past, things which have shaped our lives in the present, and for the future. There are circumstances we haven't been able to do anything about, we haven't been in control of, which have deeply affected us. Isaiah 43:18 says *"Forget the former things; do not dwell on the past..."* Also, in Isaiah 65:16, at the end of the verse, *"For the past troubles will be forgotten and hidden from my eyes."* God doesn't want us to dwell on our past failures, or disappointments. He doesn't. Dwelling on the past can cause us to believe very negative things about ourselves, and it's a trick of the enemy, who will pull up our past in front of our eyes to condemn us and to make us believe we are worthless. But God has given us new life, forgiven our past sins. Paul said, *"For everything that was written in the past was written to each of us. So that through endurance and the encouragement of the Scriptures we might have hope."* (Romans 15:4). In the Scriptures, there are many stories of people with horrible pasts, but God has changed them before our very eyes, and they joyfully go forward with renewed strength and hope in Him. These are examples of His grace that we must apply to our own lives.

Know that God created you for His purpose. He knew you before your very day of creation. Each day of your life was planned out, and your life had identity, meaning and purpose. So everything that has happened to us in the past is for a reason, but we must learn from it and move ahead. God wants us to become what He created us to be, in spite of, or because of, what we see when we look back.

NOVEMBER 18

HOLY, HOLY, HOLY...

There are so many things called "holy" in the Bible. Mostly they are items or places associated closely with the Almighty God. Objects or locations where His presence blessed, or dwelt, to be considered with awe. I just returned some months ago from Israel, the "Holy Land," as it is called, because God actually dwelt there, in person. With all the governmental unrest and hostile uprising that seems to have been going on forever there, we wonder just how holy the land really is. From the very beginning, when God had created the earth and all that was in it, *"God blessed the seventh day and made it holy, because on it He rested from all the work of creating that He had done."* (Genesis 3:3). And when Moses "noticed" the burning bush in the desert and went to investigate, God called to him and said, *"Take off your sandals for the place you are standing is holy ground."* (Exodus 3:5). Then later, God speaks to Moses again, commanding him to observe the Sabbath *"as a sign between Me and you for the generations to come, so that you may know that I am the Lord, who makes you holy."* (Ex. 31:13). So ~ we can be made *holy*? God said it. Again, the Lord says to Moses in an exhortation of laws He's been giving him, for His people, *"Consecrate yourselves and be holy, because I am the Lord your God. Keep My decrees and follow them. I am the Lord, who makes you holy."* (Leviticus 20:7-8). There is it again.

All through the Bible we read about the holy scriptures, God's holy hill, the holy temple, His holy Name, a Holy God, and the holy city. We were a little amused when visiting some places in Israel, and noticing that the people, shop-owners, still call a place "holy..." such as "The Holy Bagel," and the "Holy Rock Café." I highly doubt these places are actually holy, as God is holy. They're just capitalizing on a theme, perhaps.

In I Thessalonians 4:3, Paul says, *"It is God's will that you should be holy"* [or some translations say 'sanctified' which means 'set apart'] ...and vs. 7, *"For God did not call us to be impure, but to live a holy life. Therefore, he who rejects this instruction does not reject man, but God, who gives you His Holy Spirit."* We often think it is impossible for a human being to be holy. But if God said it is possible, and in fact He requires it and expects us to be holy, then it must be possible. I would never consider myself holy. But God sees me as holy ~ He has set me apart. I am His. After all, He says, *"Be holy because I am holy."* (I Peter 1:16). And then

His word, the Holy Bible, proceeds to tell us and show us just how that is to be done. It stems on obedience to His word, His law, and accepting His never-ending love and compassion through His Holy Spirit. We could never do it on our own. The only thing that makes it possible is the unbelievably humble sacrifice He made on the Cross.

If we come to Him in faith, believing that indeed, He can make us holy, then we will not only hear the angelic beings in heaven singing *"Holy, holy, holy is the Lord God Almighty, who was, and is, and is to come,"* (Rev. 4:8) but we will join in and sing it with them!

NOVEMBER 19

GLORY AND HONOR...

"When I consider the heavens, the work of Your fingers, the moon and stars which You have set in place, what is man that you are mindful of him [her]? The son of man that you should care for him? You made him a little lower than the angels, the heavenly beings, and crowned him with glory and honor." (Psalm 8:3-5). Did you get that? HE has crowned US with glory and honor! And just how do we glorify and honor HIM with the life He has given us? Oh, dear ~ it seems that I may be just about ready to open a huge can of worms here...

Every single day we read or hear on the news that more war and fighting is going on around the world, and right here at home, some in our own cities. Men (and women) are greedy and selfish, mostly for power, and this comes right down to our homefront ~ our very homes, if you will. We all have heard of unrest in churches and schools, and yes, in our own homes. Why do we think there is so much divorce? So much child abuse and neglect? When we are supposed to be nurturing our children and teaching them God's truths (as the Bible admonishes us) we instead are giving them everything they want (if we can afford it!...or even if we can't) instead of the valuable hours and minutes of our time, instructing them, and showing them God's love. Oh, I know there are many who do not realize this ~ many parents who are not church-goers or Christians. But here's the shocking news ~ many ARE. But parenting is not an easy thing. It's very frustrating in today's world with so many outside influences at school, work and truly, on TV.

Well, I didn't mean to get off on a tangent here, but I just want us to remember, God had a plan for families when He created us. And of course, we blew it early on. We are not God's only creation meant to give Him glory and honor. I looked at the dark clear sky early this morning and saw a sliver of moon, and the huge face of Venus shining brightly, and I had a sense of awe at how these objects are always right where they were hung in the very beginning. The clouds and sunsets take our breath away. The way some trees sway and flow in the wind, and yet others stand firm, hardly moving. How the flowers poke up out of the dirt, spring after spring, on their own, as they were designed to do from when time began. The song of each bird, and even insects (I love the crickets, don't you?), the howl of the wolf and coyote, the sweet meow of a kitten. I saw a peacock the other day, just wandering in someone's yard, and this is one of the most magnificent birds in the world... so much detail in each feather! Each one of these creatures gives glory to God because they do what they were created to do. We were all created to praise Him in our own way. Our voices were given to us to sing and shout and exalt Him.

When I think of how much I DON'T deserve the honor and glory He has bestowed on me, I try to imagine how pleased and excited the Maker was when He was creating me. How He made me so different from anyone else, how He chose my eye and hair color, my personality, and then He breathed His Spirit into me. Each one of us was created in this way. He took the time and the initiative to make each one of us as He desired. And yet, we are dissatisfied with ourselves, and with each other. We are always trying to change ourselves, and others. Let's leave that up to the Creator. Let's be who He made us to be. We are important enough to Him that He bestowed *glory* and *honor* on each of us by making us in His image. That doesn't mean we are God. He is still in control ~ otherwise this awesome universe would fall apart. He gave us Jesus as an example of how we should live. And love. And if we follow the instructions put down in the Instruction Book, the Bible, His glory and honor will show forth from our lives, and we will in turn be glorifying and honoring Him as we were created to. We need to take a little time each day to notice His creation, to see others as He sees them. And be thankful.

NOVEMBER 20

COUNT YOUR BLESSINGS...

I know I've spoken of this before, but it's important, especially at this time of the year when we are thinking of what we should give thanks for. Remember the little song we sang in church years ago, "Count your blessings name them one by one, count your blessings see what God hath done…?" Well, there's something to that I've never forgotten. And I do try to count my blessings each day, even through the hard times. Even for one thing. I thank Him for little things, and for the big things, for things that some of us don't ever observe. The fact that I can rise up in the morning and put my feet on the floor is huge to me. A new day. Rest through the night. Eyesight to see His beautiful creation. Good health. So many times we complain ~ I have found myself complaining about something almost every day. And God has big shoulders, He can handle anything. But shouldn't we first be thankful for everything he has given us? James 1:17 says, *"For every good and perfect gift is from above, coming down from the Father of lights, who does not change like shifting shadows."* God gives so much to us, but many times we don't even look for it, or notice it. But if we look for the blessings He gives, the things that trouble us will diminish.

Oh, I'm sure every one of us has blessings that come our way every day in one form or another, but we get so busy and caught up in the "stuff" of life that the end of the day comes finding us exhausted and barely taking note of our blessings. And some of them are barely noticeable. I find that I LIKE to look for little things that I can thank Him for…living in a land like America, (well, that's a BIG thing), having the freedom to worship in the church of my choice, the blessing of family and watching young grandchildren grow and learn, beautiful sunsets, stars in a black sky, seeing nature up close and personal as the deer wander through my yard every night, a car that runs well, fresh water I can help myself to all day long, friends, so many things we tend to take for granted.

What can you count today as blessings in your life? No matter if every day is the same, over and over again, or there are new adventures that come our way, view everything as coming from God's hands. Sometimes there is profound blessing in our sufferings, too. So don't think that because you have hardships, God is not blessing. He will show you in His time in ways you could never fathom *"the depth of the riches of the wisdom and knowledge of God!"* (Romans 11:33). And remember, in your hardships, you may be a blessing to others who know you.

"And I pray that you being rooted and established in love, may have power together with all the saints, to grasp how wide and how long and how high and how deep is the love of Christ, and to know this love that surpasses knowledge ~ that you may be filled to the measure of all the fullness of God." (Ephesians 3:17-19). This is the greatest blessing.

Count your blessings today!!

NOVEMBER 21

FRIENDS AND FAMILY...

"Jesus said, 'Go home to your family and tell them how much the Lord has done for you, and how He has had mercy on you.' " (Mark 5:19). This was, of course, after Jesus had delivered the demon-possessed man, who then wanted to follow, to go with Jesus. Jesus sent him away with a message. Sometimes, the most important audiences are those who are closest to us.

My husband and I were blessed to visit family members on vacation recently, spending a week with them. It was wonderful to share with them how God has been working in our lives, providing for us through our struggles. We rejoiced with each other, and prayed together, as well as doing some wonderful sight-seeing. On our way home we were able to attend our church's annual conference, and meet up with old friends, and we even made some new ones. When you share meals and free time with one another, conversation often goes right to "life," and how life is treating us. We share our experiences and struggles with one another, and we encourage each other in the Lord. It can be so helpful to share our experiences with others who may be encountering hard times as well. And as we share what God has done for us, faith is strengthened on both sides, and hope is reborn. Sometimes potential problems can be solved, even before they become problems, by sharing God's blessing with another person.

Although I missed my own church, we attended our relatives' church for two Sundays, and then the final Sunday service in our conference, and how encouraging to hear another's perspective on God's word, and know that it is the same as yours! And to get acquainted with others we haven't met, and realize God's people are the same all over.

I can imagine what Paul felt when he traveled around the Holy Land, speaking and instructing in the different churches, meeting old friends, and making new friends, sharing what the Lord had done for him. He shared many things about his suffering, his illnesses and incarcerations, the brutality…but he sought to build up the faith of the believers through his ordeals. He told some *"Therefore encourage one another and build each other up, just as in fact, you are doing."* (1 Thess. 5:11).

And, of course, my children are the first ones to hear of any miracles in my life, and yes, there have been many. I want them to know what God does for their parents, and it is our responsibility to share these things with them, and teach them, and build their faith. David prayed, *"Since my youth, O God, You have taught me, and to this day I declare Your marvelous deeds. Even when I am old and gray, do not forsake me, O God, till I declare Your power to the next generation, Your might to all who are to come."* (Psalm 171:17-18). I see miracles, small and large, every day. I am so grateful to God for each one of them, even some that may be unnoticed and unknown by others, I just have to tell others what God has done for me. God gave us family and friends ~ they are gifts. I care so much about their spiritual welfare, I can't be silent…

NOVEMBER 22

FREE GIFTS…

Some businesses offer free gifts to get you to come and shop in their establishment. Years ago we had a tire company who used to offer "free beef" if you bought tires there. It was an annual special offer, and I guess the more you spent on tires, the more beef you got.

My daughter and I went to the Mall on Saturday and stood in line for a few minutes to receive a free gift to kick off the holiday shopping season. We actually got a $10 American Express gift card apiece. Who can't use $10? Free. Well, if that wasn't enough, there was a grand opening of a new store and they were giving free morsels of their goodies, and free coffee and milkshake samples.

My husband will receive a free turkey next week from the company he works for, as an appreciation gift for his service. We receive offers in the mail for free gifts if we order.

We all love free gifts. But there is one free gift that we are sometimes hesitant to accept. That is the free gift of God's salvation, and His grace. *"For the wages of sin is death, but the gift of God is eternal life in Christ Jesus our Lord."* (Acts 6:23). Why is it we are so hesitant to reach out and take this one? Gosh, who wouldn't want a gift like that? Well, lots of people, I'm afraid...because they don't understand, I guess. It seems absurd to some people to be given a gift like that with no strings attached. Actually, there are a few, but all God asks of us is to follow Him and let Him be Lord of our life.

Some of us think we have to clean up our lives ~ our habits, our language, our friendships and our pastimes ~ in order to come to Christ. Paul told the Ephesians, *"For it is by grace you have been saved, through faith ~ it is not from yourselves, it is the gift of God ~ not by works, so that no one can boast."* (2:8-9). God gave us the gift of His Son, a priceless gift, His life's blood, shed freely so we could possess that eternal life.

During this season of gift-buying and -giving, let's remember the greatest gift of all, Jesus. We don't even need to go shopping for this one. It's free. But it's not a gift unless we receive it.

NOVEMBER 23

TRADITIONS...

I love traditions, old and new. These are the customs, beliefs and practices of people, individually or as a group or family. I think most families have certain traditions for certain holidays, and times of the year. I take comfort in them. They are familiar. Since our children were born, we have gone camping over Labor Day weekend at the same campground, and we still do...now we take their husbands and children...it is looked forward to every year with much anticipation.

And since we are coming into the Christmas season, I'll have to mention some traditions my family has had. Each year my mother would make "Scripture Cake," (I have mentioned this before, but must include it here) and after our dinner she would light candles on it and the small children (kids and grandchildren) would all sing Happy Birthday to Jesus, and then blow out the candles. When my brothers and I were little, our parents would always let us open one gift on Christmas Eve, after our dinner and baths and we were ready for bed. What an exciting night! And when my husband was growing up, his father would always read the Christmas story from the Bible, Luke 2. Of course, we left our stockings up, somewhere, even if we didn't have a fireplace, and made sure we put out cookies for Santa.

Some people take drives around their town to look at the lights, make a special annual shopping trip together to a large mall near them, the sledding trip the day after Thanksgiving to the nearby sledding hill. Some have cookie exchanges, or the telling of a story repeated every year, tromping through the snow in the woods in search of the perfect tree, or a certain recipe used only at Christmas. Some families fill up a box for the Christmas child program, to be shipped to third world countries where children do not have Christmas gifts. We have done this. As we began our family, and the girls were growing up, we started some new traditions just for our family...and were surprised when our children passed some of them along to their own families, as well as making their own. Some of the old ones are still being passed down, however. And they are important to teach our children, so they know something of their heritage.

Some traditions warm our hearts, bring memories, and make us stronger. There are others that are harmful, though. Paul said, to the Galations (1:14), *"I was advancing in Judaism beyond many Jews of my own age and was extremely zealous for the traditions of my fathers."* He was so zealous, in fact, that he would harm and persecute the Christians and the ministry of Jesus. His experience with Jesus, however, turned him away in the opposite direction from the religious traditions his fathers and grandfathers had passed down through the generations. And unbeknownst to Paul, many of his positive practices and attitudes have been passed down many, many generations. Why not adopt some new traditions in our families, or for ourselves that will glorify Jesus, and begin passing them down to our children and grandchildren?

"Since my youth, O God, you have taught me, and to this day I declare Your marvelous deeds. Even when I am old and gray, do not forsake me, O God, till I declare your power to the next generation, Your might to all who are to come." (Psalm 71:17-81).

NOVEMBER 24

THANKS GIVING...

"In everything (in all circumstances) give thanks, for this is God's will for you in Christ Jesus..." (I Thess. 5:18).

This week we will celebrate Thanksgiving all over America. And we do have so much to be thankful for. I'm afraid we all tend to take so much for granted...our freedoms, our easy access to God's word, and to worship, so much opportunity we wouldn't find in other places. It's a time when we stop and count our blessings, and all the good things God has given us.

But why do we take only one day a year to celebrate His goodness? Shouldn't thanks giving be a daily attitude? In addition to the holiday once a year when we reflect on His gifts, shouldn't thanks giving be the daily tone of our very hearts? Oh, yes, we learn to say "please" and "thank you" to each other, and even to our heavenly Father, but do we thank Him in every situation? It doesn't mean we like some of the situations we find ourselves in at times, or even that we are thankful FOR them, but God's word says to be thankful IN every situation. Thankful for the watchful eye of the Lord as we are going through a rough time, thankful for the wisdom and knowledge we will gain from the experience of learning to trust Him, for His protection, His provision. We grow stronger with each experience because we learn to go to Him earlier and earlier as we grow in His grace and experience His mercy.

This Thursday, as we gather with our families and friends to express all we are thankful for, let's strive to keep that feeling of gratitude in our hearts for the rest of the year. Pray that thankfulness will become part of your being, and that it will come easy for you. After all, God gave so much for us. It is a gift. We should be thankful.

"Let us come before Him with thanksgiving and extol Him with music and song. For the Lord is the great God, the great King above all gods." (Psalm 95:2, 3).

NOVEMBER 25

NOT AS PLANNED...

Have you ever had a day which didn't go as you had planned? I think we all have. My day was like that yesterday. We had invited several others to join our Thanksgiving feast, and everyone was excited for the day to come, but as it got closer, it became doubtful they would show. The weather and bad roads had a lot to do with it. And it's OK, I'm flexible. Just because some people I had planned on joining us didn't come, it doesn't mean my day was ruined. Far from it. The plans were just changed, slightly. We still had a marvelous meal (with way too much food), much fellowship, the kids behaved, the baby was delightful. What can I say? It was a great day.

Many times we make plans for a special day, or a special trip or visit, and we think we have it all mapped out, but then something happens to trip us up. It may be just a little glitch in the menu, or the schedule, or maybe someone has taken ill. There might have been an accident, or burst water pipes, or the truck breaks down...a disaster that is beyond our control. It is good for us to be flexible, and not depend too much on our own plans. God said, *"Surely, as I have planned, so it will be, and as I have purposed, so it will stand."* (Isaiah 14:24). Well, it works for Him, you might say. Of course it does, He is God, after all. But if we are so sure of our plans and how our day, or our trip, or our meeting, or our marriage, our *life*, will go, then we are setting ourselves up to be sorely disappointed. We cannot really trust in our day, or in other people, who often change our plans for us. But we can trust in our heavenly Father, who has a perfect plan for each one of us. He says in Jeremiah 29:11, *"For I know the plans I have for you," declares the Lord. "Plans to prosper you and not to harm you, plans to give you a hope and a future."* We can trust that.

Robert Burns said, in his poem "To a Mouse," ~ "The best laid schemes of Mice and Men oft go awry, And leave us nothing but grief and pain, For promised joy!" And, basically, what that means is to go ahead and make plans, but always have a backup plan, a Plan B. Life is full of surprises, and disappointments, turns in the road.

Proceed with your plans, but include God in those plans. In fact, it would be good to consult Him before we finalize our plans. *"Commit your way to the Lord, and whatever you do, your plans will succeed."* (Proverbs 16:3). Sounds like good advice to me.

NOVEMBER 26

THANKFUL FOR SO MUCH…

We feasted Thanksgiving Day, and we were happy and warm. My family was all around. We had plenty to eat. Good fellowship ~ no one was irritated at another. The kids all played well together. They exhibited good manners. And it felt good to share our day with our elderly neighbor who lives alone, and her son who drove 500+ miles to be with her this week. We thanked our heavenly Father for His provision.

When I think about how blessed I am, I cannot even imagine why. We have so much to eat, and will eat several more meals with the leftovers from our banquet. When I smell and taste our food, I pray for those who have none. We gathered together, friends and family, and enjoyed such sweet fellowship, laughter, merriment, but many are alone, living under a bridge, or in a shelter. Or alone in their own homes, widows, single moms, a lonely man who has lost his wife. Even some of the people we sit near on the pew in our churches are terribly alone, but we don't know it. We can look forward to a paycheck, or a reasonable facsimile, when others don't have a dime to their name. We are cozy and warm in our homes, with light and comfort, and others are cold. It shouldn't be so, but it is. How often do we pray for them? I regret to say I don't pray enough.

Proverbs 21:13 says, *"If a man shuts his ears to the cry of the poor, he too will cry out and not be answered."* Do we dare think we can ignore those less fortunate than us? God's word admonishes us to take care of the poor, and the widows and homeless among us. What better way to show God's love? Even the Proverb's 31 woman cared for the poor… *"She opens her arms to the poor and extends her hands to the needy."* (31:20). Jesus was homeless and poor, and I'm sure he was cold and lonely at times. The Son of God? Yes ~ He came as a man, in the flesh, so He could experience all we experience. There were some who ministered to His needs, and many who did not.

I think that now we are in the season of giving and it would be fitting to bless others as God has blessed us. There are so many areas where we could help ~ charities, the food bank, Toys for Tots, Coats 4 Kids, Angel Tree, Operation Christmas Child, soup kitchens, making ourselves available to drive an elderly person to an appointment, gifting of homemade bread, or a pie, or even just a phone call. We are blessed beyond measure when we begin counting. I can never get to the end of my list!

"Give and it will be given to you. A good measure, pressed down, shaken together and running over, will be poured into your lap. For with the measure you use, it will be measured to you." (Luke 6:38). God has given SO much…could we just give a little in His name?

NOVEMBER 27

THANKSGIVING IS PAST…

But is it really? We had a wonderful Thanksgiving day, a big feast, friends and family gathered and fellowshipped, and collectively, we gave thanks. We have MUCH to be thankful for ~ the freedoms we enjoy, plenty to eat, warm homes, a baby's new smile, laughter…and some are not as fortunate as we. I thank God every day for the little things I used to take for granted. When we were working we could obtain almost whatever we wished for. Now that we are not working, it's hard to even come up with what we need. But, God is so faithful to supply and meet our needs. I feel rich in His grace, as I've never felt before.

We put away all the leftovers, loaded and emptied, and re-loaded the dishwasher, put away extra chairs, and all is cleaned up once again. I have three sleeping grandchildren who spent the night and all is quiet. I am blessed beyond my imagination. And then I read *"Therefore, since we are receiving a kingdom that cannot be shaken, let us be thankful, and so worship God acceptably with reverence and awe."* (Hebrews 12:28). We are commanded many times in scripture to be thankful. We should be thankful in the hard times as well as the good times. This is crucial for me. If I didn't thank my heavenly Father in the hard times, I don't think I would appreciate the good times. And we are already part of God's unshakable kingdom ~ that should be enough to be grateful for, if there was no other reason.

So, now that Thanksgiving Day is past, let us continue to be thankful, because God's blessings don't come only on this one day. And He doesn't tell us to be thankful only on this day, but every day, all year long. *"Give thanks to the Lord, for He is good. His love endures forever!"* (Psalm 107:1).

NOVEMBER 28

GONE BUT NOT FORGOTTEN...

Today is the anniversary of my father's passage into heaven. It's hard to believe it's already been 5 years. We were all gathered around him in the hospital. He'd had a rough year. Actually the past four years, since my mother's death, were hard on him. But after suffering a series of strokes that last summer, he couldn't go home again and lived with my daughter and her teenaged children. They took very good care of Grandpa, but he was still not happy. He just wanted to go home ~ both to his home in the quiet woods, with his dog, who now lived with my brother, and to his home in heaven, where my mom was waiting for him.

He spent one last Thanksgiving with us and did very well, ate a good dinner, took a little nap on the couch, joked a little, then was ready to go "home." Six days later, my granddaughter saw him collapse in cardiac arrest. The ambulance was called and he died three hours later in the hospital. He was "home" ~ finally. And I knew he and mom were preparing to have the best Christmas celebration ever.

We never know when it will be our time to go "home." We knew my dad was getting close because of his deteriorating health, but my mom was taken suddenly and we were shocked. James says, "*Why, you do not even know what will happen tomorrow. What is your life? You are a mist (a vapor) that appears for a little while then vanishes.*" (James 4:14). Only our heavenly Father knows our future and how many days we have left to live on this earth. One day I will meet my parents, and many other loved ones in heaven, and never be separated from them again. Until then, I must live as if this is my last day on earth. I will count my blessings, give thanks, EVERY day, and try to make a difference in someone else's life. My dad did.

NOVEMBER 29

LIFE IS BUT A BREATH...(JOB 7:7)

Thanksgiving was a beautiful day of celebration for my family. We had 17 family members around our dining table(s) and everyone thoroughly enjoyed the day. I am so thankful, and blessed.

The next day we heard some disturbing news; the husband of a now-forty-something former teen girl in our church suffered a massive heart attack on Thanksgiving Day. The doctors were doing all they could to save his life. The plea was put out for prayer and many old friends, and new ones as well, were praying for this young man. The medical staff were able to keep him alive a little more than a day. He died sometime that Friday night, leaving his dear wife and two children. Much too young for a heart attack, we lament. But, death is no respecter of persons or age. Each man, and woman and child, is appointed a time to die. We never know when that will be. *"Precious in the sight of the Lord is the death of His saints."* (Psalm 116:15). Our young friend was indeed a believer, and his family looks forward to the day when they will see him again.

Since we cannot plan when our own time will come, the best advice we can follow is to always be ready for that day, or that moment. We have no promise of tomorrow. We have no assurance of even the next hour. We must be sure to always be walking with the Master, our hand in His. And to take each day as it comes. Oswald Chambers said, "If God made your cup sweet, drink it with grace; if He made it bitter, drink it in communion with Him." And know that someday, sooner or later, we will be celebrating and dining with Him at that great wedding feast. May we say, with David, *"You have turned for me my mourning into dancing; you have put off my sackcloth and clothed me with gladness, to the end that my glory may sing praise to You and not be silent, O Lord my God, I will give thanks to you forever."* (Psalm 30:11-12).

Thanksgiving will never again be the same for this stricken family, although I know, because of their deep faith, there will always be thanks giving. And the hope that they'll see their loved one again. As Jesus said to His disciples in a discourse continued in John 16:22, *"Now is your time of grief, but I will see you again, and you will rejoice, and no one will take away your joy."* Even though Jesus was speaking to His followers on a certain day, I'm sure that all scriptures are included in the Book for our encouragement and to build up our faith. So, I believe this is a promise to us, as well.

NOVEMBER 30

THE COUNTDOWN BEGINS...

Now that Thanksgiving is past, the countdown to Christmas has begun as well. 23 days, more or less, left. In fact, stores have been decorating for Christmas since September. That seems to be rushing it a little to me. We really have countdowns in a lot of areas of our lives. Of course, when we were born, our parents were counting down the days until our birth. There is a countdown for the launching of a space shuttle. There are games, and other activities in which units of time are counted off. Or when you have a list of tasks to perform before your day is completed, you cross the items off your list ~ that's a sort of countdown.

The scriptures have a little to say about this, also…in Psalm 90:10 & 12, we read, *"The length of our days is seventy years ~ or eighty, if we have the strength… teach us to number our days that we may gain a heart of wisdom."* Of course, and I repeat, only God knows the exact number each one of us will live on this earth. In fact, the whole Bible is a countdown of life, from the very beginning, through the Creation and all through the many generations of tribes and families, all down through the ages…the wars, the miracles, the way God watches over His people…the counting down to the birth of our Savior, as well as the day He was crucified, and up to the very end of time, which is foretold in the last book of the "Book of books." Feels like we are coming to the end of that countdown.

Some countdowns are fun, and some are downright scary. If you're waiting for a surgery date, it can be quite frightful. If you're counting down to an awesome trip, the days can't fly by fast enough. But we can never guarantee that tomorrow will come. It is not promised to us. The coming of the "last day," however, is spoken of all throughout God's word. *"You do not even know what will happen tomorrow. What is your life? You are a mist that appears for a little while and then vanishes."* (James 4:1). The Bible tells us not to worry about tomorrow. We should do everything we can to live today to the fullest. *"But the day of the Lord will come like a thief in the night. The heavens will disappear with a roar; the elements will be destroyed by fire, and the earth and everything in it will be laid bare."* (2 Peter 3:10). Peter goes on to say in the next verse, *"Since everything will be destroyed in this way, what kind of people ought you to be? You ought to live holy and godly lives as you look forward to the day of God and speed its coming."*

I don't mean to be a prophet of doom and gloom here, but we must be aware that our time on earth could be very short. The countdown that was begun at the very beginning of time may come to a close for some of us, or for all of us, very soon. We must be walking and talking with the Savior so we are ready for that day. If you can make a difference in someone else's day, with a smile, an encouraging word, an act of kindness, in Jesus' name, then we, and others, can count down with hope to a blessed time in eternity when there will be no more countdowns.

DECEMBER 1

SO MANY DOCTORS...

Boy, it takes a lot of doctors to keep one well these days. When I was younger we had one doctor who did it all ~ the examinations, inoculations, delivering babies, surgeries, diagnoses ~ everything. But before long, the general practitioners began sending us out to specialists, doctors who studied and became experts in one particular area of health. So, now we see heart doctors, skin doctors, baby doctors, bone, allergy, arthritis, foot and hand doctors, a doctor for anything that ails you. I guess what brought on this way of thinking for me is that I just had my annual physical exam…well, part of it, anyway! The regular girl stuff, plus a flu shot, in the doctor's office, but now I have appointments for my mammogram, colonoscopy, bone density and since I've mentioned to my doctor that I really want some relief from the sciatic pain I've had for so many years, I now have an appointment for an MRI, then to see him again right after that. Possibly a cortisone shot or surgery may follow the findings. Another doctor. My head is spinning!

It sure seemed like health care was so much simpler in the "old days." The doctor would even make house calls. I don't know, but I think if one were to want to come to the house, someone in government somewhere would rule that it wasn't feasible. Maybe that's why they don't, although I have never seen a ruling on house calls.

When Jesus walked the earth, he was called the "Great Physician" because *"He went about healing every disease and sickness."* (Matthew 9:35). He made house calls. There was no cost to the ill person, no HMOs, the patient didn't even need to make an appointment. It was like Jesus just knew where they were, and He lovingly touched them, and healed them. It was an art He was skilled in, although He didn't need to go to 12 years of college to learn it.

Jesus was asked by the Pharisees, *"'Why do You eat and drink with the tax-gatherers and sinners?' And Jesus answered and said, 'It is not those who are well who need a physician, but those who are sick. I have not come to call righteous men, but sinners, to repentance.'"* (Luke 5:30-32). He cuts away the malignancy of our wounds, hurts, disappointments and resentments. He heals our relationships with tenderness. He makes us whole. He says, *"Come to Me."* (Matt. 11:28).

We need Jesus today more than ever. I just heard of two suicides here in our area, one a 49-year old family man and popular business owner, and one

15-year old. There will be more, we can count on it. And it seems people are more despondent around the holidays. We need Jesus. He is our Healer. He can restore our bodies, our spirits, our minds to wholeness because He is compassionate. *"And when evening had come, they brought to Him many who were demon-possessed; and He cast out the spirits with a word, and healed all who were ill in order that what was spoken through Isaiah the prophet might be fulfilled, saying, 'He Himself took our infirmities and carried away our diseases.'"* (Matthew 8:16-17).

I know not all will be healed on this earth, in this life. That's up to God. But we have the hope of heaven, where we will have *"no more death or mourning or crying or pain…"* (Revelation 21:4). That will be the ultimate healing. That's what I'm excited about! It's unimaginable.

DECEMBER 2

COMPASSIONATE PEOPLE…

It says in James 5:11 that *"…the Lord is full of compassion and mercy."* He is our example. And it is possible, no matter how difficult, to follow His beautiful example. I saw some people doing this the other day. And I was moved.

I have become a substitute teacher for our school district, just as a part-time, on-call job, any school, any age group. So far I had subbed at one of the middle schools a couple of times, but Wednesday afternoon I had the opportunity to be an aide in a developmental pre-school. This is the same pre-school my grandson David attended at age 3 when he was a little behind in his motor skills because of all the surgeries he'd had. My daughter and her husband raved about the school and how much they were helping him. He quickly gained these skills back, and continued on two years as a peer in the classroom. Then my two younger granddaughters attended there as peers, as well.

On Wednesday I saw firsthand examples of the compassion the teachers and aides had for these precious little ones. The children (ages 3-5) had varying handicaps, some emotional, some physical. There was one little Downs girl I just wanted to eat up! One little boy cried and cried when his mommy had to leave him, and she talked so quietly and soothingly to him, but still he cried for about an hour after she left. The teacher, and other aide, instead of getting impatient with him, took time to comfort him and work with him…finally he entered into play with the others and was happy the rest of the time. His mommy and the teacher took the time together to think back to what might have triggered this behavior, and came to the conclusion it started when there was a terrifying fire drill two weeks before.

I saw other teachers and aides out on the playground with these little ones, all of them patient and kind with each one. I thought to myself, "these are very special people" who can come day after day and work patiently, sometimes without success, with these little precious handicapped children. What an opportunity to show God's love and mercy, and how much these children are benefiting from their unselfish care.

Another verse comes to my mind, *"Therefore, as God's chosen people, holy and dearly loved, clothe yourselves with compassion, kindness, humility, gentleness and patience."* (Col. 3:12) These teachers were and are, doing just that. They are the "unsung heroes" in our school district and community.

DECEMBER 3

FINGERPRINTS...

I had an interesting thing happen to me ~ a few years ago, when I applied to be a substitute teacher in our school district. In Idaho, you don't need a teaching certificate or degree, but they do fingerprint you and send these prints to the State Education Dept. The following Friday I received a letter saying my fingerprints had been rejected by the FBI! WHAT?! I didn't know there was such a possibility. I mean, these are the only fingers I have! So, I went back to the Sheriff's office that Friday afternoon, with my letter and my new fingerprint card in hand, and they took the prints again. The technician commented that these weren't very good either! I couldn't believe it. Certainly, if I were ever arrested, they would HAVE to do, right? I'm not going to be able to come up with any others, that's for sure.

This morning I heard the song by Steven Curtis Chapman, "Fingerprints of God," and I got to thinking that even though my own fingerprints have *worn off*, I am still unique and very special to my Maker. I am a "masterpiece that all creation quietly applauds, and I'm *covered with the fingerprints of God*." What a thought!! There has never been and will never be another person just like me. God fashioned me and perfectly planned me to be just who I am, and since my first heartbeat, He's been creating a "living, breathing , priceless work of art."

Isn't that a beautiful concept? Oh, and He's really just getting started! He will never be through with me. Or you, or any of us. We are a wonder in the making. *"I praise You because I am fearfully and wonderfully made…"* (Psalm 139:14)

So, on days when you feel like you're not so special, just remember that God has His fingerprints all over you, molding you, forming you into just the woman He wants you to be; holding you and protecting you ~ loving you!

DECEMBER 4

BIG TRUCKS…

God gave me big trucks….I prayed for them, and they came….here in North Idaho we have right around three feet of snow and most of it fell in one snowstorm, all within about 24 hours. We've hit some new records already this winter that we thought we topped LAST winter. Basically, we are snowed in. The headlines in the two local newspapers this morning are "We're In Deep" and "Buried." It was, and is, the largest snowfall in our local history. Oh, it's beautiful, all right, and I do love the snow. But today I have some responsibilities downtown and I was worried about even getting out of my driveway! Let alone trying to drive out of the neighborhood through almost three feet of rutted and packed snow.

Last night my son-in-law needed to borrow one of my husband's plow trucks (yes, my husband plows snow, and we thank God for the work!) so he could clear some area in front of his house down the street for my little granddaughter's birthday party. When he was finished, and brought the truck back, he cleared our driveway too, for which I was SO grateful. My husband had been out already about 28 hours in one stretch, without sleep, and just like any other profession, our house is the last to be serviced when he has paying customers! The street isn't his responsibility, anyway.

Worrying (a little) and wondering how I was going to get through the streets, I simply prayed that God would send the city trucks & plows, since the neighborhoods are usually the last to get plowed in every snowstorm, and this morning I whispered the prayer again, then went to look out at the street. Lo and behold! There was a city truck right in front of my house and the street had been plowed, or was in the process, anyway. Had God just dropped that truck out of the sky? There was no noise ~ of course, with this much snow, there is hardly any noise because it is so muffled...God sent the trucks!! And now I can make it in to town.

God is so faithful...He says, *"And all things, whatsoever ye shall ask in prayer, believing, ye shall receive."* (Matthew 21:22). All things? Even trucks? Yes! God cares about what we care about. If we can't trust Him, who can we trust? And thankfulness goes right along with that asking...Thank You Lord, for sending the trucks!!

DECEMBER 5

SNOWFLAKES...

God asks Job, in the midst of his complaining, *"Have you entered the storehouses of the snow, or seen the storehouses of the hail...?"* (Job 38:22). I never thought of the snow being kept in God's storehouses. Of course, the "storehouses" could simply be His unending creative ability...He is the One who "*commands the snow to fall on the earth*" (Job 37:6). He is the One who carries the clouds along and fills them with beautiful ice crystals ~ no two snowflakes are alike. I cannot even fathom how many snowflakes have fallen in North Idaho in the last week...billions. And each one is different. I haven't taken the time in my adult life to examine a single snowflake, although I notice them when they fall on my windshield, but when I was younger, I would marvel at the intricate design of each one, trying to remember what the previous one looked like before it melted away in my gloved hand.

You know, we are like that ~ there are billions of us, and yet no two of us are alike. There is even a difference between identical twins, although sometimes not visible to the naked eye! He made each one of us in His image... what a concept! That is why we will never be what He created us to be without Him. Oh, we can go along, living our lives, even being successful and admired, but we will never be fully what He intended for us without filling that special space in our hearts with *Him*.

Let's think about that as we ponder the true meaning of this season... Christmas. Christmas is not just a day, but an entire season. God sent His Son to the earth as a tiny, helpless baby with each one of us in mind. We needed a Savior. Jesus is that Savior. No matter how good our life seems to be, it will never be enough without His grace and mercy. Let's keep Christmas in our hearts throughout the whole year, and not just for a season. Just like the miracle of the snowflakes, our lives are a miracle also. May God's redeeming love fill your hearts and lives this week as you celebrate His goodness on Christmas Day. Merry Christmas, from North Idaho, filled with billions of beautiful snowflakes!

DECEMBER 6

THE WILLING SERVANT...

"I am the Lord's servant'" Mary answered. "May it be to me as You have said." Then the angel left her." (Luke 1:38)

I am sure this was not good news for a young girl, a virgin, to receive during her engagement. And I'm sure all the thoughts of "what will people think?" and "what will JOSEPH think?" passed through her mind at this shocking information, delivered by an even more shocking heavenly being. Just think of it ~ she could have been put away by her family, divorced (engagement broken) by Joseph, and even stoned to death for being pregnant out of wedlock. Her parents and Joseph, as well as herself, would be embarrassed to say the least, and Mary would have been heart-broken that the love of her life, her husband-to-be, would most certainly leave her, not understanding the whole situation.

And yet...instead of arguing with the angel, telling him God had chosen the wrong person for this job, that someone wiser should take her place, she said simply, "May it be..." Do you suppose Jesus' whole life (and suffering and death) flashed before her eyes when she accepted the news? Did she have a "knowing" of it all at the time the Holy Spirit came over her? How like her Son who said to the Father when His time had come, "Not My will but Yours..."

How many of us, when receiving a difficult assignment from our Lord, are as willing and eager to comply. Do we argue with God, as Moses did, informing Him that He has chosen the wrong person? That we aren't perfect enough, or qualified enough, or knowledgeable enough? How qualified could Mary have been to become not only a mother at such a young age, but the very mother of the Savior, the Almighty God? No, it wasn't that she was experienced, although she possessed wisdom far beyond her years...but that she was a willing and obedient servant. It shows me she had a deep relationship with God. And because of her obedient heart, God *equipped* her for the awesome task that was ahead of her. He will do the same for us. If we but say yes to what He asks of us, He will give us the strength and the means to do it ~ actually, He Himself will be doing it. We are just His receptacle. And when we come face-to-face with Jesus at the end of our life, may He then say, *"Well done, good and faithful servant."* (Mt. 25:21). Because we were willing.

DECEMBER 7

THE SEARCH IS ON...

We are deep into the Christmas shopping season now, in fact, there are just a little over three weeks until Christmas. And if any of you are like me, we haven't started our shopping yet! I began to make a list, first, of all the family members I need gifts for, then an idea or two, or three, for each one. And now I begin my search, either running around from store to store, or (and) online, looking for just the right item for that special person. I have to ask my kids for lists so at least I have a little bit of an idea what they're wishing for. I know some people who actually got up at 3:30 am on the first Christmas shopping day of the year just to stand in line to get first pick of those perfect gift items!

Do we seek as diligently after Jesus? Deuteronomy 4:29 says, *"But if from there you seek the Lord your God, you will find Him* ***if you look for Him with all your heart and with all your soul."*** What does that look like? All your heart and all your soul. It requires energy...like power shopping! And great effort. It should become the most important thing to us, the greatest priority in our life. Jesus said, *"But seek* ***first*** *His kingdom and His righteousness, and all these things will be given to you as well."* (Matthew 6:33). Many of us think we need to expend all our energy on our careers, making money to pay for the things we need and want. We put God on the back burner, knowing He will always be there, but right now we have more important things to pursue. But my Bible tells me that I must *"Seek the Lord while He may be found; call on Him while He is near."* (Isaiah 55:6).

If we seek the Lord now, the rest of our lives, our activities, our interests, will fall into place as God purposed. God will not be put off forever. If we wait, our hearts will harden and we will not feel the need for His presence in our lives. That's a tragedy. We must search for Him now, with ALL our heart and soul, while He is waiting. And maybe the gifts we give to each other will take on a new and different, eternal, meaning this Christmas season.

DECEMBER 8

GIVING TO THE POOR...

There was a beautiful story in our local paper on Christmas Day a couple of years ago, about a little boy named "Bubba" whose Christmas spirit has rubbed off on the rest of his family in a huge way. His family, as the story goes, was visiting in Seattle earlier in the year and Bubba had his first encounter with a homeless person begging on the street. He was so touched he wanted to give the man his teddy bear. Bubba was bothered by the fact that there were homeless people in the world, and so his family banned together and began collecting items that would benefit some of these panhandlers. They began carrying grocery bags of helpful items in their car, handing them out whenever they saw someone begging. Once they had run out of bags, but Bubba had his backpack and offered that. Thus began the operation of "Bubba's Backpack Brigade" and the family began collecting backpacks as well, filling them with such items as food, socks, a sweatshirt, and toiletries. This "ministry," just begun a couple of Christmases ago, has grown into a family project and their goal is to give away 25 backpacks per month in our town. It's a beautiful story. What a way to raise kids!

We have always been admonished by the Lord to give to the poor. *"A very rich man once took Jesus aside and asked Him how to inherit eternal life. Jesus told him that in addition to keeping the commandments, he must go and sell all he had and give to the poor, then having treasure in heaven. And the man went away very sad because he had great wealth."* (my paraphrase of Mark 10:17-22). Throughout the Bible, we are told that *"it is more blessed to give than to receive."* (Acts 20:35). God's word says in Proverbs 25:21, *"If your enemy is hungry, give him food to eat; if he is thirsty, give him water to drink."* He instructs us to even give to our enemies! Then how much more should we give to those who are helpless and poor? And in Deut. 15:11, His word says, *"I command you to be openhanded toward the poor and needy in your land."*

It's pretty easy to give at Christmas. We're in the spirit of giving. We've put a few dollars in the Salvation Army's buckets as we come and go from the stores. We take gifts to a shut-in neighbor, or give to charities, such as Toys for Tots, Angel Tree, Samaritan's Purse...but I think God's idea of giving to the poor is a year-long thing. People are not only needy during the holidays, but every day of the year. We are all needy, whether we are homeless or not, and God lovingly gives us His gifts every day. We are blessed with refuge in Him; He has blessed us with knowledge and learning; He gives us wisdom; He promises for our faithfulness and obedience that we will inherit the kingdom of heaven, and the earth; we will be filled with righteousness and shown mercy; we will be called sons and daughters of God. We will see God if our hearts are pure. (From the Beatitudes, Matthew 5). The blessings from God's hand are endless. Sometimes we don't recognize them, but if we persevere through our trials, we will be blessed. With God's extravagant blessings in store for us, how can we not bless others?

DECEMBER 9

OFFERING OF WORSHIP...

There are the words to a song that keep going through my head, day after day, a song from the Christmas musical our church choir has been practicing for the past few weeks...

"I bring an offering of worship to my King,
no one on earth deserves the praises that I bring,
Jesus may You receive the honor that You're due,
O Lord, I bring an offering to You..."

I got to thinking, just how does our worship become an offering to our Lord? And God brought my attention to this scripture: *"There came a woman having an alabaster box of ointment of spikenard very precious; and she broke the box and poured it on His head."* (Mark 14:3). She didn't just put a little dab of the spikenard on her finger and anoint Jesus' forehead ~ she emptied the whole box. This woman, Mary, the sister of Martha and Lazarus, is often found in scripture at the feet of Jesus. And she was unashamed in her worship of Him. She knew what real worship was.

My question...do I worship God without restrictions or reservations? Is my worship just a token gift, or from my whole heart, freely spilling out of His broken vessel which is my life? Does my life bring honor to Him? May my worship be as a sweet fragrance to Him as I lift His name high. He alone is worthy of my offering, my worship.

DECEMBER 10

PERSONAL MIRACLES...

I believe in miracles. Big miracles. Little miracles. I've seen a lot of them, both sizes, and sizes in between. I get excited when any miracle happens. I know they are from the hand of God, and He cares about what we care about.

There were the miracles of the early Bible times, the Creation was the first one, the parting of the Red Sea, the fire in front of the worshippers of Baal, manna in the wilderness, the changing of Jonah's mind and heart, the birth of Jesus, water into wine...these are some of the big ones. Then there are the ones we have experienced, healing of body and spirit and relationships, provision in our lean times, protection in traffic....God has His eye on us all the time. I don't look at times like these as coincidence or chance.

It was said of Jesus, *"Where did this man get these things?What's this wisdom that has been given Him, that He even does miracles! Isn't this the carpenter?"* (Mark 6:2). And yet, His own friends did not believe.

I experienced my own little personal miracle last night. For the last week, my favorite authors, Bodie and Brock Thoene, have been talking in their blog and email newsletter about the sights in the heavens that confirm God's existence and plans. They have been watching for and discussing the conjunction of stars with the moon daily ~ the new sliver of a moon, Venus and Jupiter. I love looking at the night sky, and the early morning, as well. Since Thanksgiving day our weather has been crummy ~ rain, then snow, then clouds and fog...for days...no way could I see the sky. After reading their blog yesterday, I voiced a little prayer that I would really love to see these heavenly beings in this unusual position. I was sitting on my couch reading in the afternoon, when the sun started shining in the window. Surprised, I looked out the window and saw that the sky was clearing . I thought how nice it was to have some sunshine. Then I realized I would be able to see the sky tonight! So, yes, my eyes were on the sky...I can see the area through my livingroom window, but when these three heavenly beings showed up at sunset, I went outside to get a better look. And about every 10 minutes, until the sky was dark, and those three showed up bright and brilliant. The last time I went to look, I couldn't see them. They were gone. Clouds had covered them.

Wow ~ God had cleared the sky for those couple of hours so I could see the beauty of Venus (Splendor), Jupiter (Righteousness) and the Holy

Spirit moon (as they are called by Bodie), and enjoy this little miracle of my own. These three were appearing within the constellation of Sagittarius (The Archer), who represents the victorious Messiah. His arrow is aimed at the heart of Scorpio, known in ancient times as the serpent.

This little lesson was for me, to know that I can still trust Jesus to see me (us) through the issues and problems in our lives right now. The wonders we see in the sky give us hope that Jesus is coming again, and maybe very soon. So, I'll keep looking up, watching for the biggest miracle of all. I don't want to miss it!

DECEMBER 11

THE SEASON FOR GIVING...

I have been having so much fun, giving my granddaughter things for her duplex. She and her little family just moved into their own place after being married almost three years and living in the basement of my daughter's home. Their own space, but not their own *place*. They need stuff. They had a nice bed, and a few pieces of furniture, but now that they're on their own, they are discovering just how much they don't have. It's perfect that Christmas is right around the corner, and better yet, her birthday is next week. Gift cards will allow her to pick out some new things she needs, but today she came over and picked up some extras from Grandma's house ~ a four-foot artificial tree (used once) and a commode to stand it on, which has been stored in our basement for nearly ten years, some tree lights and Christmas ornaments, used but still good, fabric for a tree-skirt-slash-table cloth, some potholders...I even gave her my old sewing machine, yet to be picked up. But it makes them happy, and I love to give the things I'm not using. I can't wait until Christmas morning, when my children and grandchildren will be the recipients of all the quilts I've been making for the last year or so.

My phone rang, and my little great-granddaughter was on the other end, trying to tell me in her own 2-year-old language, that she was helping mommy decorate the tree. Mommy came on and said she was having so much fun. I had some tiny doll ornaments from many years ago, again, unused, and thought she'd enjoy them. Her mommy said she had to hold and rock each one before placing them on the tree. That little seemingly insignificant detail is like a gift to me. Gave my heart a thrill.

Jesus said, *"Freely you have received, freely give."* (Matt. 10:8). He has given us so much, and much of it is undeserved. God sent His Son to give us eternal life, forgiveness, peace, His Spirit, hope. His very life's blood. We didn't do anything to earn it. We *couldn't* do anything to warrant that kind of gift. He gives it out of love. When that Baby Boy was born, over two thousand years ago, it just seemed natural for those who came to worship Him to also bring Him gifts. The wise men traveled a long distance, and brought gifts of gold, incense and myrrh. Expensive gifts. These men, who were likely kings themselves, went to a lot of trouble to find the Baby King of Kings, and to pay homage to Him. The shepherds came and worshipped, and although the Bible doesn't say whether they brought gifts or not, I wouldn't doubt that at least one of them brought a lamb. And we have the story of the Little Drummer Boy, in song, who didn't have money for a gift, but played his drum for the King. I truly believe that song could have been inspired by true events.

At this beautiful season of the year, much effort is given to fill the coffers with gifts for needy children and families, such as the food bank, coats and toys collections, soup kitchens, monetary offerings for the struggling needy families in our churches. Jesus also said, in Acts 20:35, *"It is more blessed to give than to receive."* I believe that to be true ~ at least for me. It is like a gift for me to see the delight in someone's face when I have given a gift. My grandkids are so excited. They receive each "gift" with joy, and I find these little gifts (my grandchildren) are things I certainly cannot live without.

Take advantage of the season for giving, and give not only money and material items, but give of yourself ~ time, love, encouragement, forgiveness. I know we have all received these ourselves. "Freely you have received, freely give."

DECEMBER 12

CAN WE AFFORD THAT?

We are a "buying" society. It's pretty easy to get the things we want with cash, check or credit card. There was a sign on a local car dealership a few years ago that said, "No Credit? No Problem!" Retailers are ready to offer all kinds of deals to get us to buy what they have. It doesn't matter if we can't afford it. Of course, even if the payments of a major item are affordable, when you figure in the interest over the years of the contract, it's way out there. Something that may seem affordable at the time will end up costing more than we thought, and more than it's worth in the long run. And before we know it, we are buried in so much debt, we honestly may never climb out of it. And kids don't understand this. They think parents are made of money.

Retailers will come up with a variety of offers and gimmicks to get us to purchase what they have. I'm sure most of you remember when Les Schwab Tires offered "free" beef to those who would buy a set of tires. They actually "gave away" sides of beef with your purchase. Of course, nothing is free; they just make it sound that way. The cost of the merchandise may be increased ever so slightly to make it look like it's still "on sale," but they have to make up for the cost of the free gifts, right? In the "old days" bartering, or "horse-trading" as my dad used to call it, was a way people could trade goods and services back and forth without the exchange of money. We are doing that again, to a certain extent, today. "You fix my car, I'll paint your fence."

We cannot afford our salvation. No amount of money could pay the price. It's too high. There is a chorus we sing, "Lord, You are more precious than silver; Lord, You are more costly than gold; Lord, You are more beautiful than diamonds, and nothing I desire compares to You." It's true. *"Oh, the depth of the riches of the wisdom and knowledge of God!"* (Romans 11:33). We could not repay Jesus near enough for what He did for us. No amount of work, or cash, or time could ever cancel our debt. But what He did on the Cross, spilling out His life's blood, was enough. "He came to pay a debt He didn't owe, because we owed a debt we couldn't pay." The longer we live, the deeper that debt grows. We have nothing with which to pay it. We are spiritually bankrupt. Even if we spent the rest of our lives praying, giving, and worshipping Him, we could never repay the obligation we have to Him.

The author of "Rock of Ages" penned this verse: "Could my tears forever flow, Could my zeal no languor know, These for sin could not atone, Thou must save, and Thou alone." We simply cannot afford Him. But what He gives us is a free gift. He paid IN FULL, once for all, so we could be free of the debt of sin. *"For the wages of sin is death; but the GIFT of God is eternal life thought Jesus Christ our Lord."* (Romans 6:23). All we have to do is reach out and accept it. No qualifying ~ no credit check.

DECEMBER 13

THE LION AND THE LAMB...

"Do not weep! See, the Lion of the tribe of Judah, the Root of David, has triumphed. ... Then I saw a Lamb, looking as if it had been slain..." (Rev. 5:5-6).

The lion is one of the fiercest animals on earth, king of the jungle. Very few animals will challenge the magnificent lion. The lion has been depicted as "God" in C.S. Lewis' popular book, and movie, "The Lion, the Witch and the Wardrobe." He is very wise and majestic. The lamb, on the other hand, is one of the meekest. And sheep are not considered too smart, They stick together, but become stressed when separated from their flock members. They are helpless without a shepherd. But they do know their shepherd's voice. In the time of Jesus, sheep were the desired sacrifice in the temple...a lamb without blemish ~ spotless and perfect.

You've no doubt seen pictures of natural enemies, a lion and a lamb, lying down together, in paintings, or on Christmas cards. What a serene scene. One mighty, and one gentle. There will be a day when this will be reality. It sounds incredible, but God's design for peace will allow it. I love the picture.

Jesus IS both the Lion and the Lamb. He is King and Friend. The Righteous Judge ~ and merciful. Humble, yet the Great I AM. He's the Prince of Peace, the lowly Child. Son of God and Son of Man. The perfect sacrifice, without blemish. *"The Lamb of God who takes away the sins of the world."* (John 1:29). And just as God provided a lamb for Abraham's sacrifice, He has provided a Lamb for us, as our ultimate sacrifice. The only perfect, innocent One, allowed Himself to become helpless, and cruelly killed so we could be cleansed before God through receiving His life's blood. The Lamb is also the *Shepherd* of His flock. And one day, all will hear and recognize His voice, and worship Him.

"He was given authority, glory and sovereign power; all peoples, nations and men of every language worshiped Him. His dominion is an everlasting dominion that will not pass away, and His kingdom is one that will never be destroyed." (Daniel 7:14). Jesus IS the Lamb of God, and the King of Kings!! Hallelujah! Does He reign in your heart?

DECEMBER 14

I LIFT UP MY EYES...

"I lift up my eyes to the hills ~ where does my help come from? My help comes from the Lord, the Maker of heaven and earth. He will not let your foot slip ~ He who watches over you will not slumber..." (Psalm 121:1-3). Not just any hills, mind you, for sometimes the enemy would come down from the hills in the Judean

wilderness. I believe David was talking about the hills of Moriah, or Zion, where the ark of God was, the symbol of His presence.

There are many hills in Israel…all over. My tour group walked and hiked up numerous hills. Some of them had steps hewn into the rock face, others just a path. We drove our bus up and down over many hills, as well. They are rugged and rocky, some barren as the desert, some lush with pine and olive trees, and date palms. Jerusalem is built on a hill, Moriah. David looked to God, of course, for assistance in his trouble, and for deliverance. Moriah was also called the holy hill of the Lord. *"To the Lord I cry aloud and He answers me from His holy hill."* (Psalm 3:4). The lifting up of the eyes is a prayer gesture. It expresses confidence and boldness in prayer, expectation and hope of help and salvation. People who were ashamed or hopeless could not look up, or lift their eyes or their face to God. Job's friends told him, that if he devoted his heart to God, *"then you will lift up your face without shame; you will stand firm and without fear."* (Job 11:15). And, of course, God is the Most High over all the earth, higher than the highest, above all gods. And so it is fitting to lift our eyes, our faces, up to Him in prayer, and praise.

The Temple of Solomon, the Dome of the Rock, sits on Mt. Moriah. It is a significant place of sacrifice ~ believed to be the spot where Abraham was called to give his son, Isaac, in sacrifice. And, of course, the Muslims have different ideas about what happened on the spot. It would be easy to tag such a site as a place of worship, or a place TO worship. God is not confined to a certain spot, a rock or hill or temple.

We must remember that our help does not come from the hills, nor from men. This would indeed be vain help. It doesn't come from kings or princes, or great men of the earth, and certainly not from the most powerful nations. But we must remember that our help comes from the Lord alone. God is the One who provided the "ram in the thicket" as an alternative sacrifice for Abraham's obedience. Let's be sure to fix our eyes on Jesus and give our worship and praise to Him, rather than a place, or a spot on a hill.

DECEMBER 15

HEAVEN AND NATURE SING…

I know many of you (most, at least) are not ready to talk about Christmas, and this isn't really about Christmas, although the title may suggest that. Our church's choir has been practicing our Christmas cantata for the past few weeks, and the words of "Joy to the World," specifically the title phrase for today, have been ringing through my mind as I look around at our landscape these days.

Last year we didn't have a particularly beautiful fall because the leaves froze on the trees before they had a chance to turn color and fall. We had very little color. It was eerie, almost. This year, what a glorious scene we have been privileged to behold. Our colors have changed gradually, and trees shed their leaves slowly. The color almost seemed electric, especially when illuminated by the sun. It's been spectacular. Almost "loud."

Did you ever wonder about how heaven and nature "sing?" Heaven of course, is filled with angels equipped with harps and beautiful voices, and saints who have much to sing about. So, that one is believable. But nature ~ singing? I look out at those gloriously arrayed trees in autumn, and yes, I believe that is part of nature's song. Nature praises our Creator by doing specifically what God created it to do ~ worship and praise Him, just as we were created for. The resplendent landscape is doing exactly what God designed it to do. Just as the thunderstorms we have enjoyed, with the boom like many percussion instruments, the flashes of crackling lightning putting on a show of shows. What else "sings" in nature? Of course, birds would be a universal answer, for they are truly singing their little hearts out to the Creator with every kind of song we can imagine, and cheerfully. Have you heard the coyote choirs at night when you are out camping? They make me smile because I know they are praising God in their own way ~ just as they were created. The wind in the trees, and even the twinkling stars would sound like chimes if there were no other sounds to interrupt. An earthquake can make an awful, deafening noise, adding to it boulders that tumble down a mountainside. The wild ocean waves are riotous, thundering as they rise and swell, and then recede. And of course, there is the pitter-patter, or the roar ~ the *song* ~ of the rain on the roof, on your umbrella. And how about the dance of the tornado? Awesome in its design, though very destructive.

The thing about nature…nothing holds it back. It worships with reckless abandon, not inhibited in the slightest. Not embarrassed. Praising God unashamed. When you look around at the beautiful brilliant autumn colors, try to imagine the noise of their song, the trees, the rustling of leaves. I think David felt the same way, as he said, *"Let the heavens rejoice, let the earth be glad; let the sea resound, and all that is in it; let the fields be jubilant, and everything in them.*

Then all the trees of the forest will sing for joy; they will sing before the Lord, *for He comes, He comes to judge the earth."* (Psalm 96:11-13). And Isaiah said, in 55:12, ***"All the trees of the field will clap their hands."***

Heaven and nature singing? You bet they do! Do you hear it? Take some time to look, and to listen. And then join in!

DECEMBER 16

CHRISTMAS OR XMAS?

I was curious about the origin of the term "Xmas" and so I did some research. I had heard something a long time ago about it having Christian origins, but I was not sure about this. So here is the information I discovered. It's pretty extensive, and I'll not repeat *all* of it here, but just to put our minds at ease, it is most assuredly a Christian word. The "X" is the Greek symbol for "Christ," or "chi" meaning "Xristos." In the 1400's the early church began using "X" because of the prohibitive costs of typesetting notices and publications. Each letter had to be tediously set by hand, and if they could deal with fewer letters, all the better. Later the word "Xmas" moved into general use in newspapers and other publications. In early times, this Greek symbol, "X," was written in older manuscripts. Another example is the symbol of the fish, one of the earliest symbols of Christians that has been found scratched on the walls of the catacombs of Rome. It likely originated from using the first letter of several titles of Jesus (Jesus Christ Son of God Savior). When combined, these initial letters together spelled the Greek word for fish (*ichthys*). (Oh, I even found the abbreviation "Xnty" for the word Christianity, in Webster's dictionary). So, it is not a modern invention, and it is not blasphemous, or a sign of disrespect, as it would seem. Even Wycliff used the "X" as an abbreviation for Christ.

There is no grand scheme to dilute Christianity by promoting the use of "Xmas" instead of Christmas. It is simply another way to say Christmas, drawing on a long history of symbolic abbreviations used in the church. In fact, as with other abbreviations used in common speech or writing (such as Mr. or etc.), the abbreviation "Xmas" should be pronounced "Christmas" just as if the word were written out in full, rather than saying "exmas." Although it is in no way "x-ing" Christ out of Christmas, and that's not possible anyway, I still love to write out the entire word, "Christmas" because I recognize my Savior's name at the beginning. And I don't think I could send out a Christmas card with the abbreviation on it. There would be misunderstandings, for sure. Still, it's good to know that it is not some worldly plot to overthrow Christendom.

And so, I want to focus on the issues of the Faith during the Advent season ~ the peace, the joy and the love we share in Christ's name. I am in no way suggesting that we use this symbol in our day, instead of Christmas, (although many do), but when we see it being used, we can relax and breathe easier knowing it is indeed a Christian word, and not a device to promote commercialism.

"She said to Him, 'Yes, Lord; I have believed that You are the Christ, the Son of God, even He who comes into the world." (John 11:27).

DECEMBER 17

UNSPEAKABLE JOY...

"Though you have not seen Him you love Him; and even though you do not see Him now, you believe in Him and are filled with joy unspeakable... [inexpressible and glorious]." (1 Peter 1:8). According to Peter, the joy from the Lord is impossible to truly express with words. There is a newer rendition of the Christmas song, "Joy to the World" that includes the following chorus, "Joy, unspeakable joy, overflowing well, no tongue can tell, joy unspeakable joy, rises in my soul, never lets me go." This is not a new concept, however. In 1 Chronicles 16:27 we read, *"Splendor and majesty are before Him; strength and joy in His dwelling place."* And in Nehemiah 8:10, *"Do not grieve, for the joy of the Lord is your strength."* And then of course, in the Christmas story we are reading this season, *"Do not be afraid. I bring you good news of great joy which shall be to all people."* (Luke 2:10). It's that joy unspeakable that the angel was talking about.

I would imagine that Adam felt that great joy and awe when God created Eve to be his help mate. It was rapture beyond Adam's wildest imagination. And the realization that God used Noah mightily in the flood, when no one had ever heard of rain, or knew what a flood was. And there was Mary. Here was a teenage girl, making plans for a wedding, but the angel told her God had a special and marvelous plan for her life. She was filled with joy that God would use such a simple common girl as she. And then when that Baby King was born, what deep delight and wonder she must have felt looking into that infant face of God, knowing this baby she bore would someday be her own Savior. Her joy glorified the Lord from deep within her spirit and soul. She realized just how blessed she was, and how blessed future generations would be for her obedience. And then the indescribable joy when the women went to the tomb and discovered it was empty ~ that Jesus had risen, just as He said He would.

We, as women, have felt the joy of bringing a little one into our lives, of watching them grow and develop and discover. The Apostle John wrote, *"I have no greater joy than to hear that my children are walking in the truth."* (3 John :4). God has given us many gifts that bring us joy. We are just celebrating Christmas, commemorating Jesus' holy birth. Gifts will be exchanged, songs will be sung, meals shared, and prayers given. Families are looking forward to being reunited with loved ones. These things bring us joy. But to have the knowledge that we are used of God, and see the evidence of that, and feel His Presence, there is no other joy like that. It cannot be described in any way. Joy unspeakable. God alone makes our joy complete. But according to James (1:2), we don't just find joy in the gifts and happy moments in our lives. He said, *"Consider it pure joy, my brothers [sisters], whenever you face trials of many kinds, because you know that the testing of your faith develops perseverance..."*

Many of us have experienced much sadness recently, and it seems that we just could not be joyful, no matter how hard we try, or how much we do. And that's okay. There will be those times for us, and trouble is no respecter of the season or holiday we are celebrating, or the time of year as tragedy hits. For many it is a lonely and frightening time. But just remember, Jesus died for these times. He sent the Comforter. He gives Peace in the midst of the storm. He will never leave us. He promised. He gives Joy.

DECEMBER 18

WITH CHILD...

"But the angel said to her, 'Do not be afraid, Mary, you have found favor with God. You will be with child and give birth to a son, and you are to give him the name Jesus.'" (Luke 2:30-31). I imagine Mary was terrified, trembling, at the sight of Gabriel, glowing and towering over her with this shocking news. He said she was highly favored. He told her not to be afraid. He said her child would

be the Messiah ~ the Son of God! Mary's faith was great, even for a teenager, and she was suddenly filled with joy. *"May it be to me as you have said."* (vs. 38). She believed the angel, sent from God Himself. But now she had to tell her parents...and Joseph. There would be much gossip and talk when others found out, not understanding the celestial visitor whom no one else had seen.

Teenage pregnancy ~ a scary thing. We have been there, my family. Our daughter was 17, crying as she told us. We were in shock, crying and holding her. Now what? There was much discussion, and more shock as we told the rest of the family. Her younger sisters were excited ~ a baby! One family member suggested adoption. We wouldn't hear of it. The "grandparents" visited over lunch to come up with a solution. It was decided ~ they would keep the baby and get married. This was their choice. And how would our church family react to this news? Surprisingly, or not so surprisingly, knowing God's people, they rallied, they embraced our daughter and loved her right through it. By the way, that "baby," now 22 has given us our first great-grandchild.

In this day and age, teenage pregnancy is a common thing, accepted by our society. But in Mary's and Joseph's day, she could have been stoned to death for adultery. Exiled. *"Put away quietly."* Joseph probably initially thought she had been unfaithful to him...but, surely not his Mary! Her faith was strong. She was a godly woman. It certainly put a strain on their relationship. Surely people could tell there was something wrong. But then the angel visited Joseph. I believe Gabriel had a lot to say to Joseph. He may have repeated some prophecy, talked about lineage and why Mary, an ordinary girl, would be chosen. He probably answered at least a dozen questions for Joseph. And ... *"Joseph, son of David, do not be afraid to take Mary home as your wife, because what is conceived in her is from the Holy Spirit. She will give birth to a son and you are to give Him the name Jesus, because He will save His people from their sins."* (Matthew 1:20-21). There it was. The confirmation that Mary was telling the truth about the visit from the angel. And "permission" if you will, to marry her anyway.

And we know the rest of the story. The shepherds, the wise men, signs in the sky ~ maybe this is why I love looking at the sky so much! The birth of the beautiful Christ-child was the talk of the town, the whole country, and now the whole world. A miracle from God Almighty. He has come, in the form of a baby, to redeem His people! It was foretold, *"For to us a child is born, to us a Son is given, and the government will be on His shoulders. And He will be called Wonderful Counselor, Mighty God, Everlasting Father, Prince of Peace."* (Isaiah 9:6). What marvelous news! Get ready to celebrate the birth of this holy Baby!

DECEMBER 19

GLORIFIED IN ME...

"I am the Lord's servant," Mary answered. "May it be to me as you have said." (Luke 2:38). I love Mary's heart. She was just a young girl, probably early teens, when the angel spoke to her about carrying the Savior of the world. And yet, she was willing to do whatever it took to be in God's will, and to glorify Him. How many teenagers do you know like that? I have lived 60+ years, and I still have a problem saying "whatever, Lord!" Oh, I ask Him to let His will be done in me, and I *want* to glorify Him in all I say and do, but sometimes, I forget to trust Him. Sometimes when life gets hard, or I am hurt, or I just simply want my own way...

Mary didn't have time to think about it, she just obeyed without question. Well, one little question... *"How will this be, since I am a virgin?"* (vs. 34). Satisfied with the angel's answer (who would have believed it?) she got on with it. She even sang a song praising God. She sang, *"My soul glorifies the Lord and my spirit rejoices in God my Savior, for He has been mindful of the humble state of His servant..."* (vs. 46-48). My goodness, her whole soul and her spirit were rejoicing, glorifying God, because of the shocking news the angel had brought her! I'm not even sure I can imagine my very soul being so elated about news such as this that would change my life, and the way people looked at me. Oh, it was a shameful state at first, the way the tongues wagged and people looked down at her...until that night her Baby, the Savior of the world, was born. And as her song continued to say, *"From now on all generations will call me blessed..."* (vs. 48).

Certainly this type of history will not be repeated in our lives, in any of us. There is no need for any more saviors. Jesus is the One and Only. He is enough. But, I have to think...what if God came to me with a pronouncement as shocking as this was to Mary and her family? Would I argue with God as Moses did? Would I run away and hide as Adam, Jonah and David did? Or would I suddenly feel the glow of God's Spirit coming over me as I would obediently say, as Isaiah, *"Here I am, Lord, send me."* (Is. 6:8), or Mary, *"May it be to me as you have said."* I'm thinking that when the Holy Spirit came over Mary, she may have suddenly had a rushing knowledge of all that would be coming her way. And still, she stood firm. She did not waiver in her resolve that God was honoring her. It all comes down to trusting Him to do what it is He calls us to. Imagine what this poor world would be like if everyone God truly spoke to listened to His voice and answered, "Okay, whatever, Lord!"

It seems like I have written a lot about Mary, and the shepherds, and kings, and the gift of Jesus here in these days, but there is so much news here in Luke 2. It's like I can't get enough of what God is trying to teach me through His word in the Christmas story. It is *full* of His glory. And God's glory will be there whether we glorify Him with our lives or not. I would like to be a part of His glory and offer Him all that I am. Would you?

DECEMBER 20

RICH HOLIDAY FARE...

Well, if you're like me, you've already been to some Christmas parties, and will probably go to more...the office party, luncheon with the girls, the church Christmas Tea, the neighborhood get-together, and of course, the family gatherings. We have eaten more than our share of cookies, lavish hors d'oeuvres, fruitcake, eggnog, and of course, much chocolate of all shapes and sizes. Aren't you glad Christmas only comes once a year? But those Christmas snacks seem to carry over into New Year's, and here we go again! Some of us scrimp on these rich morsels, but others just enjoy with reckless abandon. I'm kind of in between both of those types. I like to taste mostly everything, but realize I can't eat full portions of any of it!

I've read about another big party, a banquet, in fact, where it won't matter how much we eat. And there will be food we have never tried, yet we will savor each bite. *"Then the angel said to me, 'Write; Blessed are those who are invited to the wedding supper of the Lamb!' and he added, 'These are the true words of God.'"* (Rev. 19:9). It will be a feast, for sure, like none we've ever seen on earth. Actually, there may not even be food, as we know it, and it won't matter to us. Because Jesus said, *"I have food to eat that you know nothing about."* (John 4:32). It may be that we will have no need for food at all, because we'll be in the presence of our Savior in glorified bodies. But I also know that we will have *"earned the right to eat from the Tree of Life."* (Rev. 2:7). This Wedding Feast will be a celebration, as all wedding feasts are, but there will be no end to the celebration on that day of days that will flow into eternity. In the Old Testament, there were seven feasts that were celebrated regularly, the Feasts of Passover, Unleavened Bread, First Fruits, Weeks/Pentecost, Trumpets, Day of Atonement, and Tabernacles. These were very holy and sacred feasts, with much preparation and significance. Each feast was appointed by God, and provided powerful lessons that pointed toward the Messiah. But there has never yet been a Wedding Feast of the Lamb, and once we attend this feast, I believe it will never end.

It won't matter what we have, or have not, been able to eat on earth, what our health problems have been, our size, our tastes, likes and dislikes, allergies. A lot of recipes have been called "Heavenly This, or That" but this banquet table will truly be laden with everything heavenly. There will be no preservatives, peanut oil or msg that we have to worry about, we won't have to count calories or carbs, and everything will be the freshest there is, no insecticides or preservatives. David knew about this banquet, and he said, *"You prepare a table before me in the presence of my enemies... my cup overflows"* (Psalm 23:5). Have you received your invitation? It's right there in His Book of books. Make sure you R.S.V.P!

DECEMBER 21

DO YOU HEAR WHAT I HEAR...?

When I see, or hear, this phrase, I always think of the well-known Christmas song of the same title. It's a beautiful song, with a message we don't soon forget.

"Said the night wind to the little lamb
Do you see what I see
Way up in the sky little lamb
Do you see what I see
A star, a star
Dancing in the night
With a tail as big as a kite
With a tail as big as a kite".

This verse causes me to think that all of nature, from the wind to the animals, noticed the unusually large star in the sky, and I'm sure that the glorious light shining all around got everyone's attention, and they wondered together at it....

"Said the little lamb to the shepherd boy
Do you hear what I hear
Ringing through the sky shepherd boy
Do you hear what I hear
A song, a song
High above the tree
With a voice as big as the sea
With a voice as big as the sea".

And of course, the little shepherd, I imagine, was very close to his little lamb, maybe it was even his pet, his little friend, and I picture him snuggling with him during the cold night, both trying to keep each other warm. And I believe the song they could not help but notice out there on the hillside in the once dark night, was the song of many thousands of angels heralding the birth of our Savior...

"Said the shepherd boy to the mighty king
Do you know what I know
In your palace wall mighty king
Do you know what I know
A child, a child
Shivers in the cold
Let us bring him silver and gold
Let us bring him silver and gold".

That must have been a bold little boy to march right up to the king and announce the arrival of this baby-King, and suggest that they go and present him with extravagant gifts...

"Said the king to the people everywhere
Listen to what I say
Pray for peace people everywhere
Listen to what I say
The child, the child
Sleeping in the night
He will bring us goodness and light
He will bring us goodness and light".
(written by Noël Regney)

And this was indeed one very wise king, who had authority to make the proclamation and spread the word that this Child was truly the King of peace, and goodness & light. For Jesus IS Light. And He is our only Peace.

During this Christmas season, on a night that is clear and the stars are shining brightly, look up, stand still and listen carefully to see if you can hear the angel choirs. And remember that when we are singing our Christmas carols, we are actually joining in with heaven's hosts who are already singing them. Can you imagine what that sounds like to God?

DECEMBER 22

JESUS IS OUR PEACE...

"He is our peace Who has broken down every wall, He is our peace, He is our peace... Cast all your cares on Him for He cares for you...He is our peace, He is our peace." One of the old choruses we used to sing, slowly and prayerfully ~ it always touched me so deeply, and gently.

In Ephesians 2:14 it says, *"For He Himself is our peace, Who has made the two one and has destroyed the barrier, the dividing wall of hostility..."* I love it when songs are adapted straight from scripture. After singing a chorus several times, it will come to mind easily, and it aids us in memorizing scripture. Repeating...*"I have hidden Your word in my heart..."* Psalm 119:11).

If there was ever a time when we need peace, it certainly is now. Peace in our homes, in our country. Peace of mind. Peace in the midst of the storm. Many songs and hymns are written about peace. At this time of the year, we see and hear many messages about peace, greetings in the name of peace, and so on. But peace cannot be superficial. It needs to become seated deep in our souls. I only know of one Source of that kind of peace.

"He will stand and shepherd His flock in the strength of the Lord, in the majesty of the name of the Lord His God. And they will live securely, for then His greatness will reach to the ends of the earth. And He will be their Peace." (Ancient words, spoken by the prophet Micah 5:4-5). Can you imagine that kind of peace? The kind that reaches to the very ends of the earth?

This has been a very troubling year for many of us, economically, spiritually, physically...for some of us, life has taken a very disturbing turn. The future, as we see it, is uncertain. Though we try to remain positive, we can only have that true peace and deep joy, yes, in the midst of the troubles that come toward us from every direction, through Jesus Christ. "Peace is not just the absence of a storm, but the rest for our souls in the midst of the storm." (Ron Hutchcraft). He is the whole reason we are celebrating this holiday season. From Philippians 4:7, *"And the peace of God, which transcends all understanding, will guard your hearts and minds in Christ Jesus."*

DECEMBER 23

HIDDEN STARS...

I love the stars. You know that by now. I have a few favorites ~ Venus, Mars, the Orion constellation, the Big Dipper...they are so constant, and a reminder of God's creative hand and His unfailing love for us. Sometimes, the stars are hidden ~ I would say, about half the time they are obscured by clouds, rain or snow, or fog. But I know they are still up there, giving glory to God in the way they were created to. Every once in awhile, there will be a break in the clouds and I will see a few twinkling behind them. And, of course, on a clear night they shine even brighter. There are even more stars behind the ones we can see, that we will probably never see. I have been known to lie on my back on the grass in my front yard, in the dark, just gazing up at the sky. And if I'm lucky, I'll see a shooting star or two.

And there was that Star on the night our Savior was born, burning so brightly, I don't think anything could have covered it up, no rain, nor clouds ~ because that star was leading the way to the Savior. I would love to have seen that one! I can't help but imagine that the magi had to travel days, maybe even weeks to get to Bethlehem, and the only clue they had as to His whereabouts was the Star. Certainly, every night during their travel was not clear and cloudless. And yet, the Star shone brightly. *"We saw His star in the east and have come to worship Him."* (Matthew 2:2).

Sometimes, other things we are searching, or watching for seem to be hidden. Well, certain items around our house, for sure...but we often times feel that God Himself is hidden from us. We can't find Him. We are in trouble. We are sick, or scared. We pray. We wait. And yet, we don't think He hears us, or sees us. But like the stars, He is up there, we can be sure of it. He's actually all around us, right next to us. *"The angel of the Lord encamps around those who fear*

Him, and He delivers them." (Psalm 34:7). That's comforting to me. God's angels, sent by Him, are all around me. The mystery of God's love for us, though, is hidden from us because it is too awesome for us to understand. Little by little He reveals these things to us as we mature in grace and knowledge.

Do you feel as if God is hidden from you? Do you call out to Him and wait, but cannot hear His answer? Remember, His timing is perfect, and whenever He sees that we are ready for the truths and promises in His word, He will act. Do not give up. Just as you trust that the stars are hanging in the sky, even when you cannot see them, also trust that God is looking down on us all, even when we don't see or sense Him. The next to the last thing Jesus speaks in His word to us is, *"I am the Root and the Offspring of David, and the* ***Bright and Morning Star****."* (Revelation 22:16). He is the one Star that will never be hidden from us. The perfect Light.

DECEMBER 24

SANTA BOWED...GOD BOWED...

Our children's department at church just presented the most meaningful Christmas pageant I've ever seen. It was called "Santa Bowed at Christmas." On the front cover of the book is the picture we've all seen, in a snow globe or as an ornament, Santa kneeling at the manger, hatless in respect, worshiping the baby Jesus. What a poignant scene. It starts out with the town's children all gathered, waiting to talk to Santa, and discussing what they want for Christmas. Santa seems very distraught and joy-less that day, and it concerns the kids. So, they do their best to tell him the real meaning of Christmas. It's a beautiful story. So beautiful, and so powerful, that a man who was visiting tracked down our pastor right afterwards and with tears in his eyes, said he wanted what those children were singing about! He gave his life to Jesus right there in the foyer amid the crowd and coffee and cookies!

But have you ever thought about God on His knees? How about at the very beginning of time, first chapter of Genesis, when he knelt down and formed man out of the fresh soil of the new earth He'd just created? He breathed His own life into man, and blessed him. Abundantly. But man became rebellious and broke that first covenant with God, his Father. So, God sent His own Son into the world to redeem us, set us free from that first sin which has stayed with us through the generations. And in this Man, Jesus, we see God kneeling again, drawing in the sand, after a woman had been caught in adultery. He forgave her. *"If anyone is without sin, let him be the first to throw a stone at her."* (John 8:7). Then we see Him again on His knees, in John 13:5, washing the feet of His disciples. *"After that, He poured water into a basin and began to wash His disciples' feet, drying them with the towel that was wrapped around Him."*

In the longest prayer by Jesus, recorded in John 17, the "high priestly prayer," after He had spent much time with His disciples, having dinner with them, explaining God's plan to them, loving them, He prayed for the task at hand ~ the betrayal, the arrest ~ He prayed for His disciples, and for all believers. *He prayed* for you and me.

We find Jesus kneeling again, in Gethsamane, a beautiful garden, where He was seeking solitude to cry out to His Father. It's night, and His disciples were implored to keep watch. He prayed for hours. He wanted to make sure the thing He was about to do...give His life's blood for the world's sin...was truly the Father's will. Jesus' own prayers, God on His knees, bringing us to the very throne of heaven. He loves us so much!

DECEMBER 25

SHHHH...

It's Christmas morning, and everything at my house is quiet ~ that's because no one lives here anymore except my husband and myself. I still enjoy the quiet before the festivities of the day begin. We are having a real different Christmas this year. One of our daughters and her family traveled away to spend Christmas with her husband's family. My husband had to work Christmas Eve, so our Christmas Eve dinner was missing yet one more person. The ones remaining, my other two daughters and their families, will come for a big breakfast soon, followed by the gift-opening frenzy. Then most of them will go their way to in-laws and other grandparents' homes for the main Christmas dinner. So, this year we will have one lone daughter here, without her children, for our Christmas dinner. But we have invited a sweet young couple and their two little boys to share, because they have no family here. So, at least we will have bodies around our table. The others will return in the evening for desserts, visiting and games.

Shhhh…it's Christmas morning more than 2,000 years ago. In a lambing cave in Bethlehem, with no modern conveniences, no facilities of any kind, a newborn infant King lay in a manger of soft hay, snuggled up in blankets to warm Him. It is quiet, except for the rhythmic munching of animals eating their morning hay, or maybe the hushed bleating of a lamb, and possibly His mother's soft humming. And Mary, "the lady of the house," the mother of this holy Child, was silently contemplating her newborn Son and all that this experience meant. How peaceful it must have been, without all the machines beeping, and voices and hustle-bustle of our modern hospitals! I wonder if she knew how this day would evolve into a gift-opening frenzy, with lots of visitors, many of them crude and dirty, to pay homage to this little King? But come they did. Many shepherds, who had seen the great light in the heavens, received the proclamation of the angel, *"Fear not, for behold, I bring you good tidings of great joy which shall be to all people. For unto you is born this day in the city of David a Savior which is Christ the Lord!"* and had heard the celestial choir, *"Glory to God in the highest, and on earth peace, good will toward men."* (Luke 2:10-11, 14). Wise men, or kings, they've even been referred to as astrologers, traveled from far away to bring expensive gifts. I wonder what they thought when they saw that this King was born in a cave? Maybe no one even noticed. They knew He was the holy One, they had read the ancient prophets, and I don't think it really mattered to them what His surroundings were ~ which had to have literally glowed with the holy light. *"But Mary treasured up all these things and pondered them in her heart."* (Luke 2:19).

But because of this event, over 2,000 years ago, we have Christmas! Mary and Joseph would never be the same. All those guests who visited and worshipped Him would be changed forever as well. Let's come to the manger and visit Him. Look on His face. Celebrate. Worship Him. And we will never be the same, either.

DECEMBER 26

THE FIRST BABY SHOWER…

The invitation went out… *"Today in the city of David a Savior has been born to you; He is Christ the Lord. This will be a sign to you: you will find the baby wrapped in cloths and lying in a manger."* (Luke 2:11). After the shepherds had heard this pronouncement, they hurried off to Bethlehem. Others came, too. *"On coming to the house, they saw the Child with His mother, and they bowed down and worshipped Him. Then they opened their treasures and presented Him with gifts of gold, and of incense, and of myrrh."* (Matthew 2:11). Luke 2 goes on to say that when they had visited and worshipped the Baby, the shepherds returned to their fields, and they spread the word all around the countryside about the arrival of this special Baby.

Many came, along with the magi, who gave expensive and extravagant gifts ~ the shepherds were poor and brought "only" their worship. We hear the song about a little drummer boy, also poor, who gave the gift of his musical talent, which seemed to please the Baby King. I'm sure even the animals in the stable seemed to give this special Baby their attention.

Here it is, more than 2,000 years after that first baby shower, and I wonder what gift I can give Him? I don't have much money, but I do give my tithe. What about my time? Do I use it wisely and for His glory? I visit a lonely, shut-in lady in an assisted living facility who has no one, because it makes her so happy, and it blesses me to make her feel special. Can that qualify as a gift to Jesus? I contribute to a ladies' Bible study every week, sharing books and insight, wishing to be an inspiration and encouragement to others. I give free hugs to my children and grandchildren. And yet, I know this is not enough ~ my Savior deserves more. But nothing I can do will ever give sufficient glory to His name. And yet, He continues to shower lavish gifts and blessings on me. The blessings of sunrises and sunsets, the beauty of the fresh snow, budding of trees in the spring and the brilliant colors in the fall, a baby's giggle, fresh water to drink and plenty of food, friends and family to love me...the gifts never stop coming.

I want my whole life to be a gift back to Him. I don't want to become proud of all I "do" and would not want to ever receive glory for myself, but I pray the talents and abilities He has gifted me with will be used to edify, and to lift up His name. May I never forget that I cannot "earn" my salvation. It is the one true gift He has given to all. *"For it is by grace you have been saved, through faith ~ and this not from yourselves, it is the gift of God ~ not by works so that no one can boast."* (Ephesians 2:8-9). What will you bring Him? How about your heart?

DECEMBER 27

MISSING PIECES...

Did you ever put together a jigsaw puzzle only to discover when you are almost finished that there is a piece or two missing from the box? It's frustrating, and your beautiful picture is not complete. Or how about mixing up a favorite recipe, and you realize you're missing one little, but important, ingredient? One time we were putting together a Christmas present...I can't remember exactly what it was, a bike, or scooter, for one of our children, and there was a screw or bolt missing. After searching all over the floor and in the box, we realized it came that way from the manufacturer...very disappointing.

We used to move a lot when I was a child. I was able to make one or two good friends at school, or in my neighborhood, but then we had to leave, and I had to make friends all over again when we reached our new home. It was very hard for me, as I'm sure it has been for everyone whose parents are in the military. When we drove away, I felt like part of me, part of my heart, was being ripped out. To this day, I cherish my friendships, and I am so blessed to have many.

Last night we had to have our beloved dog, Angel, put to sleep. It was certainly time. But doubly hard so close to Christmas. It was so tough, but in a matter of seconds, her labored breathing was still and her arthritis- and illness-wracked body was relaxed. Our hearts were broken. We had enjoyed her loving company for fourteen-plus years. I know that her companion, our other dog, Stormy, will miss her terribly, as we will. Each time we lose something that is dear to us, a loved one, a cherished item, we feel suddenly incomplete. And that emptiness lingers for a time, often a long time. James said, in 1:2-5, *"Consider it pure joy, my brothers, whenever you face trials of many kinds, because you know that the testing of your faith develops perseverance. Perseverance must finish its work so that you may be mature and* ***complete****, not lacking anything. If any of you lacks wisdom, he should ask God, who gives generously to all without finding fault, and it will be given to him."* And Jesus said, in John 15:11, *"I have told you this so that My joy may be in you, and that your joy may be* ***complete****."*

Is there something, or someone, missing in your life that makes you feel incomplete? No doubt, there are many of us who are feeling a little lost, or blue, especially at this time of the year when families and friends gather. Most of our family was missing from our Christmas dinner table, although we saw some of them on Christmas day, at different times. But oh, the exuberance we feel when we find that missing puzzle piece on the floor, or a neighbor has that ingredient we need to finish our recipe...or when we hear from that long-lost best friend...God is there to fill that emptiness we feel. As Jude said, in that tiny book near the end of the Bible, verse 2, *"Mercy, peace, and love be yours in abundance."* And that is my wish for all of us in the midst of our "missing pieces."

DECEMBER 28

THE WONDER OF CHRISTMAS...

Do you remember what it was like when you were a child, and the sheer wonder you felt at Christmas? The lights, the snow, the tree with presents placed under it with care? The filled stockings hanging up? The caroling, the ornaments, the star on top? Helping Mom make fancy cookies and the smells that went all through the house? That unmistakable "jingle, jingle" sound? The manger scene? The story of Mary and Joseph tediously making their way to Bethlehem, not really knowing the full impact of what was in store for them?

As children, we believed it all. A story like that was easy to believe. Because a grownup said it, or read it out of the Bible, it must be true. We didn't question the huge star shining in the night over the birthplace of Jesus, the Baby Savior. We had no problem accepting the idea of thousands of angels flying around in the night sky, singing to the shepherds. Children have a great imagination, after all. They can easily picture a scene like that! How a pregnant woman could ride all that way over the desert on the back of a donkey...how three famous kings heard the news from so far away, without the help of newspapers or telephones ~ or email. Or how uneducated shepherds, men and boys who lived in the fields with sheep and never took a bath, were honored by the angels and led by miraculous signs in the sky. And it seems perfectly acceptable for a baby to be lying in a manger of hay with farm animals standing all around, and strangers kneeling on the ground.

But children grow up. They become skeptical, and adults are not as believable as they were to a little kid. A king that would actually kill all the baby boys in a country because he was afraid of losing his throne? Oh, yes...and we have even seen this atrocity in our own time, in Hitler, a "butcher king" just like Herod was. A perfect, holy Baby? A Baby born just to grow up and die on a cross? That's the story. But as we grow up, we crowd out those memories of early Christmases, the families gathering together, no matter how far they had to travel. We begin to disbelieve the story of a virgin being visited by God Himself and becoming pregnant with a holy Baby, the Savior of the world. We think that all the things we have done will just have to be dealt with, that there is no hope for us because we are "in too deep." We don't feel the awe of looking up at the lights, or the stars, crunching in the snow, hearing the hymns and carols being sung by choirs.

May I invite you to stop and smell the gingerbread? Stand still and hear the music coming from radios, loud speakers and churches everywhere. Light a few candles and see how warm and comforting that feels. Open your dusty Bible to *Luke Two* and re-read the Christmas story, just as you heard it when you were young. Don't let the cares and worries of the world take away the joy you can feel in your heart when the Savior is near. Bring back the awe and wonder of your youth. Believe it again, and forever. And make it believable for your children and grandchildren. Now's your chance to make a difference, and renew those feelings of wonder and awe you enjoyed as a child, not just at Christmas, but all year long.

DECEMBER 29

IS CHRISTMAS OVER?

As I prepare to start putting away Christmas in my home, I have time to reflect as I pack away each bauble, each snowman, the gifts, each candle and wreath, the lights, that I am really not putting away Christmas, but just the decorations of Christmas. Oh, I hate to take down my tree ~ I have enjoyed it so much, with the tiny white lights against the darkness of my living room in the early morning…But Jesus said, *"I am the Light of the world. Whoever follows Me will never walk in darkness, but will have the light of life."* (John 8:12).

Jesus came to us as a tiny baby, helpless and crying, needy, just the same as all of us. And at Christmas we celebrate the love and joy of that manger story… but Jesus is no longer a baby. *"The child grew and became strong in spirit…"* (Luke 1:80). And the longer I serve Him, the stronger His Spirit grows in me. That is why I can carry Christmas around with me, in my heart, all year long. It doesn't mean that I have to buy gifts and keep my holiday giftwrap handy, and listen to Christmas music all year, although there is nothing wrong with that ~ the Christmas songs have a beautiful message, for sure. I can still give gifts all year, in His name, the gifts of my love, compassion, mercy, encouragement… always remembering to give thanks to God for these same gifts He has given me. I can still sing the songs with the Christmas message ~ actually, doesn't all Christian music carry this message?

So, as we look back at another Christmas past, let's remember that we don't have to "put it away" but that we can carry the message of the Christ Child in our hearts all year. God bless this new coming year, and…Merry Christmas!!

DECEMBER 30

REMEMBER…

Memory is a great thing…sometimes. Mine has been failing me of late, but I ran across a little verse in a book, "How dear to the heart are the scenes of my childhood, when fond recollection presents them to view." (Samuel Woodworth). Some of us have fond memories of our childhood, some do not. But we do have them ~ memories. Sometimes they make us sad, sometimes wistful, and sometimes happy. We remember a special toy, our first pet, our first plane trip, our first love.

God told Noah and his family in Genesis 9:15, *"I will remember My covenant between Me and you and all living creatures of every kind. Never again will the waters become a flood and destroy all life."* Memory ~ God made us with a memory. And my goodness, sometimes there are so many things to remember ~ the errands we need to run, bills to pay, phone calls to make, the grocery list, meetings… but He wants us to remember HIM. Remember His covenant to take care of His people. Remember what He did for us in the Garden of Gethsemane, and on the hill called Golgatha. He wants us to remember the poor, remember His mercy and grace. *"Remember that we are but dust, here today and gone tomorrow."* (Psalm 103:14).

David said in Psalm 136:23, *"Give thanks to the One who remembered us in our low estate, His love endures forever."* His everlasting love ~ now that's a good thing to remember. Especially when it sometimes seems He has forgotten us. There is only one thing our Lord will not remember: *"For I will forgive their wickedness and* ***will remember their sins no more."*** (Hebrews 8:12). That's good news. How can we do any less?

We are right on the edge of a brand new year. Can we put aside our differences and make a choice to forget those distinctions, those hurts, and go forth in this new year with love for our brother and sister? Remember. Remember what Jesus did for us…

DECEMBER 31

WHAT'S NEW?

"What has been will be again, what has been done will be done again; there is nothing new under the sun." (Ecclesiastes 1:9). Many of us will make some "New Year's Resolutions" tonight, hoping to better our lives in one way or another. We'll lose weight, find a better job, be more patient with our kids, start saving money…sounds good, the promises we make to ourselves. But how many of us can actually follow through with our resolutions? We may even say we're going to read our Bible more, tithe, attend Sunday School…we not only make promises to ourselves, and to each other, but we promise God a number of things, usually in trade for something we know He can do for us. We think if we change our habits, or our patterns of living, everything else will change and our circumstances will improve. But it's not that easy.

From the book of Ecclesiastes, it seems a little depressing to read that *"everything is meaningless."* (1:2). But Solomon's musings showed that the things he was trying to change, the things he was seeking after, were indeed folly ~ they were what HE wanted. It's not wrong to want wisdom, which God did give him, or to desire knowledge. But Solomon seemed to be chasing after these things, and others, trying to find the meaning of life. But it all came down to God's timing. *"He has made everything beautiful in its time."* (3:11). He also realized that God "*set eternity in the hearts of men."* (vs. 11).

There will always be tears with no one to comfort; people will die, some not realizing that they have hope in Jesus; some of us will lose jobs, homes, belongings. Some will never be satisfied, no matter what comes their way. Many will not get enough to eat; others will eat too much. We will make new friends, and lose a few, for whatever reason. We will make mistakes…or get it right. But no matter what the coming year holds for each of us, we can always count on some things. The same sun and moon will continue to rise and set on each one of us, just like they have since the beginning of time. Babies will be born, and people will die. We will have happy times, and we will experience sorrow. Spring will come, followed by summer, autumn, and winter again, just as always. And one more thing remains the same…Jesus offers hope, no matter what our circumstances are. He has promised in Hebrews 13:5 to "*Never leave us or forsake us.*" And Paul reminds us, that if we accept that redemptive gift from the Lord, *"we are a new creation; the old has gone, the new has come!"* (2 Cor. 5:17). Also, in the book of Ecclesiastes, here again is the beautiful observation we have all seen, and has been listed in this collection already, about life for everyone:

"There is a time for everything, and a season for every activity under heaven;
A time to be born and a time to die,
A time to plant and a time to uproot,
A time to kill and a time to heal,
A time to tear down and a time to build,
A time to weep and a time to laugh,
A time to mourn and a time to dance,
A time to scatter stones and a time to gather them,
A time to embrace and a time to refrain,
A time to search and a time to give up,
A time to keep and a time to throw away,
A time to tear and a time to mend,
A time to be silent and a time to speak,
A time to love and a time to hate,
A time for war and a time for peace."(3:1-8).

That pretty much covers what the new year holds for us...let's just remember that God has designed each year, and each life to glorify Him…I'm excited to see what He has in store for me! Happy New Year! God bless us, every one. From my heart….

Recipe for Scripture Cake:

(JESUS' BIRTHDAY CAKE)

1 Cup Judges 5:25 (butter)
2 Cups Jeremiah 6:20 (sugar)
2 Isaiah 10:14 (eggs)
1 Cup Genesis 24:17 (water)
3-1/2 Cups 1st Kings 4:22 (flour)
2 tsp. Exodus 32:20/Luke 12:21 (baking powder)
1st Kings 10:10 (spices- cloves, cinnamon, nutmeg, ginger)
Pinch Leviticus 2:13 (salt)
2 Cups 1st Samuel 30:12 (figs, raisins ~ chopped)
½ Cup Numbers 17:8 (almonds ~ chopped)

- Mix as you would a normal cake, put in greased bundt pan. Bake at 350 45-50 min.
- When cooled, invert onto serving plate and swirl lemon & ginger glaze over the top.
- (Powdered sugar, ginger & lemon juice)

Made in the USA
Lexington, KY
21 December 2012